I0819701

IN HER PLACE

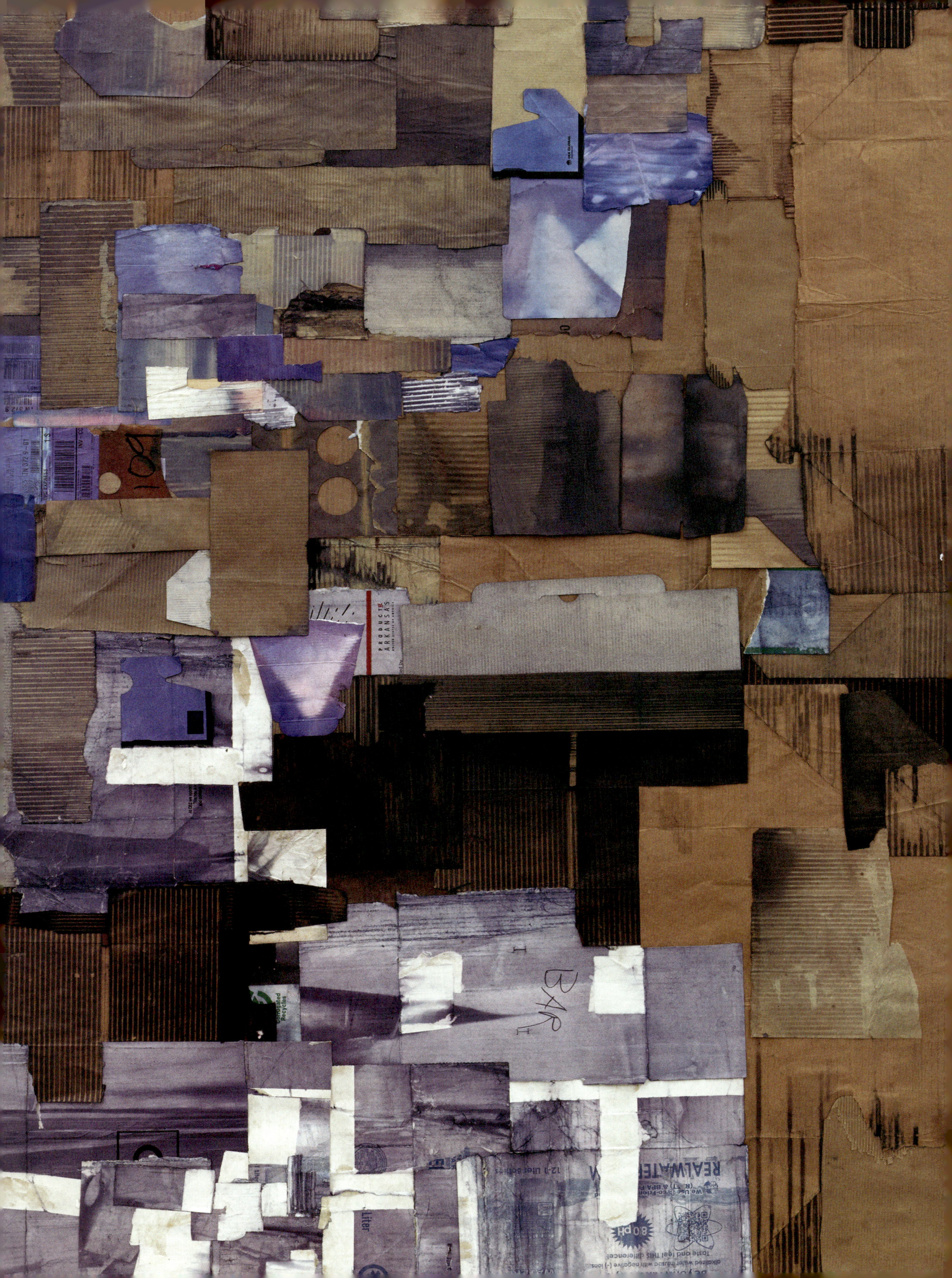
104
PRODUCT OF ARKANSAS
BAR
REALWATER
8.0 pH

IN HER PLACE

Nashville Artists in the Twenty-First Century

Edited by

Kathryn E. Delmez and
Laura Hutson Hunter

FRIST ART MUSEUM | VANDERBILT UNIVERSITY PRESS | NASHVILLE, TENNESSEE

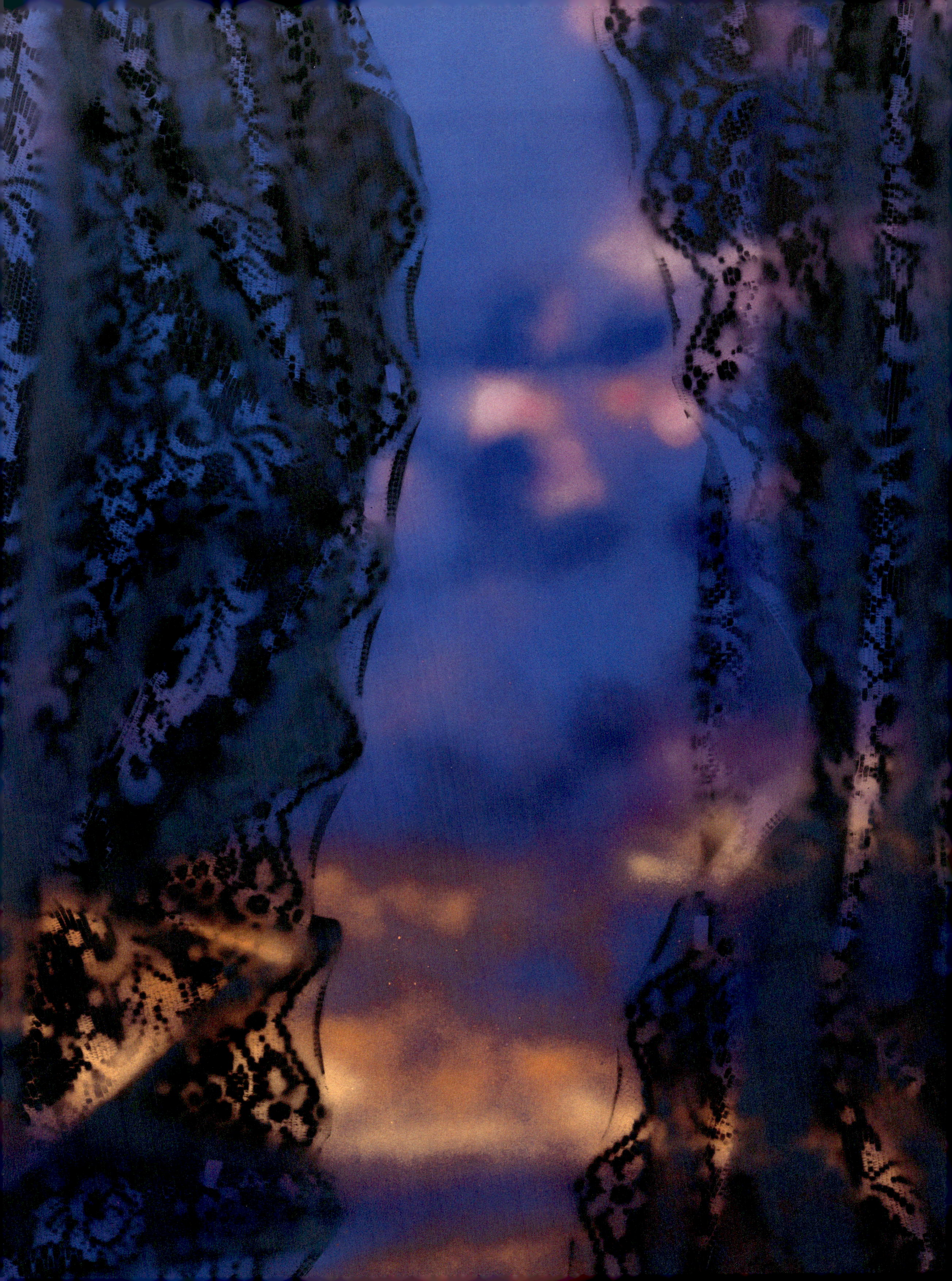

Dedicated to Susan H. Edwards

Frist Art Museum Executive Director and CEO, 2004–22

CONTENTS

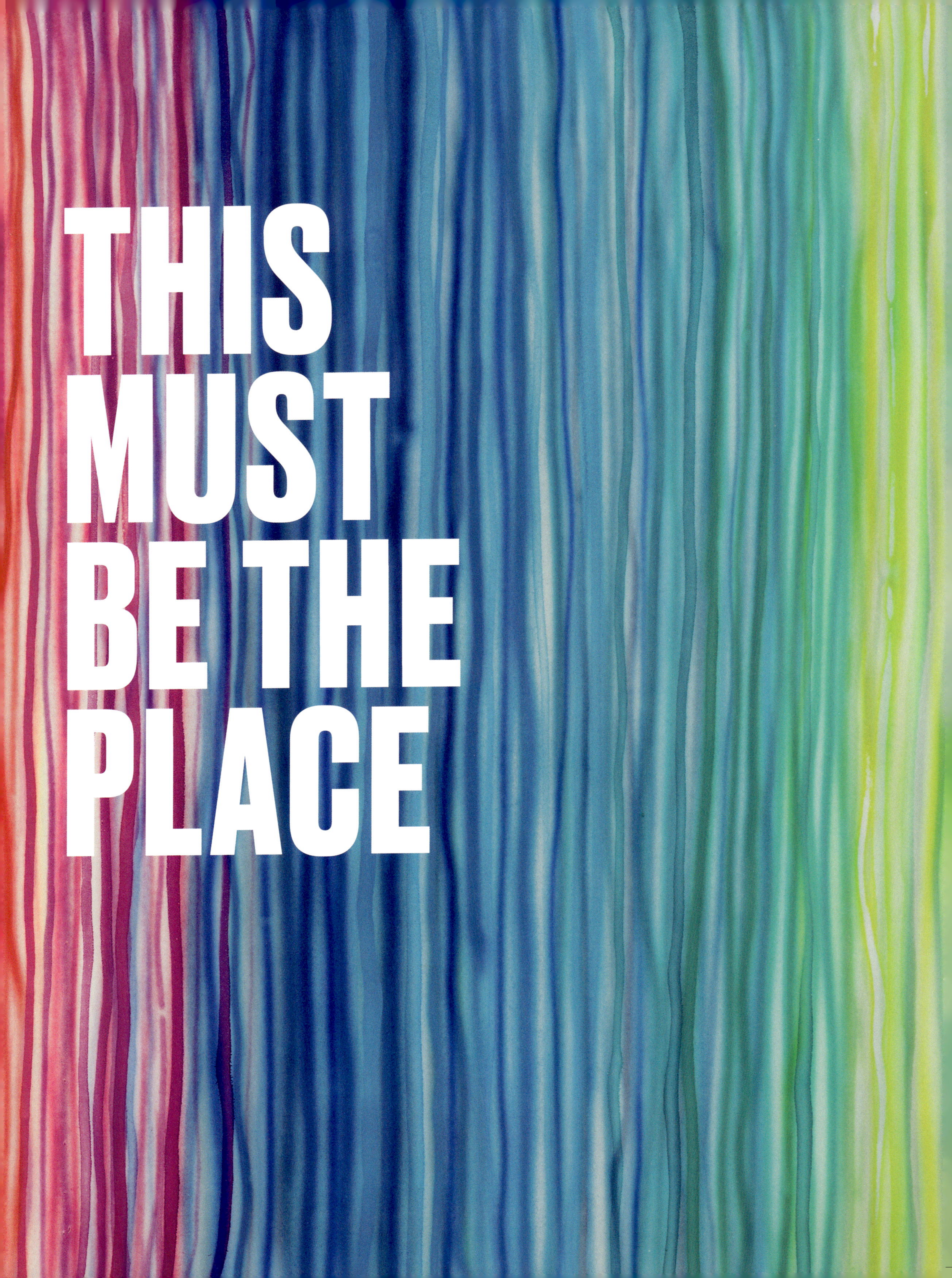
THIS
MUST
BE THE
PLACE

DIRECTOR'S FOREWORD

AND ACKNOWLEDGMENTS

"WHY HAVE THERE BEEN no great women artists?"

I first heard the question in a darkened lecture hall in the late 1990s while studying art history at Vassar College—a world away from my childhood home in Nashville. The question is the semisarcastic title of an essay written by art historian Linda Nochlin when she was teaching at Vassar in 1971 amid the rising tides of second-wave feminism. Decades later in that dim lecture hall, I watched a parade of paintings by unquestionably great French artists flicker across the screen: Jacques-Louis David, Eugène Delacroix, Gustave Courbet, Édouard Manet . . . and where were *les grandes femmes*? The question lit up the room like a lightning bolt.

Nochlin did not merely seek a corrective. Simply rewriting art history with women in it would be insufficient, she insisted, as would cataloguing the institutional impediments that kept them out. Women should not be "*grafted* on to a serious, established discipline," she wrote, though such tactics could cause a "chain reaction" that would upend what Nochlin argued was fundamentally wrong with art history: "the entire romantic, elitist, individual-glorifying and monograph-producing substructure upon which the profession of art history is based." Her question, in other words, sought to topple the reigning order of things, and to achieve something new, she proposed throwing open art history's insular spaces—darkened lecture halls and museums alike—so they could rejoin the vibrant world taking place outside. There, art would fulfill its most promising purpose: to make vital connections with the great incandescence of life.

What Nochlin wished to see was blossoming in Nashville in the 1990s, when the art scene we recognize today was first taking shape. Here, art and life seemed utterly inseparable, and women largely called the shots. Almost all the leading galleries were owned by women—Anne Brown's Arts Company, Nancy Saturn's American Artisan, Saturn's and Alice Zimmerman's downtown gallery Zimmerman Saturn, Carol Stein's Cumberland Gallery, and Janice Zeitlin's Zeitgeist Gallery, among others—and several of the most active curators were women, including Susan W. Knowles, Susan Shockley, Terri Smith, and Celia Walker. Yet it was more than the creative and enterprising presence of great women that nurtured the Nashville scene. It was also the deep connections they forged—the way they treated art as the connective tissue that gave substance to Nashville's civic and community life—that propelled the city's art world, even the city itself, toward greatness.

This placemaking is precisely what is meant by the title *In Her Place*. It refers to the city of Nashville, but even more to the community and creative interconnections that have been nurtured by Nashville's artists and provided a sense of place. Thus, in every instance, the artists shown represent positions within much wider networks, each deeply rooted in community and in Nashville.

Several have been active since early on, setting the stage and carrying things forward, while others who studied with them, both in formal and informal ways, have continued their traditions, infused them with new energy, sometimes diverged and stood in distinction from them, while always moving forward together. That dual sense of a rooted connection to place and the drive to nurture it into something new is the great aspiration of this project; it is an opportunity to explore deep connections and make new ones. *In Her Place* is therefore not only an acknowledgment of the lay of the land but also the groundwork for what comes next.

We have chosen to present *In Her Place* as the kick-off for our twenty-fifth anniversary celebration because the Frist Art Museum owes its own existence to the same creative ferment—the same sense of place—that has nurtured the artists in this exhibition. The idea of establishing a museum first gained steam in the 1990s thanks to civic-minded women arts advocates devoted to creating a sense of place in Nashville, women like Patricia C. Frist, Andrea Conte, Bernice Gordon, Martha Ingram, Judy Liff Barker, Ellen Martin, Peggy Steine, and Judy Turner, and just a few years after the museum launched, Dr. Susan H. Edwards became its second director, serving from 2004 to 2022. From the start, the Frist Art Museum was deeply invested in the women artists of our region. As art historian Vivien Fryd has noted, during the museum's first five years alone, the Frist organized seven exhibitions that foregrounded Nashville art and artists. Several artists in *In Her Place*—Jane Braddock, Alicia Henry, Carol Mode, and Marilyn Murphy—were included in those early exhibitions, as was Barbara Bullock, whose work is presented in a companion exhibition to *In Her Place* in the Gordon Contemporary Artists Project Gallery curated by Carlton Wilkinson (whose own art gallery played an important placemaking role in Nashville from 1987 to 2007).

While the museum has long prioritized our local art scene and its role in civic and community life, this presentation is more than a celebration. Much of what Nochlin denounced—fierce individualism, faith in isolated genius, normalization of the "romantic, elitist, individual-glorifying"—has come roaring into power throughout much of life itself. A project like this one is all the more urgent because it not only champions but also asserts the importance of communities built around creativity, care, and a constant drive to build a better future from the lessons of the past.

This project should therefore be seen as something more than a compendium of Nashville's leading women artists; it is an example of a creative practice that celebrates connection and community. And it is thanks in large part to creative leaders like Senior Curator Katie Delmez that such connections have been nurtured and now thrive. For her entire career, Delmez has developed an inclusive curatorial practice that, while leveraging her individual expertise, decenters her own voice by cultivating a broader, participatory community and thereby ensuring her projects express a shared perspective, not just her own. *In Her Place* is no exception.

For this project, Delmez assembled a curatorial team early on, and we are grateful to Sai Clayton, formerly the museum's first Susan H. Edwards Curatorial Fellow, and Shaun Giles, the museum's director of community engagement, for working as cocurators and sharing their knowledge, expertise, and deep connections. In addition to serving as this catalogue's coeditor, Laura Hutson Hunter also broadened the curatorial vision, and for her innumerable contributions—not least of all her deep commitment to the creative life of Middle Tennessee through her own writing and curatorial work—we are deeply appreciative. This team is joined by an array of catalogue contributors who share fresh insights and perspectives, and we are grateful to each of them: Mac Cooper, Michael J. Ewing, Michelle Millar Fisher, Vivien Green Fryd, Katy Hessel, Susan W. Knowles, Joe Nolan, and Mouminatou Thiaw. Photographer Ashley Holstein made beautiful new headshots of the artists. Editor Ben Thomas brought his usual calm demeanor as well as his sharp eyes to the project, and publications manager Karen Bovie carried it across the finish line for the Frist team. Special thanks to Mac Cooper, who began working on this project as a Frist intern in 2024 and stayed on as curatorial assistant through the summer of 2025. Her dedicated support has been invaluable. For helping shape the catalogue and bring it to light, our appreciation also goes to Gianna F. Mosser, Betsy Phillips, Patrick Samuel, Joell Smith-Borne, and Alissa Faden at Vanderbilt University Press.

None of these connections would be made without the stimulating and sustaining work of artists, and each artist in this project, along with many more that are no less vital to our community, made this project possible. To each of them, we are thankful beyond words. Nashville's thriving arts community also relies on the support of collectors based in the city and beyond it who invest and believe in Nashville's artists. For their critical support of our art community and for lending to this exhibition, we thank Sheila Aminmadani; Sandra Ballentine; Fadi Braiteh; Mollye Brown and Paul Polycarpou; Jesse Hale; Jodi and Hal Hess; Hines – T3 Wedgewood Houston Collection, Nashville; Anne Joyce and Peter Lawrence; Andrew Le; Emily Leonard and Sloane Southard; Kylie Manning; Eliot Michael; Melanie and Chris Moran; Alf and Clara Naman; Jennifer and Lee Pepper; Sasha and Charlie Sealy; Roya Shanks and Aaron Bender; Matthew Steer; Jason Stopa; Cal Turner; Fara White; and collectors who wish to remain anonymous, along with several galleries and administrators who facilitated these loans and shared their connections: the Alicia Henry Estate, David Lusk Gallery, Christine Gostowski and Jamaal Sheats at Fisk University, Nina Johnson Gallery, Night Gallery, Red Arrow Gallery, Tinney Contemporary, and Trépanier Baer Gallery.

That the Frist is able to present such a project speaks to the ongoing faith our supporters have in what makes Nashville such a great place, and it is a pleasure to acknowledge that *In Her Place* has been generously supported by the Frist Art Museum's board of trustees, in particular Chair and President Billy Frist. For their steady and enduring support of the museum, I am also pleased to acknowledge the Frist Foundation, the Tennessee Arts Commission, which receives funding from the National Endowment for the Arts, and the Metro Nashville Arts Commission.

Seth Feman, PhD

EXECUTIVE DIRECTOR AND CEO,
FRIST ART MUSEUM

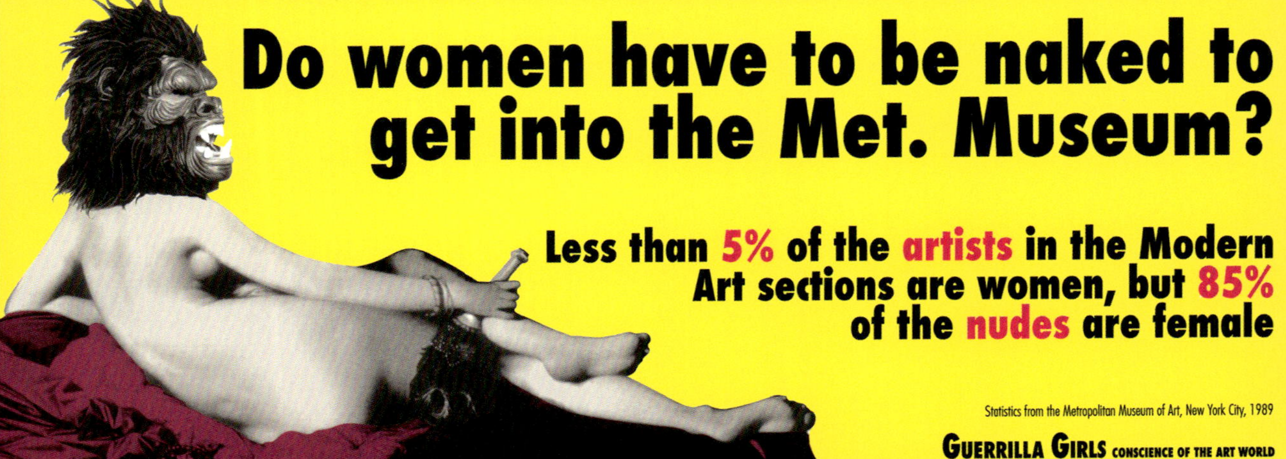

FIGURE 0.1. Guerrilla Girls. *Do Women Have to Be Naked to Get into the Met. Museum?*, 1989. Photo-offset lithograph on paper; 10⅞ × 28 in. Courtesy guerillagirls.com

FOREWORD KATY HESSEL

WHY STAGE AN ALL-WOMEN ARTISTS EXHIBITION IN 2026? Are we not beyond this; have we not spent decades—centuries—campaigning for women's inclusion, and the right to be in the history books, the museums, and collections worldwide?

It was a staggering fifty-four years ago that the trailblazing feminist art historian Linda Nochlin catalyzed women's art history into the mainstream with her essay "Why Have There Been No Great Women Artists?" And forty years ago, in 1985, the activist-artist collective Guerrilla Girls burst onto the scene. Disguising their faces in gorilla masks and protesting the outrageous treatment women receive in the art world, the group creates posters—to this day featuring their iconic bold text and images—listing statistics that state the truth of what was and is happening (fig. 0.1). One poster pointed out that the Museum of Modern Art, in 1985, was the only major New York museum to stage a single exhibition of a woman artist's work.

And now? In 2022, the Burns Halperin Report found that, of the acquisitions made by thirty-one prominent US museums between 2008 and 2020, 11 percent were by female-identifying artists, while only 0.5 percent were by Black American women.

Where I live in London, just 1 percent of our National Gallery's collection comprises work made by women artists. The city's oldest museum, the Royal Academy of Arts, has dedicated just one exhibition to a woman artist in the entirety of its main galleries since it opened in 1768. There is still clearly work to be done.

In addition to my Instagram account and podcast *The Great Women Artists* and 2023 book *The Story of Art Without Men*, last year I released a set of museum audio-guides with the Metropolitan Museum of Art, the Hirshhorn Museum and Sculpture Garden, Tate, and others spotlighting women and gender-nonconforming artists in these collections. While it wasn't to say this is the only route, it was intended to lend visitors the option of seeing women they might have missed. Because if you're not seeing art by a wide range of people, then you are not seeing society as a whole. And not only that, but you are also just missing out on great art.

While the pronoun in the title *In Her Place: Nashville Artists in the Twenty-First Century* might give away that visitors will witness exclusively women artists in this exhibition at the Frist Art Museum, it's not prescriptive, nor does it put them into a box. It celebrates and spotlights—showing a whole range of artists working in everything from ceramics to multimedia installation, from painting to fiber, and creating scenes ranging from unsettling-but-intriguing domestic and private spaces to futuristic dreamscapes where a new world can seek to exist.

The first known all-female US exhibition was *31 Women* at Peggy Guggenheim's Art of This Century Gallery in 1943. The artist lineup included the likes of Frida Kahlo, Louise Nevelson, Meret Oppenheim, and Dorothea Tanning. Eighty-three years later, how far have we come? Let's find out.

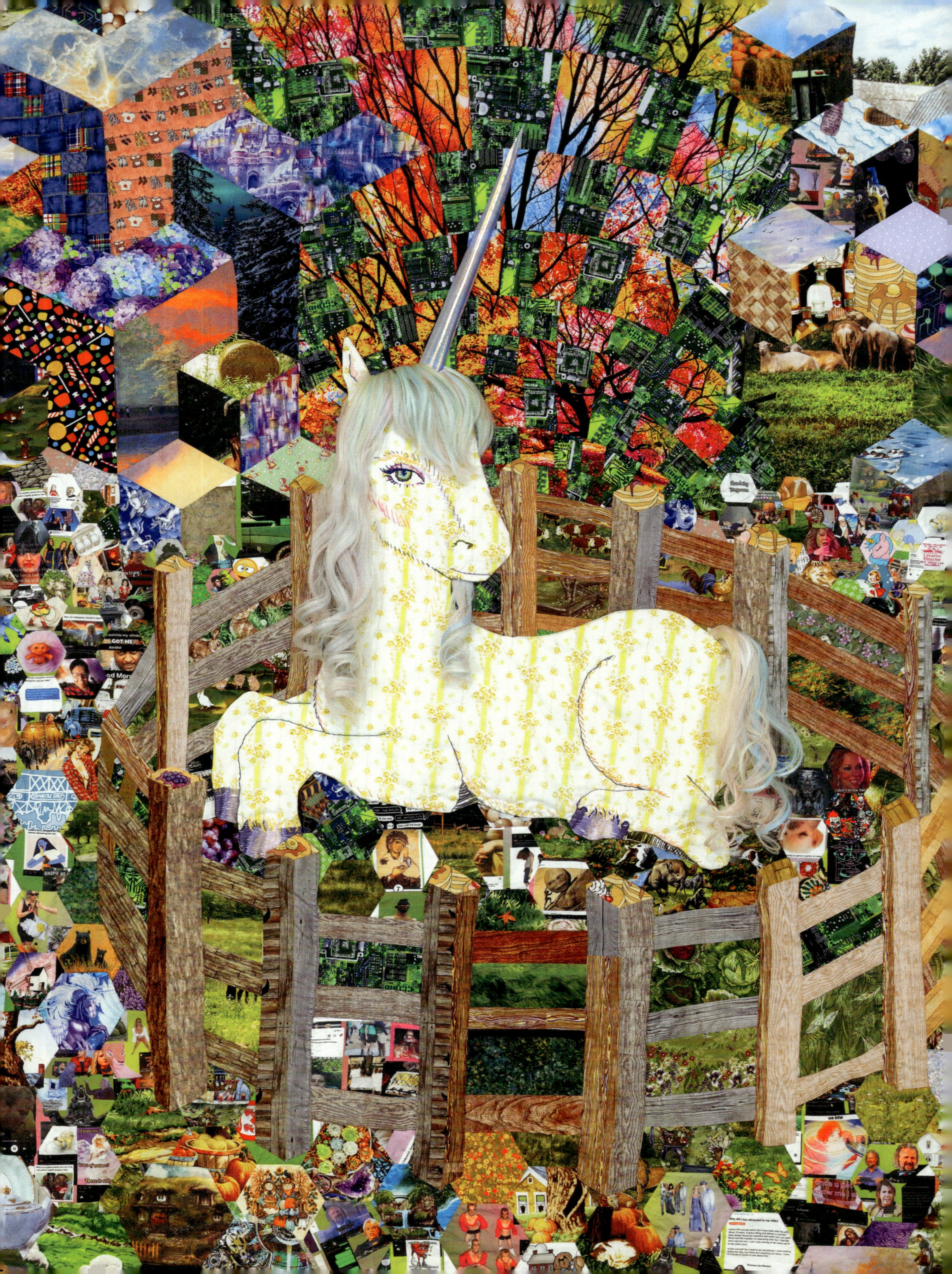

Sai Clayton and Kathryn E. Delmez

INTRODUCTION

NASHVILLE'S MAGNETISM IS ITS MYSTERY

IN DECEMBER OF 2016, Jana Harper and Vadis Turner invited arts writer Sara Estes and Frist Art Museum curator Katie Delmez to coffee. Over the course of the conversation, they casually noted that the leading artists, curators, and writers in Nashville are women and proposed a year-long program of monthly studio visits with those figures. Delmez immediately realized that Harper and Turner were correct—while many men have contributed significantly to the local creative community, women indeed play an outsized role throughout the city's arts ecosystem.[1] At that time, cultural institutions such as Cheekwood, the Frist, the Parthenon, and the Tennessee State Museum were led by women.[2] Delmez and Trinita Kennedy had been curators at the Frist for fifteen and nine years respectively, joining a local tradition of longtime women curators that includes Susan W. Knowles, Susan Shockley, Terri Smith, Celia Walker, and others. Erica Ciccarone, Estes, and Laura Hutson Hunter were leading arts writers at the *Nashville Scene* and—following in the footsteps of pioneering gallerists such as Anne Brown, Nancy Saturn, Carol Stein, and Alice Zimmerman—Julia Martin, Katie Shaw, and Susan Tinney were transforming the commercial gallery scene.

At the center of this vibrant and growing community, however, were the women artists themselves, and ten years later, they maintain that central position. With robust studio practices, it is primarily these artists whose work is being shown in museums, galleries, and art fairs across the country and the globe; who are receiving prestigious grants, residencies, and awards; and who are being written about by respected critics and art historians (fig. 1.1). Many have also dedicated years or even decades to teaching or to building impactful community organizations.

Harper and Turner's observation planted the seed for this exhibition that celebrates the prominent position of women artists within our city and beyond. The title *In Her Place* challenges the long-held exclusion of women from the art world by asserting that these artists belong in museums, in critical conversations, and at the forefront of contemporary art. And it asserts that each artist is making this place, Nashville, their own by reshaping it as a city not

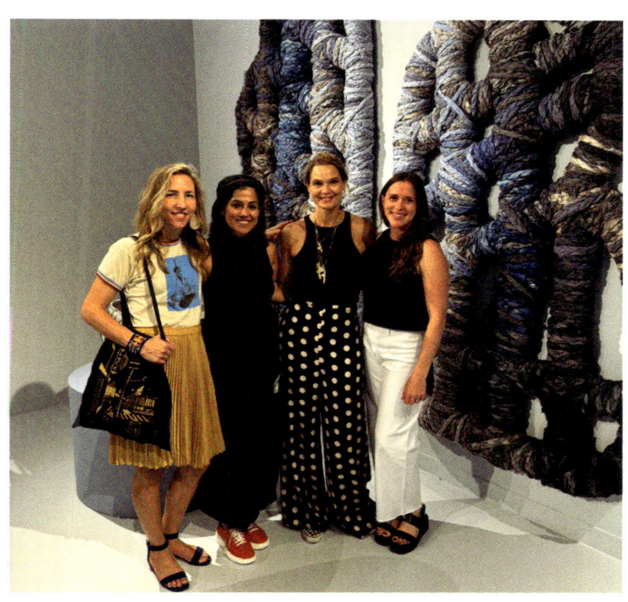

FIGURE 1.1. *Left to right*: Andrea Zieher, Raheleh Filsoofi, Vadis Turner, and Karen Seapker at Design Miami, 2024

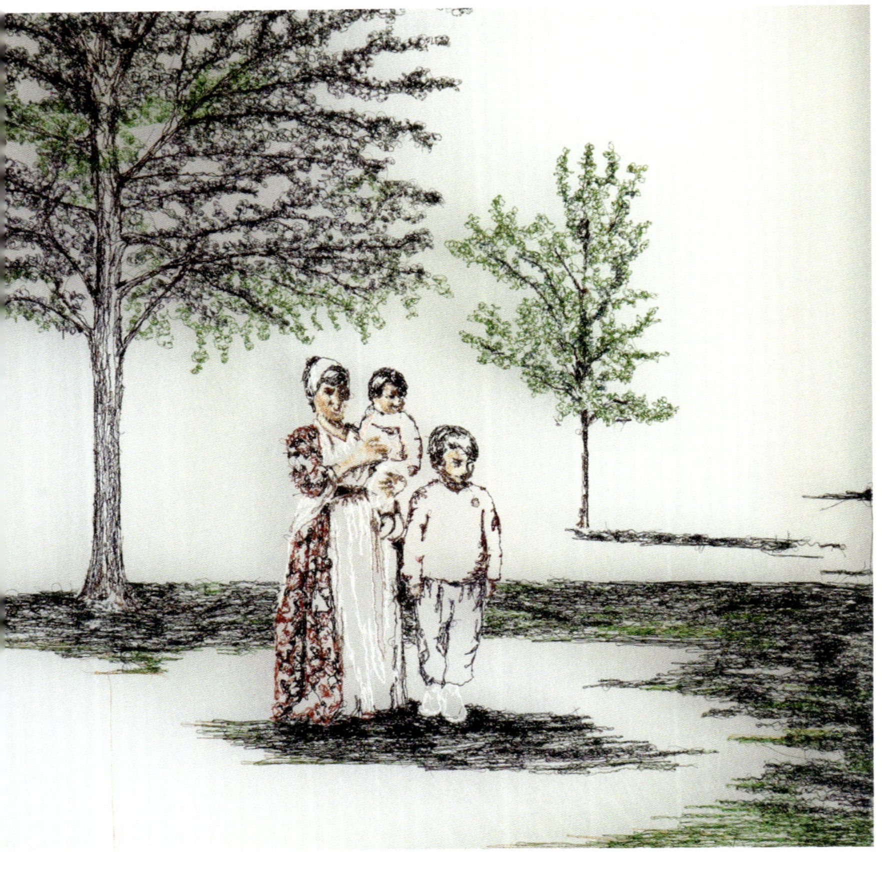

FIGURE 1.2. Beizar Aradini. *1994*, 2022. Thread and tulle; 24 × 20 in. Courtesy of the artist

only for musicians but also for visual artists working at the highest caliber. Ten years in the making, *In Her Place* is an important recognition of the decades-long impact women artists have had in defining Nashville's creative landscape.

Initially, Delmez proposed an exhibition devoted to Nashville-based women artists to accompany the Frist's 2022 presentation of *Alma W. Thomas: Everything Is Beautiful*. Because the suggested Conte Community Arts Gallery is jointly curated with the museum's Education Department, she asked longtime community engagement director Shaun Giles, who has cultivated deep relationships throughout the city, to serve as a cocurator. After one day of studio visits, however, Delmez and Giles realized that more time and more space would be required. The Frist's exhibitions committee agreed to move the project to the Upper-Level Galleries in 2025 and, at the recommendation of Kennedy, Delmez and Giles invited Sai Clayton, the Frist's first Susan H. Edwards Curatorial Fellow, to join the curatorial team. In addition to continuing the mentorship begun during her 2021–22 fellowship, partnering with Clayton brought a young voice to the project as well as the vital perspective of a second-generation Nashville artist (Clayton and her parents are all artists). Continuing this collaborative approach, the three curators then invited arts writer and independent curator Laura Hutson Hunter to coedit this catalogue.

With the curatorial team in place, work on the project began in earnest. Along the way, the location and timing changed once again. The exhibition moved to the Frist's largest gallery space, the ten-thousand-square-foot Ingram Gallery, and was rescheduled for 2026, coinciding with the museum's twenty-fifth anniversary—a timely demonstration of the institution's ongoing commitment to Nashville's creative community. *In Her Place* also aligns with the second iteration of the Tennessee Triennial, connecting the featured artists with the state's larger contemporary art dialogue.

As the team spent time on research and studio visits, they were drawn to artists that address notions of place in their work—whether a literal place, such as the garden outside a studio window; a place in time; the influence of living in the American South; or a connection to an ancestral homeland. They also decided to limit themselves to fewer than thirty artists to allow for a more-than-cursory look at each figure through the presentation of several works or an expansive installation.

From the beginning, the curatorial team acknowledged the sensitive nature of the project, especially with an art scene as tightly knit yet diverse as Nashville's. There is a network of working creatives in this city pushing their community forward at every level, and it would be impossible to include all the worthy artists, even restricting the parameters of the exhibition to women. Of the selected artists, the majority are middle aged and mid-career—in the midst of it all—but a handful of artists who have been making art in Nashville since long before it was dubbed "It City" by *The New York Times* are included, as well as a few younger artists to reflect the future of the growing art scene. This exhibition, then, serves as a microcosm of the greater intergenerational network of women artists and makers supporting and paving the way for one another.

Why Nashville?

The question *Why Nashville?* can't be answered from a single perspective. The reasons artists live and work here are as varied as the individuals whose work is included in the exhibition. Looking at the stories of how and why these artists came to Nashville reveals a web of connections: the need to prioritize family, economic opportunities, and ease of living. And despite Nashville seemingly lacking the creative infrastructure of other large cities, these artists have found community and support.

The New Nashville art community is increasingly global. Nashville has become a destination for migration and is home to many immigrant populations; the city has even been called an Ellis Island of the twenty-first century.[3] For its ever-expanding and diverse population, Nashville offers a new look at the strengths and shortcomings of Southern hospitality. Beizar Aradini was born in a Kurdish refugee camp and in 1992 moved with her family to Nashville, which has the largest Kurdish population in the

United States. In material, technique, and subject, Aradini's work draws from memories and stories of women in the camp, where they lived after fleeing Saddam Hussein's regime, adding a fresh and personal perspective to an enduring cultural legacy (fig. 1.2). Sisavanh Phouthavong Houghton was born in Laos and lived in a refugee camp in Thailand in the wake of the Laotian Civil War before coming to the United States at the age of four. Through a sophisticated visual language of abstraction and glitches, she aims to tell untold stories in her paintings, focusing especially on the Secret War in Laos while also addressing immigration, the broader Southeast Asian diaspora, and the connections between wars past and present (fig. 1.3). Kimia Ferdowsi Kline was born in Nashville to parents that came to the US from Iran after the 1979 revolution as refugees from religious persecution. Her practice blends Persian miniature painting and Euro-American modernist traditions. For the artist, the stylized forms she creates with bright, densely pigmented colors represent a way of "repairing a certain sense of cultural amputation from my place of origin, and reclaiming a central element of my identity."[4] Puerto Rican–born Yanira Vissepó blends Caribbean and Tennessean botanicals in her fiber- and print-based tapestry-like work as a way of reflecting the mysteries of the natural world and the duality she often feels as a Nashvillian still connected to her home island. María Magdalena Campos-Pons likewise continues to feel the pull of Cuba, where she was born, despite emigrating to the US in the early 1990s. Since 2017, Campos-Pons has made the American South her home; in recent work, she combines archetypal vegetative symbols of both lands—the palm tree and the magnolia. Raheleh Filsoofi left Tehran for the United States after completing her undergraduate studies. Although based in Nashville since 2020, she considers herself an itinerant artist, and her work challenges physical, political, social, and even creative boundaries in a multidisciplinary practice that centers on clay—the material of the land—and sound, often Middle Eastern music.

While Kline was born in Nashville and Aradini and Vissepó were brought here as children by their families, Campos-Pons, Filsoofi, and Phouthavong Houghton moved to Nashville via other US cities to teach at one of Middle Tennessee's many universities. Nicknamed the Athens of the South because of its numerous institutes of higher learning, Nashville is home to Belmont, Fisk, Lipscomb, Tennessee State, Vanderbilt, and other universities that have arguably brought as many people to the region as the music business.[5] In 2003, Phouthavong Houghton began teaching at Middle Tennessee State University in nearby Murfreesboro, and exhibition cocurator Sai Clayton is among the many students she has taught over more than two decades there. Campos-Pons and Filsoofi are more recent academic transplants. Campos-Pons was recruited from her longtime position at the School of the Museum of Fine Arts at Tufts University to become the Cornelius Vanderbilt Chair of Fine Art at Vanderbilt University in 2017, and Filsoofi started as an assistant art professor there in 2020.

Nashville's universities drew several other artists featured in this exhibition to the city as well. Carol Mode moved here in 1967 after her husband, Robert "Bob" Mode, accepted a position teaching art history at Vanderbilt University. Marilyn Murphy came to Vanderbilt in 1980, and her precisely rendered drawings and paintings of surreal scenes reference places where she has lived or visited, including Australia, Oklahoma, and Tennessee. In 1997, Alicia Henry began teaching at Fisk University, indelibly making her mark at Nashville's oldest higher learning institution.[6] Alex Blau moved to Nashville in 2011 and has taught, primarily at Vanderbilt, for many years. In 2013, Jana Harper left the Kranzberg Illustrated Book Studio at Washington University in St. Louis for a professorship at Vanderbilt.

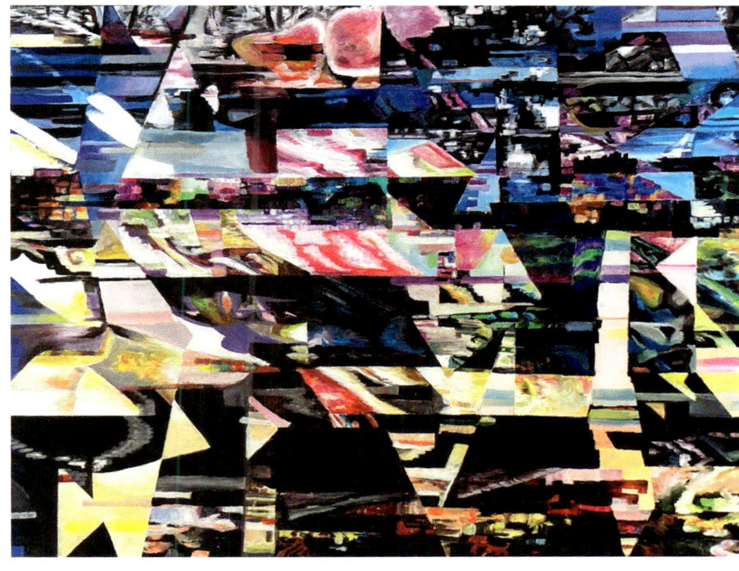

FIGURE 1.3. Sisavanh Phouthavong Houghton. *Memorial #2*, 2022. Acrylic and spray paint on board; 19 × 24 in. Courtesy of the artist

Aside from being recruited to academic positions, artists have come to Nashville because, compared to larger metropolitan centers, it is a relatively affordable, growing city with an array of opportunities and ease of living. While some expected their move to be temporary, they've found themselves putting down roots in a welcoming ecosystem of musicians and other cultural workers that compose a healthy creative class. Elisheba Israel Mrozik moved to Nashville from her hometown of Memphis for a retail position after graduating from Memphis College of Art in 2007. She remembers, "[As] soon as I landed I began to learn about the incredible history and legacy of creativity behind North Nashville. I planted my roots here . . . North Nashville is home."[7] She quickly became the first licensed Black tattoo artist in Middle Tennessee. Through her multimedia studio practice, prolific public mural commissions, and founding of the North Nashville Arts Coalition, Mrozik is dedicated to telling the stories and honoring the people of North Nashville, one of the city's primary historically African American neighborhoods.

Jodi Hays, Briena Harmening, and Lauren Gregory were all born in small Southern towns, and Nashville offered them an opportunity to be close to family while living in a larger urban environment. Originally from Arkansas, Hays moved to East Nashville from Boston in 2005 after completing her MFA and began working as a faculty member and gallery director at Tennessee State University. Hays sees her current practice of working with bleached and stained cardboard boxes as a personal dialogue with the international arte povera movement, but her layered collages also connect to such rural Southern traditions as quilting and creatively repurposing scarce resources. Similarly, Briena Harmening, who was born in McMinnville, Tennessee, came to Nashville in 2014 after completing her MFA in Knoxville.[8] Like many, Harmening grapples with her relationship to the South, and her text and textile work exposes hypocrisies and failures as well as the beloved vernacular quips of women from her hometown. Born in Oak Ridge, Tennessee, Lauren Gregory is a self-described "country mouse" who had been living and working in New York City for more than ten years as an artist, animator, and educator before she moved to Nashville in 2021. Here, she reconnected with familial art-making practices (she learned quilt making and painting from her mother and grandmother) and the physical landscape of the state. An army brat who relocated often as a child, Mandy Rogers Horton moved to Nashville in 2003 after graduate school to be closer to her family, who had recently settled in the area. Her current work depicts the temporality of a city witnessing development at a breathtaking scale and speed. The shifting landscape of Nashville thereby serves as a metaphor for the constructed and transitional elements of our lives, although ironically Nashville has also become Rogers Horton's most long-term home.

Now a Nashvillian for more than forty-five years, Jane Braddock found solace in the city's slower pace during a weekend visit while she was based in New York as a textile designer. When she relocated here in 1980, her art making completely shifted to a studio practice that now reflects the serenity and balance she was looking for. Decades later (in 2013 and 2018, respectively), Karen Seapker and Emily Weiner both moved to Nashville from New York City with their musician husbands. Weiner realized that "living in NYC with a small child and an artist's income wasn't tenable in the long term."[9] Initially uncertain if they would stay in Nashville, both have come to appreciate the vibrant music and visual-art communities they have found. Seapker has also become deeply connected to her garden, witnessing the changing seasons and life cycles through her studio window and capturing them in many paintings, including the one featured on the cover of this book.

And, finally, there are the Nashville natives, sometimes half-jokingly referred to as "unicorns" because of the rarity of finding people born or raised in this city of transplants. Aside from Lanie Gannon (who moved to Nashville from Detroit as a small child), Kristi Hargrove, and Kit Reuther, these artists moved away and lived in major metropolitan areas for extended periods of time. But Nashville has a funny way of luring its natives back.

Painter LiFran Fort returned to Nashville from Chicago in the 1980s to care for her aging parents and was offered a position at Fisk University, her alma mater, shortly thereafter. She has continued to teach at Fisk for more than forty years while making striking acrylic paintings with bands of radiating color reminiscent of those made by her former professor, Harlem Renaissance giant Aaron Douglas. Although Shannon Cartier Lucy left Nashville to study painting at New York University and lived in New York for many years before moving back to Nashville in 2011, home has long been at the heart of her practice. Beautifully rendered, otherwise tranquil domestic scenes are infused with a jolt of the absurd with such elements as a fishbowl on a turned-on stove or a woman sitting on a burning couch. Lakesha Calvin returned to Nashville in 2013 after living in St. Louis, Knoxville, and Saint Thomas, US Virgin Islands. Her practice has shifted recently from realistically rendered portraits of family and friends in these places to more abstract collages, sculptures, and paintings reflecting on personal health challenges, motherhood, and aging parents.

Kimia Ferdowsi Kline, Vadis Turner, and Kelly S. Williams attended the same high school and were influenced by the same art teacher, Rosie Paschall—a small-town trope that feels all-too-familiar to longtime Nashvillians. Turner, whose mixed-media sculptural works disrupt gendered narratives surrounding domestic materials, studied in Boston and lived in New York for ten years before moving back to Nashville in 2015. She returned to her hometown not only to be close to family but also because she recognizes the importance of making challenging work outside of the so-called art capitals of New York and Los Angeles. Similarly, Kelly S. Williams lived in New York state and Chicago before moving back to Nashville, where she makes patterned abstractions, often based on family textiles; observational genre paintings; and trompe l'oeil objects that question viewers' perceptions of reality.

Returning home isn't always easy. Kline lived for many years in New York but returned to Nashville during the pandemic, which she notes has been "a complicated experience for me. It's where my family rebuilt their lives after losing everything during the Iranian Revolution. . . . Living here means continually navigating the space between what was lost and what was rebuilt—both personally and historically. It's complicated to be a minority in a place where racism is woven into its roots, where the legacy of exclusion still lingers. Nashville holds my family's story of survival, but also challenges me to exist fully in a place that hasn't always made room for difference."[10]

Figurative painter Ashley Doggett considers herself a daughter of Nashville even though she was born in Texas. Doggett's grandmother was a Nashvillian and told her what it was like to be raised in poverty and segregation here in the 1950s—stories that reappear in Doggett's work. Despite the current surge of gentrification and erasure of many of Nashville's historic neighborhoods and identities, Doggett still finds herself drawn to the city's complex history. She explains: "I chose to stay in Nashville because, for all its growth and challenges, it has given so many a sense of purpose and belonging. I see it as a city in transition, one that holds both the promise of transformation and the responsibility to honor its past. In many ways, my decision to remain here is an act of investment—in community, in education, and in the possibility of shaping a more inclusive and equitable future."[11]

Nashville's magnetism is its mystery. For those of us born here, or who have been here long enough to see the city's cycles of change,it may have been easy at various points to ask ourselves, *Why would anyone move here?* If you're a musician, the answer is easy enough. But for the artists in this exhibition, a move to Nashville doesn't guarantee a clear path to being a successful career artist. Perhaps it is the existing framework of gig-worker musicians who make the untraditional life and career of an artist more feasible. Maybe the air of "artists just trying to make it" on Broadway has permeated the other neighborhoods, creating a network of creators that support each other's wildest dreams.

Nashville has long been a repository of stories and perspectives that continue to shape the city. This exhibition reflects the generations of women artists who have influenced one another—as professors and students, mentors and peers—and whose ideas and determination galvanize the following generations. It is a reminder of the importance of creators who have been part of this ecosystem long enough to foster these relationships and recognize the city's evolving artistic identity. *In Her Place* affirms that Nashville is, and will continue to be, a place for artists.

The twenty-eight artists featured here make visible the complexities of our belonging, identities, and histories, offering us new ways to see Nashville and, by extension, ourselves. Their work urges us to reconsider what it means to claim space, to make a mark, and to leave a legacy. In doing so, *In Her Place* stands as both an homage and a challenge to continue expanding the narrative, to recognize the creative forces that have always been here, and to ensure that their influence endures. This exhibition invites us to ask: Who else needs to be seen? What other stories demand recognition?

NOTES

1. Some particularly active men in Nashville's art scene include Sam Dunson, Jamal Jenkins (Woke3), David Lusk, Joe Nolan, Jerry Dale McFadden, Mark W. Scala, Jamaal Sheats, and Lain York.
2. Susan H. Edwards was the executive director and CEO of the Frist Art Museum from 2004 to 2022; Ashley Howell became the executive director of the Tennessee State Museum in 2017 after Lois Riggins Ezell's retirement following thirty-five years in the position; Jane O. MacLeod became the president and CEO of Cheekwood in 2010; and Wesley Paine was the director of the Parthenon from 1981 to 2021.
3. This moniker was brought to the team's attention by Grace Aneiza Ali, the 2024–25 curator of María Magdalena Campos-Pons's transinstitutional partnership, the Engine of Art, Democracy, and Justice. See Leah Donnella, "Reporter's Notebook: The South Is Home to a Growing Black Immigrant Population," NPR, May 12, 2023, https://www.npr.org/2023/05/12/1165055943/black-immigrants-memphis-nashville-tennessee.
4. Kimia Ferdowsi Kline, "Q&A with Kimia Ferdowsi Kline," interview by Emily Burns, *Maake Magazine*, accessed April 11, 2025, https://www.maakemagazine.com/kimia-ferdowsi-kline.
5. For more information on this nickname, see Sarah Arntz, "Nashville Is the 'Athens of the South' . . . but Why?" *Nashville/Community History* (blog), Nashville Public Library, October 1, 2019, https://library.nashville.org/blog/2019/10/nashville-athens-south-but-why.
6. Henry's death on October 17, 2024, during the planning of this exhibition, was a devastating loss to Fisk, the local community, and the larger art world that was being increasingly exposed to her work through recent exhibitions in Canada, Europe, and elsewhere.
7. Elisheba Israel Mrozik, text message to Kathryn E. Delmez, March 13, 2025.
8. As discussed in Shaun Giles's essay in this publication, Harmening has taught high school for many years. During her years at Hillsboro High School, she taught art to cocurator Sai Clayton, who recalls skipping other classes just to be in her art room.
9. Emily Weiner, email message to Curatorial Assistant Mac Cooper, March 13, 2025.
10. Kimia Ferdowsi Kline, email message to Curatorial Assistant Mac Cooper, March 2025.
11. Ashley Doggett, email message to Curatorial Assistant Mac Cooper, March 12, 2025.

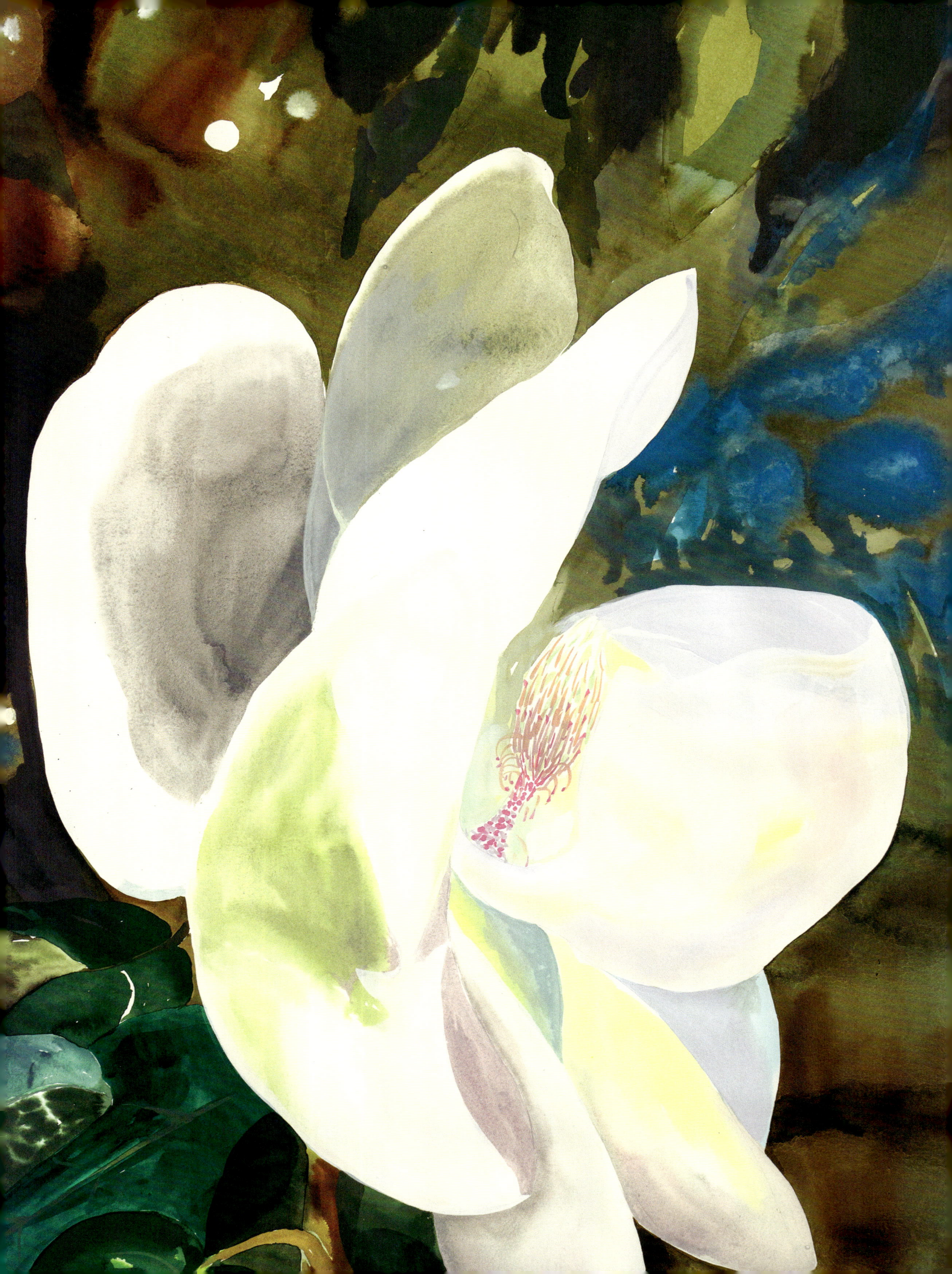

Laura Hutson Hunter

SOUTHERN ARTISTS AND THEIR DISCONTENTS

Why Place Still Matters

WHETHER OR NOT IT WAS ever their intention, all the artists of *In Her Place* are making their work in the American South.

In Her Place charts a network of artists working at a high caliber with deceptively specific criteria—they are all women, and they all work in Nashville, Tennessee. The plurality of styles, subjects, and media they choose to work in is so diverse that grouping them together proves that, if anything, there are as many differences among these artists as there are similarities.

But isn't that what it is to be Southern? Hasn't life in the American South been a quagmire of contradictions from the very start?

The South has always been defined as much by what it isn't as what it is, in much the same way that women have been defined by how they are not like men. The standard for an American artist—and perhaps for a person in general—seems to be a white, straight, cisgender man of vaguely Northern residence. Anything that deviates from that criteria needs to be justified, pointed out, turned into something exceptional in order to simply be visible. It is refreshing, then, that this exhibition does not wallow in the stagnant waters of Southern stereotypes. The artists of *In Her Place* are legion. They include a Tehran-born sculptor making vessels out of Tennessee red clay, an artist from Arkansas working with cardboard and references to unsettling histories, and a Nashville-born painter whose images of civil-rights-era sit-ins read just as poignantly in 2026 as they would have in 1960.

If anything ties these artists together, it is not their gender or their location. It is their shared ingenuity and the comfort with which they subvert.

Scott Romine's 2008 essay "The Real South: Southern Narrative in the Age of Cultural Reproduction" posits that the perception of the South as relatively behind the rest of the country has placed it in the avant-garde of contemporary culture.[1] It is true that being from the South creates a familiarity with outlier status that can serve an artist well. Even when there's nothing markedly Southern—whether in subject or application—about their work, that underdog identity can carry through in various ways.

In her large-scale mixed-media works, Arkansas-born artist and longtime Nashvillian Jodi Hays grapples with working-class values and the history of abstract expressionism and arte povera. It's a unique combination that forces viewers to accept both rural culture and high-brow art history references as part of the same conversation. *Elaine* is a 76-by-52-inch collage of fabric, cardboard, and paper pieced together like a scattershot quilt (pl. 5). According to Hays, its title could be either an homage to abstract expressionist painter Elaine de Kooning or a reference to Elaine, Arkansas—the small town in Hays's home state that, in 1919, was the site of a massacre in which an estimated 237 Black people were killed by rampaging white mobs. In Hays's work, there is little need to differentiate among sources. A kind of folk-culture reverence is inherent as she slips in allusions to her grandfather's boarded-up grocery-store windows and a legacy of handmade signs. There is something radical in making art that cares so little for pretensions, yet so precisely borrows from the same traditions that Robert Rauschenberg deified. Upending expectations is what being a Southern woman has long been about.

Nashville-born artist Vadis Turner uses materials like bedsheets and ribbons in unexpected ways to show how materials can misbehave with extraordinary results. Her freestanding *Window Figure Scylla* incorporates curtains, gravel, resin, and acrylic to make a windowpane figuration that seems to be equal parts Sheila Hicks's imposing textile-based pillars and Louise Bourgeois's spindly bronze spiders (fig. 2.1). There's nothing inherently Southern about her work, but Turner's personal history with Tennessee courses throughout the piece. The studio where she constructs her works—massive sculptures that she often has to build as two separate pieces and fasten together after they're completed—is on the ground floor of her spacious family home just outside of Nashville on Old Hickory Lake. The house was commissioned by her grandparents in 1968 and is based on a design by architect Braxton Dixon, who made a mirror image of the home for Johnny Cash, a close family friend. Turner's grandfather ran Starday, a popular country and rockabilly label in the

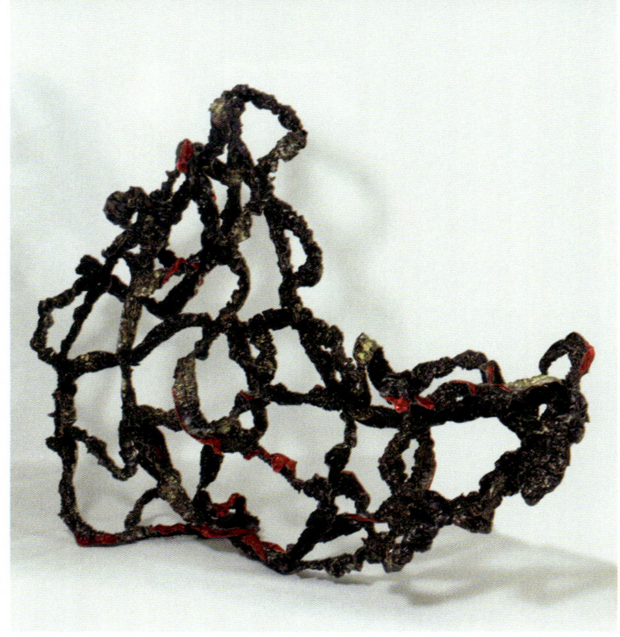

FIGURE 2.1. Vadis Turner. *Window Figure Scylla,* 2022. Curtains, gravel, resin, acrylic, and steel; 78 × 112 × 30 in. Courtesy of the artist

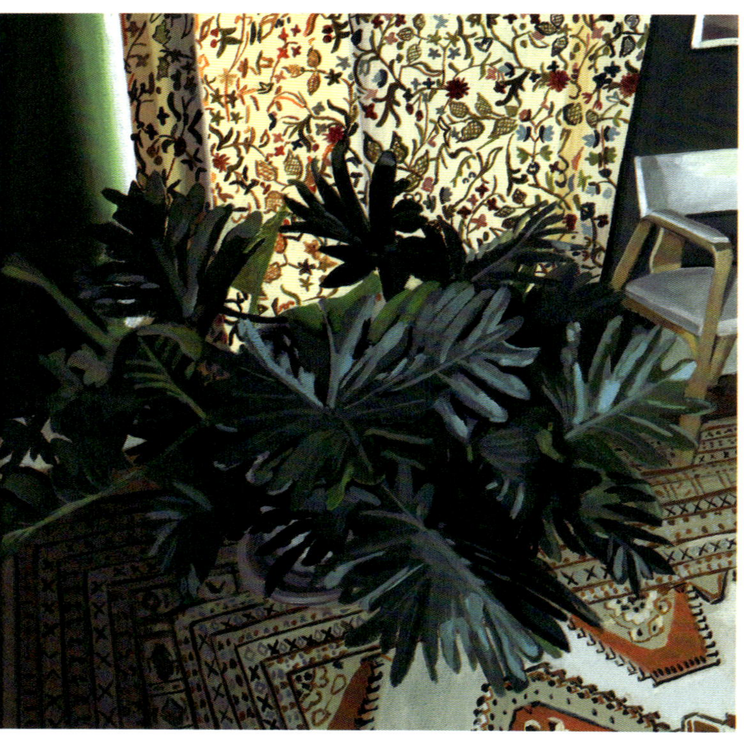

FIGURE 2.2. Kelly S. Williams. *Francine,* 2021. Oil on canvas; 6 × 6 in. Collection of Melanie and Chris Moran

1950s and '60s.[2] These days, the house is swarming with Turner's two young sons and their friends, but its shag carpet and bold architectural flourishes remain intact, preserving the late-sixties mod aesthetic like a time capsule. It's a reminder that there is always room for the avant-garde in the South—you just have to build it on top of everything that came before. Turner often hosts crafting parties for local kids, setting up stations for building clay models, making beaded lanyards, letter writing, and more on the same dirty floor where she creates her massive sculptures and where her grandfather once hosted his country music–industry friends. The way Turner has navigated her life to both incorporate and subvert her family's history is emblematic of the way it feels to make anything in the contemporary South.

When considering a group of artists as an entity, it can be easy to cast generalizations that narrow, rather than expand, the understanding of the artwork at hand. Karen Seapker, Yanira Vissepó, and Kelly S. Williams all make work that touches on similar themes of botany, home, plants, growth, and decay. But each of them uses those themes in very different ways.

In the Hallmark Channel–version of the South, a Tennessee garden might be a backdrop for domesticity and tradition. Seapker sees the garden as the ultimate nonconformist arena. Her current artist's statement references Octavia E. Butler, who wrote that "the only lasting truth / Is Change."[3] That's a comforting idea, Seapker says, in an era when rights are being stripped away and hard-won freedoms are being denied. Perhaps the United States is like a garden, and the need for regenerative phases—times when conditions seem dark and dormant, but growth is stirring just beneath the surface—is part of its cyclic trajectory.

Vissepó uses garden imagery to evoke politics and colonial history by showcasing the biodiversity of her native Puerto Rico. With an idiosyncratic combination of methods that include cyanotype and resist dying, she pieces together linocut prints of floral arrangements that incorporate both the Caribbean and the American South. Home, in Vissepó's artworks, is a coalescence of places.

Williams brings plants indoors with her photorealistic still lifes. She is well-versed in multiple painting styles, from abstract tondos based on the patterns of textiles passed down from her grandmother to trompe l'oeils of tarot cards. But her paintings of ordinary contemporary life that seem culled from gloriously candid snapshots—unmade beds, open magazines, piles of paperbacks and unremarkable views from kitchen windows—contain the most authentic representations of home. In works like *Francine* (fig. 2.2), flowers are the stuff of chintz wallpaper and embroidered tablecloths.

Narratives of the South can be conjured by objects, images, and products—quilts and Cracker Barrel restaurants and Mason jars. The reality of the South is complex and steeped in liminality. But there are artists who upend those signifiers of Southernness and use them to reassert the multiple identities of Southern women.

Lauren Gregory is a third-generation Southern woman artist. Gregory, her mother, and her grandmother have all referred to their passion for painting as "the curse," and her work reflects that self-deprecating but unrelenting essence. She borrows content and techniques from traditional tapestries and quilts but uses contemporary references in her textiles. Her *Unicorn in Captivity* (pl. 14) borrows its subject from late Gothic tapestry, but instead of fine wool and gilded threads, Gregory uses mass-produced textiles like those you might find in a scrap bin at a local fabric store. Some of her quilt squares include images culled from the internet, like Britney Spears dancing on an Instagram post, in addition to images from medieval art.

Tennessee-born artist Briena Harmening sees herself as a collaborator with the women who made the materials she reclaims in her work. She scours secondhand shops for the kinds of bedspreads, afghans, and quilts she grew up around, then augments them with her own deadpan country wisdom. As she twists the blankets around forms and screen prints quaint turns of phrases onto them, she acts as a punk interlocutor. The gently coded language of quilting is upended, and Harmening pulls away the artifice and makes it irreverent. She is an intervenor, conspiring with the women before her by picking up what they spent time on so many years before her. In her work *Second, Minute, Hour, Day, Month, Year, Decade* (pl. 45), Harmening has stenciled the words *One day we won't be here* onto an otherwise ordinary quilt, turning a simple phrase into an ominous declaration that recalls text-based

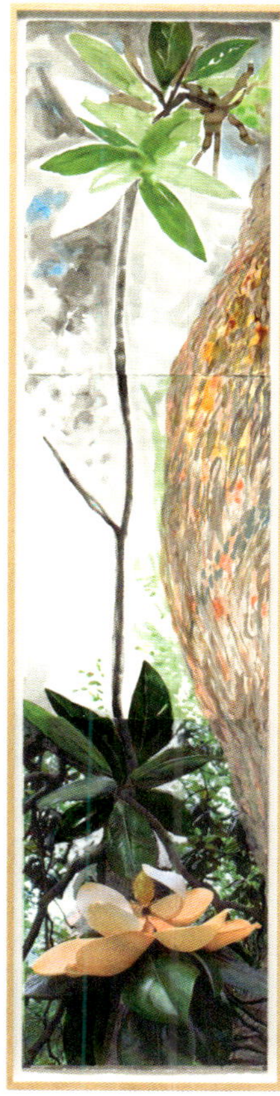
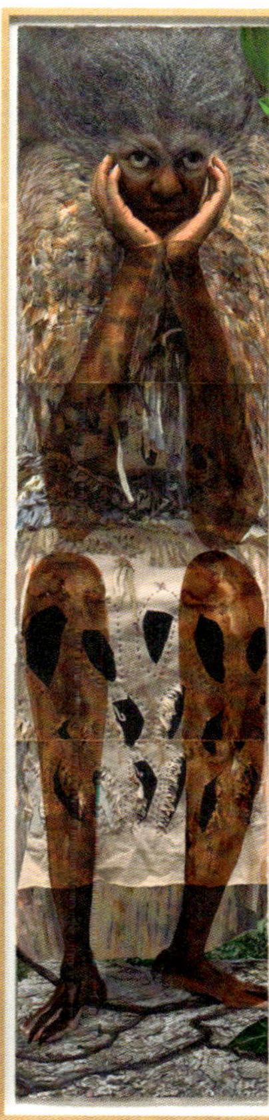
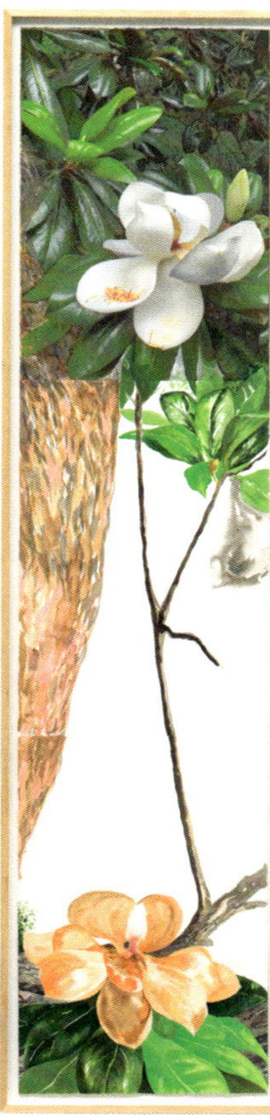

FIGURE 2.3. María Magdalena Campos-Pons. *Secrets of the Magnolia Tree*, 2021. Watercolor, ink, gouache, and digital printing on three panels; 132 × 90 in. overall. The Museum of Modern Art, New York, Latin American and Caribbean Fund and gift of Ronnie Heyman 2022

works from Jenny Holzer and Wayne White. The quilt becomes a conversation with the past—a simple *we were here* carved into an old school desk—and it makes you wonder whose quilt this was, and why it was so small. Was it unfinished? Was it perhaps made for a child? Where is that child now? Who has she become?

In any discussion of art and place, it is important to consider not only the location of an artwork's production but also the time in which it was created. The twenty-first century is brimming with contradictions, and the artists of *In Her Place* are making their work in the middle of it all. As Vadis Turner has said in conversation, artists working in Tennessee right now are in the teeth of America.[4]

Cuban-born artist María Magdalena Campos-Pons has said that we are all "voyeurs of our times. . . . Everyone is a participant in the narration of time. No one is excluded."[5] In a 2011 talk she gave during the run of a solo exhibition at the Frist that included her foundational work *Spoken Softly with Mama*, Campos-Pons told the audience that the first line we ever draw as people is the umbilical cord, a connection to our mothers.[6] The observation that people have the innate, biological ability to create, but not control, their connections is a perfect example of how Campos-Pons

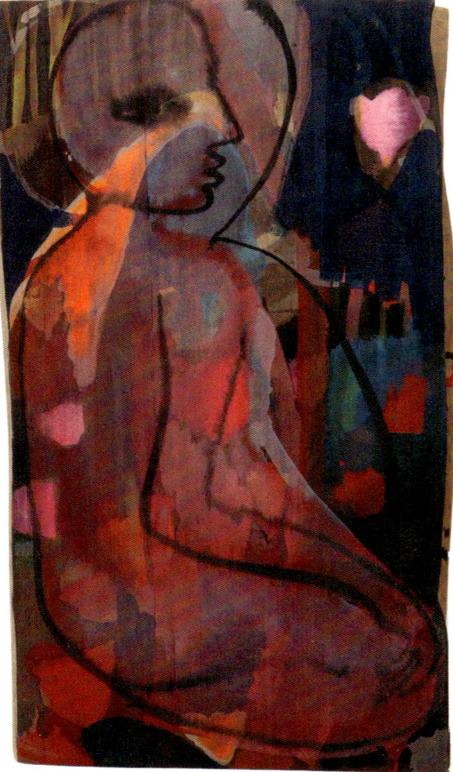
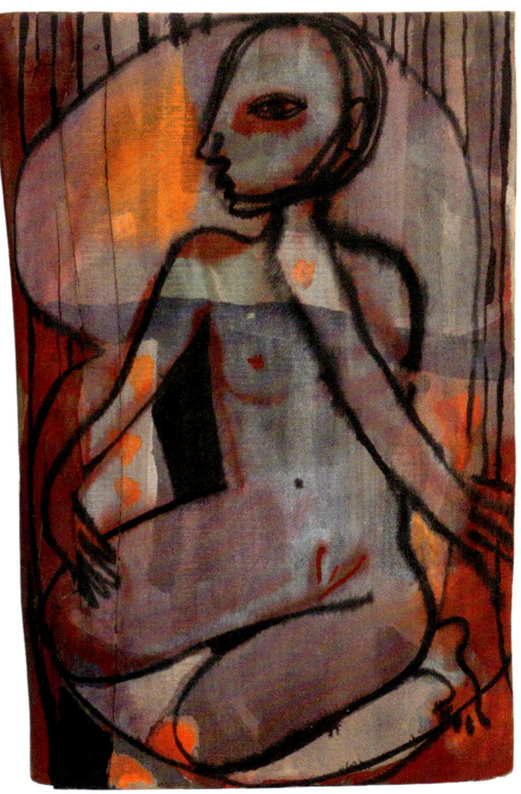

FIGURE 2.4. Kimia Ferdowsi Kline. *October* (diptych), 2024. Ink on carved wood; 22 × 28½ × 3 in. Courtesy of the artist

approaches her art. She presents something familiar and creates a ritual that gives it a symbolic dimension. Since moving to Nashville in 2017 to become the Cornelius Vanderbilt Endowed Chair of Fine Arts at Vanderbilt University, Campos-Pons has incorporated Southern imagery into her works. The university grounds are located on an arboretum, to which she attributes the recurring symbol of the magnolia tree—a symbol that seems to haunt her recent work. *Secrets of the Magnolia Tree* is a 132-by-90-inch multipanel piece that envisions the artist as a monumental owl-faced oracle (fig. 2.3). But even as it incorporates stories and images from her days in Nashville, her work remains connected to her deeper roots in Cuba and her ancestry in Nigeria and China. As an artist, Campos-Pons is drawing lines across countries and through time.

Memory is also explored in the work of Ashley Doggett, a painter whose practice incorporates ideas of Blackness and the history of Nashville as a site of political unrest. Curator Miranda Lash writes in her essay "What Do We Envision When We Talk About the South?" that the civil rights movement of the 1960s was a major turning point in how the "spirits" of the South were seen and understood, simply because of the outpouring of images that were broadcast and circulated far beyond the region.[7] Doggett's paintings of photographs made during the Nashville sit-ins of 1960 express the discontent and violence of that era but also show how images can carry stories across geographical lines (pls.49–53).

Jana Harper, who was born in Washington, DC, to a family with roots in the Mackinac Bands of Chippewa and Ottawa Indians, explores the ways ancestries can blend in her multimedia series of works *Blood, Memory, and the Power of Naming*. The sumi ink and gouache on rag paper artwork *Memorial for Mackinac* charts the names of every Mackinac individual accounted for in a census from 1870 and 1908 (pl. 34). Squares of red, black, and yellow reference the Indigenous tradition of the Medicine Wheel as well as the flattened geometric compositions of Piet Mondrian. Harper has piled each name onto the last until the list becomes a wash of indecipherable lines. Her own imperfect-but-calligraphic handwriting recalls drawings by Cy Twombly, while the increasingly illegible quality of the names nods to Glenn Ligon's *Untitled (I am an invisible man)*.

The theme of place intersects with ideas of both time and memory. As events unfold in a location, they can lend the place its specific significance. Sometimes that significance can simply come from an artist's own autobiography.

Kimia Ferdowsi Kline was born in Nashville to Iranian parents, and her work draws from two visual traditions: a flat, decorative style inspired by Persian miniatures and carpets, and an approach to the body derived from European figurative painting. She speaks of this blending as a mirror of her own dual identity as an Iranian American.[8] Her ink-on-carved-wood diptych *October* shows two figures facing each other like sisters from across time (fig. 2.4). They may be ancestors, lovers, or even different facets of the same person. In Kline's saturated stained-glass colors and bold lines, her family's heritage is transmuted into her own expression of personhood.

The surreal situations in the stirring paintings of Nashville-born artist Shannon Cartier Lucy reflect a desire to recapture the feelings of her childhood. In her artist's statement, Lucy says that her father's advancing schizophrenia is a major influence in the uncanny combinations she paints: "It was customary in my home to find a toaster in the freezer or the Holy Bible in the dishwasher."[9] Works like *Our New Home*, which shows a goldfish bowl set atop a stove, or *New Home (Oven)*, which shows a pair of bright red women's panties draped over the middle rack in an oven, demonstrate how artists can sometimes find place inside their own minds (pl. 55).

Tehran-born artist and ceramicist Raheleh Filsoofi can trace her autobiography over Iran's political timeline. A toddler during the 1979 revolution, she came of age during the wars between Iran and Iraq. After finishing her undergraduate studies in ceramics in Tehran, Filsoofi moved to the US in 2002. She has taught ceramics at Nashville's Vanderbilt University since 2020 and in that time has begun a new body of work that incorporates earth she's collected from multiple sites in and around Nashville.[10] It would be unimaginable to say that Filsoofi's art has ever abandoned her Iranian heritage. Rather, living in Nashville has helped her develop a body of work that looks different than it would have had she stayed in Tehran but is no less *of* Tehran.

When you look at the work the artists of *In Her Place* are making, it is clear that there are more differences than similarities. There are large-scale sculptures constructed from inherited curtains, oil paintings of impossibly bizarre domestic arrangements, and interpretations of medieval tapestries pieced together from bargain-bin fabrics. The same is true for the artists themselves—aside from making work in the same location at the same time, there are few direct similarities among them. Does that mean that place no longer functions as a reliable marker of work? Perhaps it means that place is more expansive than it was before everyone was connected online, airfare was relatively cheap, and art centers began moving away from major coastal cities. Place is additive, not subtractive.

Perhaps place means more, not less, than it used to. It is where you are from and also where you choose to be. It is a setting for human behavior. Place—that particular point of view that can ground an artist—is more important than it has ever been. It just looks different now.

NOTES

1. Scott Romine, "The Real South," in *When the Stars Begin to Fall: Imagination and the American South*, ed. Thomas J. Lax (Studio Museum in Harlem, 2014), 118.
2. Libby Callaway, "Gimme Shelter: Vadie's Place," *Nashville Scene*, November 10, 2016, https://www.nashvillescene.com/arts_culture/coverstory/gimme-shelter-vadies-place/article_5b1f8ae7-cb1c-52e9-8fb7-b7c74979cf51.html.
3. Octavia E. Butler, *Parable of the Sower* (Open Road Media, 2012), chap. 1.
4. Vadis Turner, telephone call with author, December 14, 2024.
5. Laura Hutson Hunter, "Fall Guide 2024: María Magdalena Campos-Pons Talks 'Behold,'" *Nashville Scene*, September 19, 2024, https://www.nashvillescene.com/arts_culture/coverstory/mara-magdalena-campos-pons-behold/article_9d587d02-7524-11ef-baf0-cb0aa3ec4854.html.
6. Laura Hutson Hunter, "María Magdalena Campos-Pons Explores Memory with a Video Installation at The Frist," *Nashville Scene*, October 20, 2011, https://www.nashvillescene.com/arts_culture/mar-a-magdalena-campos-pons-explores-memory-with-a-video-installation-at-the-frist/article_2be601d9-2413-5dc5-93fc-acdc438850d4.html.
7. Miranda Lash, "What Do We Envision When We Talk About the South?," in *Southern Accent: Seeking the American South in Contemporary Art*, ed. Miranda Lash and Trevor Schoonmaker (Nasher Museum of Art at Duke University, 2016), 25.
8. Kimia Ferdowsi Kline, email message to author, January 3, 2025.
9. Shannon Cartier Lucy, "Artist Statement," 2019, https://www.shannonlucy.com/artist-statement.
10. Laura Hutson Hunter, "Raheleh Filsoofi Talks Memory, Ceramics and Winning the Joan Mitchell Fellowship," *Nashville Scene*, November 16, 2023, https://www.nashvillescene.com/arts_culture/visualart/raheleh-filsoofi/article_a5239e22-8326-11ee-87de-230508c40be9.html.

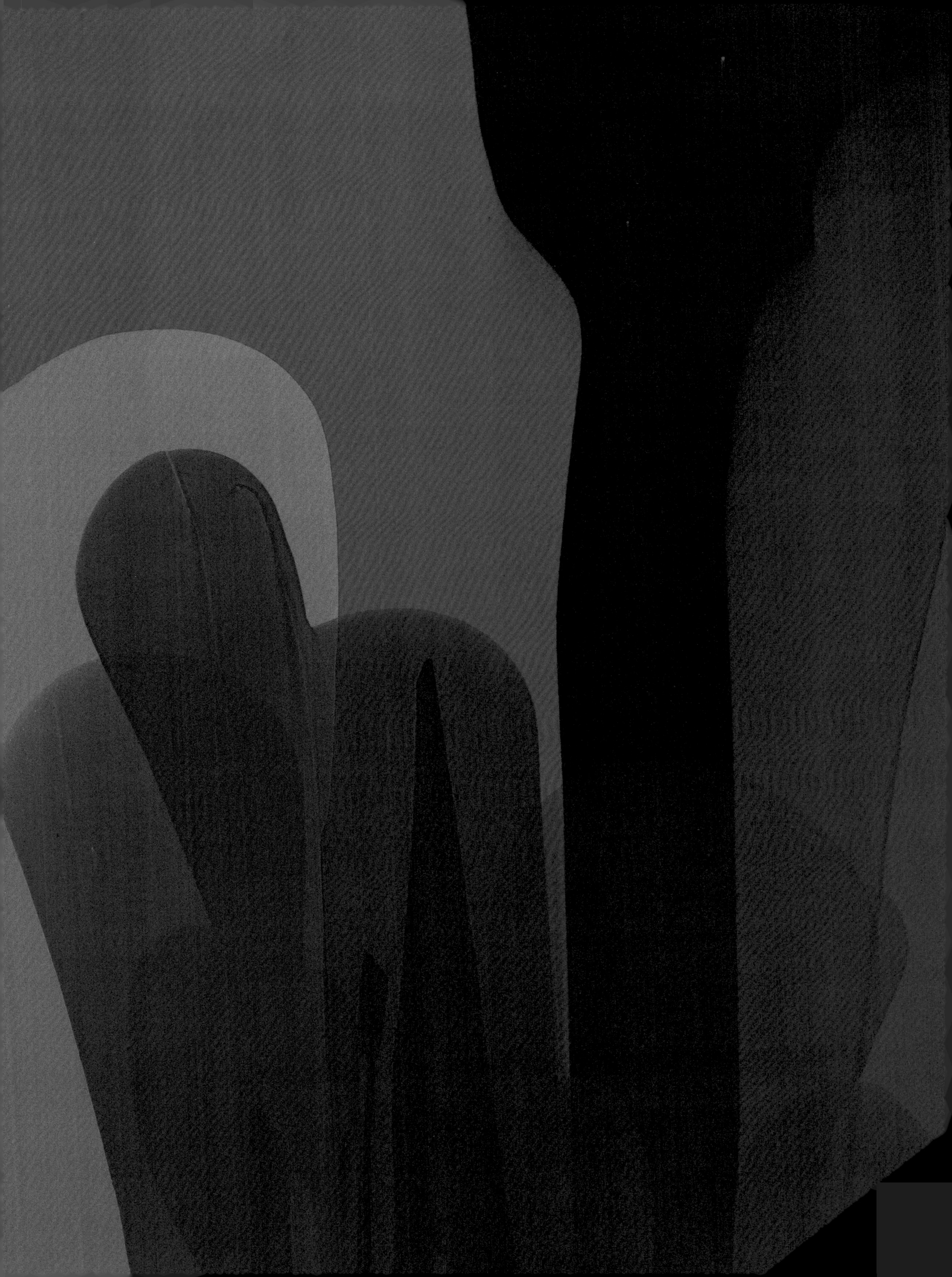

Vivien Green Fryd

NASHVILLE'S "GOOD-OLE-GIRL" NETWORK

Art Leaders at the End of the Twentieth Century

IN APRIL 2001, ARTIST CAROL MODE AND I jumped for joy at the opening of the Frist Art Museum, then the Frist Center for the Visual Arts, in the grand, newly renovated building that once housed Nashville's postal headquarters. We were thrilled over the existence—*finally!*—of a major institution dedicated to bringing global art to Middle Tennessee. The Frist's opening in the heart of downtown Nashville was the culmination of a growing community of artists, exhibition spaces, and viewers over the previous two decades. Looking back, I see it as the beginning of a new chapter that has resulted in the vibrant Nashville art scene of today.

When I arrived in Nashville in the summer of 1985 to be an assistant professor of art history at Vanderbilt University, the city had some pockets of visual artistry, but no large-scale, centrally located nexus. What is now called Cheekwood Estate & Gardens existed as the primary art institution, but its location ten miles from downtown in the affluent Belle Meade neighborhood made it inaccessible to many. Smaller art collections, primarily of American art, were dispersed around town, including the Cowan Collection at the Parthenon, the Stieglitz Collection in the Carl Van Vechten Gallery at Fisk University, and the Belmont Mansion, which houses nineteenth-century American neoclassical sculptures. In 1970, the Country Music Hall of Fame commissioned Thomas Hart Benton to create *The Sources of Country Music*, a mural now installed in the downtown institution's rotunda. Only a few galleries, such as Cumberland Gallery, Zimmerman Saturn Gallery, and In the Gallery, exhibited contemporary art.

Change was coming, though. The following years witnessed new galleries and exhibition opportunities. Notably, it was primarily a "good-ole-girl" network that contributed to the blossoming Nashville visual arts community, leading to the opening of the Frist at the turn of the twenty-first century. I derive this term from an article published in a 1986 issue of *Premier* magazine. The writer recounts a conversation among Enid Katahn, pianist at Vanderbilt's Blair School of Music; Marilyn Murphy, professor of studio art at Vanderbilt University; Carol Stein, the owner of the Cumberland Gallery; and Clara Hieronymus, art correspondent for *The Tennessean*. Murphy, who initiated this discussion, explained that she "started thinking about the people who have become the leaders in the Nashville art world," realizing, "almost without exception, all were women."[1] This examination of the Nashville arts scene from 1980 to 2001—a scene dominated by women artists, curators, and gallery owners—derives mostly from artist resumes, exhibition catalogues, gallery invitations, newspaper and local journal articles, and oral history.[2]

Nashville Woman-Operated Exhibition Spaces, 1980–2001

During the eighties and nineties, Jane Braddock, Lanie Gannon, Carol Mode, and Marilyn Murphy exhibited in various Nashville venues. Murphy noted that, when she moved to Nashville in 1980 to teach at Vanderbilt, many artists in the community felt like they worked in a vacuum.[3] When she arrived, "about five artists

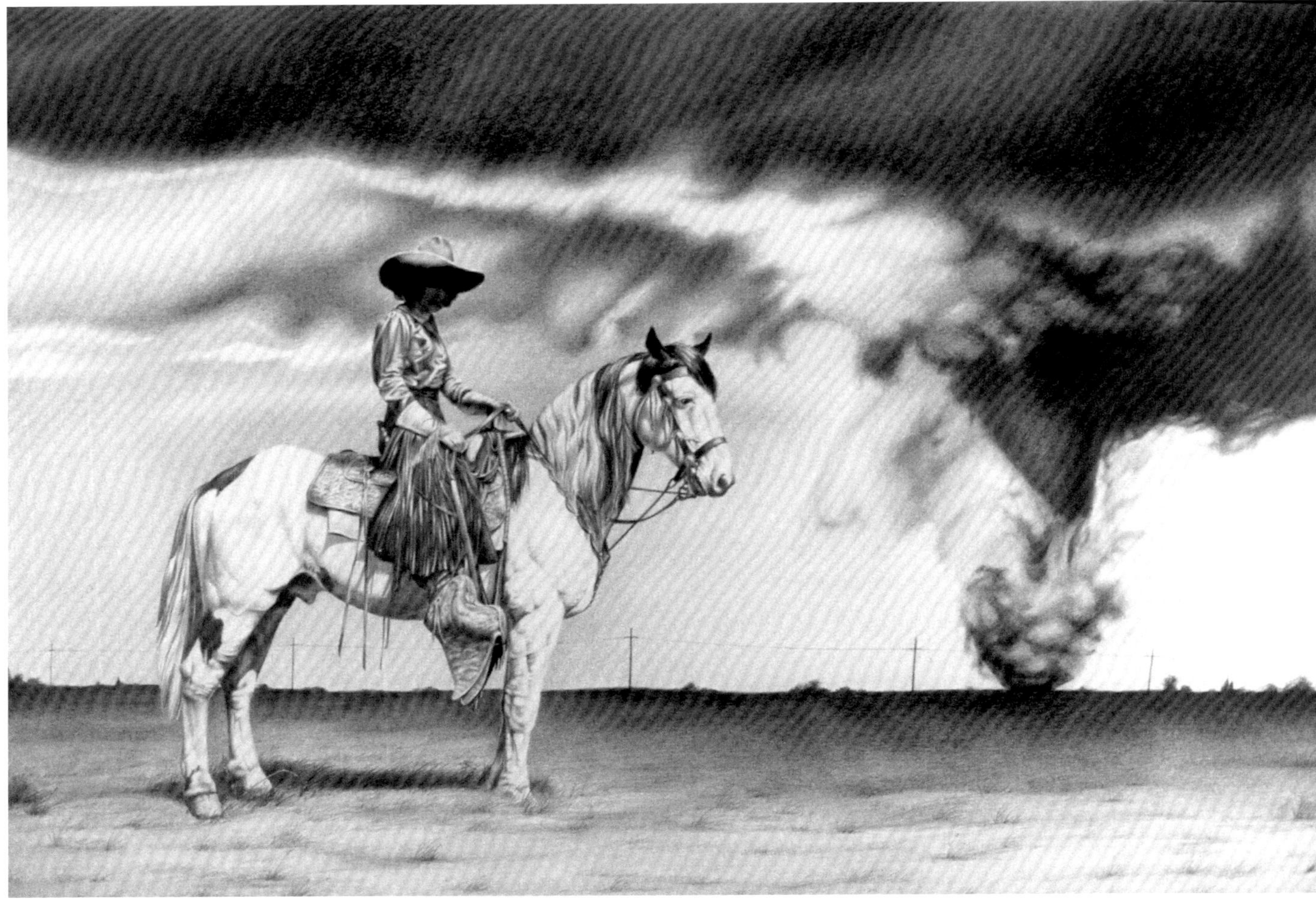

FIGURE 3.1. Marilyn Murphy. *101 Ranch Twister*, 1993. Graphite on paper; 25 × 38 in. Collection of Walter and Mary Schatz

in town formed a close-knit group."[4] Because few opportunities existed for artists to show their work, she curated during this decade six group exhibitions of local artists, which each lasted one weekend, in buildings on Vanderbilt's campus.[5] These were "guerrilla openings" and "bring-your-own-wine parties."[6]

During this time, women owned and ran two of the leading commercial galleries in Nashville.[7] When Carol Stein moved to the city in 1972 from New York City because her husband began teaching at Vanderbilt University School of Medicine, she recognized that no commercial galleries existed and in 1980 opened Cumberland Gallery in Green Hills.[8] Along with contemporary American and European artists from outside Nashville, Stein included in solo and group shows local artists such as Braddock, Gannon, Mode, and Murphy.[9] Nancy Saturn and Alice Zimmerman opened the Zimmerman Saturn Gallery downtown in 1985, highlighting work mostly by non-Nashvillian artists.[10] Their gallery closed in 1992 because it turned out to be financially inviable. As Saturn explained, they sold "art with a capital 'A.' But we just didn't sell enough. Now everyone says it was ahead of its time."[11]

Women continued to dominate the art scene over the next decade and a half. Zeitgeist Gallery, founded by Janice Zeitlin in 1994, exhibited works by many *In Her Place* artists.[12] The Arts Company, founded by Anne Brown in 1996, showed art by Gannon and Murphy. Brown, dubbed a "one-woman artist committee," also served as the founding executive director of the Metro Nashville Arts Committee, cofounded with Zimmerman the Summer Lights festival, and in 1988 initiated Arts at the Airport, which showed Braddock, Alicia Henry, Mode, Murphy, and others.[13] In 1996, Terri Smith inaugurated the Temporary Contemporary exhibition series at Cheekwood. Its opening reception attendance increased from five hundred in 1996 to 3,500 when Smith left in 2005, indicating expanding community interest.[14] Smith created an important dialogue between local artists—including Barbara Bullock, Mode, and Henry—and well-known artists from elsewhere.[15]

Nashville Women Artists, 1980–2001

Marilyn Murphy became central to Nashville's art scene, not only through her pop-up shows but also by exhibiting her own work in the city's galleries and museums. Extolled by Mark W. Scala, then curator of American art at the Frist, as "one of Nashville's most compelling artists," her art is notable for its meticulously detailed realistic figures, domestic settings, and clothing inspired by 1940s and '50s mass-media images.[16] She often includes faces obscured by coverings and shadows, cropped compositions that cut heads out of the picture frame, or body positions viewed from behind or at abrupt angles. Her film-noir evocations highlight fires, tornadoes, and unknown scientific studies, as well as flying papers, balloons, buildings, objects, and people, to create a sense of unease, danger, and mystery.[17]

Having grown up during the 1950s in Tulsa, Oklahoma, what Murphy calls "the heart of Tornado Alley," she created works that convey "psychological tension" and sinister external forces.[18] This is evident in *101 Ranch Twister*, in which a cowgirl on horseback in the foreground of a Great Plains landscape surveys a farm demarcated by the fence in the middleground (fig. 3.1). She seems oblivious to the impending disaster: a tornado barreling forward in the background. Murphy's drawing references nineteenth- and early twentieth-century images in which equestrian cowboys explore and settle the American West, evoking conquest of the frontier. Murphy notably rewrote and subverted this history by replacing the triumph of US conquest with the threat of natural disasters, thereby troubling the romanticization of Western settlement. She also replaced the heroic frontiersman with an isolated frontierswoman who is not a Madonna-like mother such as those typically found in earlier images of the West. At the same time, *101 Ranch Twister* conveys the angst of baby boomers' post–World War II and Cold War zeitgeist and Murphy's own personal disruptions.[19]

Fire is a recurring theme in Murphy's art. In *Air and Dreams* (pl. 59), she created a suspended narrative (a characteristic of many of her works) in which the viewer cannot know if the blazing cane fire seen in the right background will destroy the romantic and seemingly peaceful cabana in the foreground. For Murphy, her fire images convey the power of US industry and people's ability to design and build "remarkable things," an association derived from childhood visits to a variety of factories and plants.[20] Seeing how farmers in Australia would set fire to sugar cane prior to harvesting, which she witnessed while joining her husband in that country in 1992, further inspired this subject. She created dualities between safety and danger, calm and upheaval, "fire and water, hot and cold, [and] acidic reds and yellows with quiet greens and blues that are opposites on the color wheel."[21]

From fire, Murphy moved to other ephemeral motifs, especially clouds, evident in *Call in the Night* (pl. 61). This drawing again shows a suspended narrative: a woman, hovering in the sky, talks on a telephone with a surprised facial expression. This could be interpreted as a "dream state" or an emergency phone call.[22]

Jane Braddock also moved to Nashville in 1980 and participated in the pop-up shows initiated by Murphy. After working for fifteen years in textile design in New York City, she and her then-husband, John Baeder, decided to move, having been inspired by a visit with Alice Zimmerman one weekend.[23] Upon relocating, Braddock became a full-time abstract painter. In 1996, Braddock took a trip to India, Nepal, and Tibet. She subsequently began her large-scale *Shakti* series. The former moniker is Sanskrit for the divine female force of creation. As with her earlier textile works, for these *Shakti* paintings, she focused on repeated patterns, color and light vibrations, and texture. They evolve spontaneously from an "internal place," creating a meditative mood in which the viewer becomes immersed in its color field.[24] Braddock initially used small brushes to create these all-over compositions with no central focus, and later began painting with her fingers as well. The *Text* series contains block stencil lettering in the Phantom font, in which she quotes passages from various sources and cultures. She explains these "text fragments express underlying values, ideas, and beliefs," which she considers "provocative, arresting, or spiritually potent."[25] She elaborates elsewhere that the typography in a grid format forms "another layer of patterning" that "only secondarily" is "perceived as text."[26] She achieves this "by eliminating punctuation and running words together."[27]

Braddock next created her *Drip and Pour* series, again creating layers with a sense of "fluidity . . . and opacity."[28] This intuitive, experimental, and spontaneous process consists of dripping and spattering, the opposite of her controlled *Text* series. In some works, she combines words with her signature fingerprint and drip process. Sometimes the text appears legible while elsewhere color, drips, and shadows of letters in different hues obscure the writing.

Braddock does not always create triptychs intentionally, but after completing works, she recognizes relationships among canvases in terms of colors, compositions, and textures. She thus often exhibits three canvases together, as can be seen in plate 98, which combines works from her *Sanskrit*, *Drip and Pour*, and *Text* series. Here, Braddock honors the acclaimed Muscogee (Creek) Nation poet Joy Harjo and includes in the right panel some passages from her publication *Crazy Brave: A Memoir* (2012).

Carol Mode began her painting career while living in Venice for a year with her husband, Robert Mode, who was researching on a Fulbright fellowship. They moved to Nashville in 1968 when he began teaching art history at Vanderbilt University. She too

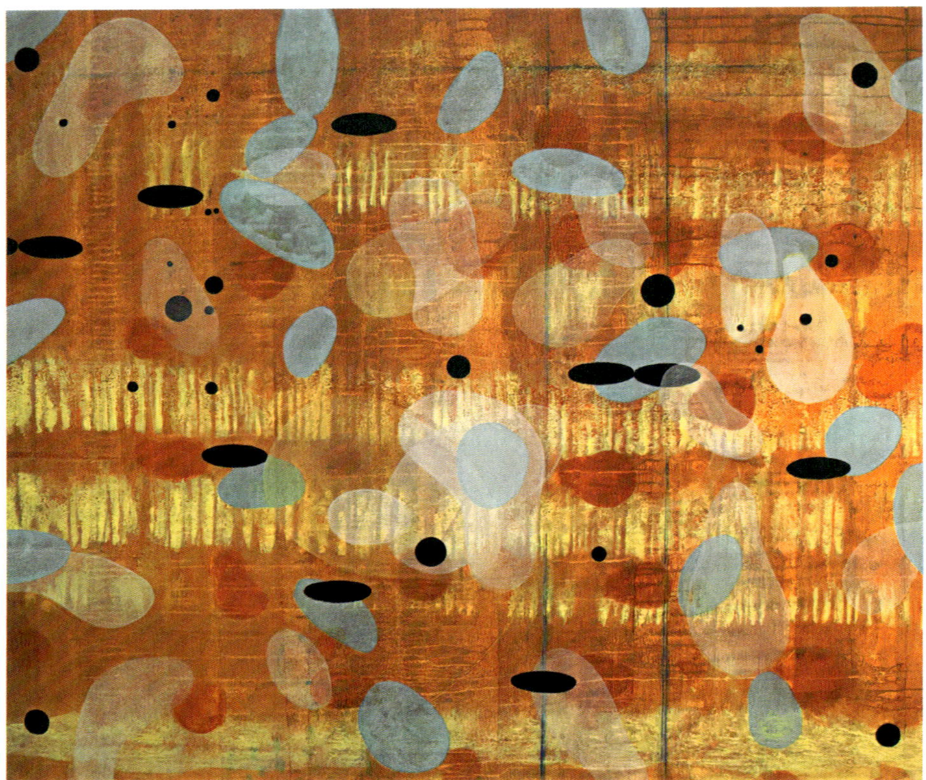

FIGURE 3.2. Carol Mode. *Araby*, 2006. Acrylic on canvas; 60 × 72 in. Courtesy of the artist

FIGURE 3.3. Lanie Gannon. *Girt*, 2002. Wood, acrylic, and rope; 6 × 10 × 6 in. Courtesy of the artist

FIGURE 3.4. Barbara Bullock. *The Hate That Hate Produced*, 1992. Acrylic on canvas; 50 × 38½ in. Collection of Dr. Albert Z. Holloway

participated in Murphy's exhibitions in the 1980s, showing colorful acrylic paintings with layers of floating, transparent, abstract, and fluid forms that hover in space, as well as works that include geometric shapes with hard edges. To create "unpredictable passages of pure process," she often paints using sandpaper, sponges, brushes, and scrapers, "uncovering, excavating, and rebuilding" motifs.[29] She also presses pigmented bubble wrap, rubber stamps, and rubbings to create "pattern repetitions."[30]

When doctors diagnosed Mode in 1999 with a rare retina condition that causes visual distortion, double vision, and lack of focus, she created a series of works to convey the "interactions of vision and place" through her "layers of irregular 'floaters' or black spots moving about freely." This results in "transparent veils occupying multidimensional spaces."[31] *Araby* (fig. 3.2) evolved from her experience with this condition; as Scala notes, "her symptoms have become a part of her artistic vocabulary."[32] Here, black, light blue, and white amoeba-like spots float on the surface against horizontal, atmospheric veils of color. Black, which usually conveys distance, hovers on the surface, while orange and yellow, which usually project forward, establish the background.

Lanie Gannon, who has lived in Nashville since elementary school, initially created sculptural figurative pieces made from wood and burlap. Rather than glorify a statesman or military hero as manifest in the classical tradition, in *Girt*, Gannon depicts an anonymous and androgynous elongated bust attached by burlap to a wooden plank (fig. 3.3). For her, wood and cloth are "materials of the earth . . . that anchor images." This highly polished disembodied wooden head, restrained and bound by rope, signifies "displacement, and the fate of all refugees . . . coercion and forced exile."[33]

Starting in 2005, Gannon began experimenting with other media, creating "more colorful and energetic visual expression[s]" that expose "internal structures and inner workings."[34] For *doily* (pl. 86), inaugurated at Zeitgeist Gallery, she used readily available materials—"a pair of scissors" as "a drawing tool, cutting a line" to create "shapes that can be fastened, linked, and connected [by fasteners, clips, snaps, tape, and glue] into a structure."[35] This eleven-foot installation appears as a headless feminine anthropomorphic being with four loose appendages that hang down to the floor, evoking both vulnerability and strength. Circular shapes made of paper reference the titular doilies that the artist associates with her grandmother.[36] The work's title, along with its concentric circles—pastel and bright pinks, yellows, and shades of green—and the use of scissors and paper, suggest a feminine craft, which could be seen as either a celebration or critique of such binary associations. Paper, according to the artist, "can be so delicate" and yet also "so strong and versatile." In this work, Gannon overlapped, wove, and fastened paper to form "a skin," creating "a scaffolding or a skeletal structure" and "bestowing materiality on the 'invisible.'"[37] The concentric circles in the center with open spaces between them form what she calls a "rib cage" or spine surrounded by "a corset or armor that warps and wefts into

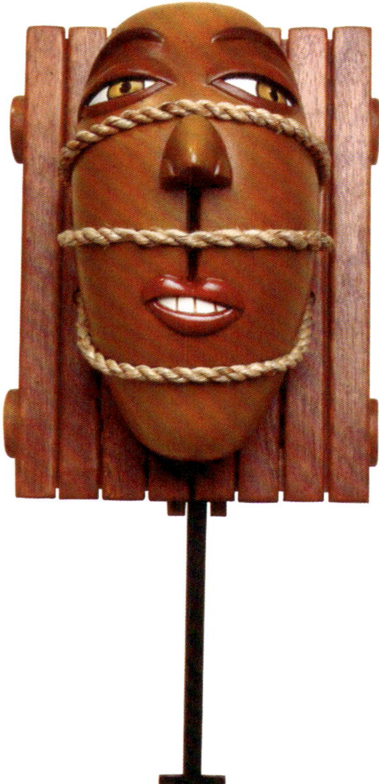

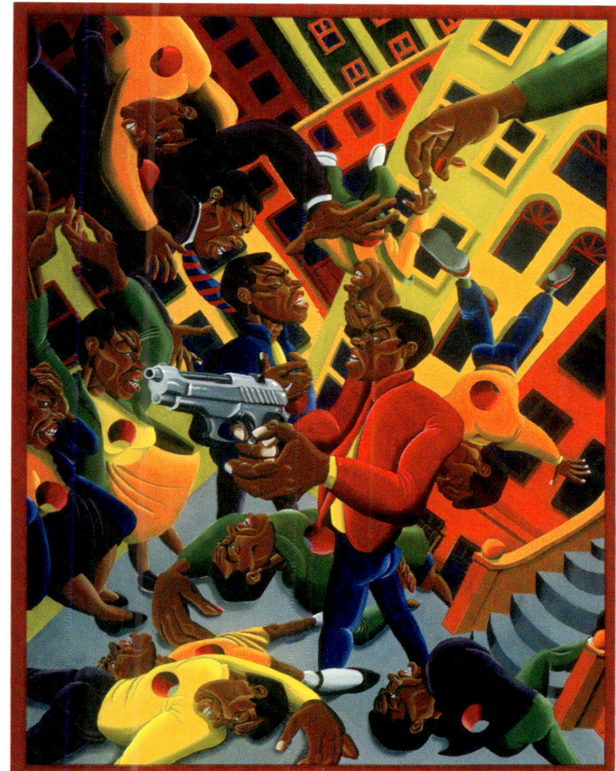

a woven synthesis of color, pattern, decorative trim, ornamentation, frippery, and finery," creating "a diversion, a coverup, a decorative camouflage with teeth."[38]

North Nashvillian LiFran Fort studied as an undergraduate at Fisk University with the renowned Harlem Renaissance artist Aaron Douglas, graduating in 1966. After earning an MA from the University of Chicago, she worked a variety of jobs in that city before returning to Nashville in 1980 to care for her ailing mother. After teaching studio art at Tennessee State University, she returned to Fisk in 1985, where she still is an instructor. In her figurative and abstract graphite, oil, and acrylic works, Fort explores "planes of the picture surface by allowing the viewer to see through layers of the foreground, middle ground, and background simultaneously." She derives this "layering [of] diaphanous images" from the style of her mentor, Douglas.[39] Her works address themes of race and misogyny "in a quiet way," she explained, elaborating that "if something touches me" such as "justice not being done," she will consider subtle strategies for their inclusion in her works.[40] Fort admitted that she was "never fully involved in the outside art [exhibition] world," although she had a show in 1985 at Nashville's Designer Collections on West End Avenue, a group show at In the Gallery in 1986 or 1987, another one at the Parthenon, and a solo exhibition at Fisk.[41]

Barbara Bullock (1946–1996), another important African American artist working during this time, is featured in a solo exhibition curated by Carlton Wilkinson, presented in the Frist's Gordon Contemporary Artists Project Gallery concurrently with *In Her Place*. She moved to Nashville in 1969 to attend the George Peabody College for Teachers, majoring in fine arts. According to Scala, her acrylic painting *The Hate That Hate Produced* (fig. 3.4), exhibited in the Frist's *Art of Tennessee* show (2003), displays a "colorful and scathing brand of social realism" that addresses "poverty, racism, or violence."[42] A Black man slightly off-center aggressively holds a huge gun, having killed and injured multiple Black people in a crowded urban space. In this topsy-turvy world, the victims express their anger and grief over what Bullock saw as the chaos and destruction caused by hundreds of years of systemic racism. Dead men lie in distorted poses on the floor while other men and women float upside down or stand on the left side. In both clothing and shifting skyscrapers, the primary colors of bright red, orange, pale green, light and dark blue, and yellow clash, further underscoring the sense of mayhem. As Scala assesses, "had Bullock lived longer . . . she might have come to be regarded as one of the most original artists to emerge in the Southern United States."[43]

The close of the twentieth century saw what is arguably one of the most important moments in Nashville's art scene: Alicia Henry—who, like Bullock, sadly died from cancer in her fifties—moved to Nashville in 1997 to teach at Fisk University.[44] Henry stitched together multilayered figures made from pieces of paper, leather, and fabric that were often shades of brown and gray. Typically named *Untitled*, her textile sculptures, pinned onto walls, address family relationships, race, and identity, as well as themes of isolation, interaction, and "pain and healing."[45] Her anonymous faces were inspired by West African masks, which she saw while working in the Peace Corps in Ghana.[46] Scala curated a show of Henry's work in 2003, noting that Henry "is more an anti-portraitist, who depicts the exterior facade as a shield protecting the selves that will always remain hidden beneath the surface."[47]

Twenty-five years after the Frist's opening, I agree with Murphy's 2017 observation, "now I don't even know all . . . the art crawls. It's amazing."[48] Along with the Frist, more than fifty art venues exist not only downtown but also clustered in other areas, many of which Joe Nolan's essay later in this publication addresses. Nashville's art community has indeed changed since these artists and I moved to Nashville in the 1980s and 1990s, but it continues to be largely charted by women.[49]

NOTES

1. "The Good-Ole-Girl Network," *Premier* (Spring 1986), 36.
2. I would like to thank the following people for sharing information with me: Jane Braddock, Lanie Gannon, Susan Knowles, Linda Lou Marks, Carol Mode, Marilyn Murphy, Adrienne Outlaw, Robyn Rubinoff, Samantha Saturn, Mark W. Scala, Jamaal Sheats, Terri Smith, Carlton Wilkerson, Lain York, Janice Zeitlin, Anna Zeitlin, and Manuel Zeitlin.
3. "Good-Ole-Girl Network," 36.
4. "Good-Ole-Girl Network," 36.
5. The exhibitions were *Mayday Invitational*, Cohen Memorial Art Gallery, Vanderbilt University, 1981; *Music City Biennial*, Cohen, 1981; *Dangerous Works*, Cohen, 1982; *Second Music City Biennial*, Cohen, 1982; *Microwave Invitational*, Vanderbilt Fine Arts Gallery, 1985; and *Four x Four: Four Women Artists*, Tenth Anniversary of the Women's Center, Vanderbilt University, 1988. The following participated in these pop-up exhibitions: John Baeder, Jane Braddock, Carol Mode, Marilyn Murphy, and David Ribar. See Jim Ridley, "Domestic Disturbance," *Nashville Scene*, October 21, 2004, 27.
6. Marilyn Murphy, email message to author, November 15, 2024.
7. Carlton Wilkerson opened In the Gallery in 1987 and closed it in 2006. Having grown up in Nashville, he realized that, as an African American, his "art was always excluded just because of who [he was] . . . there was nobody who was going to show my work unless I did it myself." In the Gallery sold art of the African diaspora, including works by Barbara Bullock and LiFran Fort. See David Maddox, "Home for the Homeless Artist," *Nashville Scene*, October 12, 2006, https://www.nashvillescene.com/arts_culture/home-for-the-homeless-artist/article_8a2cca72-1340-5664-8ec4-920622f35fd3.html.
8. Carol Stein, initially with Susan Hammond and Susan O'Neill, opened the Cumberland Gallery in the Green Hills area. She became the sole owner a year later. In 1985, the gallery moved to another area in Green Hills, where it remained until 2019 when Stein retired.
9. The Cumberland Gallery exhibitions were *Carol Mode: Recent Paintings*, 1982; *Lanie Gannon and Teresa Bucy-Reed*, 1983; Murphy in *Metropolis*, 1984; Murphy and Mode in *Media Variations*, 1985; *Jane Braddock*, 1985; Murphy in *Southern Realism*, 1985; Braddock, Gannon, Mode, Murphy, in *Artists Select*, 1985; *Jane Braddock*, 1987; *Carol Mode: New Work*, 1987; *Marilyn Murphy Recent Works*, 1988; Braddock, Gannon, and Murphy in *Small Packages*, 1988–89; *Jane Braddock: Paintings and Oil Pastels*, 1988–89; Murphy and Mode in *Prints of the Eighties*, 1989; Gannon, Murphy, and Mode in *Ten Year Retrospective: Group Exhibition*, 1990; *Lanie Gannon*, 1991; *Carol Mode: New Paintings*, 1991; *Carol Mode: New Work*, 1995; and *Carol Mode: Air Layers*, 2000.
10. They also showed some local artists: John Baeder, Hank De Vito, Marla Faith, and Linda Lou Marks. Linda Lou Marks, text message to author, December 29, 2024.
11. Mary Hance, "American Artisan Owner Crafts Unique Niche in Business World," *Nashville Banner*, December 8, 1994, D-3. Nancy Saturn and her husband, Alan, moved to Nashville from Washington, DC, in 1969, for Alan's job as a lawyer. In 1970, she began the American Crafts Festival, and, in 1971, she purchased Craft Cranny on Bandywood Drive, which she transformed in 1981 into the American Artisan—*the* place to purchase crafts until it closed in March 2009. Zimmerman moved to Nashville from Atlanta in 1960 with her then-husband because of his business. They began collecting art in the early 1970s, and she continued to do so throughout her life, which led to her opening with Saturn the Zimmerman Saturn Gallery in a building on Second Avenue owned by her husband. Zimmerman selected the "fine" artists they represented, while Saturn chose the high-end "crafts." She served as executive director for the Metro Arts Commission and cofounded the annual Summer Lights music and arts festival that lasted from 1981 to 1997. See "Alice Zimmerman of Nashville, Tennessee, 1939–2024, Obituary," Crawford Funeral Home, August 2024, https://www.crawfordservices.com/obituary/alice-zimmerman.
12. From the beginning, Zeitlin wanted to provide an open conversation about architecture design (her husband, Manuel, is a notable architect) and create a network not just for the visual arts but also musicians, dancers, and spoken-word artists.
13. A 2002 Joint House Resolution called Brown a "one-woman arts committee." See Tennessee House Joint Res. 716, March 11, 2002, submitted by Jere Hargrove, https://www.capitol.tn.gov/Bills/102/Bill/HJR0716.pdf. Brown moved to Nashville in 1968 to teach at Fisk University and became a leading figure in the city's arts community. She sold The Arts Company in 2019 after twenty-three years. As Erica Ciccarone and Laura Hutson Hunter assessed, "In its 23 years with Brown at the helm, The Arts Company has helped define downtown Nashville as an arts destination." See Erica Ciccarone and Laura Hutson Hunter, "Downtown Mainstay The Arts Company Abruptly Changes Hands After 23 Years," *Nashville Scene*, November 21, 2019, https://www.nashvillescene.com/arts_culture/downtown-mainstay-the-arts-company-abruptly-changes-hands-after-23-years/article_1c89b9f2-00c9-5b23-a725-6c314f2c8282.html.
14. Terri C. Smith resume, shared in personal communication with the author.
15. Nashville women artists shown at Cheekwood include Carrie McGee (1996), Barbara Bullock (1996), Carol Mode (1999), Adrienne Outlaw (1999), and Alicia Henry (2000).
16. Mark W. Scala, "Acknowledgements," in *Marilyn Murphy: Suspended Animation*, exh. cat., ed. Mark W. Scala and Lucy R. Lippard (Frist Center for the Visual Arts, 2004), 4.

17. Murphy explained, "I want my works to look like a film still. . . . It's up to you as the viewer to figure out what is going on. There's realism in this approach, but also a lot of surprise." John Pitcher, "Murphy's Law: Realism Subverted and Short Stories," *Nashville Art Magazine* (February 2017), 55. See also Linda Leaming, "Marilyn Murphy: Surrealism and Dangerous Deserts," *Nashville Arts Magazine* (2010), and Peter Frank, in *Marilyn Murphy, Realism Subverted*, exh. cat. (Vanderbilt University Fine Arts Gallery, 2017).

18. "The heart of Tornado Alley" quote from Murphy email to author; "psychological tension" quote from Mark W. Scala in Jim Ridley, "Domestic Disturbance," *Nashville Scene*, October 21, 2004, https://www.nashvillescene.com/arts_culture/domestic-disturbance/article_466626f7-be1c-5980-91c2-b03b91590579.html.

19. Murphy stated, "My subjects fairly often are symbols of what's happening in my life." Quoted in Lucy R. Lippard, "Mapping Morphea," in Scala and Lippard, *Marilyn Murphy: Suspended Animation*, 11.

20. Mark W. Scala, "'Nostalgism' and Identity," in Scala and Lippard, *Marilyn Murphy: Suspended Animation*, 12.

21. Murphy email to author.

22. Murphy email to author.

23. John Baeder and Alice Zimmerman had attended the same high school in Atlanta and ran into each other at the OK Harris Gallery in New York City, which represented Baeder. Jane Braddock, conversation with author, December 11, 2024.

24. Bascove, "A Conversation with Artist Jane Braddock," *Stay Thirsty Magazine*, vol. 101 (Summer 2008), https://staythirstymagazine.blogspot.com/p/bascove-braddock-conversation.html.

25. Jane Braddock, "Statements," accessed December 2024, http://www.janebraddock.com/statement/.

26. Bascove, "Conversation with Jane Braddock."

27. Braddock, "Statements."

28. Braddock, "Statements."

29. "Unpredictable passages" from Carol Mode, artist's statement for *Continuum: New Work by Carol Mode*, Tinney Contemporary Gallery, Nashville, 2014; "uncovering, excavating," from Carol Mode, artist's statement for *Amber Waves* (2001), artist's archives.

30. Carol Mode, artist's statement for *Carol Mode and Emily Mode*, Sarratt Gallery at Vanderbilt University, November 5–30, 1998, artist's archives.

31. Carole Mode, artist's statement for *Pulse: Paintings by Page Coleman and Carol A. Mode*, Austin Peay State University, January 24–February 13, 2005, artist's archives.

32. Mark W. Scala, "The Fragile Species," *The Fragile Species: New Art in Nashville* (Frist Center for the Visual Arts, 2005), 4.

33. Lanie Gannon, "Traversing the Grain," artist's statement, 2006, artist's archives.

34. Lanie Gannon, "Words on Paper," artist's statement for exhibition at Zeitgeist Gallery, November 2–30, 2024.

35. Lanie Gannon, "Words on Work," accessed December 2024, https://laniegannon.com/page/1-words%20on%20work.html.

36. Lanie Gannon, conversation with author, November 30, 2024.

37. Gannon, "Words on Paper."

38. Gannon, "Words on Work."

39. LiFran Fort, text message to author, January 7, 2024.

40. LiFran Fort, telephone conversation with author, January 12, 2025.

41. Fort, telephone conversation with author. See also Clara Hieronymus, "'Diaphanous Images' Go on Display Today," *The Tennessean*, April 19, 1985. Fort does not remember the dates for these shows, nor does Carlton Wilkerson.

42. Mark W. Scala, "New Directions: Contemporary Art in Tennessee," in *Art of Tennessee*, exh. cat., ed. Benjamin H. Caldwell Jr., Robert Hicks, and Mark W. Scala (Frist Center for the Visual Arts, 2003), 349.

43. Mark W. Scala, *Real Illusions: Contemporary Art from Nashville Collections*, exh. cat., ed. Mark W. Scala (Frist Center for the Visual Arts, 2002), 13. Murphy and Bullock were neighbors and friends. As Murphy remembered, Bullock had a "wry sense of humor and . . . keen interest in social statements. At one point, she asked me and Susan Knowles to pose for one of her paintings. . . . She posed us so that I held Susan like a frightened mother shielding her young daughter by what she saw outside the window which were African American men. Barbara took Polaroids of us that day as source material." Marilyn Murphy, email message to author, December 20, 2024.

44. María Magdalena Campos-Pons assessed, "She's an icon. One day her work will be regarded as some of the most important that was produced in this city." Quoted in Laura Hutson Hunter, "The Talented Professor Henry: On Enigmatic Artist Alicia Henry," *Nashville Scene*, July 6, 2023, https://www.nashvillescene.com/arts_culture/coverstory/the-talented-professor-henry-on-enigmatic-artist-alicia-henry/article_0e5da854-1772-11ee-a616-73ea79bbee4e.html. In Nashville, Henry had solo exhibitions at Cheekwood's Temporary Contemporary (2000), the Nashville Airport (2002), the Frist (2003), Zeitgeist Gallery (2005, 2012, 2016, 2021), and Fisk University in conjunction with the Tennessee Triennial (2023). At the Frist, her work was also included in the group shows *Art of Tennessee* (2003) and *Phantom Bodies: The Human Aura in Art* (2015). Information from Henry's resume, accessed December 2024, https://www.tiwani.co.uk/usr/library/documents/main/artists/48/alicia-henry-cv-2025.docx-1-.pdf.

45. Mark W. Scala, *Black and Blue: Recent Works by Alicia Henry*, exh. cat., ed. Mark W. Scala (Frist Center for the Visual Arts, 2003), 3.

46. Alex Greenberger, "Alicia Henry, Artist Whose Modest Works Asked Big Questions about Visibility, Dies at 58," *ARTnews*, October 21, 2024, https://www.artnews.com/art-news/news/alicia-henry-dead-1234721745/.

47. Scala, *Black and Blue*, 1.

48. Pitcher, "Murphy's Law," 53.

49. "Nashville Art Crawls," Nashville Convention & Visitors Corp, updated 2025, https://www.visitmusiccity.com/things-to-do-in-nashville/nashville-art-crawls.

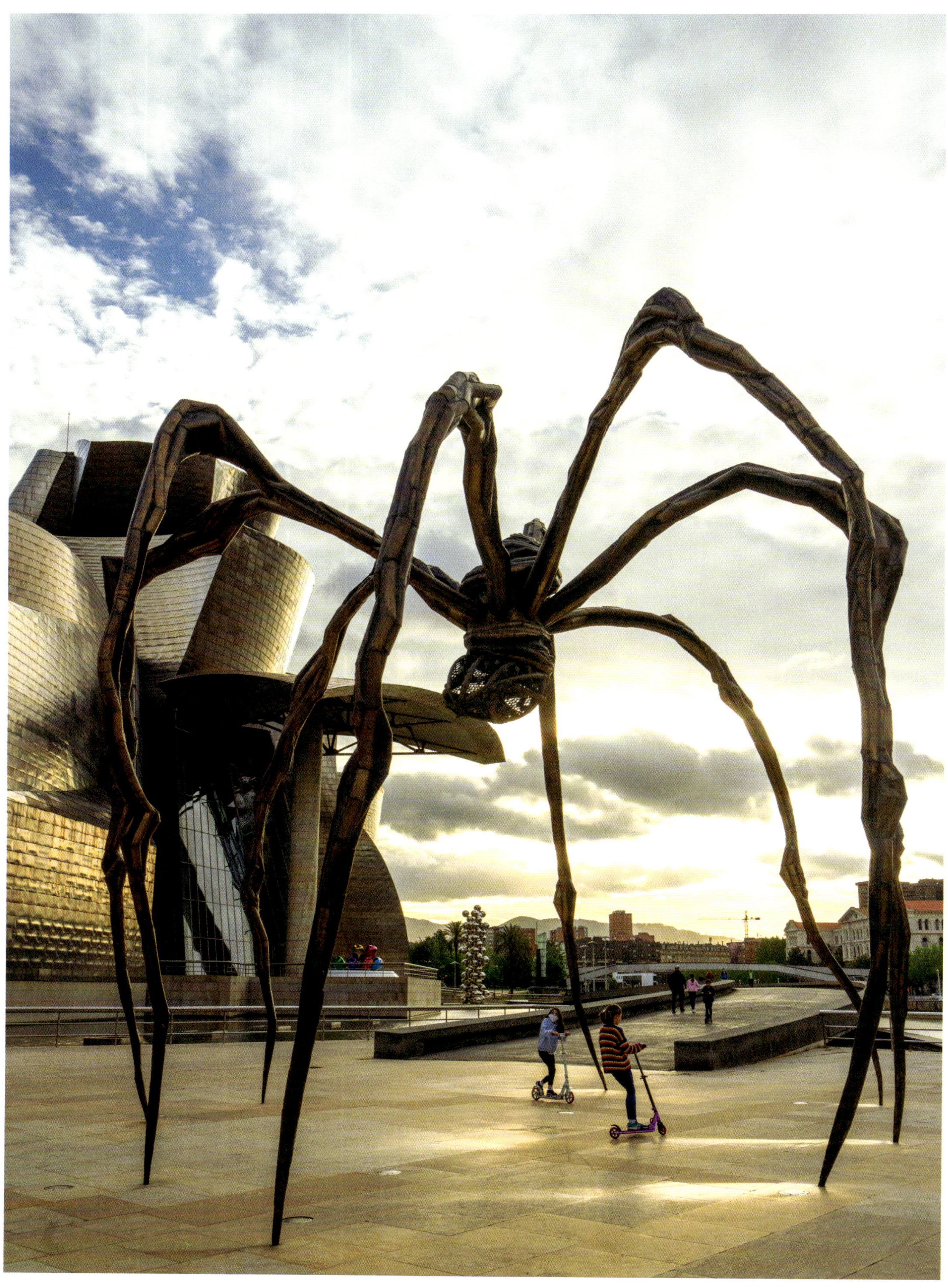

FIGURE 4.1. Louise Bourgeois. *Maman*, 1999, cast 2001. Bronze, marble, and stainless steel; 29 ft. 4⅜ in. × 32 ft. 1⅞ in. × 38 ft. ⅝ in. Museo Guggenheim Bilbao: GBM2001.1

Michelle Millar Fisher

TENDER LOVING CARE

Notes on Art Work and Care Work

16:05 Daughter and I play and make the contact we both need . . . This moment. I wonder if our days could have more of them if I didn't have so much to do . . . I wish for a cleaner.

14:20 Leave slightly late for workshop, 40 minute drive away. Frustrated that I've had to abandon my workshop prep.

1:43 PM Husband goes back to work. I head back to studio with tea, weave 20″ and hem-stitch one row and read an article on weaving history.

3:00 PM Drive to pick up preteen.[1]

AS PART OF AN ONGOING PROJECT called *Mother's Days*, artist Lenka Clayton asked the members of An Artist Residency in Motherhood to journal their days on Monday, July 15, 2019. Eighty-one artist-mothers from nineteen countries who had children ranging in age from six weeks to thirty-three years old responded. The resulting book describes lives that arc between normalcy and urgency; that encompass responsiveness, routine, and riot; and that occur in spaces that serve (and sometimes do double duty) as homes, workplaces, and studios. In making art out of care work and acknowledging the care that art making demands, too, the project demonstrated the inextricable ebb and flow between the types of labor that straddle an art practice and mothering.

It's worth immediately pointing out that this entwined labor would be recognizable to most artist-parents, regardless of gender. However, it's especially true for those who identify as women. Writer Alex Bollen rightly argues in her recent book *Motherdom* that women, regardless of whether they parent or not, have been socialized from their youth to provide caregiving labor across generations and needs. Quoting the sage Sheila Heti, Bollen points out the sheer inevitability of this expectation, one that reaches beyond biology and nuclear family structure: "The hardest thing is actually *not* to be a mother—to refuse to be a mother to anyone."[2]

It thus tracks that the precarious balance of such unremunerated and undervalued care much more often forms the context for—if not the outright subject of—artwork made by women. Clayton founded her residency program in her own home seven years before the publication of *Mother's Days* and shortly after the birth of her first child. It was a firm riposte to the lazy stereotype that the domestic sphere is a killer of creativity.[3] It also highlighted the way so many art-world structures—from openings and lectures and classrooms to the material support that ensures time for art making itself—were (and often still are) firmly closed to those with all types of care responsibilities.[4]

Like so many brilliant artists before and after her, Clayton looked at the material conditions at hand and made work from them. This included *The Distance I Can Be From My Son* (fig. 4.2), in which she films her toddler as he strays from her side in a park and a supermarket; *All Scissors in the House Made Safer* (2014), in which she hand-felted multiple pairs of the eponymous tool; and *63 Objects Taken from My Son's Mouth* (2013), in which she collected and displayed acorns, cigarette butts, screws, and other things rescued from mastication when her son was between eight and fifteen months of age.

In its unabashed foregrounding of the care work that exists as an indelible and interconnected part of her art practice, Clayton's work has plenty of foremothers in the art world. They range from

Mary Kelly, whose influential 1972 *Postpartum Document* included her infant son's fecal matter (replete with descriptions of his daily menu prepared by her) pinned to a gallery wall to María Magdalena Campos-Pons, who creates powerful meditations on ancestral mothers. Yet artists choose many different conceptual catalysts and media, so artworks are not always as direct about the conditions of their conception.

Many of the artists in the *In Her Place* exhibition have produced their works while mothering children of various ages and stages, from infants to those past college. All the artists in this exhibition have attended to someone else in or out of their homes while pursuing their work. Evidence of this unpaid labor, however, is not always apparent, even as it remains inescapable context.

In her art-making practice, Carol Mode—now in her early eighties—does not explicitly reference the two children that she gave birth to and nurtured to adulthood; neither does Sisavanh Phouthavong Houghton, a professor at Middle Tennessee State University, nor Alex Blau, even though both are mothers too. Instead, each experiment with color, form, and abstraction to different ends in their paintings. Formalism has long been a way for artists to refuse didactic demands to justify their work or explain their identity to audiences.[5]

The mother of a young son, painter Emily Weiner moved to Nashville from New York "for the family support and ease in living" when her income as an adjunct professor no longer stretched to cover bills once daycare became a factor.[6] After she became a parent, Kimia Ferdowsi Kline, whose artwork connects to mothering most profoundly in the manner in which she nurtures discarded materials back to life, moved from New York back to Nashville, her home city, for similar reasons amid the early COVID-19 pandemic lockdowns.[7] East Tennessean Lauren Gregory similarly left New York and relocated to her home state during the pandemic, soon after making a short animated film, *Ol' Splashy* (pl. 16), that explores the emotional and physical work of pregnancy loss (and resurrects the best parts of Maria Lassnig's 1970s animations in the process).

Weiner goes to her studio in her home not when creative impulses strike but "as soon as my son goes off to school." She works "until 4 PM when my alarm goes off telling me to pick up my kid," her studio time hard-won and finite. Her dreamlike, symbol-laden paintings bordered by beautiful handmade ceramic and wood frames reveal none of this at first glance. It's the imagery of a magician's white rabbit and a melancholy Pierrot clown that hint at Weiner's state of mind as a performer conjuring whatever is required—salary, dinner, comfort—on demand.[8]

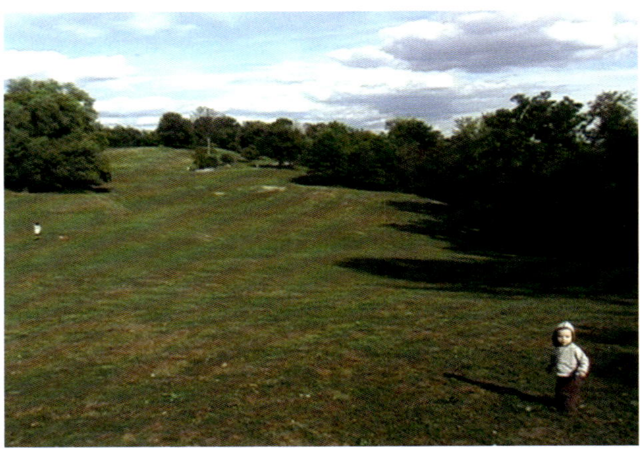

FIGURE 4.2. Lenka Clayton. *The Distance I Can Be From My Son (Park)* (video still), 2013. Video. Courtesy of the artist

Jodi Hays's three children are not at all self-evident in her collaged and painted cardboard works, which simultaneously evoke Southern quilting ("generally mother-made," as the artist notes) and Rauschenbergesque readymades.[9] One must look further back in her oeuvre to a boldly hued painting of an outdoor trampoline for hints of the children with whom she shares her home (fig. 4.3). It is from an interview, rather than from looking at her work, that I glean Hays's studio is in her backyard, a setup like that of so many other artists with care responsibilities.[10] Her current primary material, recycled cardboard, is a cipher for the interconnectedness of the domestic doorstep where packages arrive, especially since the beginning of the COVID-19 pandemic, and far wider networks of commerce and capital.

When Hays says she could, like other carers, "write a book" on experiences during the pandemic, I am reminded of Louise Bourgeois, who reclaimed wood from rooftop water towers abutting her New York townhome from which to carve her earliest tall, slender *personage* sculptures in the late 1940s. She had two young sons to care for and, like both Clayton and Hays, worked with what was at hand while struggling to make time for her own work among the expectations society and her family had placed upon her. Made much later in her career, Bourgeois's immense bronze arachnid, *Maman*, stands on its pin-prick legs as a cipher for the powerful yet precarious relationship between the artist and her own mother (fig. 4.1). When I first encountered these works as a young art historian stuffed too full of theory and formalist methods, they showed me how one's own life and matrilineal inheritances might meaningfully inflect the shape of one's work. I decided never to belittle my own biography (or an artist's) ever again.

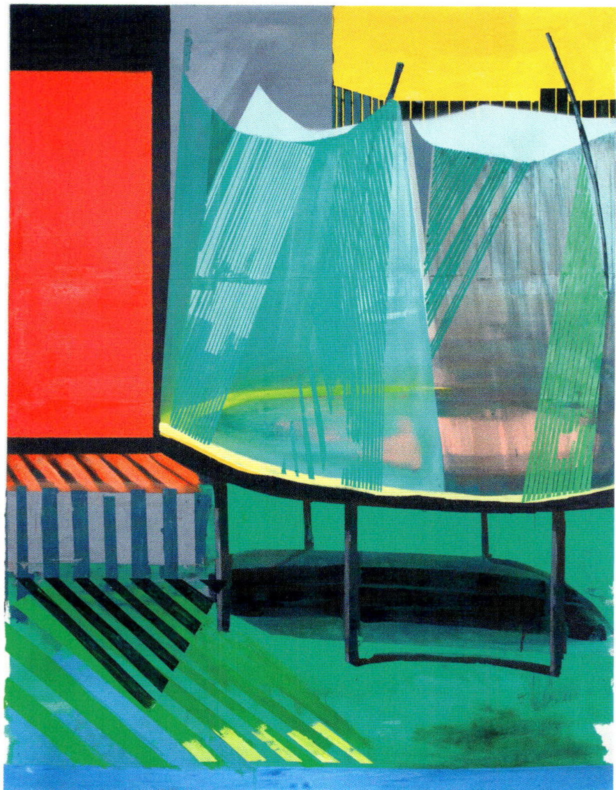

FIGURE 4.3. Jodi Hays. *Turf (Entrance/Exit)*, 2017. Oil and spray painting on sewn canvas over panel; 64 × 48 in. Courtesy of the artist

Even giants like Bourgeois are still cautionary tales in an art world that continues to skirt or neuter unpalatable embodied experiences, including care work. Just as women are socialized to undertake such labor, they have also long been told that it is embarrassing, insular in focus, unserious, and thus not valuable enough to constitute the basis for art making. If I had a dollar for every time I've heard artists across multiple generations tell me some version of a story in which their mentor, or professor, or partner, or peer reinforced this message, I'd no longer need my job as a curator. When Hays notes that the primary goal "is to be defined by one's work, not one's gender, pedigree, race, geographic location—any of these biographical ideas that have been used against an artist to limit how large their vision might be," she articulates a sentiment that is still necessary armor.[11] Many of us will spend our life's work attempting to dismantle this paradigm.

The labor of art making and mothering connects in more directly practical ways for some artists included in *In Her Place*. Campos-Pons, who has nurtured generations of students through her teaching practice, took lessons from her own child as she balanced being a parent and an artist. Inspired by the Legos and blocks in his young hands, she decided that "I could work like him. I could build big things out of very small parts."[12] So too Lanie Gannon, whose graduate training was in woodworking at Tennessee's renowned Appalachian Center for Craft, but who gravitated toward the immediacy of tools that are mainstays of children's activities: construction paper and scissors. And in some of Karen Seapker's paintings, scrawled messages written by her children are embedded within scenes of nature that suggest the life cycles of growth and decay that underwrite all our parent-child relationships (fig. 4.4).

Seapker is adamant that caring for her children and caring about her art making mutually inform one another. After all, she says, making a firm connection between the conceptual and the corporeal, "the painted mark can't be made without a body."[13] Mandy Rogers Horton, the mother of four children, affirms similar rhizomatic and mutually reciprocal relationships between herself, her children, her art practice, and the forms of care work that weave between them. As she tells it, tending to her children "is a kind of tending to myself in many ways . . . there's this necessary time out with them," forcing a different pace and perspective that in turn informs her approach in the studio (fig. 4.5).[14] The question of how to share such space and time is often baldly practical. A photograph of Seapker's two young children, Ellis and Iris, shows them among canvases in her workspace intently applying felt-tip pens and stickers to scrap paper fixed to the wall with blue painter's tape. How many other artist-mothers have a version of this image of the fruits of their labor and their loins, their hands, hearts, and minds side by side?

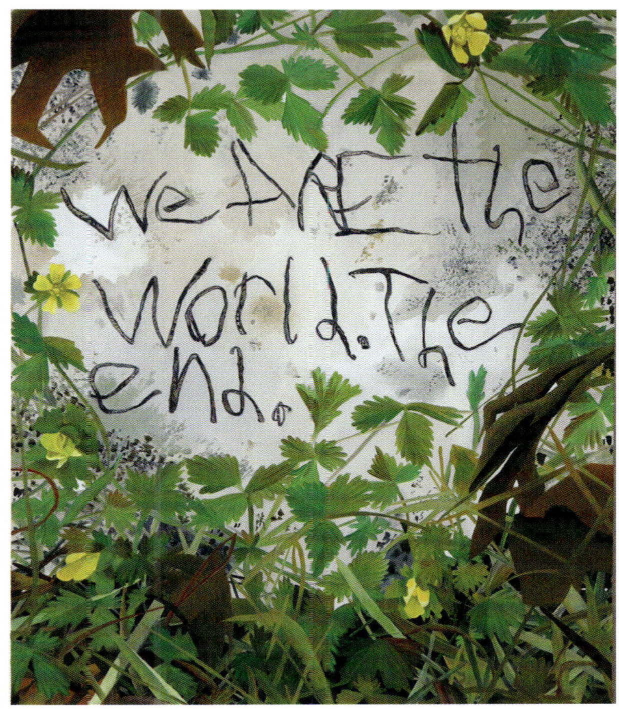

FIGURE 4.4. Karen Seapker. *Epilogue*, 2023. Oil on panel; 20 × 16 in. Courtesy of the artist

The divorce between mothering and creative work is a cultural construction rather than a biological imperative or an inevitability. Author Nicole Graev Lipson addresses this in a recent essay on the synthesis between mothering and thinking, two activities that are inextricably linked. It's a bond that social forces like patriarchy and misogyny have tried to break to marshal care work and human capital for their own ends. Lipson argues that she loves her children fiercely but, she tells us firmly, "being a mother requires more than love . . . [it] is fundamentally an undertaking of the mind. For we are thinkers before we are mothers, and it is from our thinking that our mothering is born."[15]

I affirm Lipson's formulation. For as long as I have held a pencil, I have loved to write my way into new worlds, turning words over on my tongue to pick the choicest ones for the page. As I shape stories, the patterns and rhythms of language that chatter through my mind help to quiet other thoughts that have sometimes threatened to overwhelm me. Writing keeps me happy and healthy. Hundreds of thousands of words have poured out of me as a child, a young adult, and now, at the age of forty-three, as a new mother to a six-month-old baby.

As I sit down to write this essay, I have bartered with my husband (who also has deadlines) for time—minutes, rarely hours—in evenings and weekends to write in chunks. I read through and edit with a breast pump in one hand or, sometimes, a squirming baby at my nipple. A few minutes alone in the shower offers time to reflect on a paragraph rewrite that I dictate while I towel off. Full-time daycare affords me an hour on my commute to finish up footnotes, and the fee for writing this essay pays for, among other things, a playpen so my daughter can safely explore beside me as I write some more. I read through these paragraphs I've managed to corral, and they resonate momentarily before desiccating before my eyes as soon as the baby cries out from upstairs.

As the essay nears completion, I message back and forth with the formidable painter Joan Snyder, now in her eighties and still as active in the studio as she ever was, who confirms that the push and pull of mothering and making never ends. In 1997, when her daughter Molly left home for college, Joan reflected on this reality in a poem written for the occasion:

> There is the deepest part of me that won't let you go –
> there is the shallow part of me that sees you off
> gladly so I won't be responsible
> each & every day for a child.[16]

(Joan and Molly—and now Molly's son, Elijah—remain inseparable.)

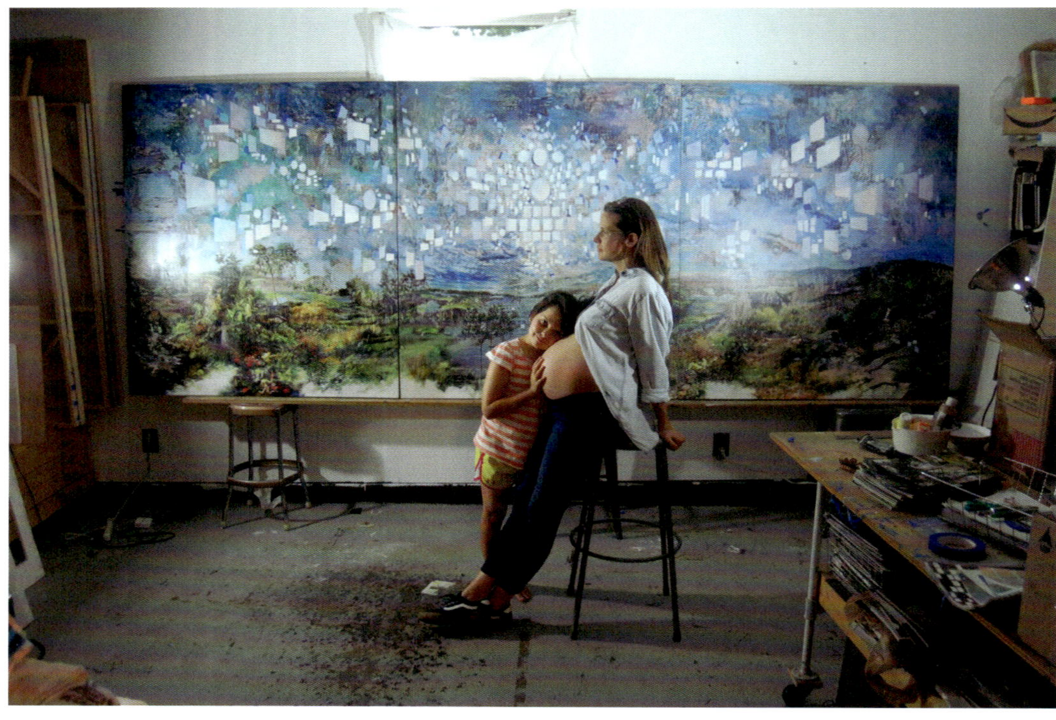

FIGURE 4.5. Mandy Rogers Horton in her studio with her oldest child while pregnant with her fourth and last child about a week before his birth, June 2018

While Lenka Clayton's respondents to her *Mother's Days* project each had their own unique twenty-four-hour journal entry, there was one universal constant between them all, and Clayton herself, and Joan, and me, and everyone who has ever tried to care for people and ideas simultaneously. Unveiling these concurrent labors of love reveal and re-center their interconnectedness. Care work might not be the subject of every artwork, but it's central to everyone's ability to make any form of art. Chronicling that fact is a political act that has the power to reshape whole worlds, not just art worlds.[17]

NOTES

1. Excerpted from three separate mother-artist diary entries in Lenka Clayton's *Mother's Days, July 15, 2019* (An Artist Residency in Motherhood, 2020), back cover, 137, and 385.
2. Alex Bollen, *Motherdom: Breaking Free from Bad Science and Good Mother Myths* (Verso, 2025), 5. For a nuanced discussion of how male-identifying people are also culturally and biologically attuned to care work, see the excellent work of evolutionary anthropologist Sarah Blaffer Hrdy, *Father Time: A Natural History of Men and Babies* (Princeton University Press, 2024).
3. There was, according to British playwright Cyril Connolly (1903–1974), "no more somber enemy of good art than the pram in the hall."
4. Grants and residencies that support those with care responsibilities are still too few, though kudos should be given to those that do exist. Hettie Judah's book, *How to Not Exclude Mother Artists (and Other Parents)* (Lund Humphries, 2022) is a useful resource.
5. Though he spoke of a racial rather than maternal identity, British Guyanese painter Frank Bowling turned to abstraction as a space of "thoughtful speculation addressing itself to aesthetic realizations" and as a way to resist external demands that he foreground his Blackness as part of what he derided as "those rotten ethnic shows" that grouped artists based on racial identity rather than conceptual affinity. Frank Bowling, "The Rupture, Ancestor Worship," *Arts Magazine* 44, no. 8 (summer 1970): 34.
6. AWT Editors, "Painter Emily Weiner: Reframing Symbolic Images Through a Feminist Lens," *A Women's Thing*, June 13, 2023, https://awomensthing.org/blog/emily-weiner/.
7. Emily Wilson, "Pregnancy Shaped Artist Kimia Ferdowsi Kline's New Show 'Mother Tongue,'" *48hills*, June 17, 2021, https://48hills.org/2021/06/pregnancy-shaped-artist-kimia-ferdowsi-klines-new-show-mother-tongue.
8. Weiner's frames also stem from an impulse to recognize hidden and gendered labor. She loves "more modest materials, such as fabric and pottery, historically made by artisans and women (now anonymous). These tactile and handmade objects might not be the motivation for most museum pilgrimages, but they have important and unsung histories of their own." AWT Editors, "Painter Emily Weiner."
9. In 1971, Rauschenberg decided to focus on a single material for a year: the cardboard box—easily obtainable and discarded after fulfilling its mission to contain something. Rauschenberg relished the chance to work directly with "a material of waste and softness." Rauschenberg quoted in Robert Pincus-Witten, "Robert Rauschenberg," *Artforum* 10, no. 5 (January 1972), 79. Hays notes that Southern quilts are "generally mother-made" in Robert Alan Grand, "Big, Dirty, Beautiful, Defensive, and Obsessed: A Q&A with Jodi Hays," *Oxford American*, March 27, 2024, https://oxfordamerican.org/web-only/jodi-hays-robert-alan-grand-interview.
10. Like several artists in *In Her Place*, what keeps Hays in the South is "affordable housing; family; childcare help." Grand, "Big, Dirty, Beautiful."
11. Grand, "Big, Dirty, Beautiful."
12. Campos-Pons continues: "If you look at my work carefully, all the work I have done, I'm like a little kid putting things together. I don't have a big studio or something like that. And money, I'm sometimes short for that as well. But I have managed to do things that are large in scale because they are like accumulations, or assembled gestures put together in this idea of building with blocks." María Magdalena Campos-Pons, "On Letting the World Be Your Studio," interview by T. Cole Rachel, *The Creative Independent*, January 25, 2019, https://thecreativeindependent.com/people/visual-artist-maria-magdalena-campos-pons-on-letting-the-world-be-your-studio/.
13. Kaylan Buteyn, host, *Artist/Mother Podcast*, episode 67, "Making 'serious' work without sacrificing play," June 16, 2020, https://artistmotherpodcast.com/podcast/67-making-serious-work-without-sacrificing-play-plus-more-wisdom-on-art-and-motherhood-from-dana-oldfather-karen-seapker-and-allison-reimus-at-red-arrow-gallery/.
14. Kaylan Buteyn, host, *Artist/Mother Podcast*, "On Intentional Tending," episode 38, October 7, 2019, https://artistmotherpodcast.com/podcast/38-on-intentional-tending-painting-and-parenting-practices-live-panel-recording-with-vivian-liddell-mandy-rogers-horton-and-jodi-hays/.
15. Lipson continues, "On the sidewalk, a mother will wait while her son rescues a caterpillar from the path of pedestrians, and we will see her thinking. At the playground, two mothers will make a game for their children of picking up plastic water bottles, and we will see them thinking. Pediatricians will acknowledge the acuity of mothers' thinking. Mothers will be hired, promoted—elected—for the maternal agility of their thinking. . . . Which thinker will you recognize for her mothering? Which mother will you recognize for her thinking? Stop her. Tell her. Make her eyes burn. Across the world the chain will grow, like so many synapses firing." Nicole Graev Lipson, "Thinkers Who Mother," in *Mothers and Other Fictional Characters* (Chronicle Prism, 2025), 136–37.
16. Joan Snyder, "For Molly Entering College (August 1997)," in *The Mother Reader: Essential Writings on Motherhood*, ed. Moyra Davey (Seven Stories Press, 2001), 247.
17. There are so many recently created resources that help drive this point home, including Angela Garbes's brilliant book *Essential Labor: Mothering as Social Change* (Harper, 2022) and Jenny Brown's *Birth Strike: The Hidden Fight over Women's Work* (PM Press, 2019). This essay is dedicated to my friend Cat Ricketts. The provocations I took from her beautiful book *The Mother-Artist: Portraits of Ambition, Limitation, and Creativity* (Broadleaf Books, 2024) are woven throughout this essay.

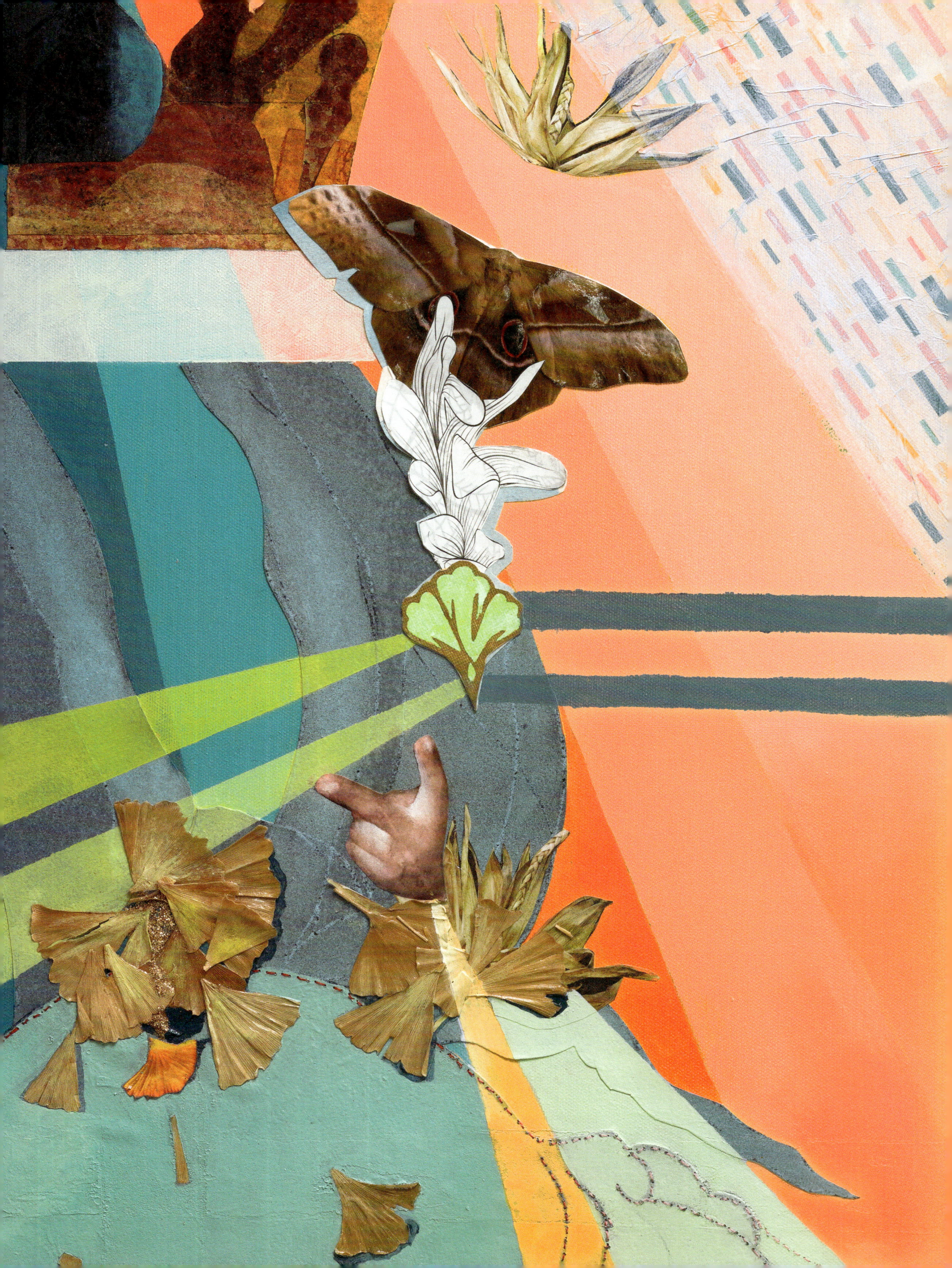

Shaun Giles

THE POWER TO IMAGINE

The Artist-Educators of *In Her Place*

IN THE PAST, TEACHING WAS ONE of few viable career options available to women who wanted to be taken seriously, secure a stable income, and build a reputation as an art professional. Today, many of the leading figures of Nashville's art community are women, and several work as teachers—but not because they have no other options. These artists teach because they love teaching, and they are committed to helping develop the next generation of artists.

The dual roles of artist and art educator can intersect or even merge into a single identity and practice. What happens in the classroom may inform what takes place in the artist's studio and vice versa.

Jana Harper, interdisciplinary artist and professor at Vanderbilt University, states, "In some ways making art and teaching are the same because at their root, they are both about transformation. Transformation of materials, ideas, and even, possibly, paradigms or consciousness" (fig. 5.1).[1]

Classrooms can also become creative communities in which artist-educators and their students grow together. When Lakesha Calvin began teaching at Fisk University in 2022 after several years at Tennessee State University, she gained well-respected colleagues in artists LiFran Fort—who studied under legendary Harlem Renaissance artist Aaron Douglas—and Alicia Henry, who taught at Fisk from 1997 until her death in 2024. For more than fifteen years, Calvin, a painter and collage artist, has been a full-time arts educator. She is inspired by her students and says that engaging with them "keeps her work honest." Part of Calvin's mission as an educator is to "lift students up so their stories of life and growth can be seen and heard."[2]

Similarly, Sisavanh Phouthavong Houghton's art practice and work in the classroom are tied together. The painting professor at Middle Tennessee State University in Murfreesboro has taught at the university level for twenty-five years. "I enjoy talking to my students about problem-solving for their projects and speaking to them about technical and professional developmental skills," she says. "As a practicing artist, my experience helps inform my upper-division students about what it takes to be a professional artist. These intense and meaningful conversations remind me of my struggles as an artist, and I practice what I preach."[3]

Teaching also encourages art educators to stay up-to-date as educators and artists. Harper is always reading and researching.

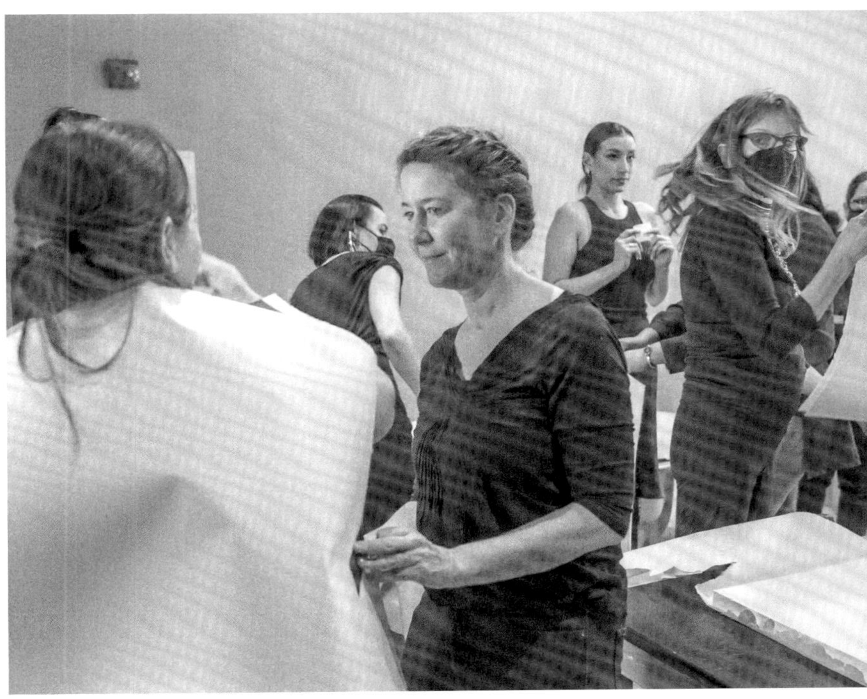

FIGURE 5.1. Jana Harper leads a performance workshop in 2022 at the International Museum of Art and Science, McAllen, Texas, with students from the University of Texas, Rio Grande Valley

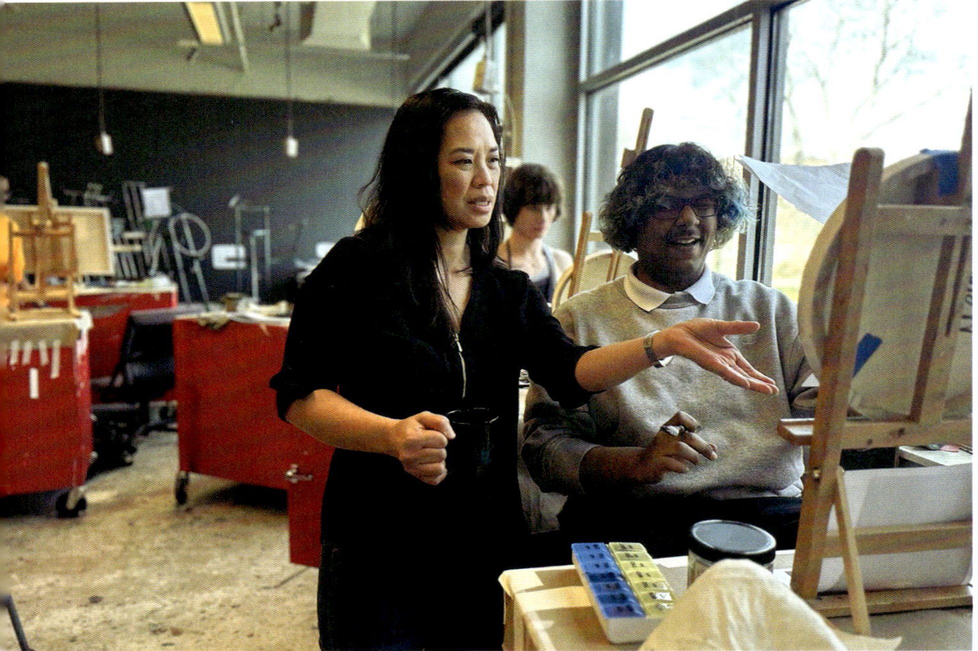

"I get to explore and develop alongside them, making it all worthwhile. I have some outstanding students with big ideas, and I thrive on their energy. They constantly support me as much as I support them, and that mutual respect is why I continue to teach."

FIGURE 5.2. Sisavanh Phouthavong Houghton engages with Mena Tanious in her painting class at Middle Tennessee State University, 2025

"That research also informs my own practice because sometimes I learn about neglected or forgotten histories or inspiring projects that I might never have come across in daily life," she notes.[4] Mandy Rogers Horton, painter and assistant professor of art at Watkins College of Art at Belmont University, acknowledges that through teaching, "I am following conversations in contemporary art and considering how to add to it meaningfully. Observation, research, and sensitivity to our ever-evolving culture are practices I aim to help students develop."[5]

Such a synergy between art teacher and art student is not only found in the university classroom. Briena Harmening, a text-based textile artist and art teacher at James Lawson High School in Nashville, credits teaching with enhancing her studio practice. In an interview for the *Drawing South* podcast, she said, "I think I got better [as a teacher] because I was looking at more work myself and that was translating to me showing the kids more work . . . when I was making soft sculpture here [in my studio], we were making it in school."[6]

Community

Building technical skills and preparing students for a future in the arts is a goal for many teachers, especially for those teaching at the university level, but artist-educators also place great importance on fostering a sense of community. Harmening works to create a safe and trusting environment for her high school students. "I think it really came from wanting to create an atmosphere of trust and freedom," she says. You know, if you don't have that, then they don't want to make stuff in front of each other."[7] A trusting environment breeds inquiry, exchange, and collaboration—key factors in any learning environment and often critical qualities of a professional art practice as well.

Such environments are also inspiring to artist-educators who may be encouraged by their students to experiment and approach their work with fresh eyes. Phouthavong Houghton reflects on her creative experiences in the classroom: "Being in a creative atmosphere and community is always lovely, regardless of your level. They [students] remind me to continue experimenting and enjoy the craziness of being a process mixed-media artist. I get to explore and develop alongside them, making it all worthwhile. I have some outstanding students with big ideas, and I thrive on their energy. They constantly support me as much as I support them, and that mutual respect is why I continue to teach" (fig. 5.2).[8]

Harper contemplates what collaboration and community mean to her art practice and her teaching: "In my studio practice, I am interested in collaborating with ancestors and natural elements, but this kind of thinking or collaboration represents a paradigm shift for many people."[9] For her, teaching can be part of her creative process, and it does not need to happen in an academic setting. In 2020, she made *This Holding: Traces of Contact*, a film that addresses burdens, anxieties, and hopes during the COVID-19 pandemic. "For my project *This Holding*, I led dozens of community movement workshops with a wide range of people," she explains. "At the university, you have a job to do—an obligation to convey certain information or teach certain skills—but in workshops, you can have more of a reciprocal relationship, pose questions that you are asking in your own practice and then share outcomes."[10]

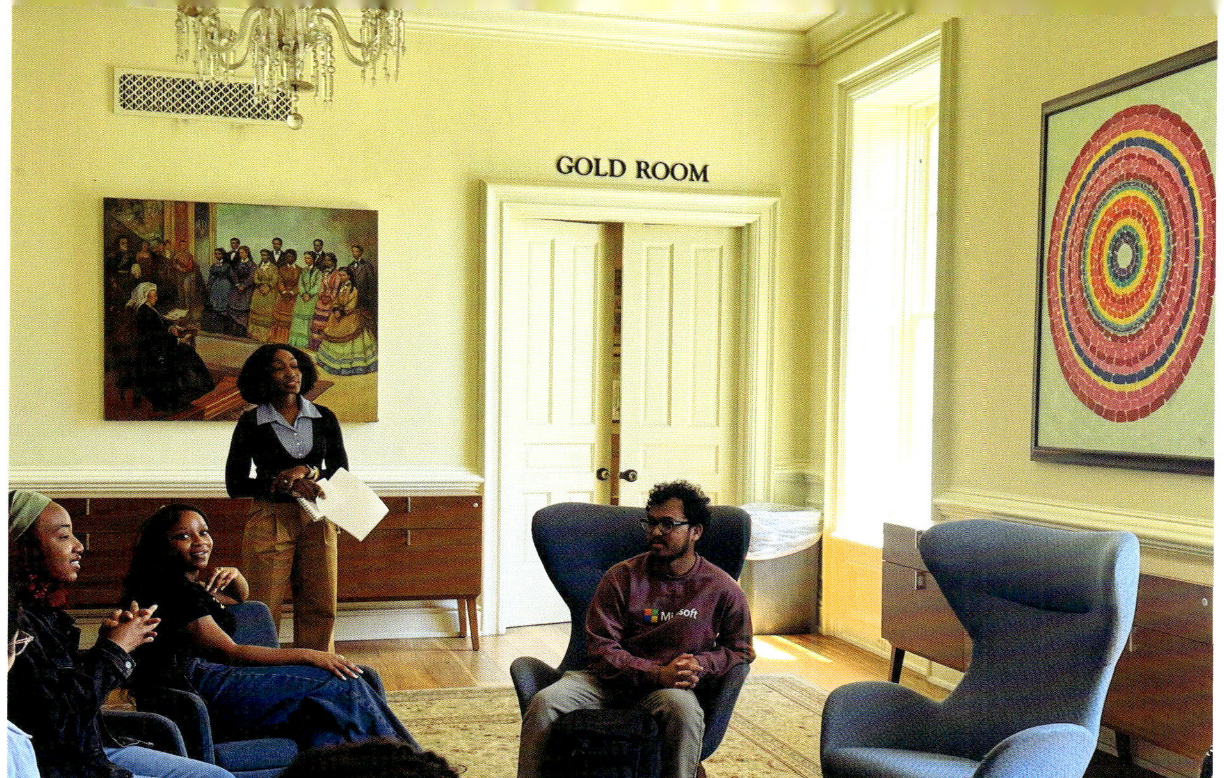

FIGURE 5.3. Lakesha Calvin with students in Jubilee Hall at Fisk University, 2025

Future Generations

Artist-educators grow as artists while laying a foundation for the next generation. They teach because they are deeply invested in their students. They grow in community with their students while evolving as artists.

Harper is committed to the Indigenous concept of *seven-generations thinking*—that is, a responsibility to three generations in the past and three in the future. "This relates to teaching because we study the past in order to understand and make work in the present," she says. "But our students represent the future, so I try to see the world through their eyes and think about what they will need to carry them through."[11] Through her art-making and teaching practices, Harper expresses the desire to find beauty in the discord around us. "Teaching is a constant reminder of this," she says. "The power of art is the power to imagine new worlds, and we have to give future generations the skills to keep dreaming."[12]

Art requires discipline and commitment. Calvin encourages consistency and curiosity (fig 5.3). She tells young artists to have a disciplined practice of making art every day, asking questions, and sharing experiences with others in order to continue developing as artists. Phouthavong Houghton encourages students to face challenges and uncertainty while they develop as artists.

"I believe that if you don't have some self-doubt, then you haven't lived the life of a creative person, and your journey is rich with experiences along the way," says Phouthavong Houghton. "I continue to teach and follow the path of a creative human because I believe I can still make a difference in this chaotic world."[13]

NOTES

1. Jana Harper, email message to author, January 26, 2025.
2. "Virtual Exhibit: *Lakesha Moore Calvin – I Am/ We Are*," Tennessee Arts Commission, February 2, 2023, https://tnartscommission.org/news/virtual-exhibit-lakesha-moore-calvin-i-am-we-are/.
3. Sisavanh Phouthavong Houghton, email message to author, January 24, 2025.
4. Harper, email.
5. Mandy Rogers Horton, email message to author, February 5, 2025.
6. mikewindy, host, "Conversation with Briena Harmening," *Drawing South* (podcast), episode 28, June 18, 2024, https://creators.spotify.com/pod/show/drawing-south/episodes/Conversation-with-Briena-Harmening-e2l1ql0/a-abcavom.
7. mikewindy, "Conversation with Briena Harmening."
8. Phouthavong Houghton, email.
9. Harper, email.
10. Harper, email.
11. Harper, email.
12. Harper, email.
13. Phouthavong Houghton, email.

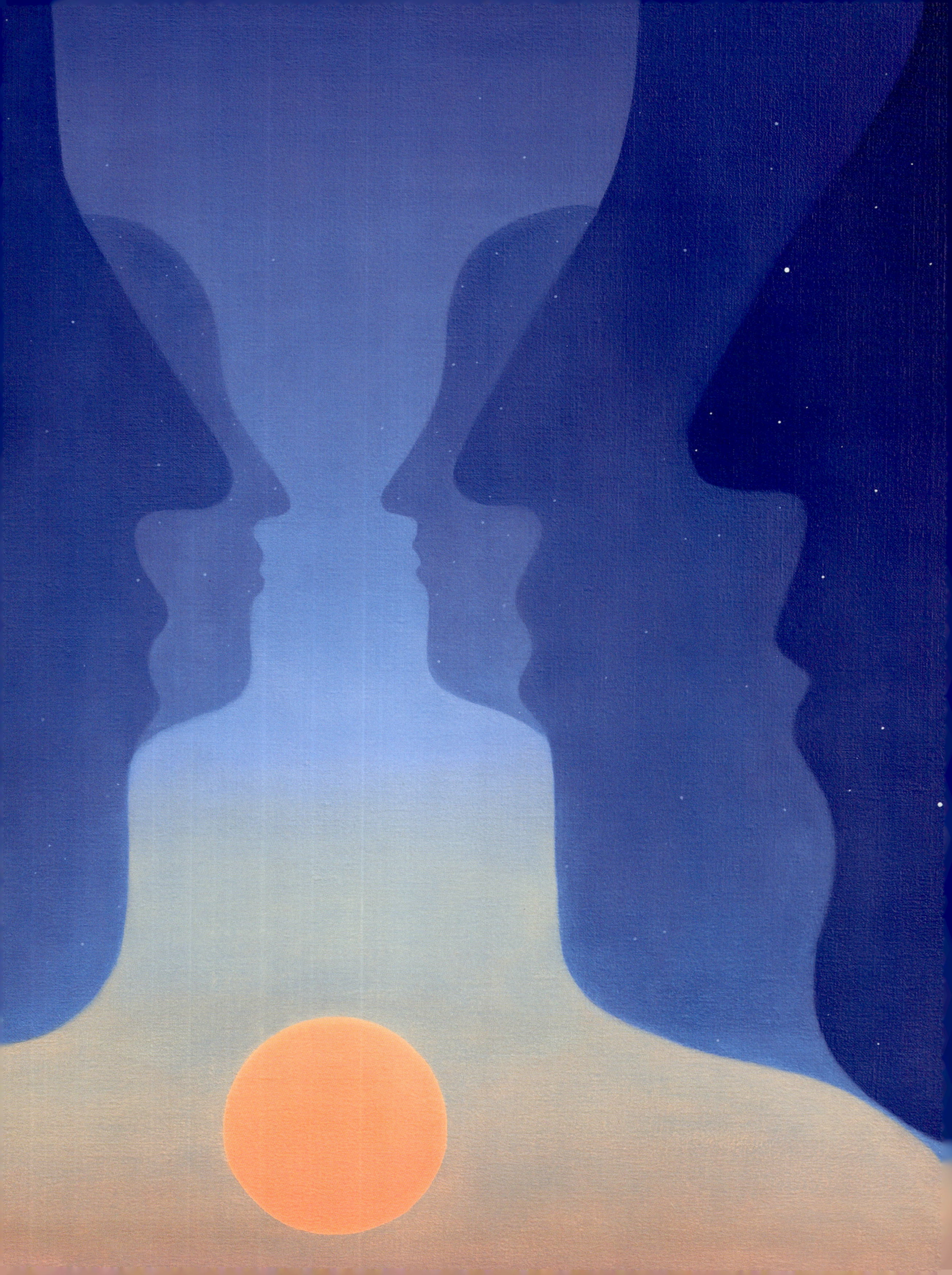

Joe Nolan

GENERATION NEXT

Women Art Leaders in Twenty-First-Century Nashville

I'VE BEEN WRITING ABOUT contemporary art in newspapers, journals, exhibition catalogues, and books for almost twenty years. Some of the things I most enjoy about covering visual art in Nashville and the Southeast are spotting trends and identifying the communities that are making an impact on visual culture. Who is creating new opportunities? Who is making the scene more sustainable?

The art gallery and institutional infrastructure that emerged from Nashville's contemporary art renaissance at the end of the twentieth century was primarily founded and run by a collection of local women art leaders, as discussed in Vivien Green Fryd's essay. Now we see new trends and new players emerging—today, the next generation of Nashville women are helming the city's visual-art institutions and creative gallery scene. They're joined by women—curators, writers, educators, and organizers from around the country—who've been drawn to Nashville to participate in our contemporary art community and take it to new heights in the twenty-first century.

Mothers and Daughters

Nashville's modern and contemporary art collectors had very few local resources before Nancy Saturn and Alice Zimmerman founded Zimmerman Saturn Gallery on Second Avenue in downtown Nashville back in the 1980s. Saturn also founded the American Artisan craft gallery in Green Hills along with its annual festival that was long held in Centennial Park. Zimmerman Saturn Gallery was known for connecting Nashville collectors to the national art scene, and the American Artisan Festival celebrates its fiftieth anniversary in 2026.

In the years since Saturn's passing in 2010, her daughter, Samantha Saturn, has stepped into her mother's role, folding the

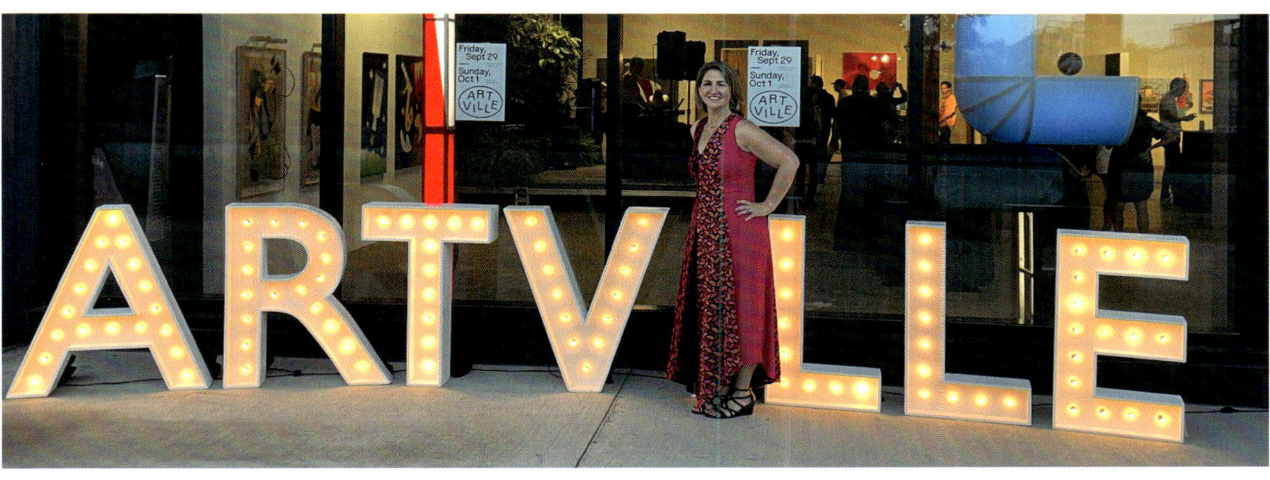

FIGURE 6.1. Samantha Saturn at the opening of the inaugural Artville, September 28, 2023

American Artisan Festival into a greater vision she calls Artville (fig. 6.1). Artville is a three-day celebration of Nashville's contemporary art community that takes place in the Wedgewood-Houston neighborhood and downtown on the last weekend of September. It debuted in 2023 with a neighborhood-wide event that included murals, performances, outdoor interactive installations, and a menu of creative programming. A who's who of local creators, including Jodi Hays and Vadis Turner, were commissioned to create site-specific works for the event. The American Artisan Festival once seemed inseparable from its traditional location in Centennial Park. But by making the festival part of the Artville happenings, Saturn has renewed the craft fair and correctly connected it more directly to Nashville's larger contemporary art scene. It's another example of how this next generation of Nashville's women art leaders are preserving and updating the foundations of the city's contemporary art renaissance, making sure that yesterday is a part of today's conversations about the art scene we want to live, play, and work in tomorrow.

In the early 1990s, Nashville didn't have many shiny new contemporary art spaces that showed equally up-to-the-minute art. That was before Janice Zeitlin opened Zeitgeist Gallery at the front of her husband Manuel Zeitlin's architectural office in Cummins Station, just behind what is now the Frist Art Museum, in 1994. The white-walled showroom quickly became known as a striking space for seeing contemporary art. Zeitgeist moved to Hillsboro Village in 1999, and the gallery's 2002 exhibition *Switchyard* secured its long-term reputation as an iconic Nashville art destination by opening up to local emerging artists who were just on the verge of new careers, as well as being a place where established artists were encouraged to take chances.

Janice's daughter Anna Zeitlin became the gallery's manager in 2012, working alongside gallery director and Nashville art-scene stalwart Lain York. One of the reasons that Zeitgeist was a top Nashville gallery space was its willingness to support the careers of locals, including *In Her Place* artists Alex Blau, Lanie Gannon, Alicia Henry, Karen Seapker, and Vadis Turner. It's a practice that kept the gallery's roster dynamic and relevant. Zeitgeist also put a spotlight on a diverse selection of up-and-coming creators like photographer David S. Piñeros and the multimedia Barbarian collective. They opened their gallery to independent curators like Marteja Bailey, Evan Roosevelt Brown, and Brooke Hoffert, who gave an array of young and emerging artists the opportunity to hang their work on some of the most storied gallery walls in the city.

Zeitgeist Gallery celebrated its thirtieth anniversary in 2024, just months before Janice announced that it would close its doors at the end of 2025. Under its mother-daughter leadership, Zeitgeist was emblematic of the best of contemporary art in Nashville.

Homegrown

Beth Gilmore and Caroline Vincent were already familiar faces in the local art scene when they helped to create the movement that brought artists and galleries to Nashville's historic downtown Arcade. In 2004, Gilmore and Vincent's Twist Art Gallery joined artist Daniel Lai's newly opened Dangenart Gallery in the Arcade, a covered shopping center built in 1902. Born and raised in Nashville, Gilmore was busy raising two young daughters and finishing her bachelor's degree at Watkins College of Art. Her studio was just up a back alley from the Arcade in the Downtown Presbyterian Church, where Gilmore was an artist in residence. Vincent was the respected curator of the Arts at the Airport program, but she'd been anxious to find a space of her own to curate and collaborate in.

Twist debuted the same night that musician-gallerist Jerry Dale McFadden opened the new location of his TAG Gallery across the street from the Arcade on Fifth Avenue. As an afterthought, the artists and galleries announced a district-wide art crawl. They were overwhelmed by throngs of art lovers, tourists, curious collectors, and broke young creators grazing cheese trays and refilling glasses with boxed wine. The artist-led spaces at the Arcade became a big draw with their often uncommercial and always unconventional programming. Twist and its spinoff gallery, Twist Etc., were known for featuring women artists and feminist displays, often programming locals like *In Her Place* artists Mandy Rogers Horton and Kelly S. Williams. Twist was at the forefront of the Arcade scene, and its penchant for immersive installations was emblematic of the Arcade's irreverent spirit.

Adrienne Outlaw was a prime mover in Nashville's contemporary art renaissance and one of the artists who helped to create the studio community at the former May Hosiery Mill on Chestnut Street in Wedgewood-Houston. The artists at the "Chestnut Building," as they called it, were among the first to demonstrate how the derelict industrial structures in that area might be reimagined as workspaces for artists, galleries, artisanal startups, and creative incubators.

Outlaw was born in Orlando, Florida, but she grew up in Nashville. When she returned after graduating from the Art Institute of Chicago in the late 1990s, her art practice focused on figurative multimedia sculptures, offering a feminist examination of female bodies. Her Chestnut Street outpost also attracted a steady stream of women artist-collaborators, including a number of young artists and art school students who volunteered at the studio, learning the ins and outs of creating a sustainable creative practice. Outlaw founded the Seed Space creative lab in 2009 with the assistance of her apprentices and interns, which included Rachel Bubis and Laura Hutson Hunter. She invited artists, curators, and writers from far-flung art centers to come to Nashville to create and collaborate on installations in a dedicated gallery space within her working studio.

Seed Space morphed and transformed from one creative experiment into another. It introduced Nashville's art scene to a cadre of creatives from all over the US, including Sonya Clark and Benton C Bainbridge, and it moved to a stand-alone space in Wedgewood-Houston's Track One building before joining with the Locate Arts project, which eventually formed the Tennessee Triennial. Outlaw also worked as an art journalist in Nashville, producing radio reports for local NPR affiliate WPLN and contributing reviews and columns to various print publications and art blogs. Through her own art, curation, writing, and leadership, Outlaw made a lasting impact on the city's contemporary art scene while also guiding and inspiring a creative new generation of Nashville's women art leaders before she moved to St. Louis, Missouri, in 2014.

Susan Tinney wasn't born in Nashville, but her family moved to town when she was eight years old. Tinney has a degree in molecular biology, and as a young career woman helping to build Nashville's booming biotech sector, she became a passionate art collector. So passionate, in fact, that she started hanging work by local artists on the walls of her living room and hosting her own opening reception parties from her kitchen. These earliest Tinney-curated displays were part of a long tradition of domestic art venues in Nashville that includes everything from William Edmondson's front-yard sculpture studio on Fourteenth Avenue South in the 1930s to garage art installations at Garage Mahal in East Nashville's Five Points neighborhood in the 2000s. In 2008, when Tinney's curatorial ambitions had outgrown the walls of her living room, she opened the doors at her signature gallery in Nashville's downtown visual arts district, across from the Arcade, on Fifth Avenue North, now Rep. John Lewis Way.

The Downtown Presbyterian Church's artists-in-residence program and Anne Brown's The Arts Company gallery, which opened in 1996, established Fifth Avenue North as an art district in the 1990s, and Brown went on to lead the charge to have the street dubbed *Fifth Avenue of the Arts*. In 2006, the First Saturday Art Crawl downtown united the artist-led spaces in the Arcade with the galleries on Fifth Avenue. The monthly event marked a

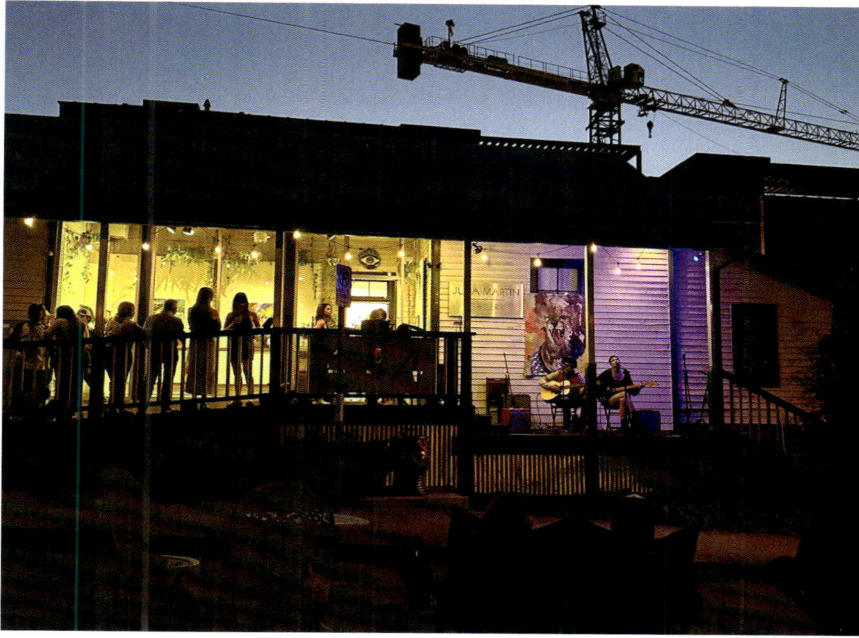

FIGURE 6.2. Opening at Julia Martin Gallery in the Wedgewood-Houston neighborhood

mainstream breakthrough for the city's contemporary art scene, attracting a class of casual gallerygoers who started planning their Saturday nights around multiple art exhibitions like Nashville music lovers hopping between honky-tonks. Tinney Contemporary made a splash, quickly establishing itself as a groundbreaking commercial art gallery in the downtown arts district. Tinney's programming felt innovative alongside the other commercial galleries downtown, but it also felt familiar and accessible when compared to the often chaotic and stridently noncommercial happenings in the Arcade. Tinney's roster and exhibition calendar have remained relevant after the temporary closure of the Arcade art spaces and some of Tinney's Fifth Avenue gallery neighbors, and the emergence of the Wedgewood-Houston neighborhood as the new center of Nashville's contemporary art scene.

Tinney's curatorial program at Bobby Nashville, just down the block on Fourth Avenue, has made the hotel into another downtown visual-art destination. And after Arcade Arts and Mollye Brown brought an artist-in-residence program back to the Arcade in 2024 following two years of renovations, Tinney cofounded the Second Saturday Art Crawl downtown in 2025. Tinney Contemporary will celebrate its twentieth birthday in 2028.

When Nashville-born Julia Martin founded her namesake gallery in Wedgewood-Houston in 2013 (fig. 6.2), it joined several new and established art spaces moving to the neighborhood, including Zeitgeist and a new outpost of the Memphis-based David Lusk Gallery. This concentration of creative venues shifted focus away from the downtown arts district, making Wedgewood-Houston the hub of New Nashville's contemporary art scene. An artist first, Martin began her career in the studios in the May Hosiery Mill building on Chestnut Street. She opened her signature space after

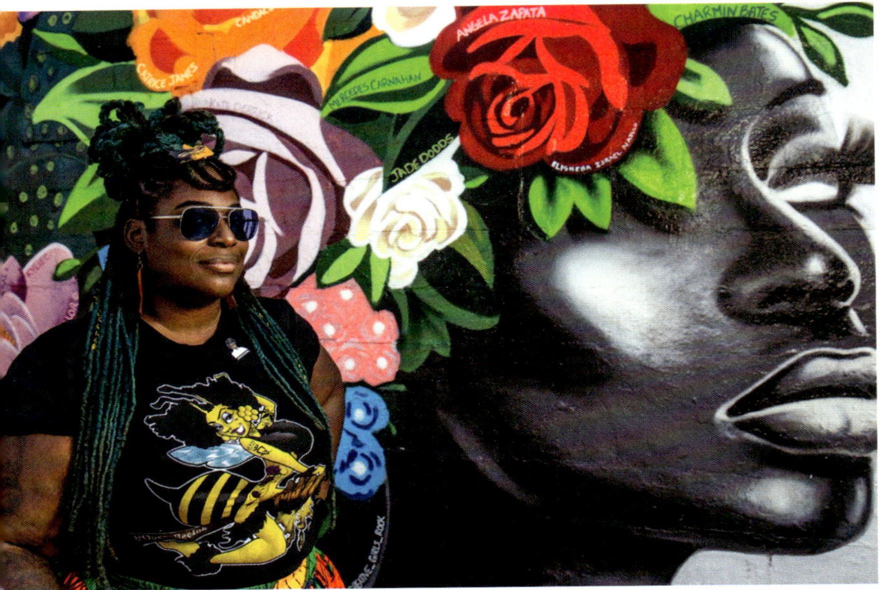

FIGURE 6.3. Elisheba Israel Mrozik outside of Slim & Husky's The Rollout on Buchanan Street in front of a mural she created with Creative Girls Rock, October 9, 2021

a road trip, a personal crisis, and a stint in the movie business that caused the artist to drop her brushes for three years. Martin transformed what had formerly been a residential space into a painting studio and showcase gallery that would allow her to act as her own art dealer. The grand opening of Julia Martin Gallery was a smash—so much so that the artist sold through her entire inventory. That was the start of Martin's path to becoming an artist-curator—a tried-and-true strategy in the building of Nashville's independent art infrastructure.

Martin has hosted iconic displays by legendary *Pee-wee's Playhouse* designer Wayne White as well as celebrated local heroes like Samuel Dunson and Kevin Guthrie. Her artist receptions run on Southern hospitality and regularly include great musicians performing on her front porch; everyone from Cassie Berman and Bonnie "Prince" Billy to Pavement's Bob Nastanovich have performed for her patrons. She's introduced new painters, craft and jewelry artists, printmakers, and creators of every stripe to her community of collectors and collaborators. Martin's gallery has welcomed countless regional artists to Nashville, helping to connect our scene to new networks and opportunities, partnerships, and inspirations. Of course, it's also the best place to see Martin's unmistakable mixed-media-and-oil portraits in pastel palettes—colorful and layered, just like the artist.

The New Arrivals

In 2001, the Frist Art Museum—then the Frist Center for the Visual Arts—opened under the leadership of executive director and CEO Chase Rynd, and it's hard to imagine a better ambassador to introduce the institution to the city. But the job of establishing the museum's identity—not to mention its place in Nashville's art scene and in the larger community—fell to Susan H. Edwards. Edwards became the museum's executive director and CEO in 2004 after leading the Katonah Museum of Art in Katonah, New York. For eighteen years, Edwards guided the Frist in achieving the seemingly impossible task of making the museum into a place with something for everyone in our diverse and relentlessly growing city. During Edwards's tenure, the museum achieved accreditation from the American Alliance of Museums and hosted more than two hundred exhibitions from prestigious institutions such as the British Museum; the Centre Pompidou; the Musée d'Orsay; the Musée Picasso; the Museum of Fine Arts, Boston; the Los Angeles County Museum of Art; and the Victoria and Albert Museum, among many others. Edwards-curated exhibitions like *Tina Barney: The Europeans*, *Vesna Pavlović: Projected Histories*, and *William Eggleston: Anointing the Overlooked* point to the former director's versatility as a talented and passionate curator, art historian, and writer as well as a skilled executive and effective fundraiser. Edwards brought a democratic and multifaceted vision to the Frist, making it a regional arts and education leader, a destination for artists and institutions from around the globe, and an organizer of original exhibitions that have toured to the Solomon R. Guggenheim Museum; the Museum of Fine Arts, Houston; the Phillips Collection; the Baltimore Museum of Art; the Cleveland Museum of Art; and more.

Elisheba Israel "Queen Bee" Mrozik is an artist, entrepreneur, and community organizer in North Nashville (fig. 6.3)—a historically Black neighborhood home to three historically Black colleges and universities and, at Fisk University, Nashville's premier collection of modern art. Originally from Memphis, Mrozik moved to Nashville in 2007 after graduating from Memphis College of Art. Networking in North Nashville, she connected with the Jefferson Street creative scene—which included the Norf Art Collective, Thaxton Waters's Art History Class Lifestyle Lounge, and Woodcuts Framing and Gallery—and the artists and entrepreneurs who were building the Buchanan Arts District. In 2011, Mrozik became the first Black licensed tattoo artist in Middle Tennessee and opened One Drop Ink Tattoo Parlour & Gallery. Tattooing put Mrozik's creativity to work and put her studio art on display in her shop, but she also made room on her walls for other neighborhood artists, friends, and the Queen's ever-growing list of collaborators. The shop hosts a collective of tattoo and piercing artists, and Mrozik has fostered that same communal approach as a cofounder of the Jefferson Street Art Crawl, participant in the North Nashville mural art movement, and founder of the nonprofit North Nashville Arts Coalition. Mrozik sees artists as workers, and her community networking and outreach are guided by her conviction that art scenes can also be labor movements. Mrozik's talents for networking and organizing won her a reputation as one of the principal artist-curator-founders of a new wave of contemporary art in North Nashville.

East Nashville's Red Arrow began as the first art gallery in downtown Joshua Tree, California. The pioneering space was founded by Katie Shaw in 2007, and its reputation as a destination for contemporary art soon outgrew its isolated, eccentric high-desert community. Originally located in a building that was recognized for its fifteen-foot sign shaped like a red arrow, the gallery took its name from the landmark before moving to a bigger location in Joshua Tree Village in 2010. This was the beginning of a prosperous pattern of gallery growth and relocation: Red Arrow opened its doors for the first time at its original East Nashville home in Riverside Village in 2014, and the gallery moved to their current location on Gallatin Avenue in 2015. Red Arrow is now considered one of the best art galleries in the state, and that status reflects Shaw and gallery director Ashley Layendecker's winning lineup of women painters, including *In Her Place* artists Lauren Gregory, Karen Seapker, and Emily Weiner. The gallery's opening receptions are can't-miss events on the First Saturday art calendar, and Red Arrow's recent splashy turns at international art festivals like Future Fair, NADA Miami, and Zona Maco Mexico City have kept the news of Nashville's contemporary art renaissance in the national art conversation (fig. 6.4).

María Magdalena Campos-Pons moved to Nashville in 2017 after being named the Cornelius Vanderbilt Chair of Fine Arts at Vanderbilt University. The Cuban-born artist has won a global audience with her multifaceted creative practice, exploring subjects from migration to motherhood using painting, sculpture, photography, performance, and more. The arrival of an artist with an international reputation was emblematic of a larger trend that saw artists, curators, gallerists, and museum professionals coming to Nashville from various locales to join the city's buzzing art scene.

Nashville was in the habit of losing artists in the 1990s and the early twenty-first century. People routinely established a presence in the local art community only to move out of town to earn an MFA or find sustainable gallery sales, reliable public art funding, or a collector base that saw the value of investing in emerging artists. Campos-Pons has shown her commitment to building Nashville's art scene by founding initiatives like the Engine for Art, Democracy, and Justice—a transinstitutional partnership with Fisk University, the Frist Art Museum, Millions of Conversations, and Vanderbilt University—curating the inaugural Tennessee Triennial in 2023, and opening the Begonia Labs gallery. At the same time, a wave of emerging and established artists, including *In Her Place* artists Raheleh Filsoofi, Karen Seapker, and Emily Weiner, have found their ways to Nashville from different points of departure to become educators, establish studio practices, and join local collectives and organizations. And many new-to-Nashville artists have landed on the rosters of gallerists and organizers who are themselves newly arrived and just beginning their journeys in the city's art scene.

A squad of women leaders stepped into founding roles in Nashville's slumbering art scene in the 1980s and 1990s, and they created a small network of commercial galleries and art festivals in the early days of Nashville's contemporary art renaissance. Pioneers like Anne Brown, Nancy Saturn, Carol Stein, Janice Zeitlin, Alice Zimmerman, and more nurtured the Nashville we know now—a city with a one-of-a-kind art scene with national reach and a creative community that's known for its collaboration and Southern hospitality. In the twenty-first century, the next generation of Nashville's women leaders has toed the line, bringing new visions to established venues and happenings and founding the new places and events that are shaping the future of Nashville's art scene. Nashville's twenty-first-century women art leaders are both homegrown and far-flung. They're ambitious and homespun. They're experimenting and innovative, but with an eye to how we all got here.

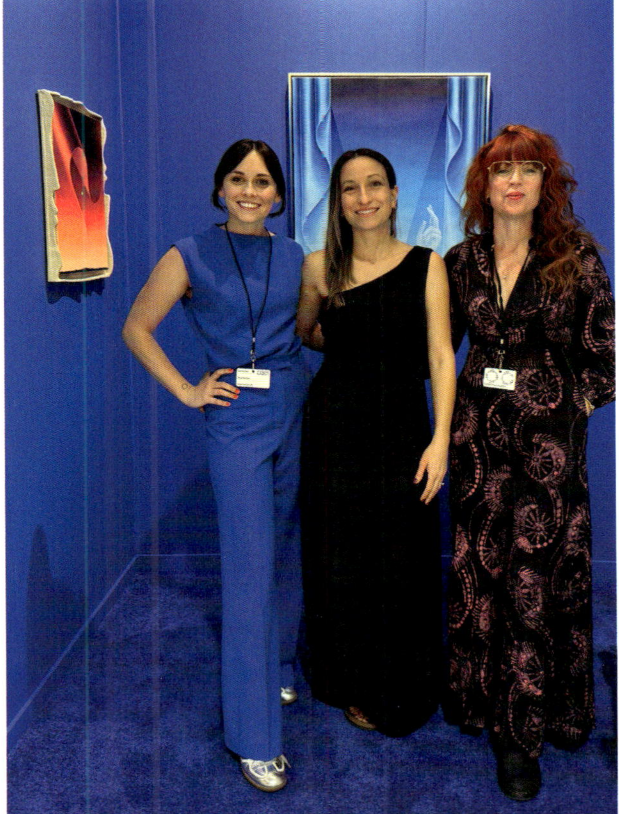

FIGURE 6.4. *Left to right:* Ashley Layendecker, Emily Weiner, and Katie Shaw at NADA art fair, Miami, 2024

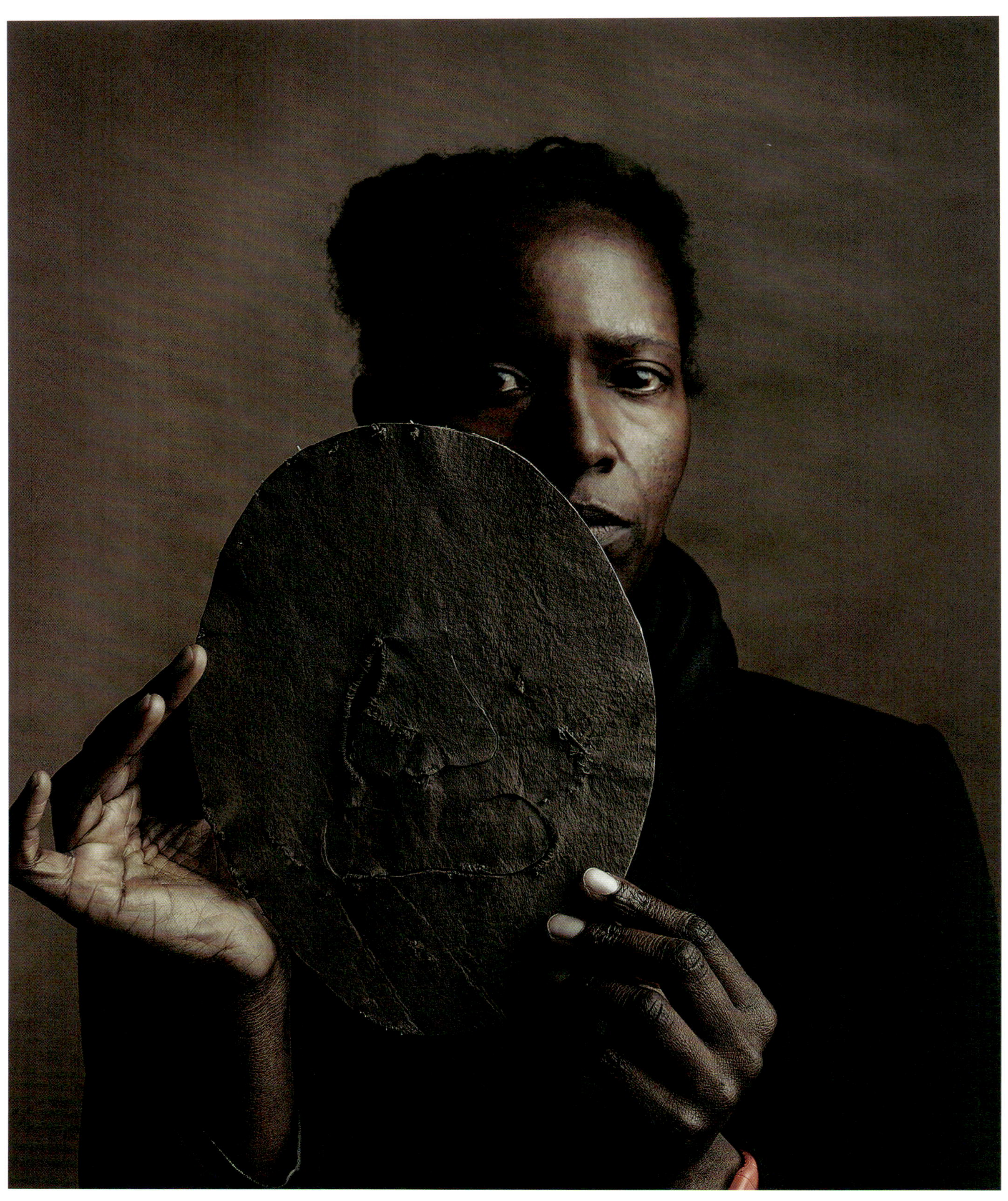

FIGURE 7.1. Gina R. Binkley for *Nashville Arts Magazine*. Portrait of Alicia Henry, 2016

Michael J. Ewing

SILENCE IS A FORM OF COMMUNICATION

Voices on the Life and Art of Alicia Henry (1966–2024)

ONE DECISIVE MOMENT REPLAYS in my mind whenever I think of Alicia Henry (fig. 7.1). At the time, I was a student in her painting class, and I had once again found myself avoiding my canvas and asking my classmates questions, reflecting on what I saw in their work, and offering suggestions about what it might be. As I walked back to my canvas—still blank—my mind was full of thoughts and ideas about what my classmates were creating. Professor Henry broke the silence; "Have you ever considered being a curator?" she asked. I didn't fully understand what a curator's role was, but the next semester, I took her Arts and Ideas course, and in that class, we curated an art show for Fisk's Spring Arts Festival. All at once, every part of me—my abundant questions, my deep observations, my vivid imagination—had purpose. I saw a career path full of exploration and expression. I knew then that she saw me as only a person who really saw themselves could: she saw what I bring to the world, and she wanted others to experience it. That one moment, and Professor Henry's one question, changed the trajectory of my life.

In the decade-plus that I knew Professor Henry, we shared relatively few words outside the classroom. But ask me how many lessons she communicated to me outside of words—those moments are almost innumerable.

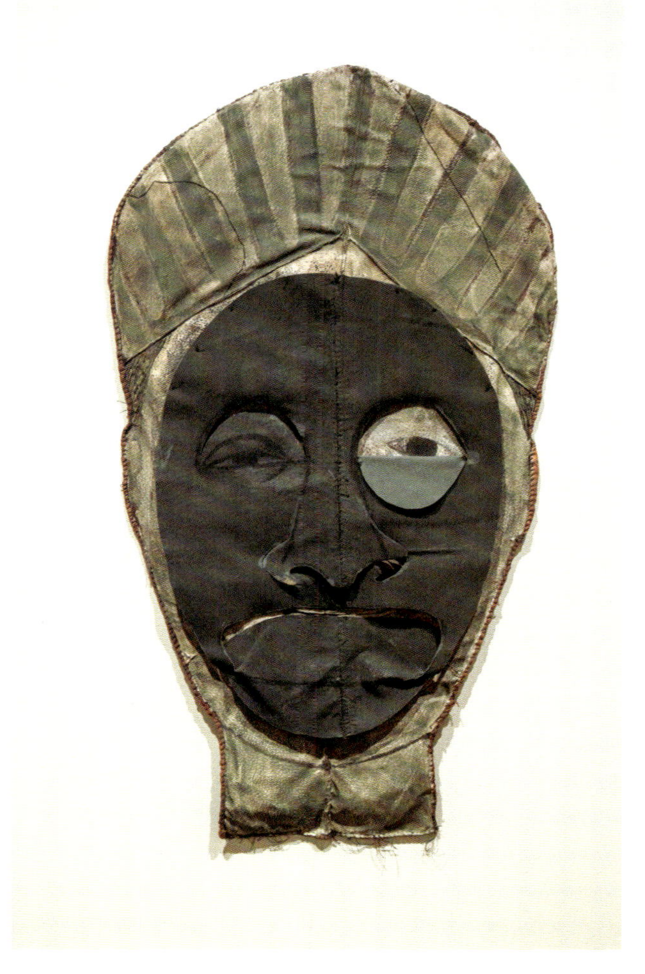

FIGURE 7.2. Alicia Henry. *Untitled*, 2005. Acrylic, leather, thread, and yarn; 28½ × 16 in. Collection of Michael J. Ewing. *The author has a tattoo of this work, which the artist gifted to him months before she passed away, on his forearm.*

That nod. That full, light smile that left you comforted and activated. Silence is a form of communication, one that Professor Henry expressed fluently.

Her silence was never empty. It was filled with the space she held for others to take up space without shame or judgment. She listened. She gave thoughtful insights, but mainly she asked questions to deepen your exploration. She would leave you in silence to affirm that you didn't need her, or anyone else's, permission to be. She taught me that the questions we truly need to answer require that we sit with ourselves and then sit a while longer.

Silence is spacious in her untitled works with simple descriptions that read like closed captions—[*acrylic, cotton, denim, felt, leather, thread, and yarn*] (pl. 2). Figures with absent limbs to be drawn in with the mind's eye are pinned at eye level for intimate encounters or towering in reverence.

Silence is full in the spatial tensions between works grouped in communities of kinship or spaced in silos of isolation. The many layers (fig. 7.2):

a face behind a mask behind a face,
a mask behind a face behind another mask,

muted colors registered boldly,
frequencies through texture,

cut out eyes, open eyes,
eyes closed—a gaze ever-present yet not always visible,

all punctuated by a quiet presence.

The labors of Professor Henry's hands—her work as an instructor, mentor, and artist—were one and the same. The voices recorded here testify not only to the power of her work, but also to her humanity and to the brilliant imprint she made on the many lives she touched.

THE FOLLOWING REFLECTIONS FROM FRIENDS AND COLLEAGUES OF ALICIA HENRY HAVE BEEN EDITED FOR LENGTH AND CLARITY.

LiFran Fort

Born in Nashville, LiFran Fort graduated from Fisk University in 1966. She has taught art at Fisk since 1985 and was Alicia Henry's next-door neighbor for twenty years.

I got a call from South Dakota in the late summer of 1997. I was immediately intrigued, because I don't think I'd ever gotten a call from South Dakota. Alicia Henry came on the phone. She was looking to join the staff at an HBCU, and she had sought us out. I was obviously impressed and passed her name along to the appropriate administrators. She joined the faculty in the fall of that year.

Almost immediately, I was struck by Alicia as a human being. My father died on January 8, 1998, and I had known Alicia for about five months at that point. That day in January was a fairly rainy day, and Alicia did not have a car. That evening, my doorbell rang, and Alicia Henry was standing at the door. I said, "Alicia, how'd you get here?" She said, "I walked." Now this is a seemingly small thing, and just a window into who she was, but it was the beginning of my knowing her as a human being.

I can say, without hesitation, that Alicia Henry was one of the best human beings I've ever known. I never heard her say an unkind thing about anyone. She did not suffer foolishness. She did not engage in gossip of any kind. She was as straight an arrow of a person as you can imagine. Out of this kind of a human being came her art.

The day before she passed, I was walking out of her bedroom after having visited for a couple of hours, and I was about to leave. She said, "I love you." This was sort of uncharacteristic. We'd said those words before from time to time, but not a lot. I stopped, and I turned slightly, and I looked around and said, "I love you too. You know that." Those words, and that person, will live in my heart forever.

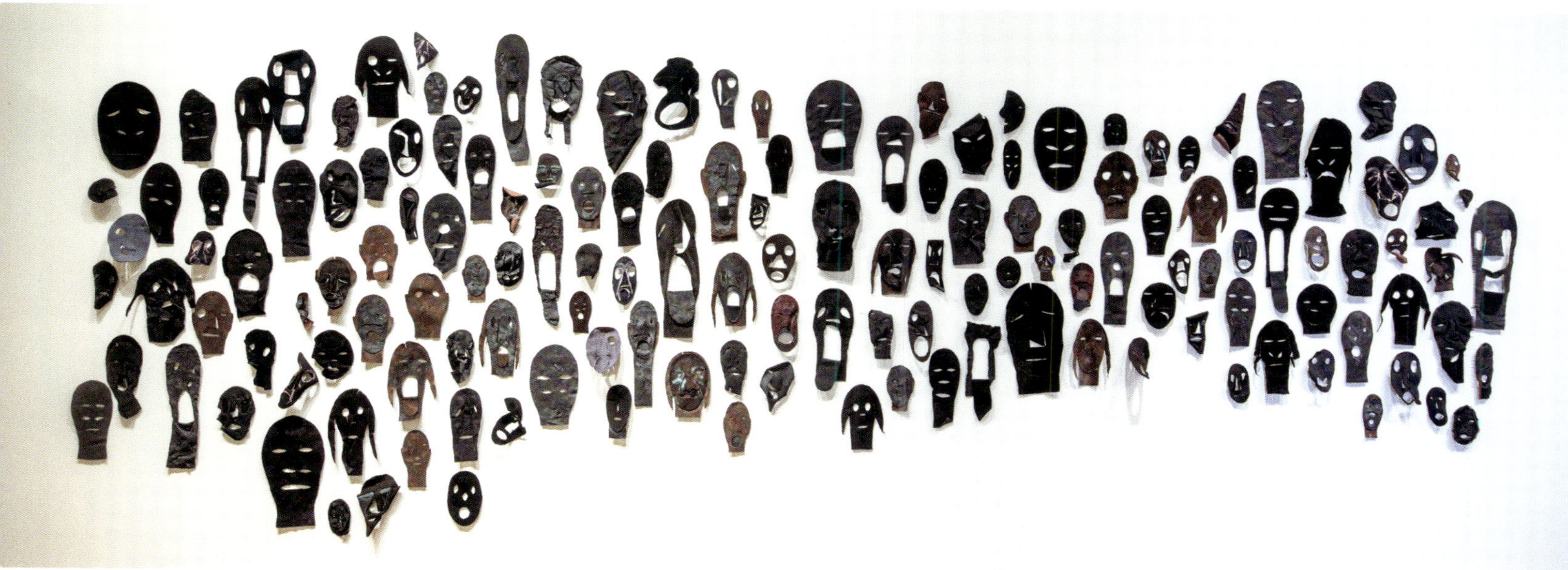

FIGURE 7.3. Alicia Henry. *Analogous II*, 2020. Acrylic, dyed leather, thread, and yarn; dimensions variable. University Art Gallery, UC Irvine

Jamaal Sheats

Jamaal Sheats graduated from Fisk University in 2002 and joined the faculty in 2015. He is currently the director and curator of the Fisk University Galleries. He curated Alicia Henry's 2023 solo exhibition, *Alicia*.

She never talked about her work. She had a clear and beautiful spirit and was your champion in why you were in the studio; she gave you clear feedback but pushed and challenged you at the same time. But as a teacher, she was very mysterious. She was just so guarded. And technology averse! I remember there was a red dot on her computer's power button, and she did not want to touch it to turn it on. I can remember in 2004 when Obama gave the DNC speech, we had a wonderful conversation about what it sounded like, because she would only listen to it on the radio.

After graduate school, I returned to Nashville. I had this idea that I wanted to teach contemporary art practice. I mentioned it to her, and she simply said, "Tomorrow, I want you to come back and teach a class." And that's how it all started.

On campus, almost no one called her by her first name. She was beloved by both faculty and staff. Even though her work was widely exhibited and collected, she never talked about it. I'd often learn about her exhibitions online. I'd share the news with my students, only to realize they hadn't seen her work either. Surprisingly, many faculty members hadn't seen it.

The first time I encountered her work was in 2003 at the Frist Art Museum. It was a series of cut-out paper figures—some missing an arm, others missing a leg. In that moment, I realized I wasn't just looking at images; I was looking at a language, a code. That was my first glimpse of understanding her work.

Years later, in 2015, I was curating an exhibition called *Topography*, which included her work. At that point, she had just started making the small masks—the beginning of a body of work she later called *Analogous* (fig. 7.3).When you saw these masks together, they functioned like words on a page, forming a visual language. But their complexity was only fully revealed up close. Some were crafted from a single strip of leather, while others were made of multiple layers sewn or sutured together. Spots of color, touches of velvet—each detail acted like punctuation within the composition.

That was when I fully understood how deceptive her work is. At first glance, it seems simple, but as you engage with it, you're led into multiple layers of meaning. Her work always returned to beauty—contested beauty, redefined beauty. From a distance, it seemed singular, but the longer you looked, the more you saw—her meticulous attention to detail, her delicate yet deliberate touch. The work was beautiful, and she was an incredible artist. She was deeply committed to bringing out the best in her students. She had a unique way of guiding you—not forcefully, but with a quiet insistence—leading you to the place you wanted to be. She was always curious, asking questions that made you think more critically about your work and process. Professor Henry created space for regular check-ins, ensuring her students remained connected and engaged beyond the classroom.

Her legacy is one of quiet, unwavering impact. She didn't seek recognition, but she shaped generations of artists through her guidance, her support, and her dedication.

María Magdalena Campos-Pons

María Magdalena Campos-Pons is an internationally acclaimed Afro-Cuban artist and the Cornelius Vanderbilt Chair of Fine Arts at Vanderbilt University. She has received a MacArthur Fellowship and curated the 2019 Havana Biennial.

I always perceived Alicia as an individual whom I would define as stoic, extremely vulnerable, and delicately fragile. For that reason, I was always very careful about what I needed to say to her, what I needed to hear from her, because—some way, somehow—everything was said in other ways.

There was something extraordinary about how much Alicia Henry could say in silence, and how much that was translated and embedded in the materiality of her work. I knew about her before I came here, and I always thought that she should have more of an international presence than she had. When I started working on the Biennial in Cuba and involved Nashville, I immediately knew I was going to invite her to participate. I had many conversations with other colleagues internationally about Alicia's work. She was always in the center of those conversations.

She had the courage to make entire pieces like the one that is going to be on the front wall of *In Her Place*, in which she dared to take a centimeter—a dot—of a paper and attach it to the wall. There is bravery, there is courage, there is an incredible understanding of the intangibility of things that are not stable. All that is silence. To understand that, and to be able to make that visual, you need to have an incredible understanding of silence.

And in some ways, for me, that is what Alicia Henry is. Alicia Henry understood the dimensionality of silence. She understood the interiority of things, and how to make it vulnerable, make it fray, and make it in a way that we could access. Yes, of course, you're going to pass, and a piece of paper is going to move. Yes, of course, you're going to build this face of all men and all liars and all truth that is a clown, and it's going to be falling apart layer by layer. And it is so many things at once. But the level and the depth of the work is indescribable.

I am very honored and pleased that I shared a tiny little bit of time in Alicia's presence.

Mark W. Scala

Mark W. Scala is the Frist Art Museum's chief curator. He curated the 2003 exhibition *Alicia Henry: Black and Blue: Recent Works*.

Right away, I recognized the incredible originality of Alicia's work and approached her about a solo show that became *Black and Blue*. Even then, she seemed to be somebody who was in the league of Betye Saar, Alison Saar, and Renée Stout—artists who were finding a language that bridges the ocean.

I was so thrilled to see that, after going to the Art Institute of Chicago and Yale, she had spent time in the Peace Corps. I could see that had had an extraordinary influence on her life, and certainly on her work. You could see it in the work she did with families, and when you see groupings on a wall—these figures are kind of isolated in a group. I think that may be not just a reflection of a cultural experience but also a personal experience. And for her, I've never tried to separate the personal from the cultural. I think that it's all packed together.

I love the idea of silence, but I also love the idea of nothingness. The surfaces of her works are the works, but there's always something implicit behind them—this invisible presence. You have this sense of being watched by something behind these layers of fabric, behind these flat, mask-like forms. For me, it was magical that an artist would be able to imbue everyday materials with this quality of sentience. So much so that, in a way, it was almost like Alicia was watching you.

Her language stayed constant in many ways, but it became deeper and deeper and richer and richer. I thought that showed she was more interested in art making as a form of life living in a way that goes beyond being a professional artist. I could never separate her from her work. They seem to be the same thing.

Lain York

Lain York is a painter and the director of Zeitgeist Gallery. He has represented Alicia Henry since 2003.

One of my first memories of her was when she brought her students down to the Fugitive Art Center here in Wedgewood-Houston. I liked her right away—she's just so cool.

Later, when we invited her to be part of a group show at Zeitgeist, I got to learn more about her. Her works are very visceral. These objects were so interesting because it wasn't clear which side we would want to show—both were so gorgeous. She'd say, "You're the professional, you can decide how to hang it." At that time, the gallery was on Twenty-First Avenue, and I just ran across the street to this dress shop and got some dress pins, and that's how we installed the work. To this day, that's the way we've always installed her work—with those pins.

She was quick to say that she was making work as an African American woman and that her process was something of a kitchen-table process—a crafted thing, an area relegated to women. At the time, I was presenting her work in a very measured, museum style. Later on, she became more specific about how her work was presented on the wall. Like Kara Walker—the wall is a canvas, and she's activating the space.

She guarded her studio time. She was all about the work. But Alicia always had an oblique relationship with the art world, maybe with the world outside her studio. I remember seeing her do a talk at Cheekwood—that was the most I'd ever heard her talk about her work. She talked a lot about her time working with the Peace Corps in Africa—seeing so many people with missing limbs and how that figured into her work.

When she started making flowers and bouquets around 2020, it made total sense. It's about the fragility of life. So many people would look at her work and think, "Oh my God, it's so heavy." There was a very particular gravity to those figures and those masks, and the bouquets might have lightened that. But also, knowing Alicia, it's interesting that those flowers could also be interpreted as even heavier. I may be a bit biased—and maybe it's my response as a painter—but I just thought there was such joy in her work.

Lakesha Calvin

Lakesha Calvin is an artist and the chair of the Fisk University Art Department. She has worked at Fisk since 2021.

I was encouraged to meet Alicia Henry by our mutual friend Brandon Donahue-Shipp. I knew her work and her work in art education. I knew how committed she was to students—not just in North Nashville, and not just at Fisk, but all over. I was still at Tennessee State University, but I wanted her mentorship. I felt a little awkward, and we had exchanged some emails, but we were still sort of circling each other. When the position at Fisk opened up in the fall of 2021, I interviewed with Alicia and Jamaal Sheats. It was a really good conversation. I was so excited to meet her. Me, I show my emotions on my sleeve. But with her, there's this kindness. There's this beauty and calmness that's just kind of like a blanket over everything. Strong, but very mild. There's a strength that's palpable, but it wasn't overwhelming. She is intentional in her walk, but it seemed effortless.

During studio visits, it was almost surreal to see her work all laid out and to be in that space with the materials she worked with—fabric, wood, ceramics—and the visual language that she'd developed over the years. I was struck by how she would formulate these meaningful images that were very simple, but the complexity was still arresting. I don't think I'd ever been in an artist's space that was quite like that.

One thing she always encouraged me to do was work—even if it's only thirty minutes a day, do something in the studio. I saw that consistency, over time, of that effort and that play. When she brought the work to the gallery, it was even more interesting—the work was so monumental in its home; to transport it to this temporary home and place it on the wall was so clearly a labor of love.

I don't know the year her home was built, but it's an older home, and it's large. The upstairs is divided into three rooms, and right after you come up the stairs, there's work. There wasn't a space you could turn where you wouldn't see work. It was almost like a theater or a playhouse of sorts, with all these characters that are laying down on the floor, resting against the wall, all waiting for their turn. With those elements that were chosen, it was like saying, "It's your time, now. You can work your magic and share what you have to share with the world." They felt like living creatures, almost.

IN HER PLACE

All works are courtesy of the artist unless otherwise noted.

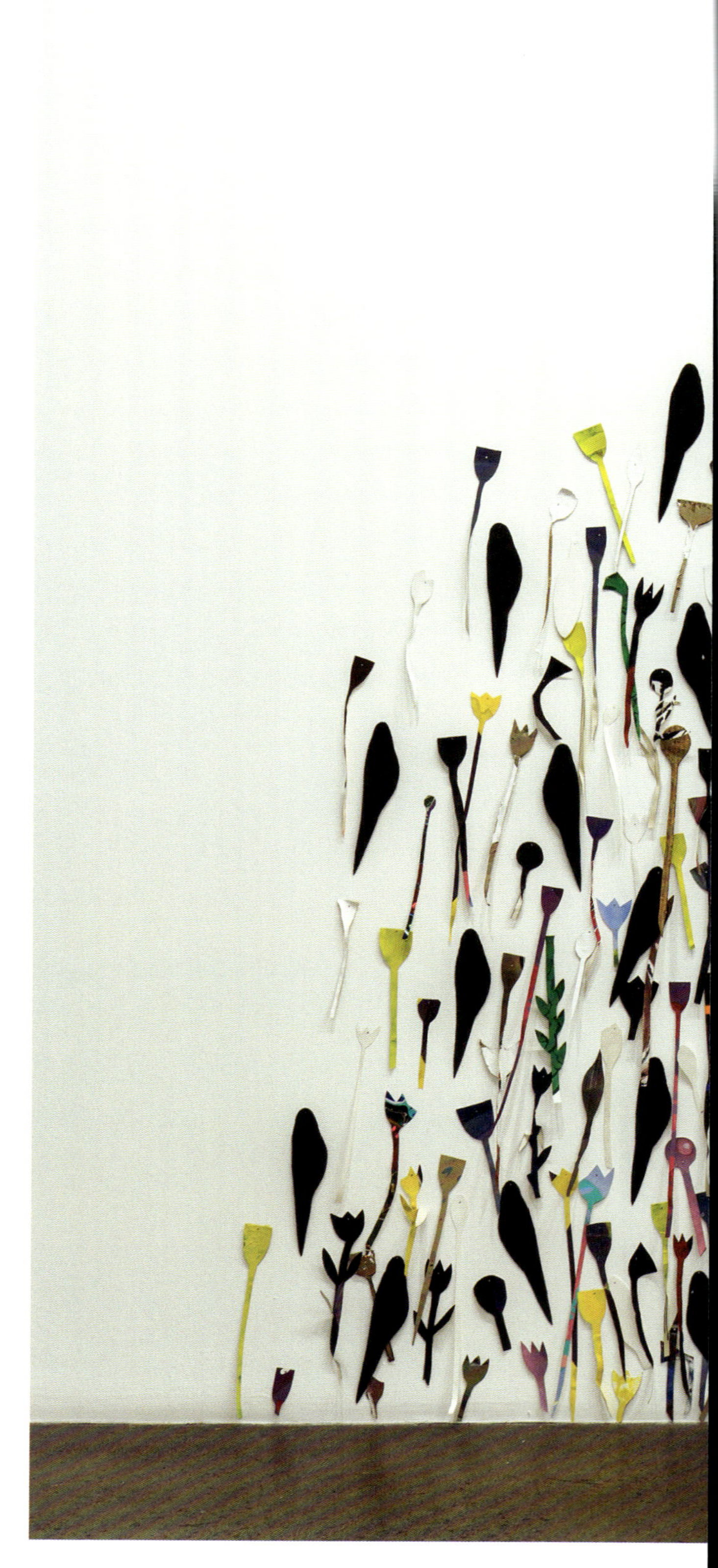

1
Untitled (Inspiration for Clerestory), 2018
Mixed media
96 × 120 in.
Courtesy of Trépanier Baer Gallery, Calgary

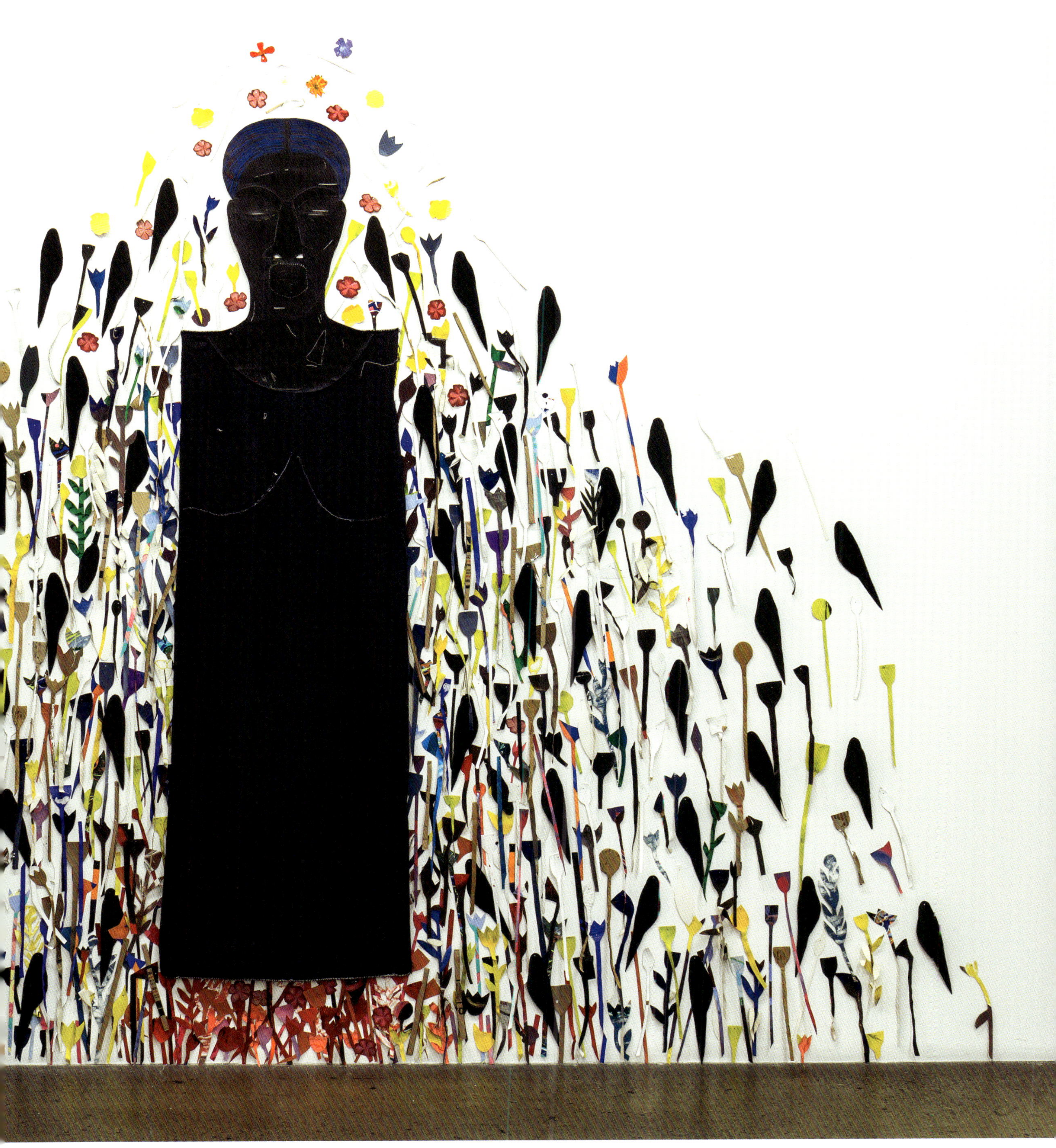

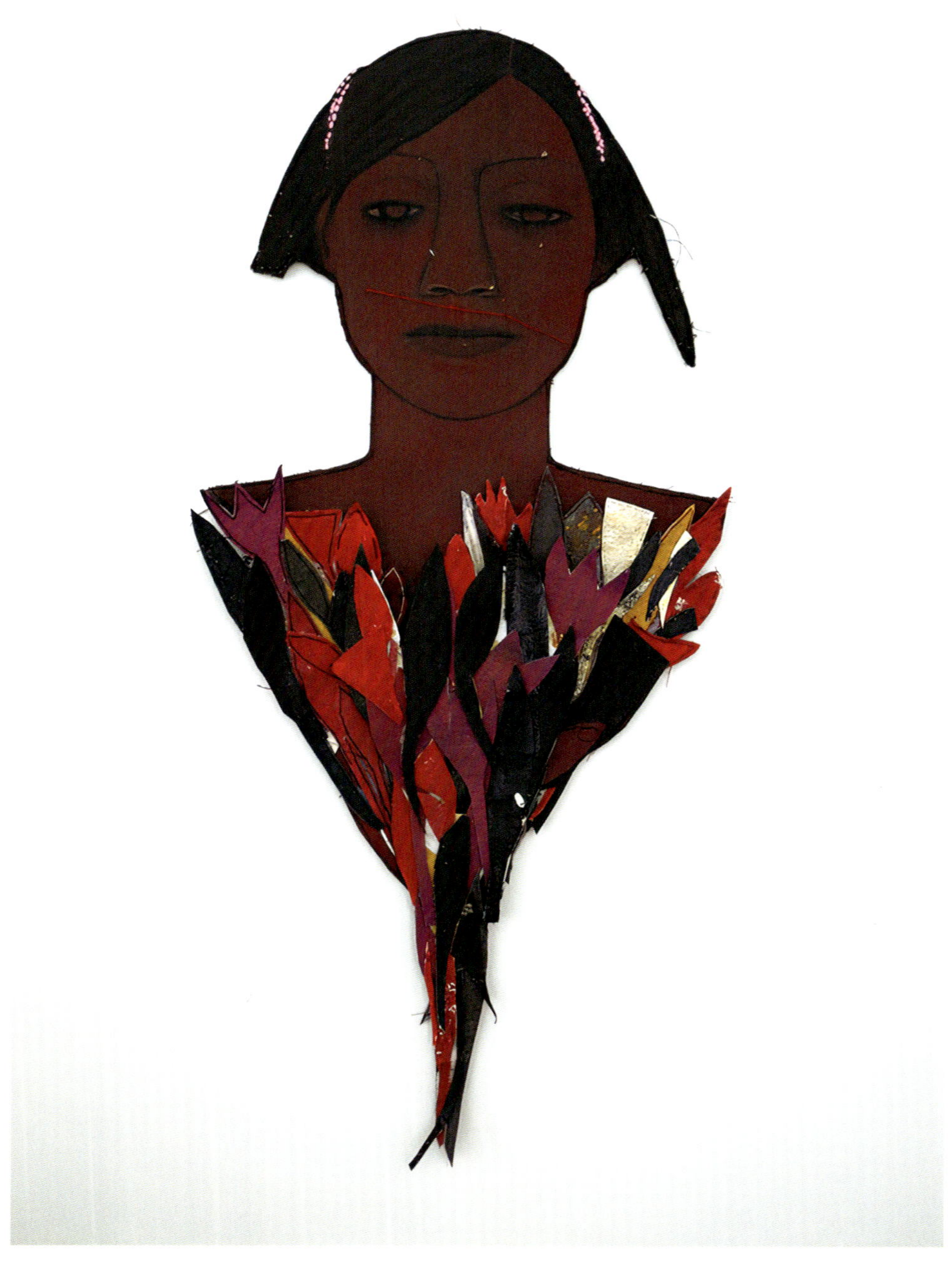

2

Untitled (Figure with Flowers), undated

Mixed media (dye, acrylic, fabric, thread, felt, leather, and paper)

36 × 16 in.

Collection of Sasha and Charlie Sealey

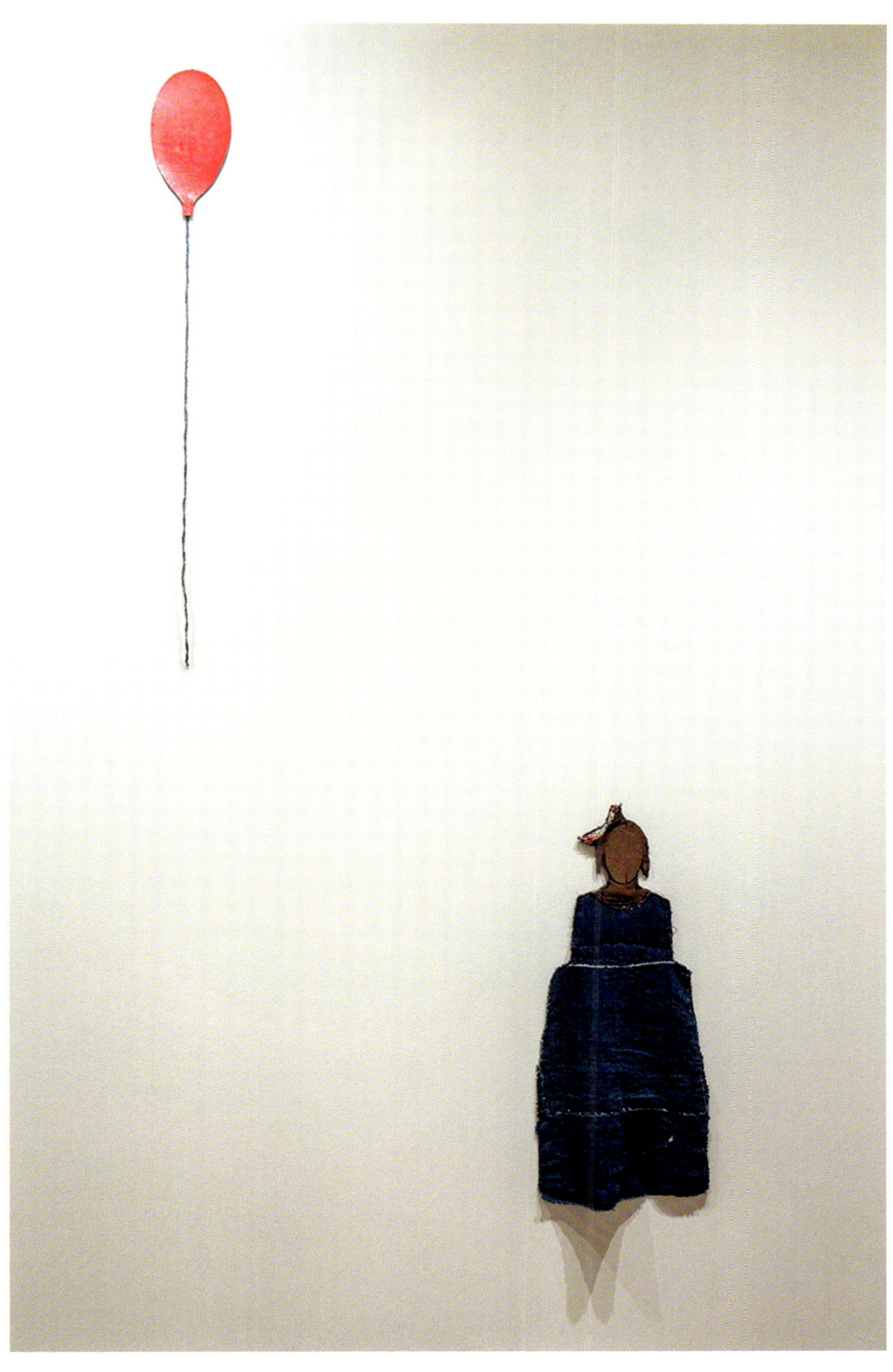

3

Untitled (Girl with Balloon), 2020–23

Mixed media (acrylic, cotton, denim, felt, leather, thread, and yarn)

Dimensions variable

Collection of Jodi and Hal Hess

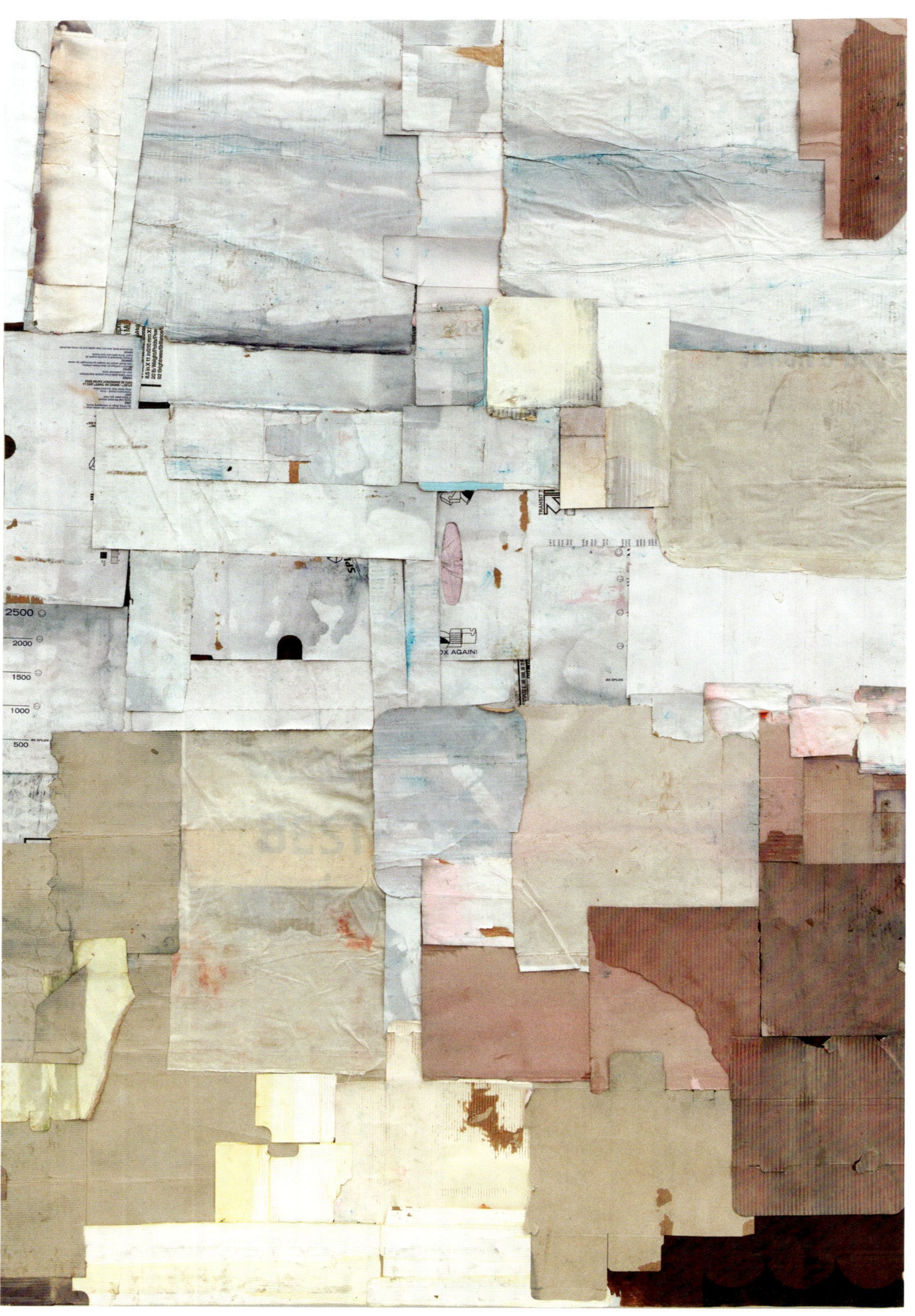

4

Twenty-Two Child Bride, 2022

Dye, paper, fabric, and glitter collage on custom strainer

76 × 102 in.

Courtesy of the artist and David Lusk Gallery

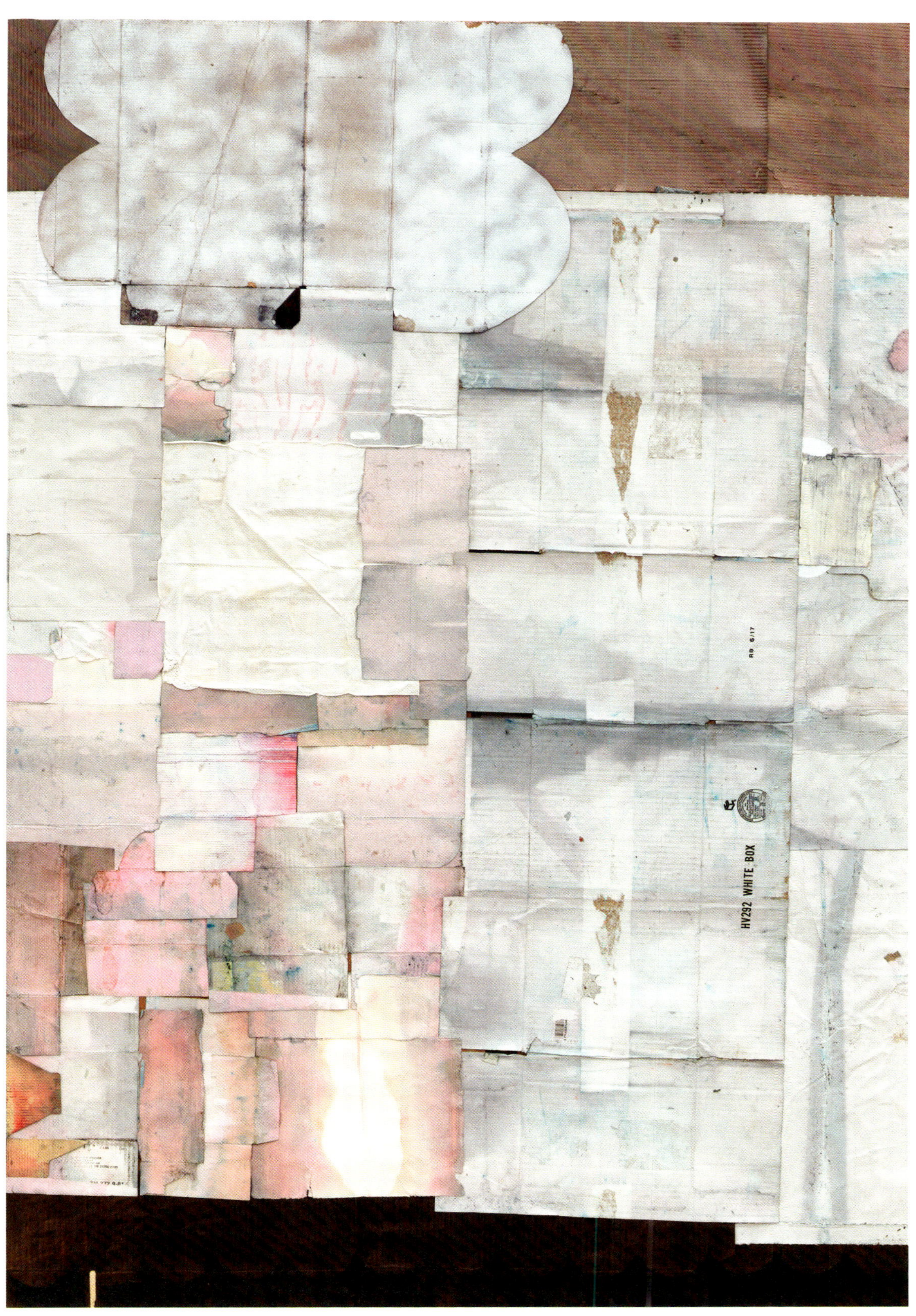
HV292 WHITE BOX

5

Elaine, 2022

Dye and cardboard collage on custom strainer

76 × 52 in.

Courtesy of the artist and David Lusk Gallery

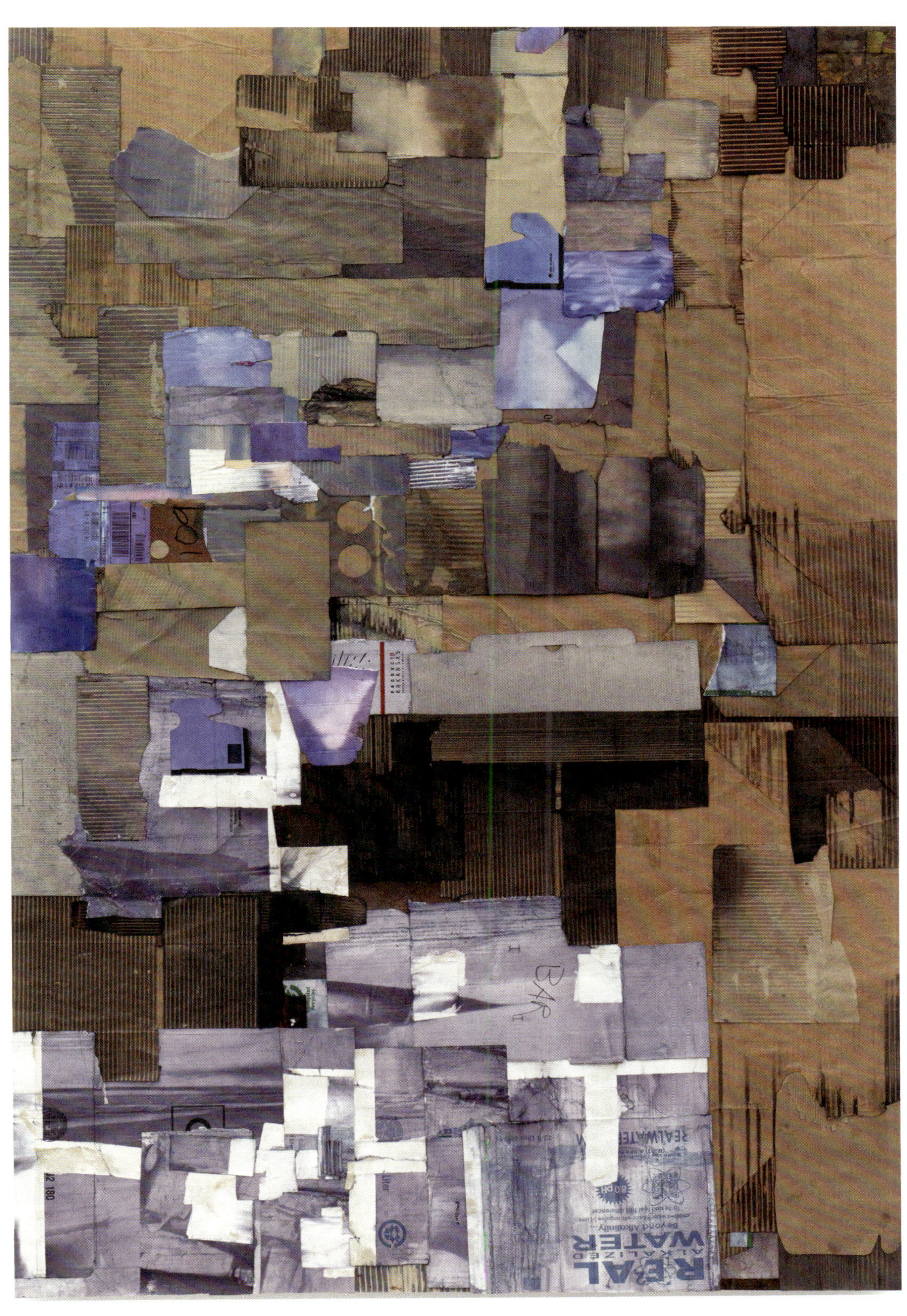

51 JODI HAYS

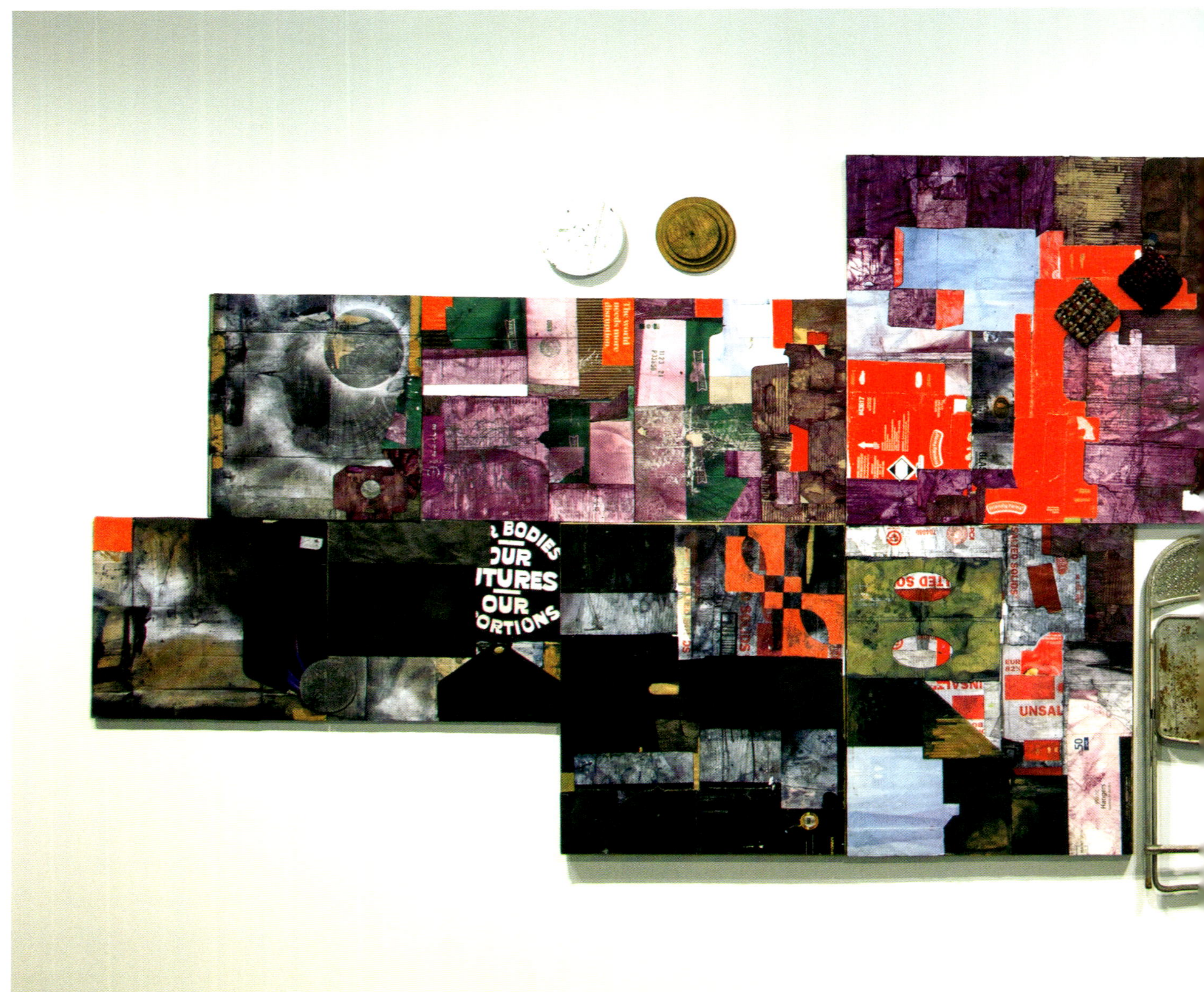

6

Lamentation (Aches, for P. and D.), 2025

Canvas, cloth, textile, jar lids, magnets, dye, T-shirt, spray enamel, gouache, leather, paper, cardboard, found wood, handmade pot holders, and wire collage on industrial aluminum strainers with metal chairs

88 × 264 in.

Courtesy of the artist and David Lusk Gallery

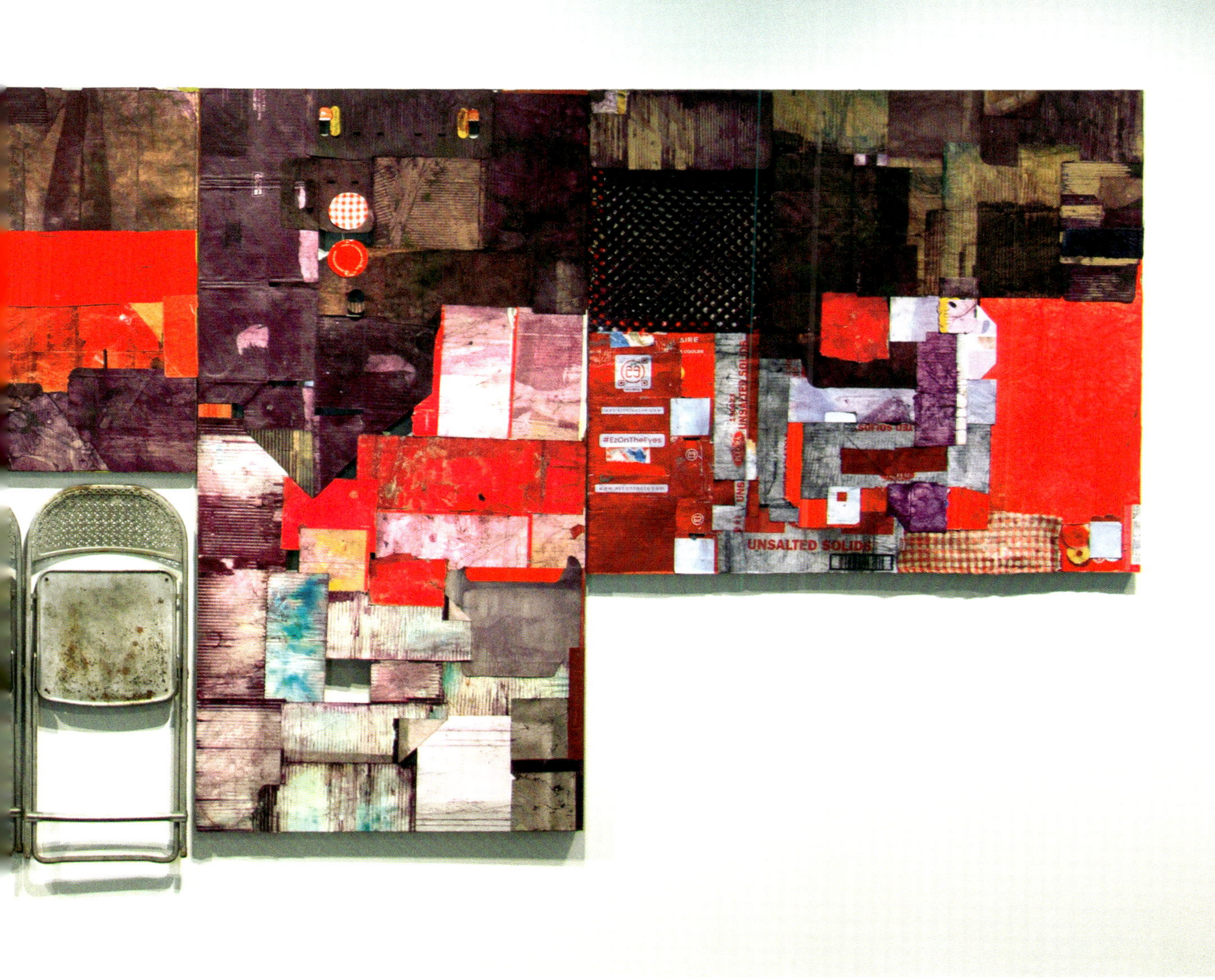
#EzOnTheEyes
UNSALTED SOLIDS

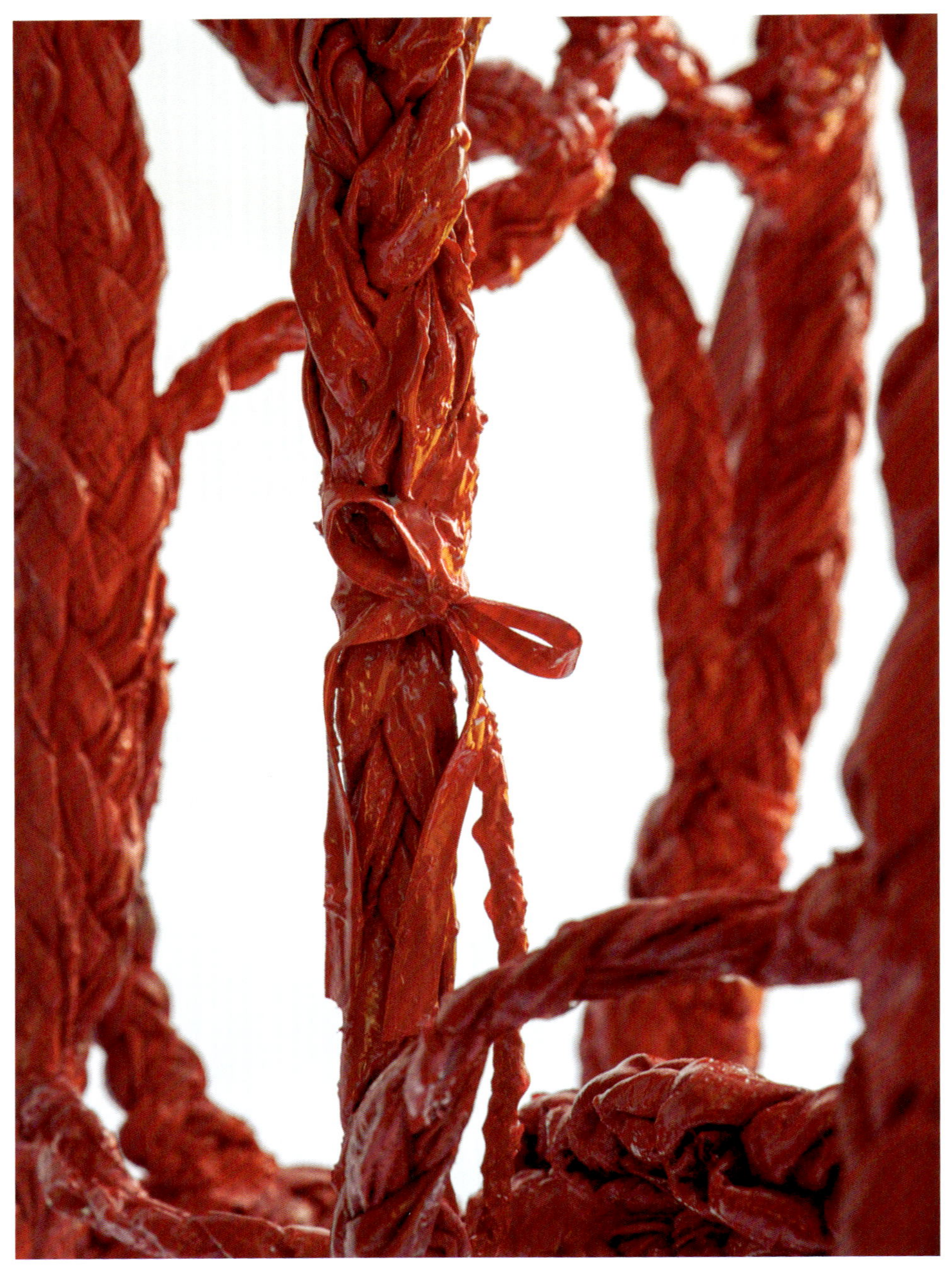

7
Venus Rising, 2025
Bed sheets, dining plates, steel, and mixed media
108 × 51 × 12 in.

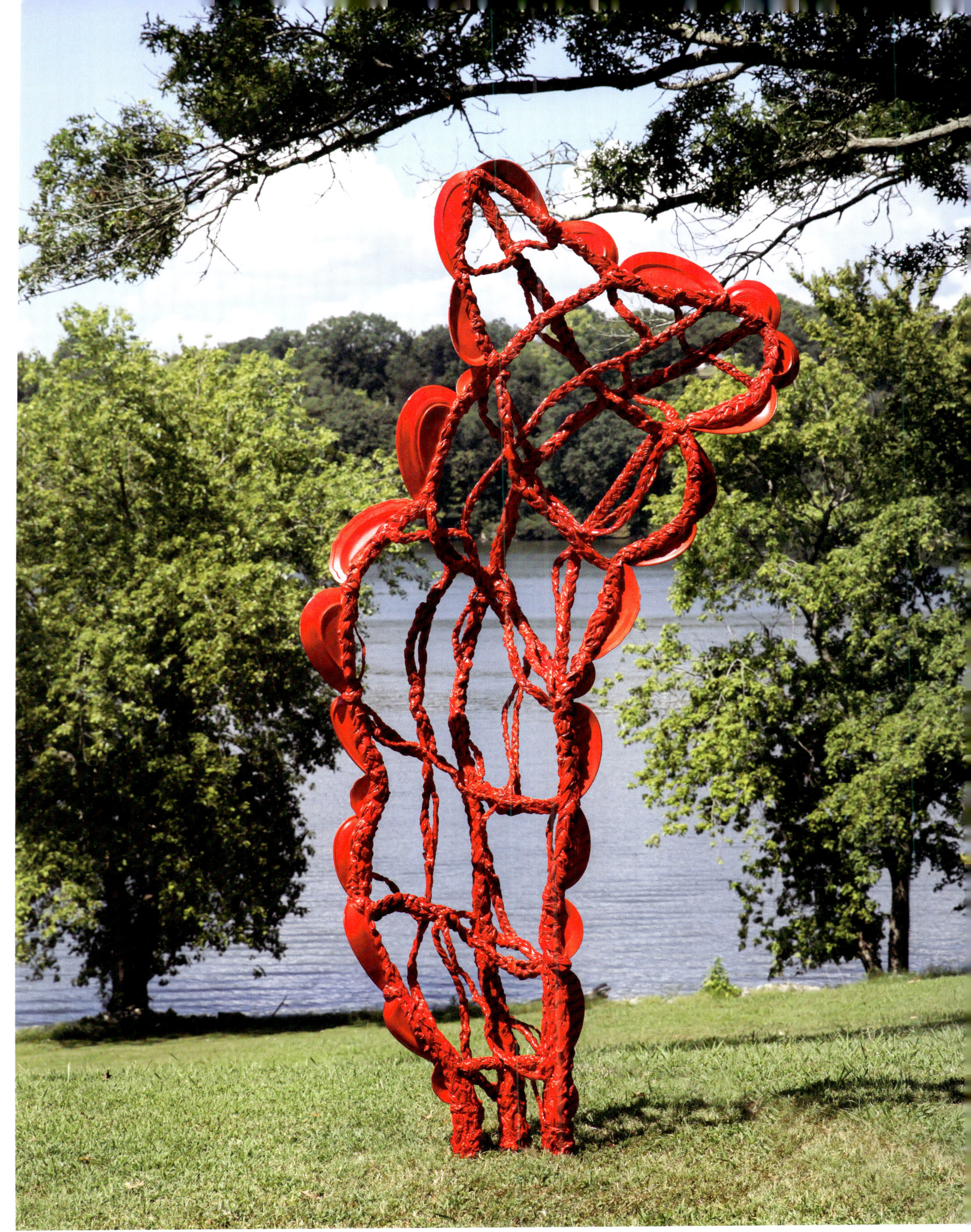

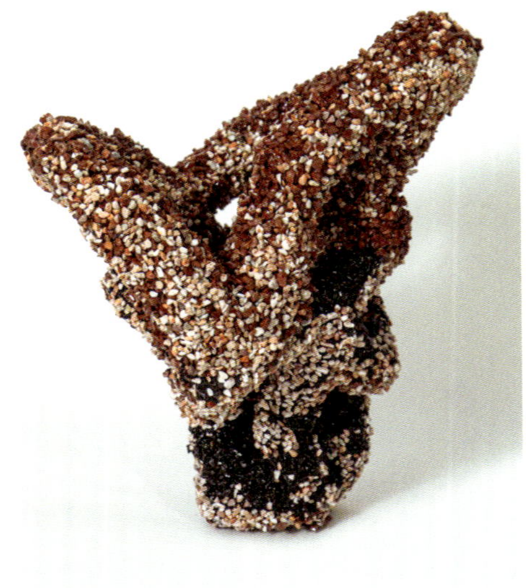

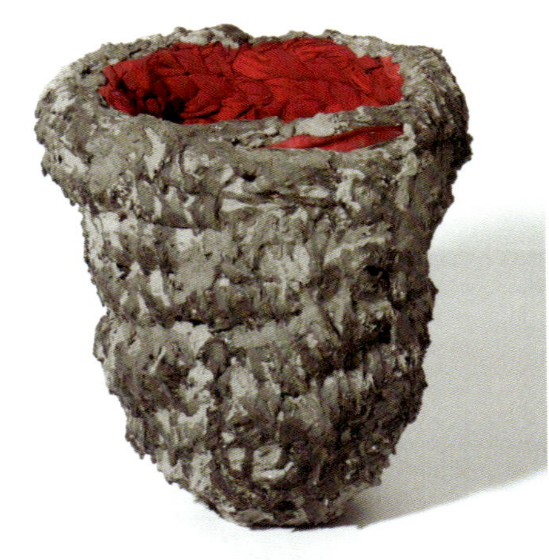

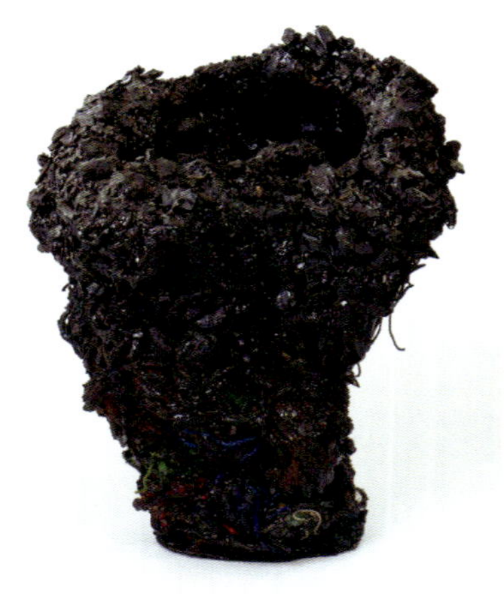

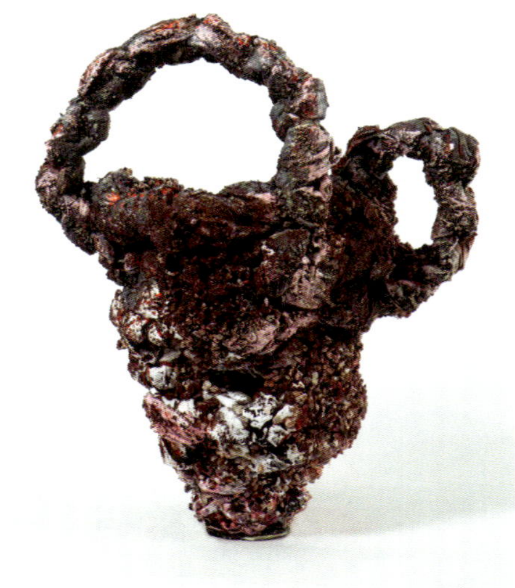

8
Pink and Gray Gravel Vessel, 2023
Bedsheets, poly fil, gravel, resin, thread, and mixed media
23 × 21 × 15 in.

9
Bedsheet and Concrete Vessel, 2022
Bedsheets, concrete, dye, resin, and thread
13 × 12 × 11 in.

11
Small Unruly Vessel, 2019
Charred wood, yarn, acrylic, resin, and mixed media
13 × 11 × 10 in.

12
Charon Vessel, 2022
Curtains, brick dust, gravel, cement, acrylic, resin, and mixed media
21 × 18 × 12 in.

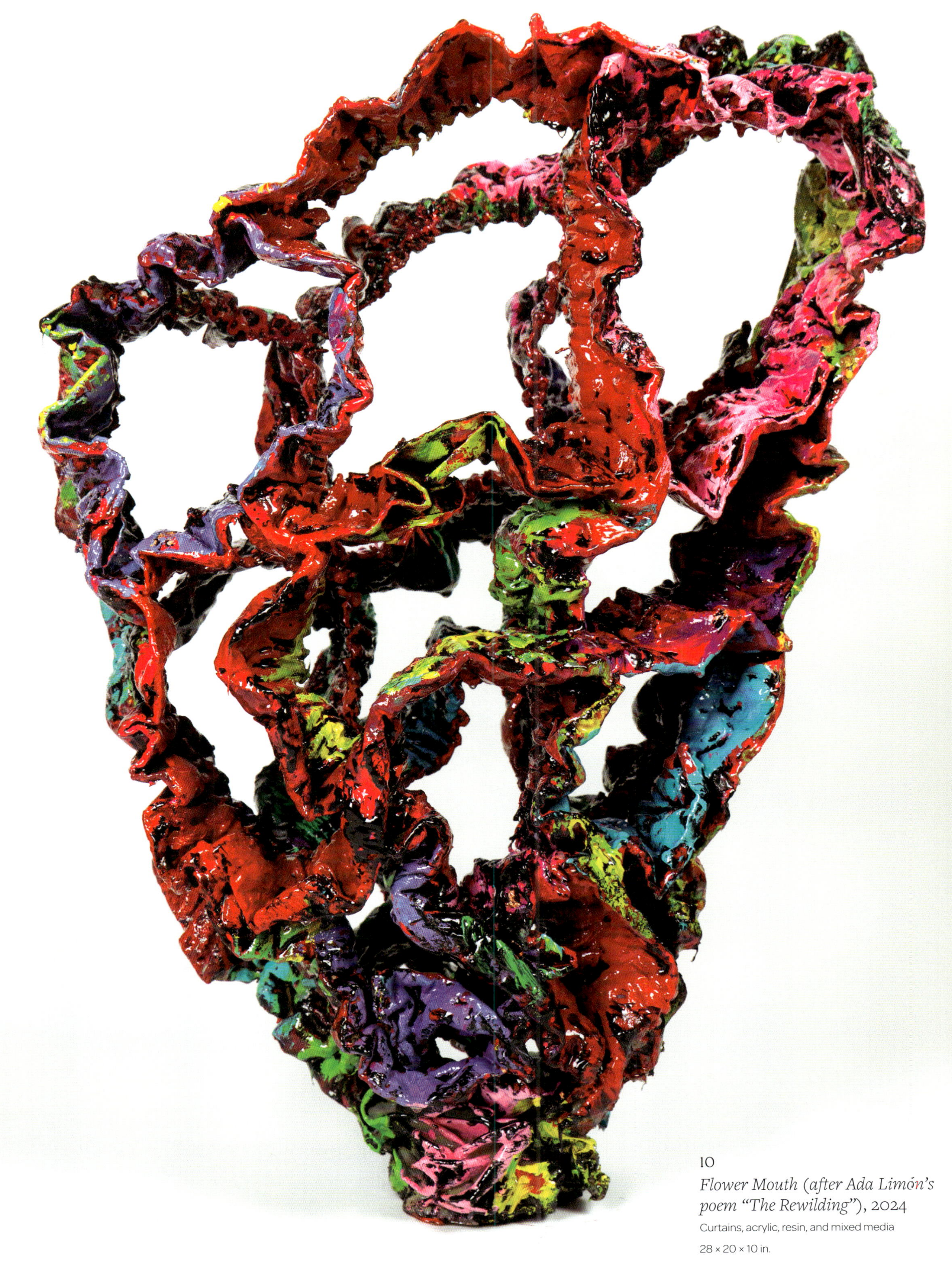

10
Flower Mouth (after Ada Limón's poem "The Rewilding"), 2024
Curtains, acrylic, resin, and mixed media
28 × 20 × 10 in.

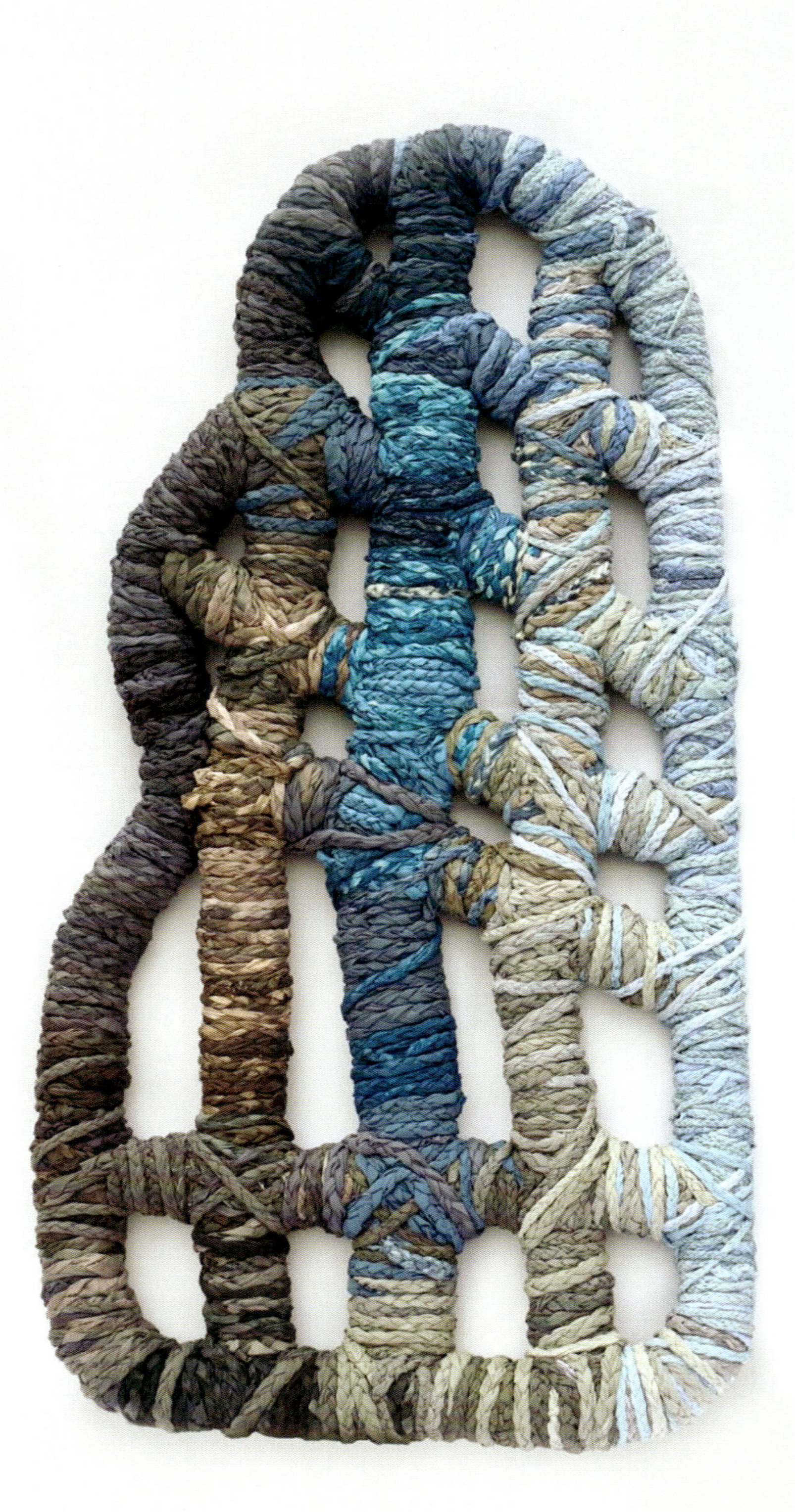

13

Celestial Megaliths, 2024

Bed sheets, dye, thread, resin, Tyvek, and aluminum

105 × 113 × 6 in.

Courtesy of the artist and Mindy Solomon Gallery, Miami

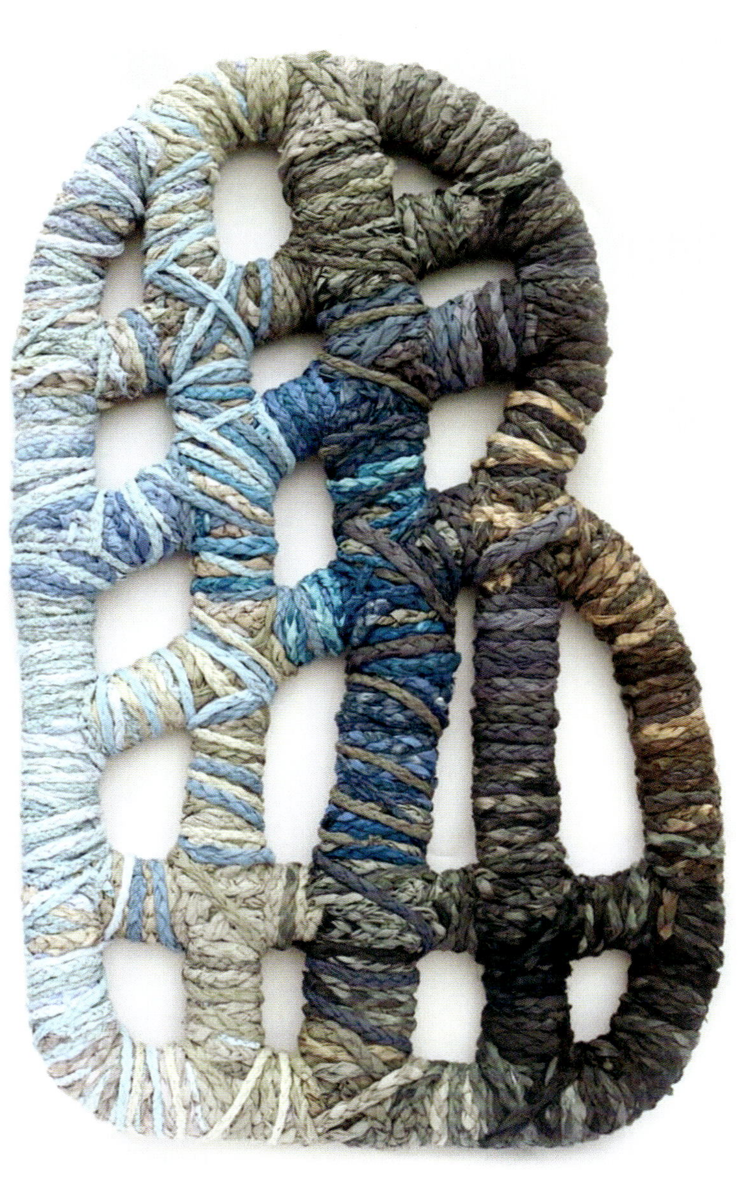

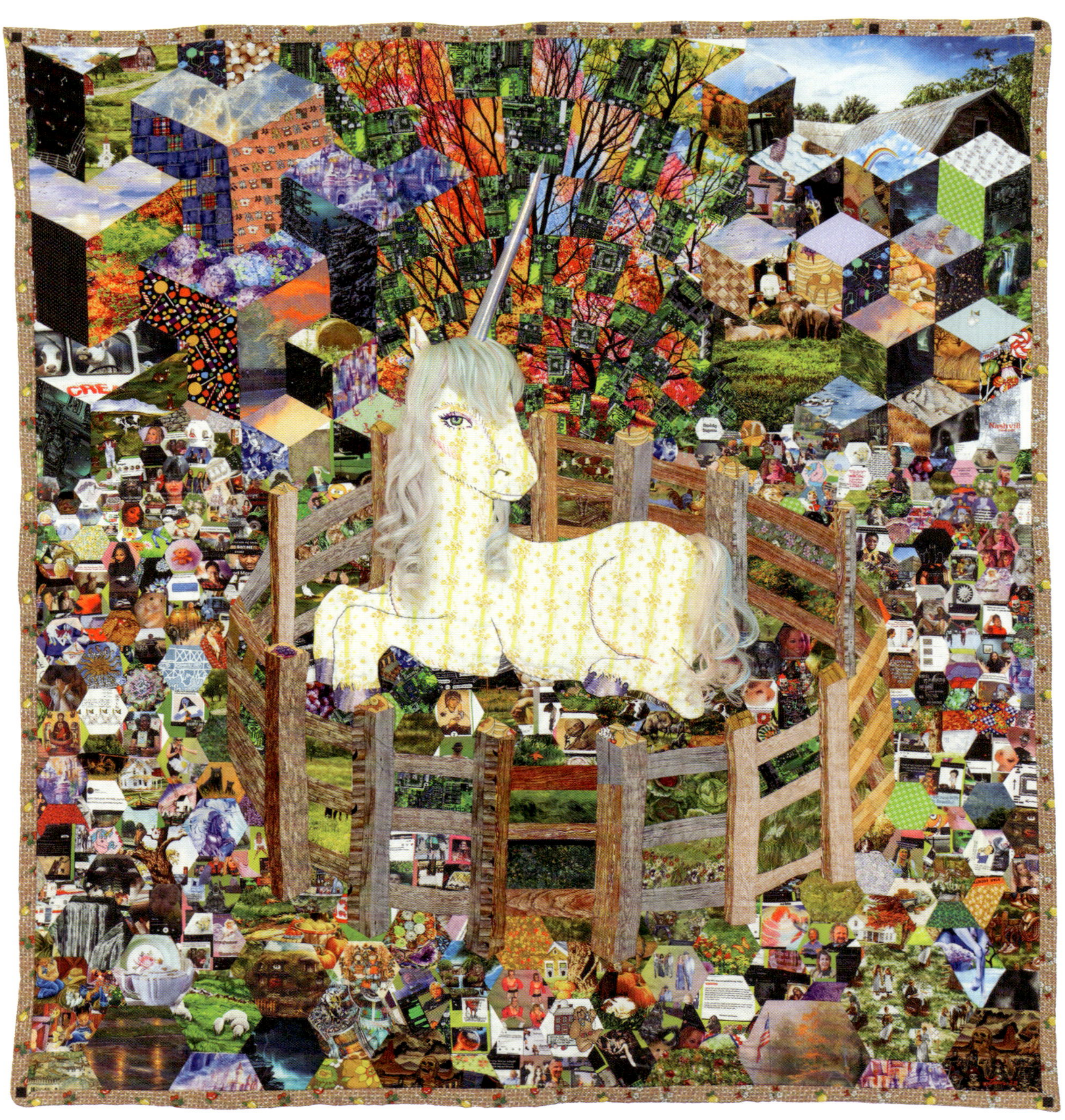

14

Unicorn in Captivity, 2024

Cotton, batting, thread, beads, and wig

90 × 85 in.

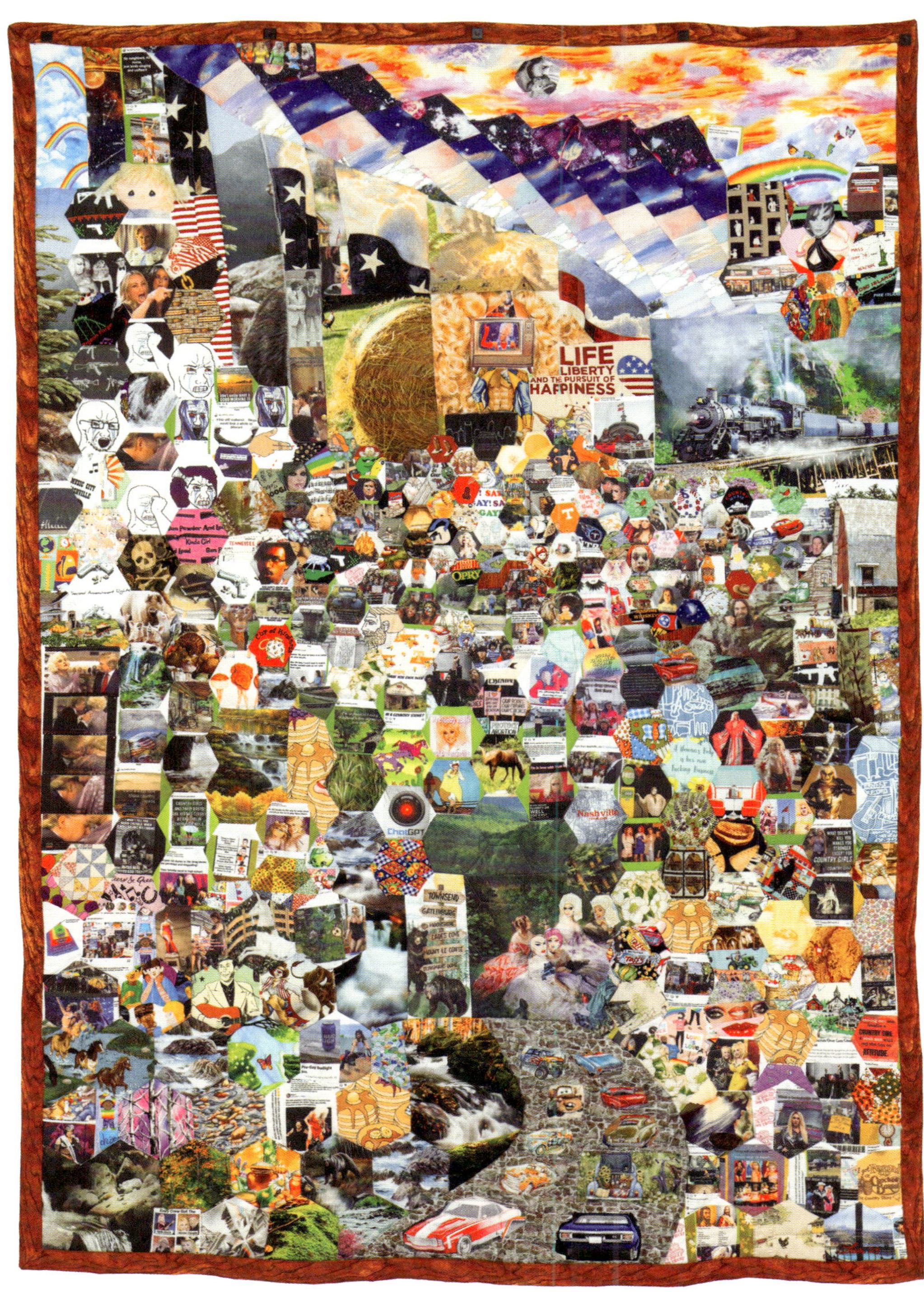

15

The State of Tennessee, 2023

Cotton, batting, and thread

86 × 61½ in.

Collection of Jennifer and Lee Pepper

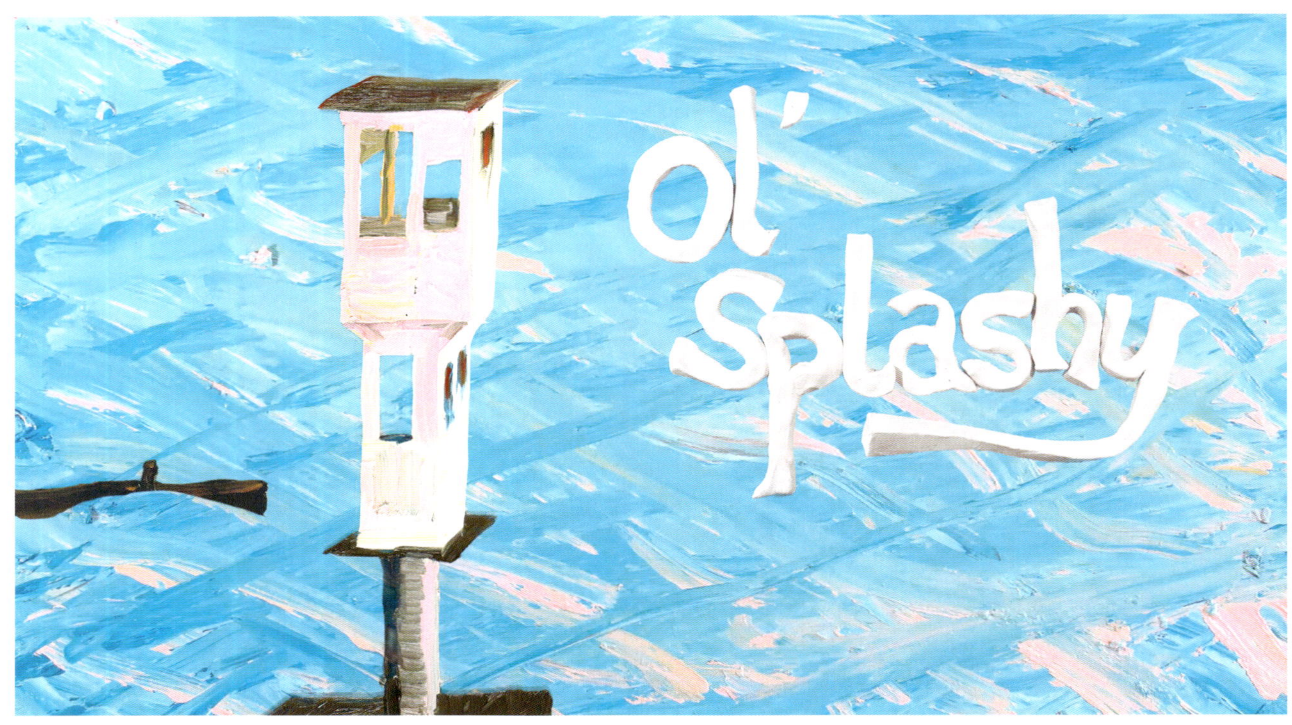

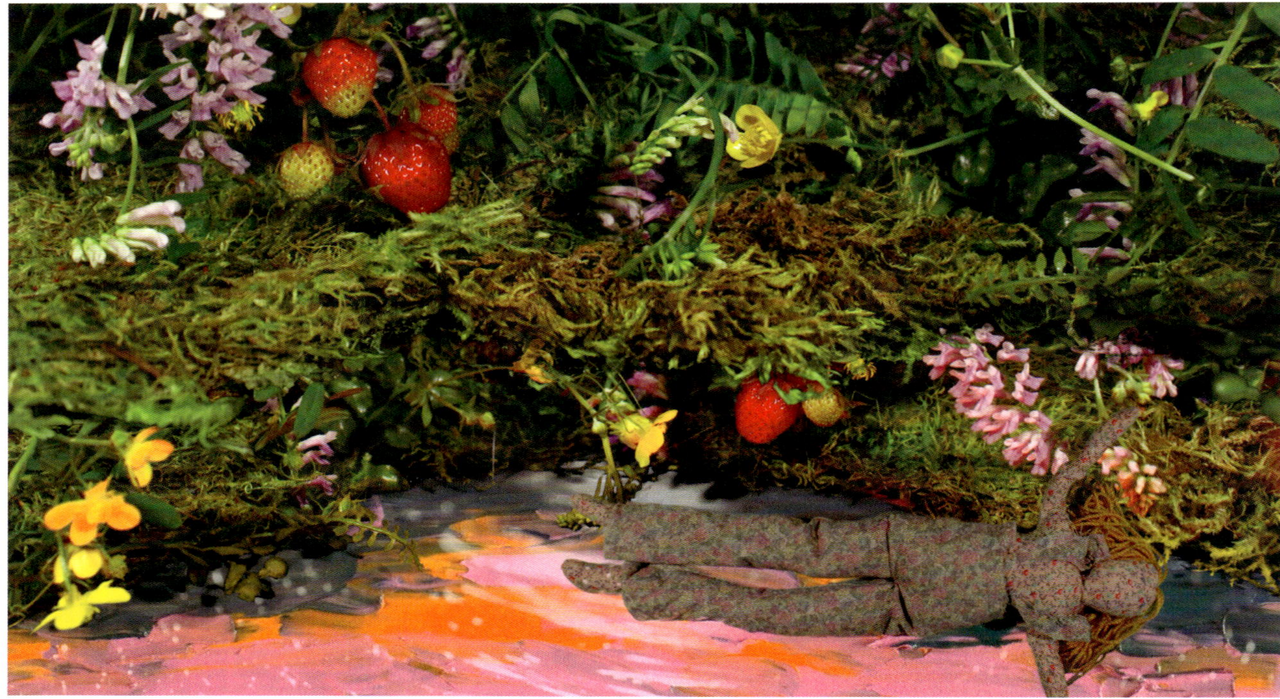

16

Ol' Splashy (video stills), 2021

Short animation film

Running time: 8 min., 41 sec.

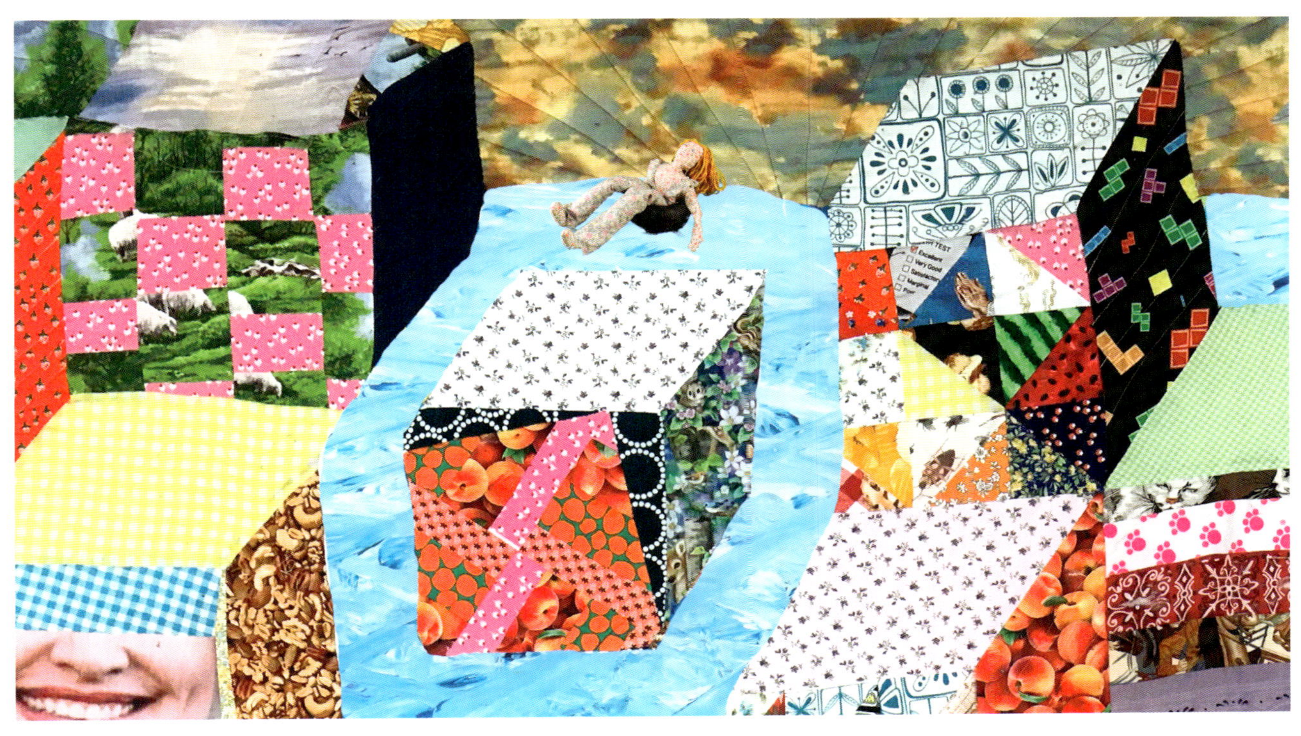

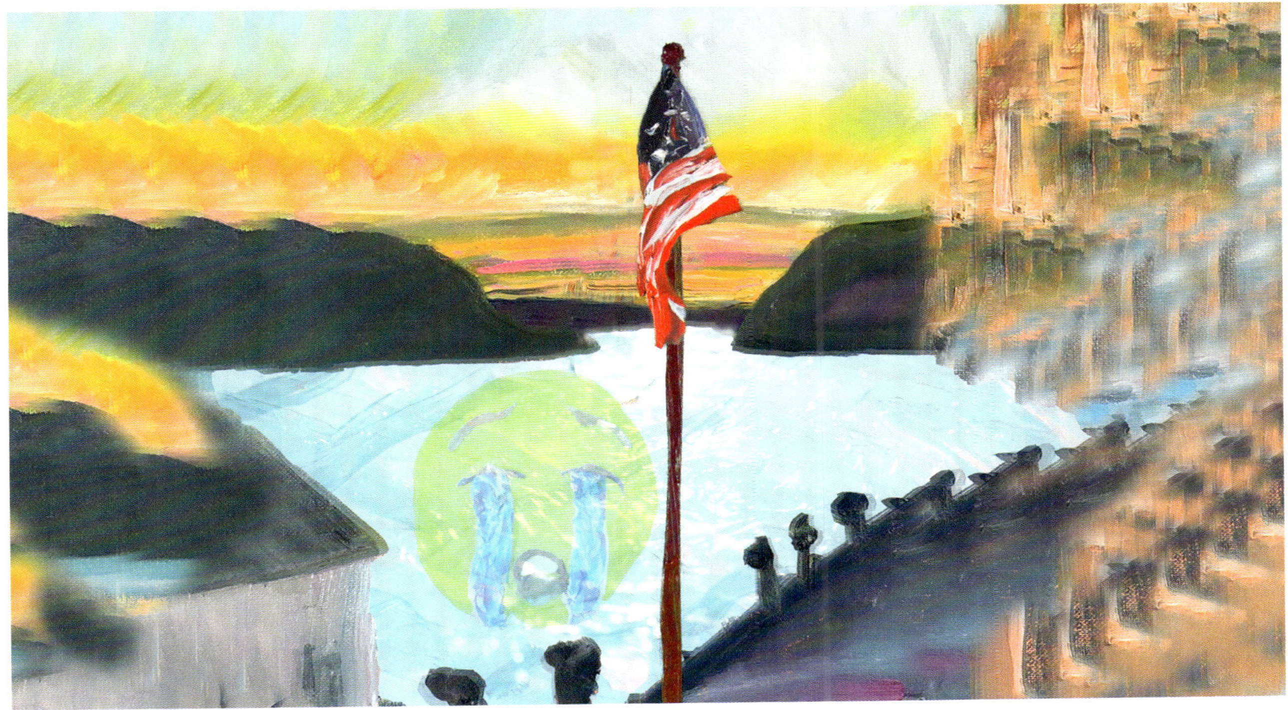

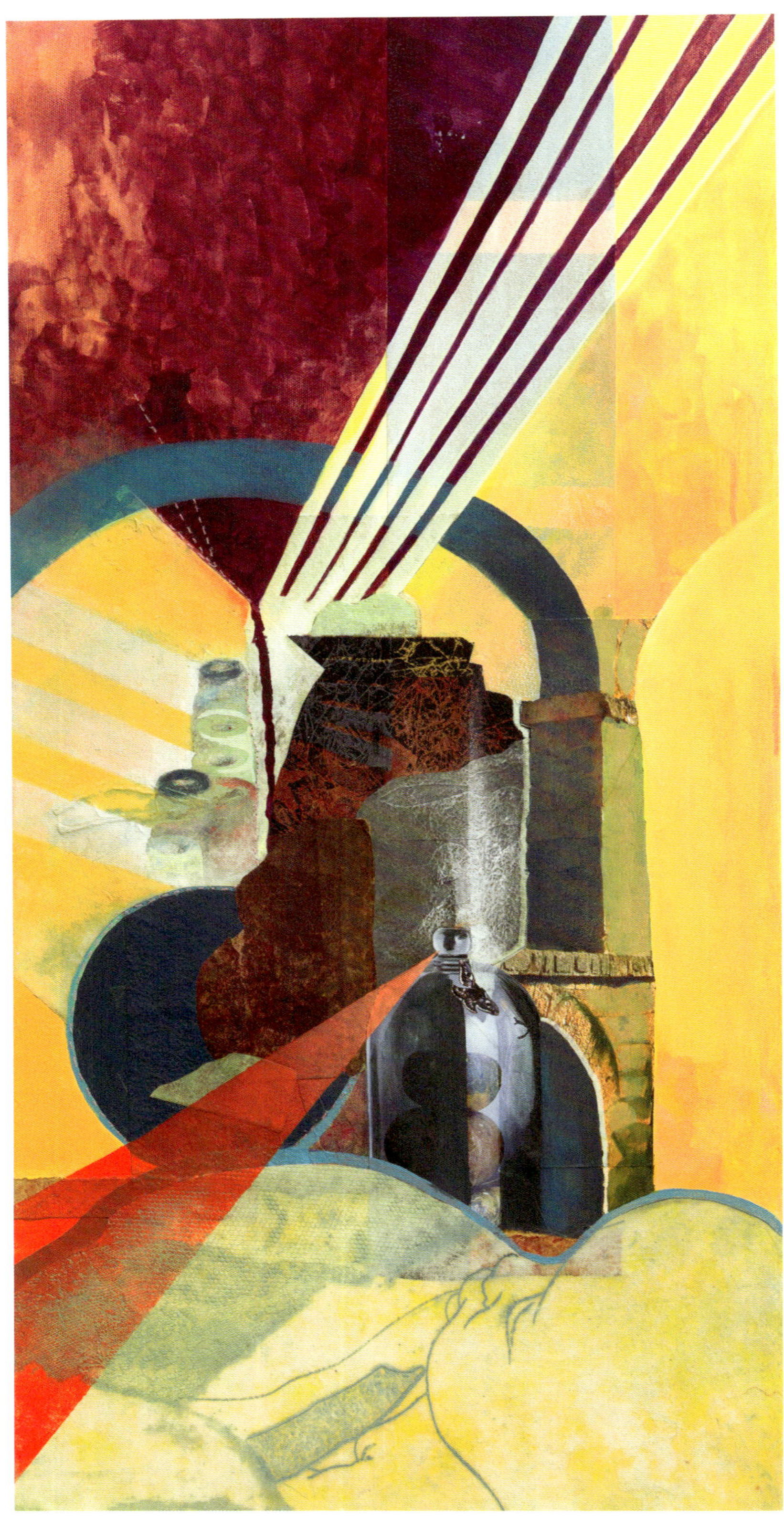

17
Cadence, 2025
Mixed media
31½ × 16½ in.

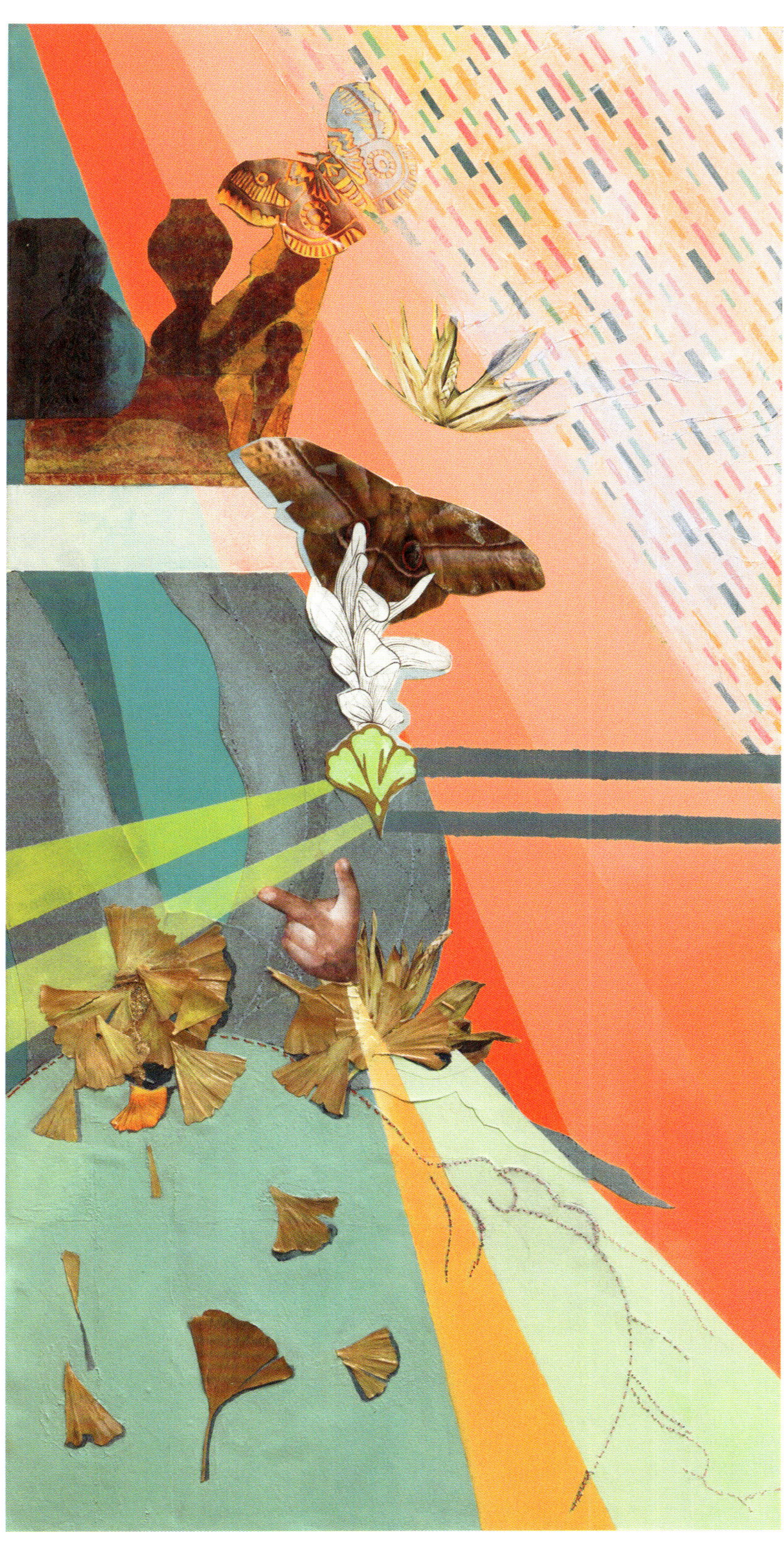

18
Revival, 2025
Mixed media
31½ × 16½ in.

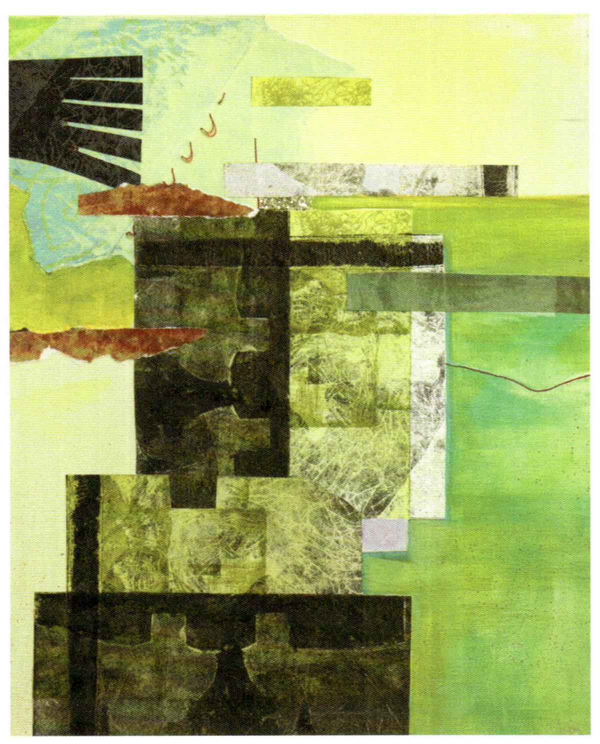

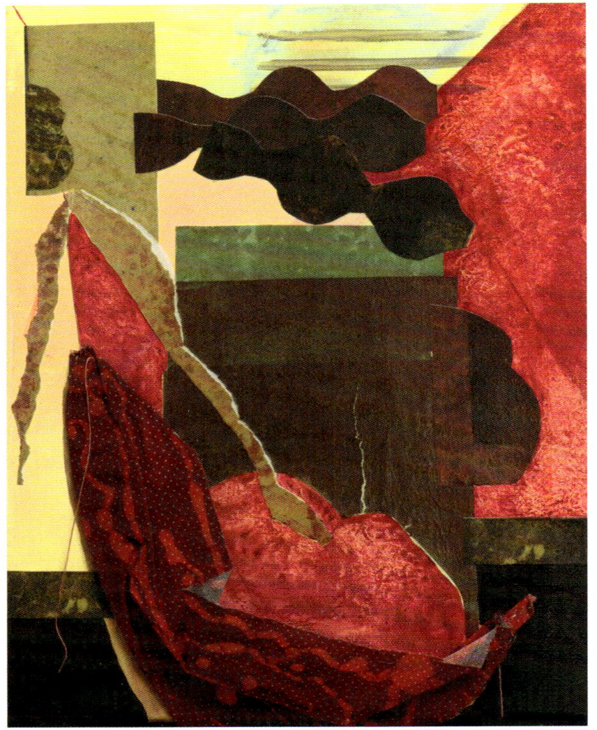

19

Connecting, 2023

Acrylic on canvas, fabric, handmade paper, old prints, and ink

12 × 9 in.

20

Cradling, 2023

Acrylic on canvas, fabric, handmade paper, old prints, and ink

12 × 9 in.

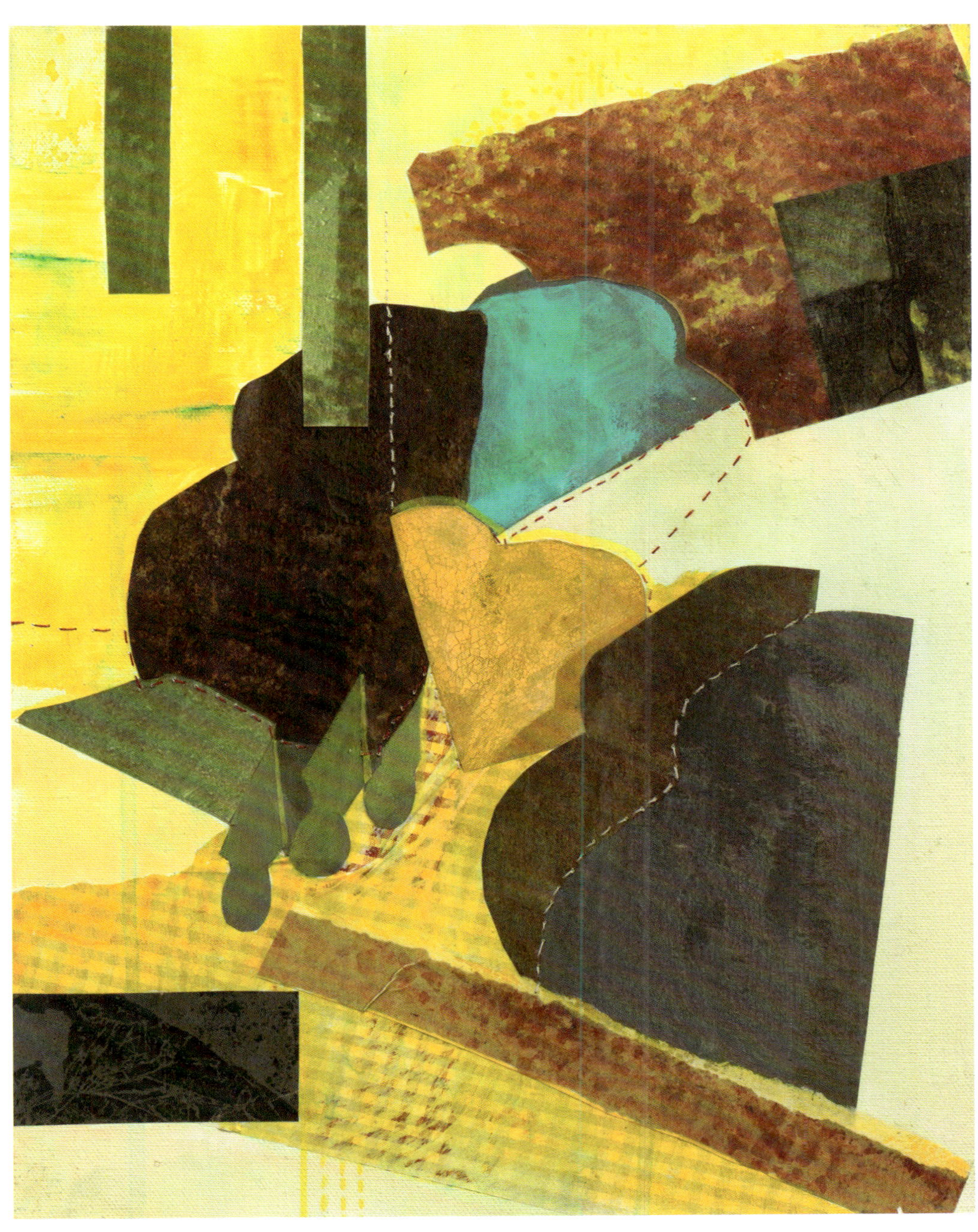

21
Reconstruction, 2022
Acrylic on canvas, fabric, handmade paper, old prints, and ink
12 × 9 in.

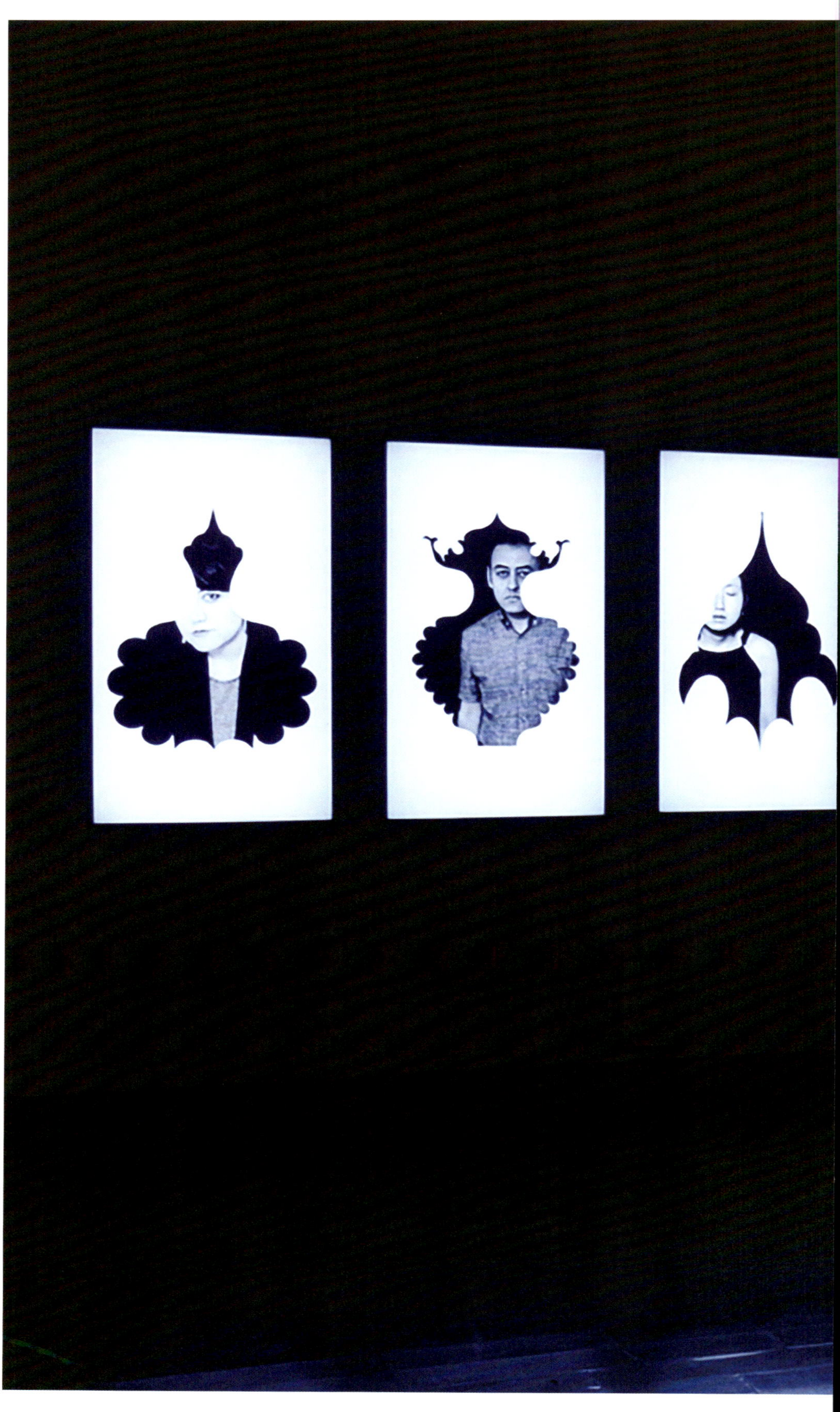

22
Imagined Boundaries, ongoing since 2017
Nine-channel videos
Dimensions variable

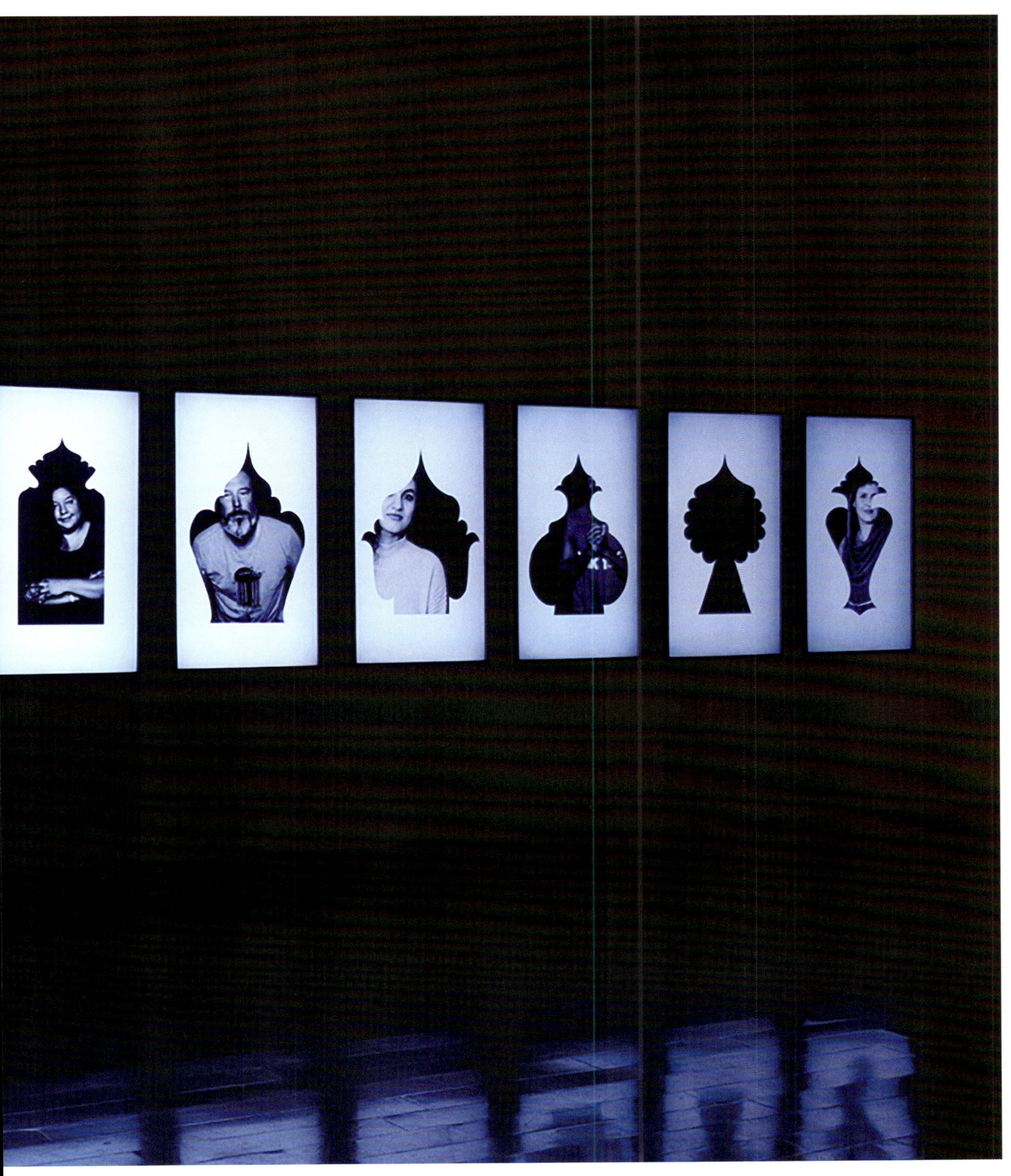

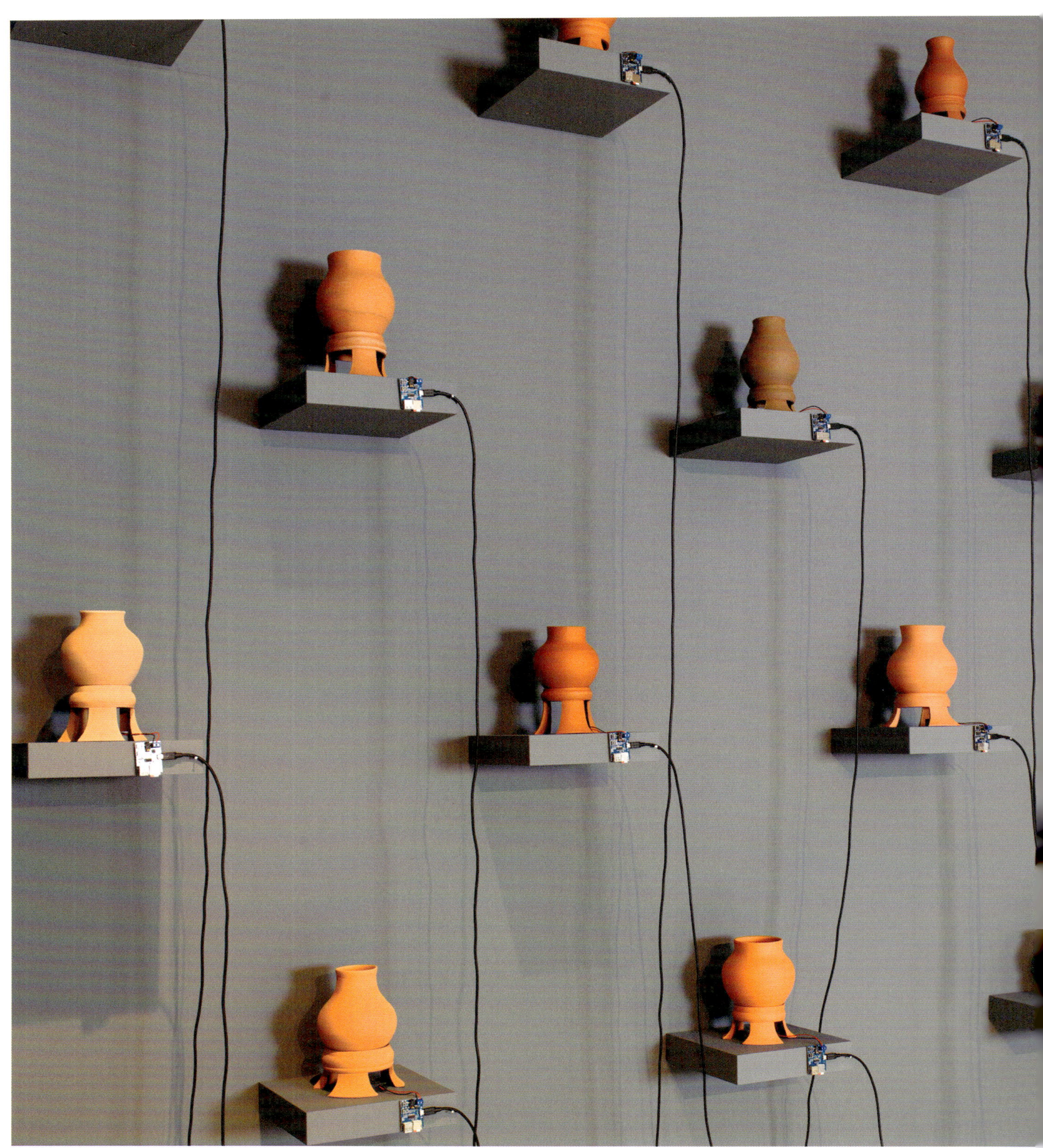

23
A Transient's Paradox, ongoing since 2022
Video, sound, ceramic vessels, and wires
Dimensions variable

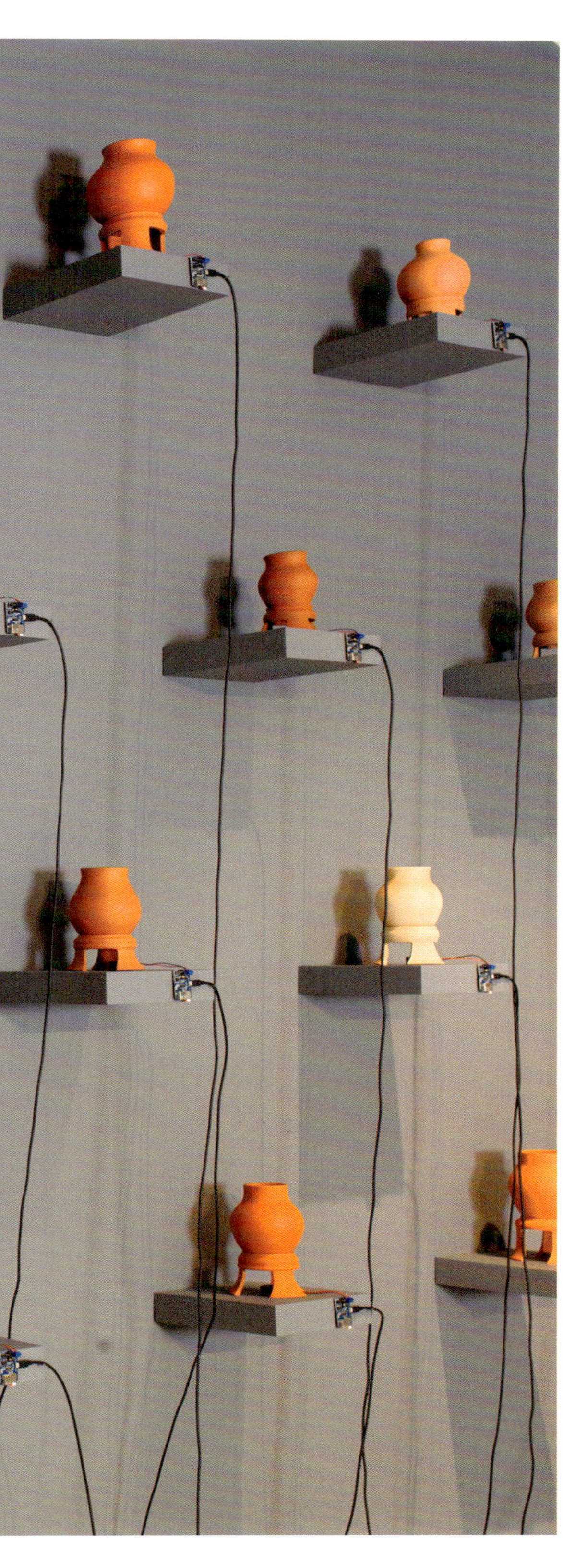

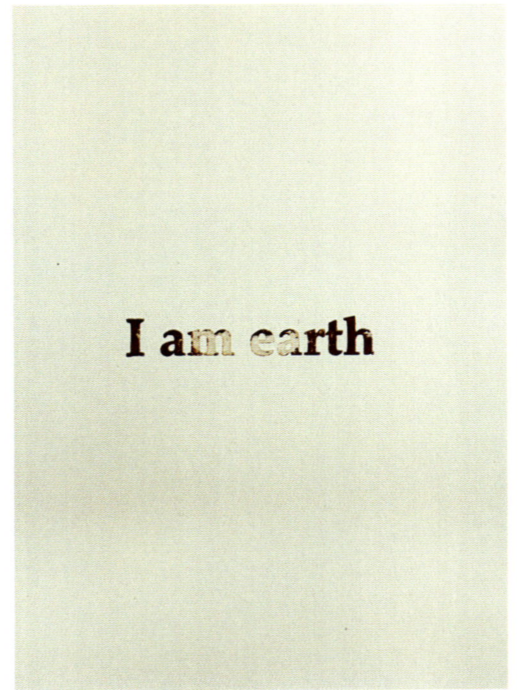

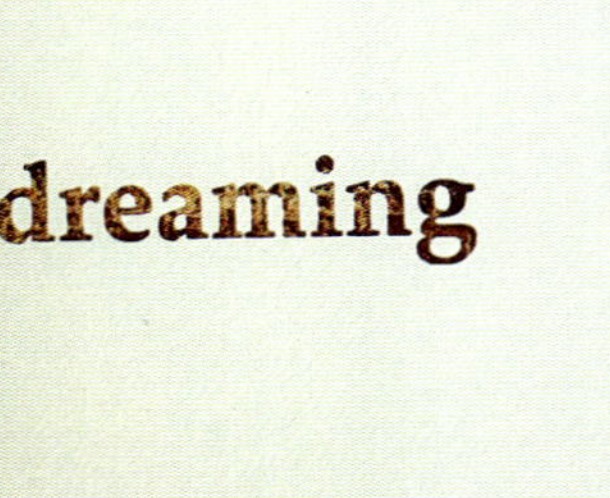

24
I am earth, dreaming, dreaming, dreaming to be a woman, 2024
Argillotype (clay print)
Five parts: 16 × 12 in. each

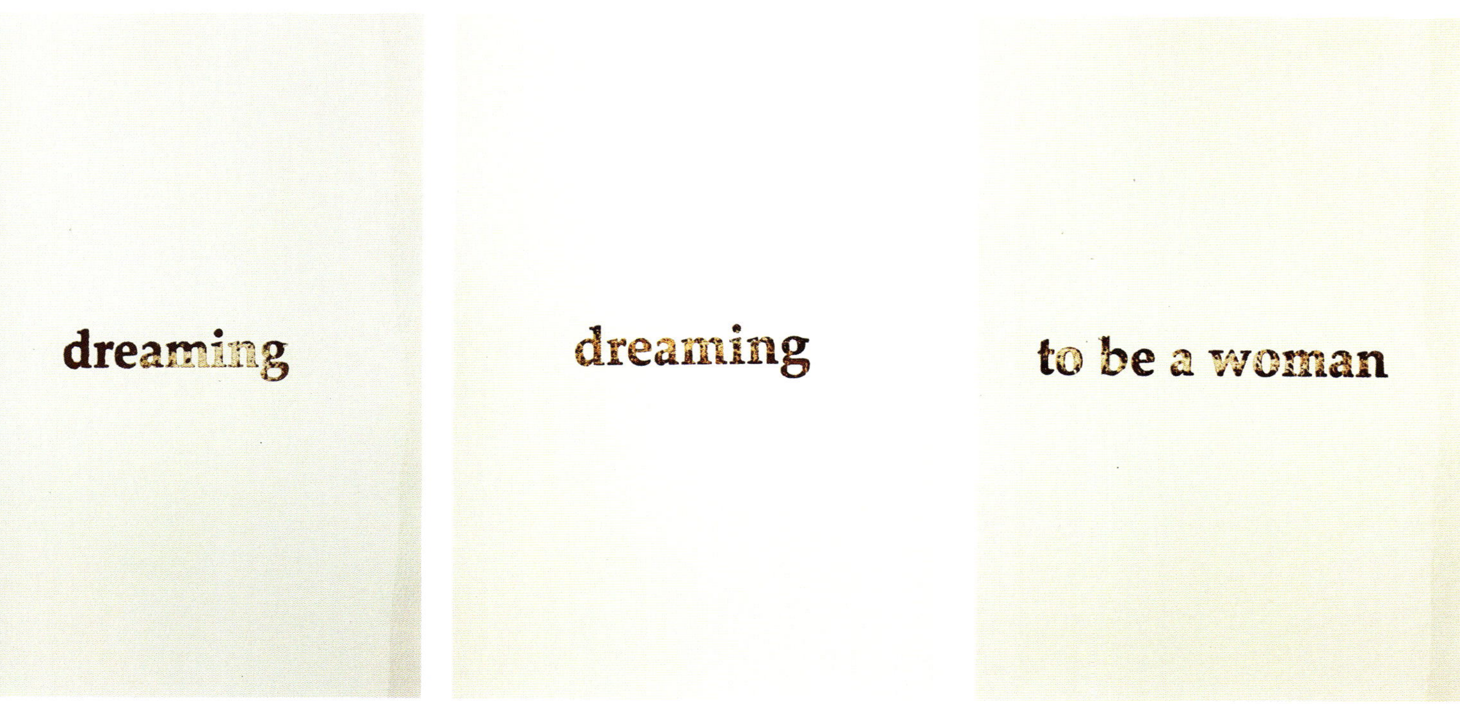
dreaming
dreaming
to be a woman

25

Forest of Solitude, from *Secrets of the Magnolia Tree Series*, 2022

Watercolor, ink, gouache, and digital printing on paper on three panels

Approx. 132 × 90 in. overall

Courtesy of the artist and Gallery Wendi Norris, San Francisco

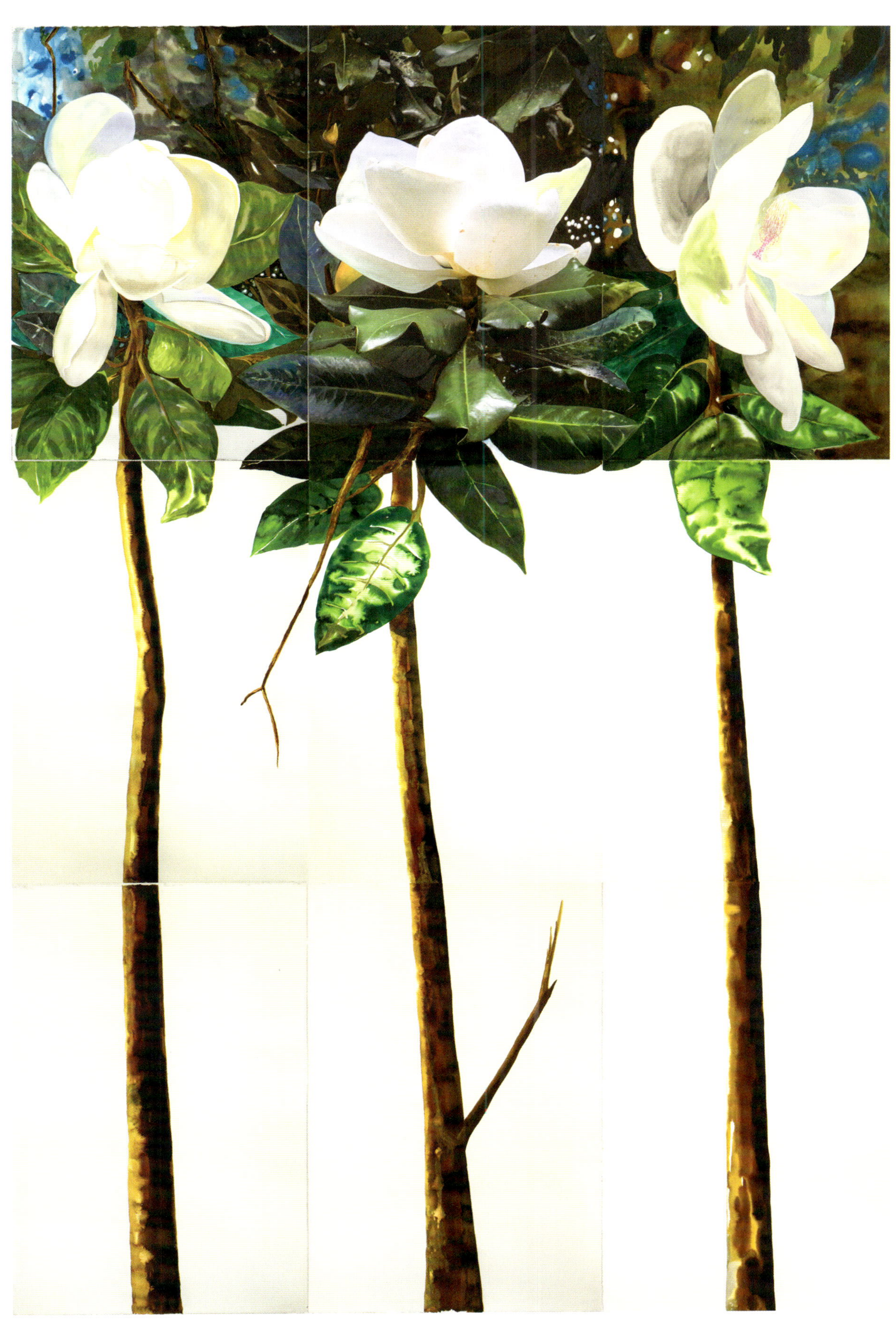

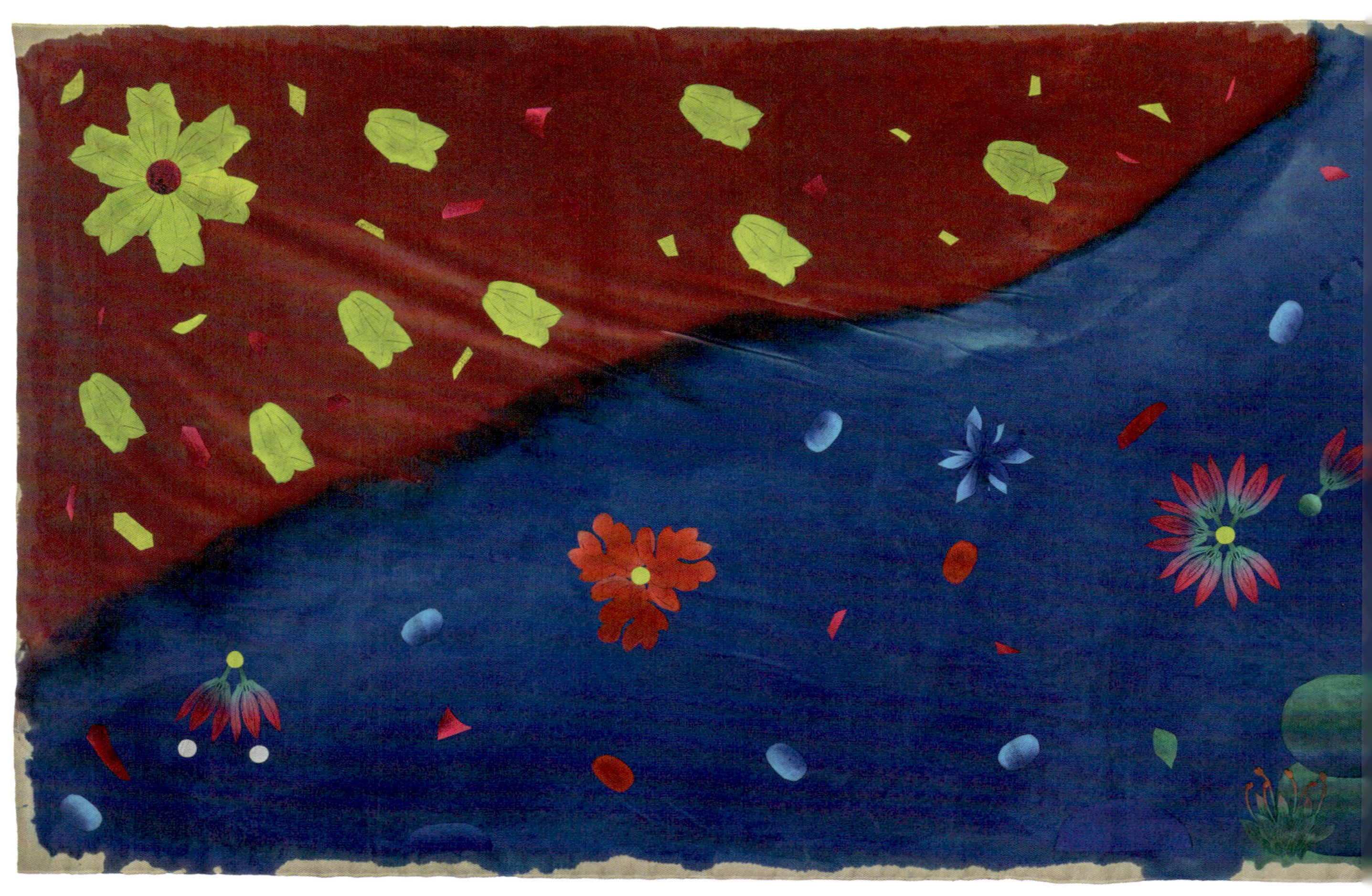

26

Water Meadow, 2025

Acrylic, oil relief, and embroidery on raw linen

72 × 226½ in.

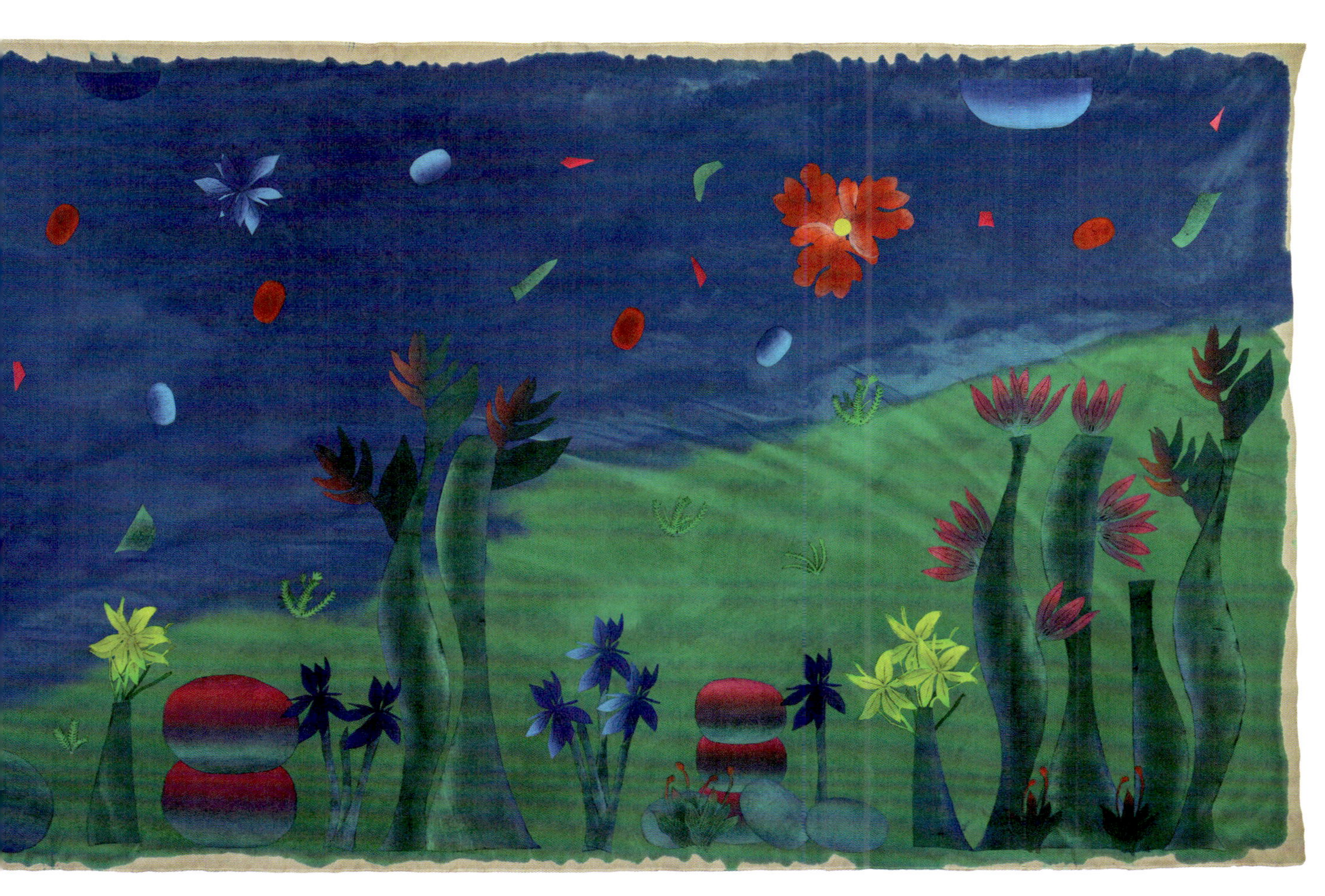

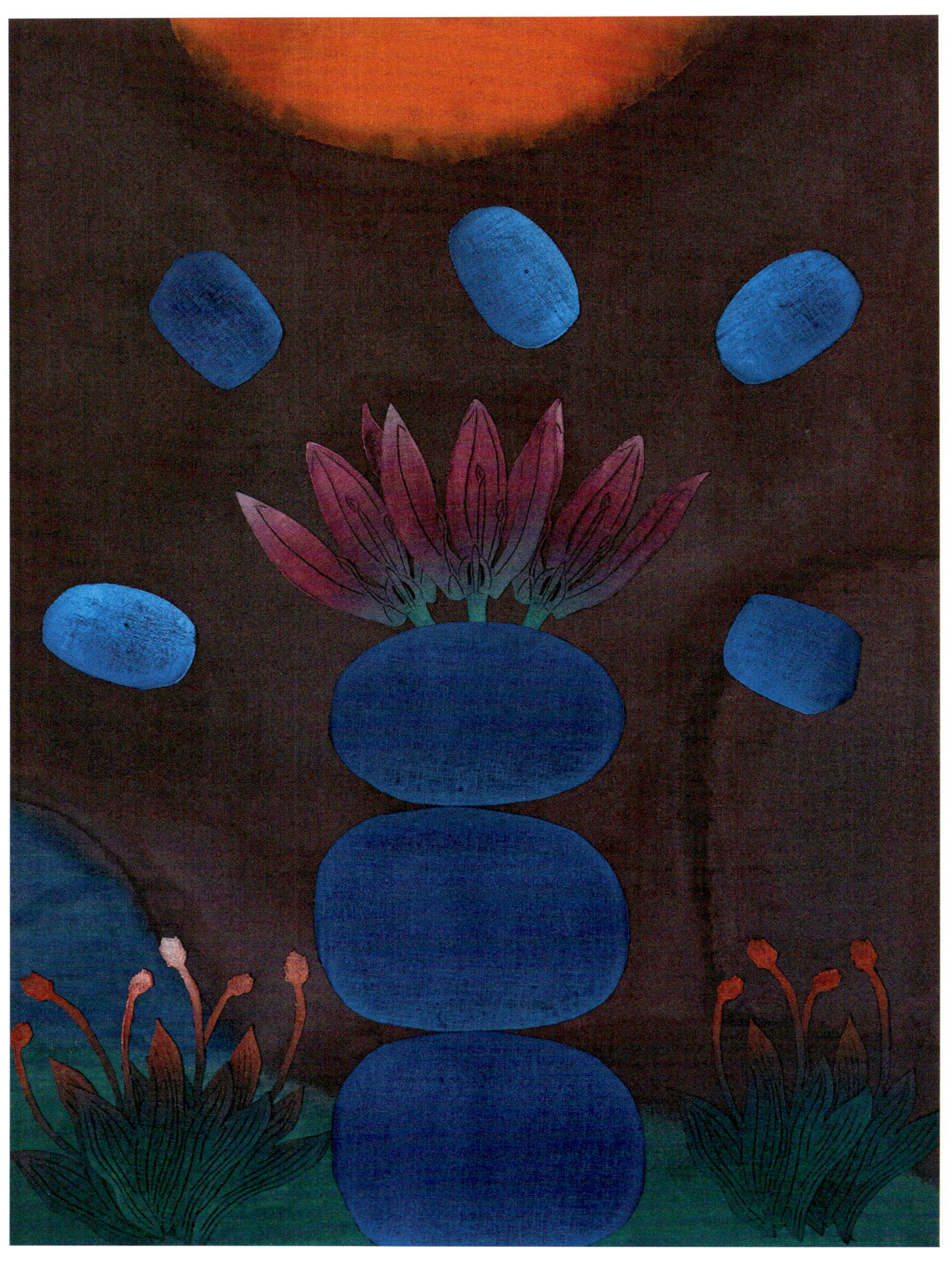

27
Beam Me Up, 2025
Acrylic and oil relief on raw linen
33 × 22 in.

28
Star Seed, 2025
Acrylic, oil relief, and embroidery on raw linen
33 × 23 in.

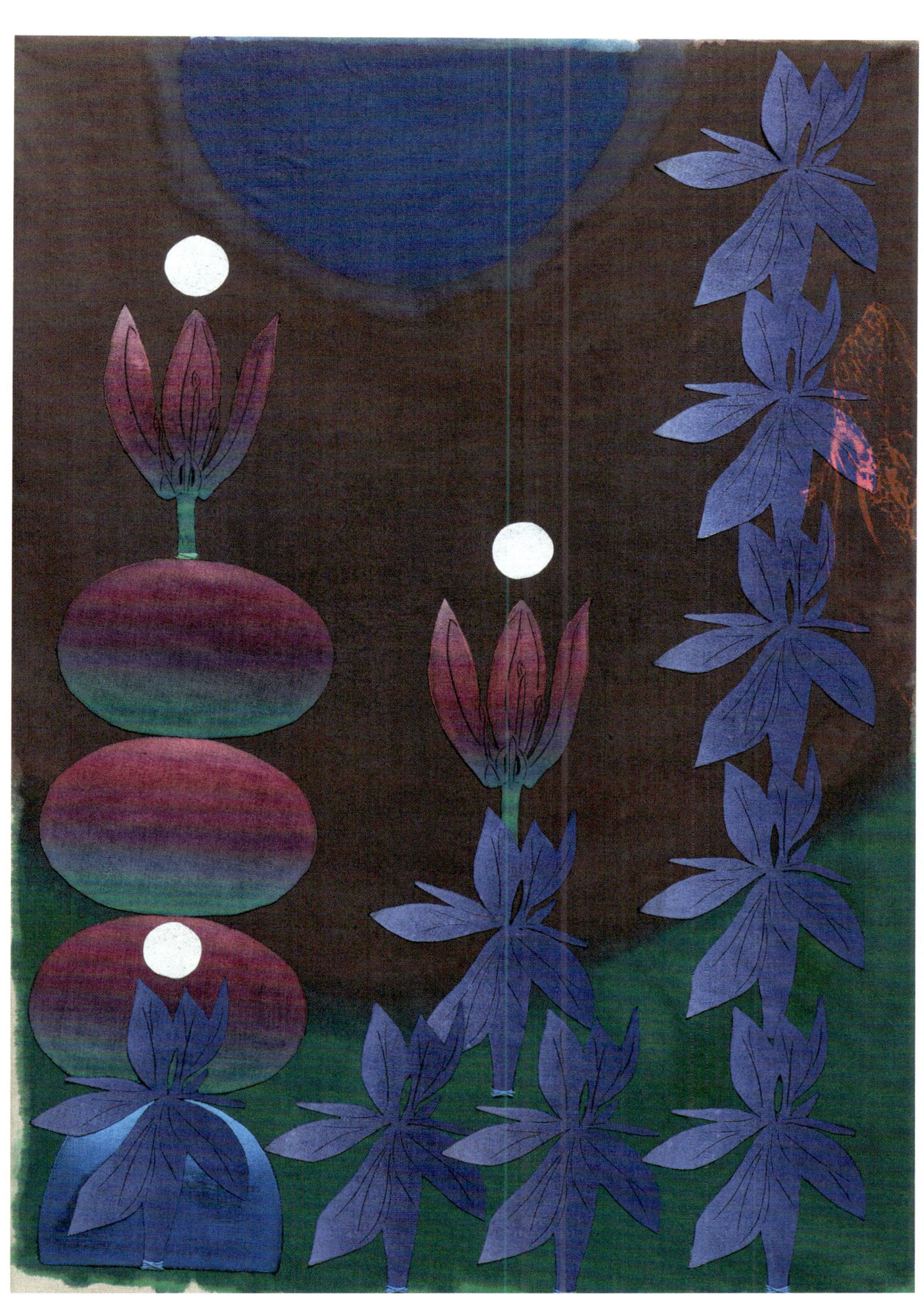

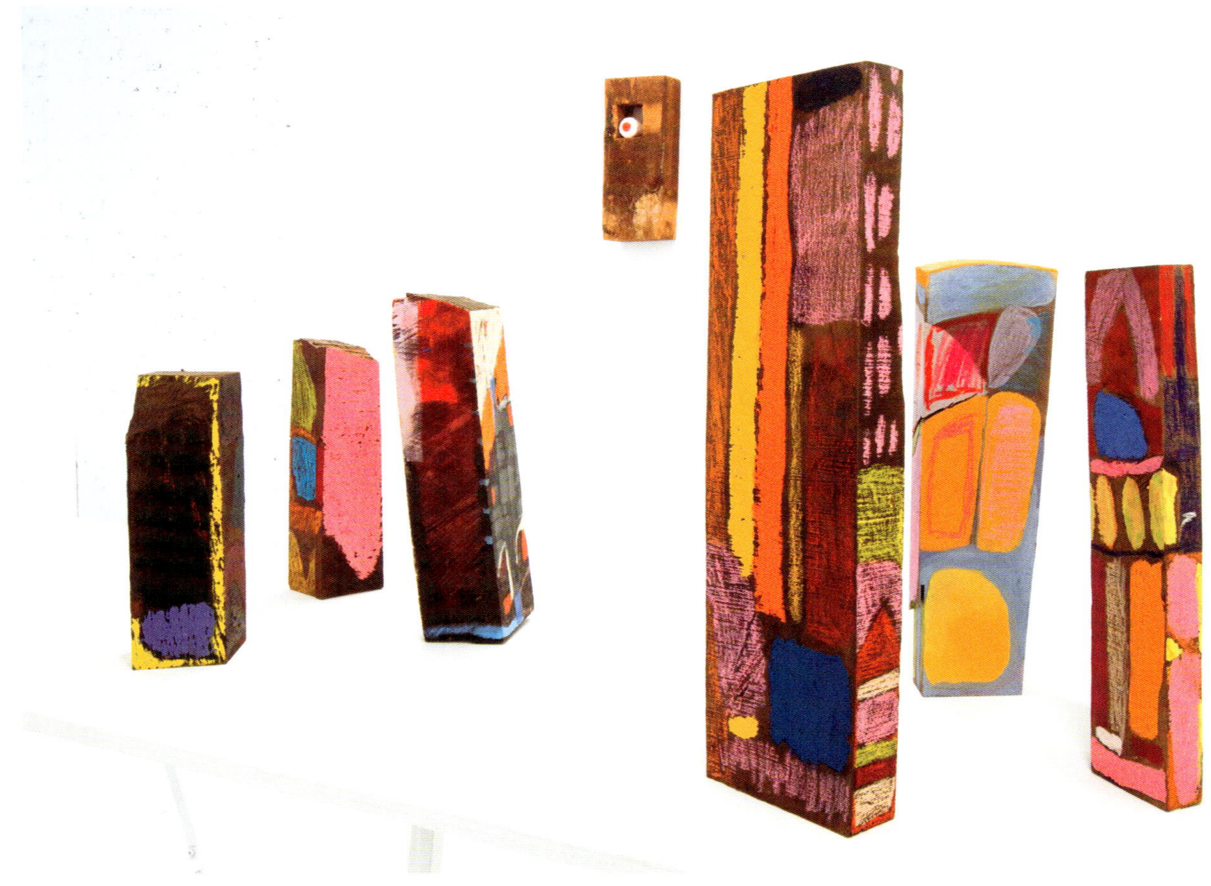

29

Elbow Room, 2018

Oil, wax, and oil stick on salvaged wood

Dimensions variable

Courtesy of the artist and Sheila Aminmadani, Anne Joyce and Peter Lawrence, Kylie Manning, Roya Shanks and Aaron Bender, Matthew Steer, and Jason Stopa

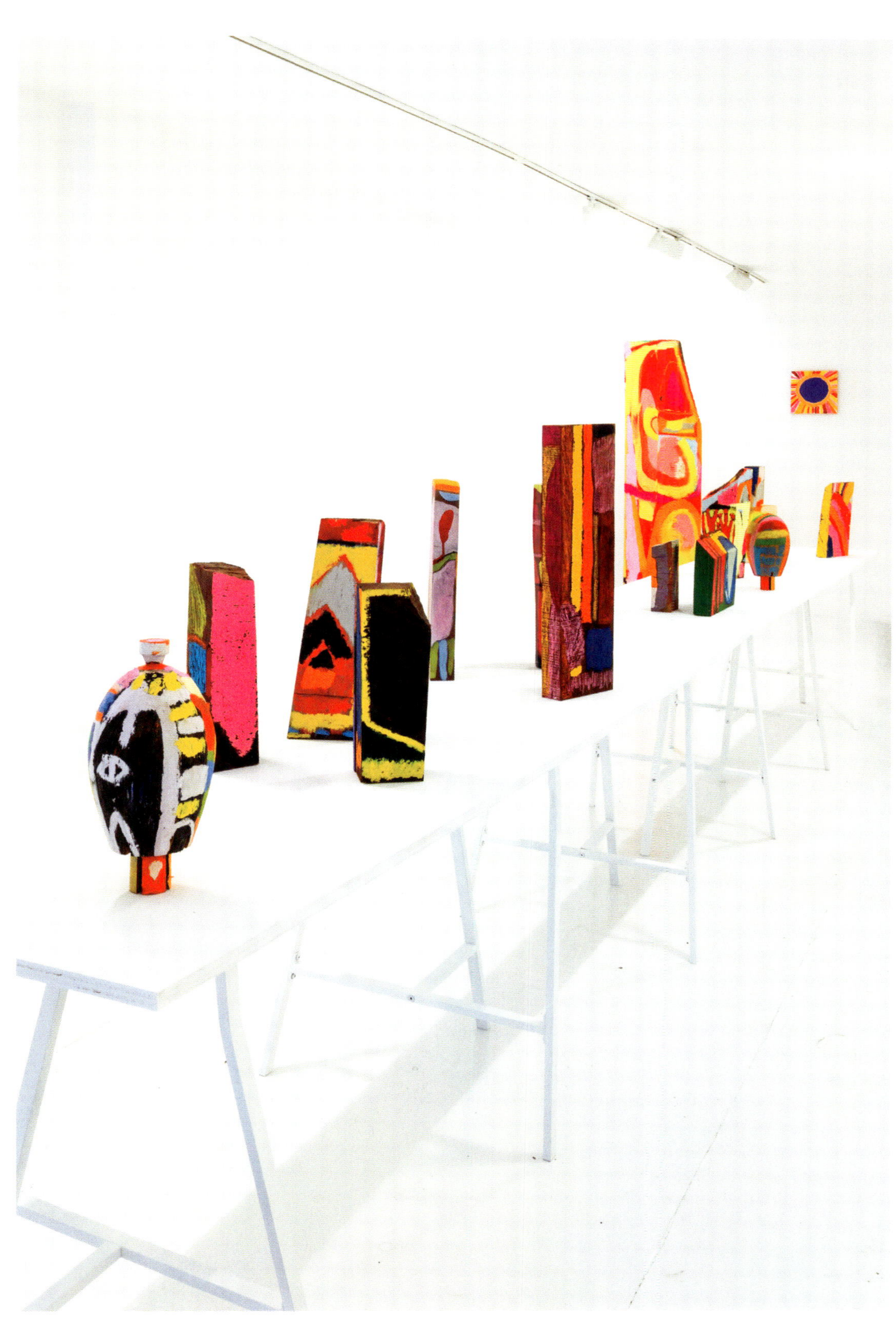

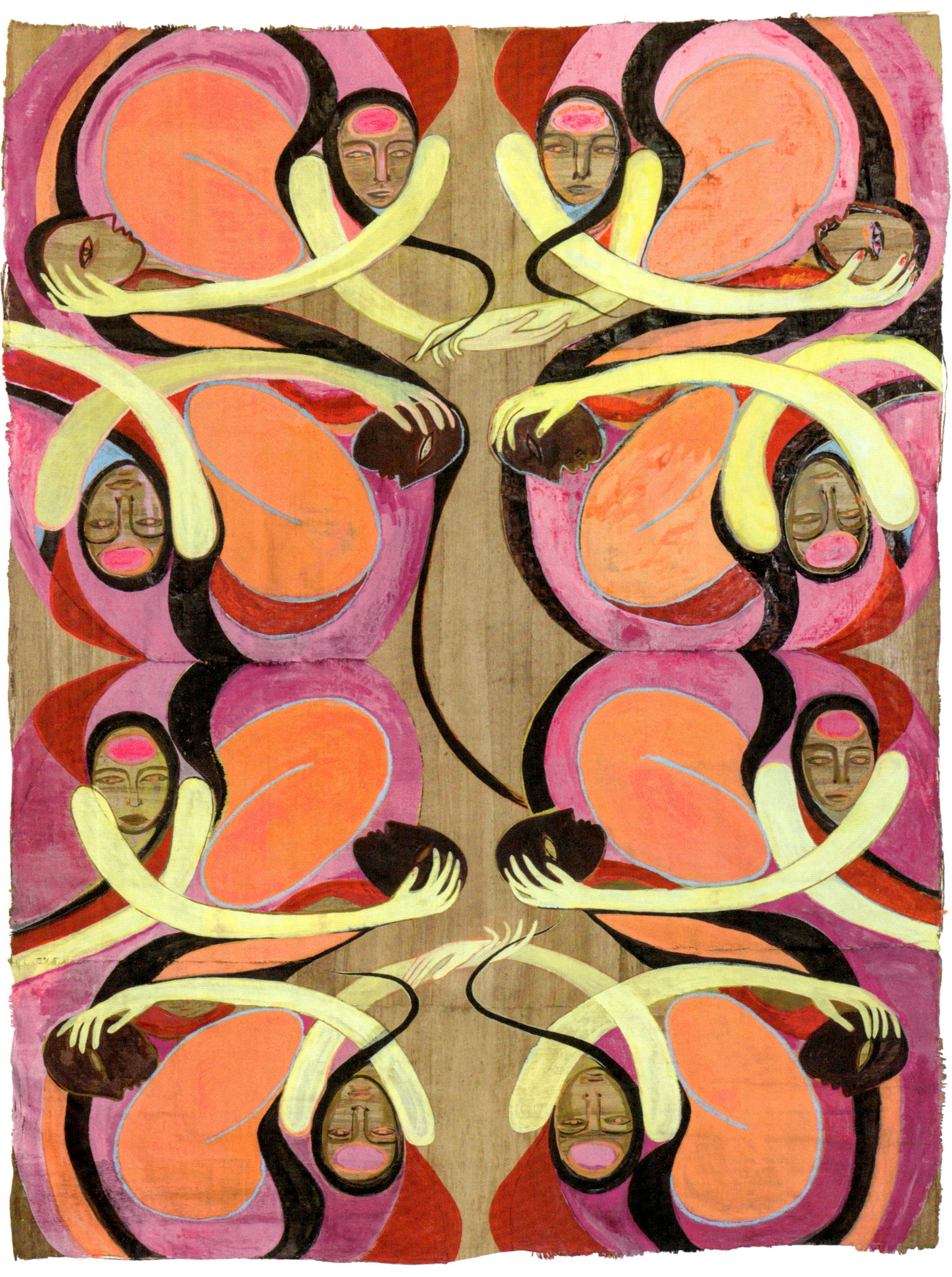

30
Leave a Light On, 2025
Ink and oil pastel on papyrus
95 × 71 in.

31
Hex, 2022
Ink, acrylic, and oil on carved wood
55 × 40 × 3 in.
Private collection, France

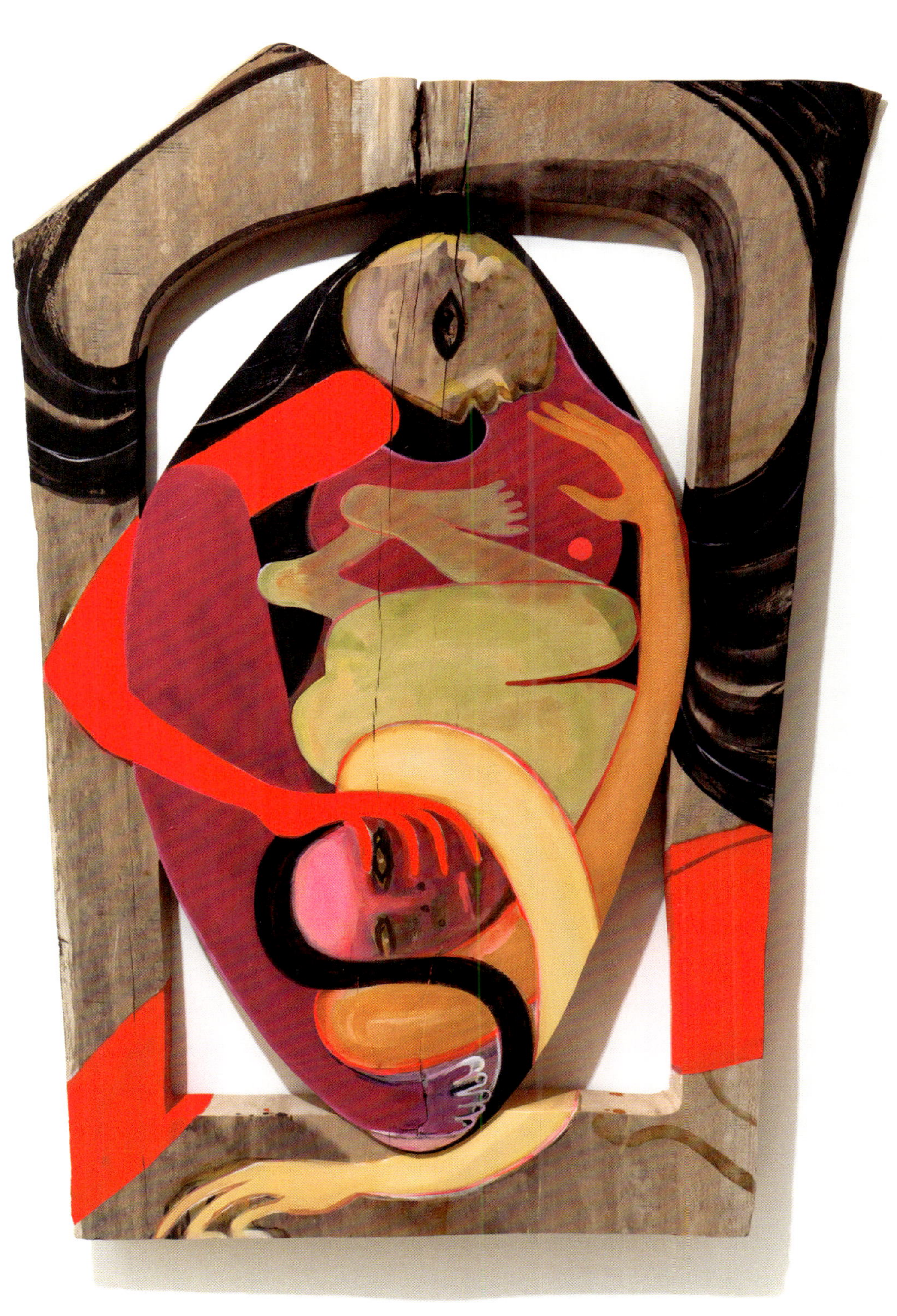

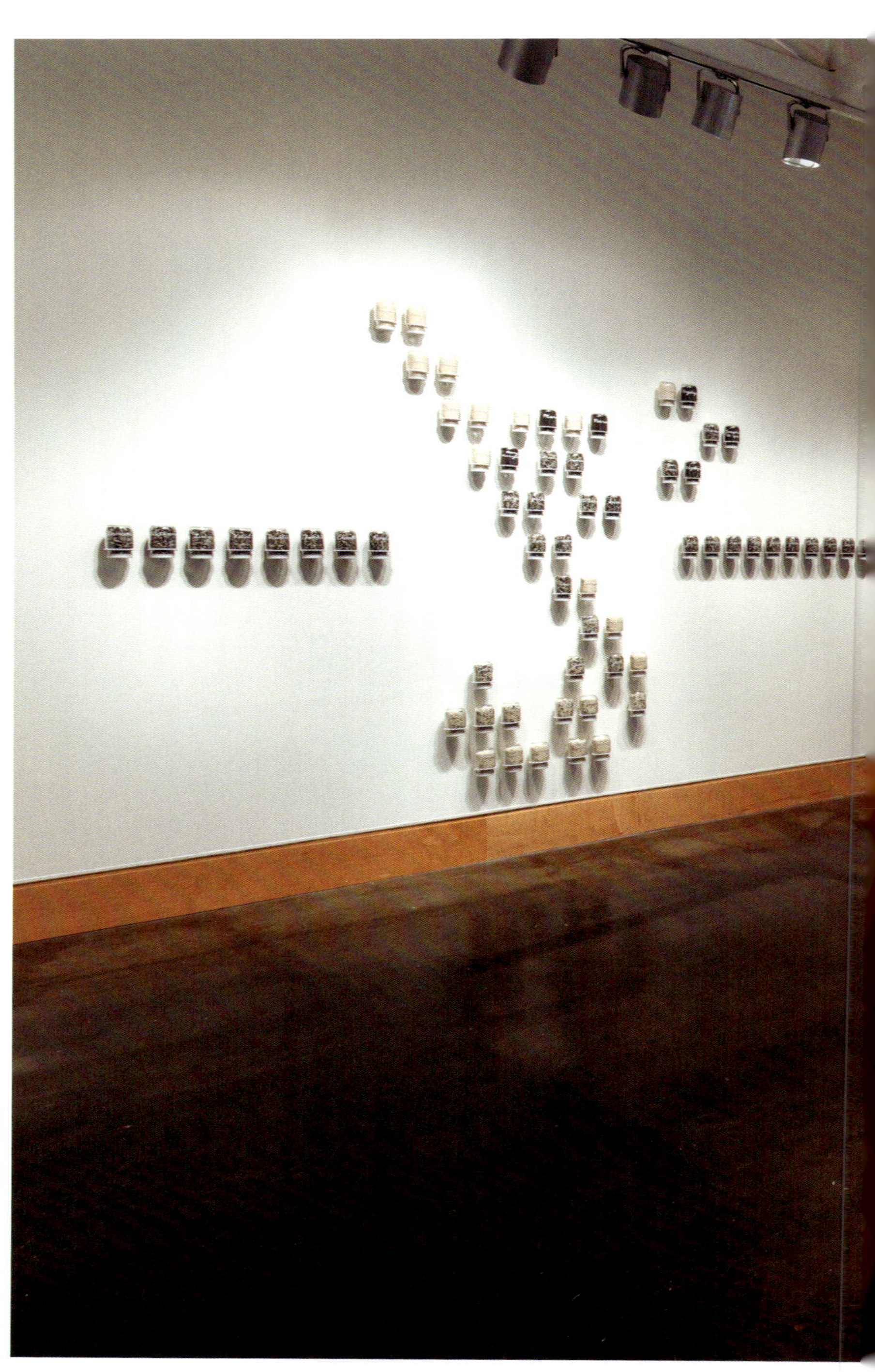

32
Blood, Memory, and the Power of Naming, 2021
Installation view, Space 204, Vanderbilt University, 2021

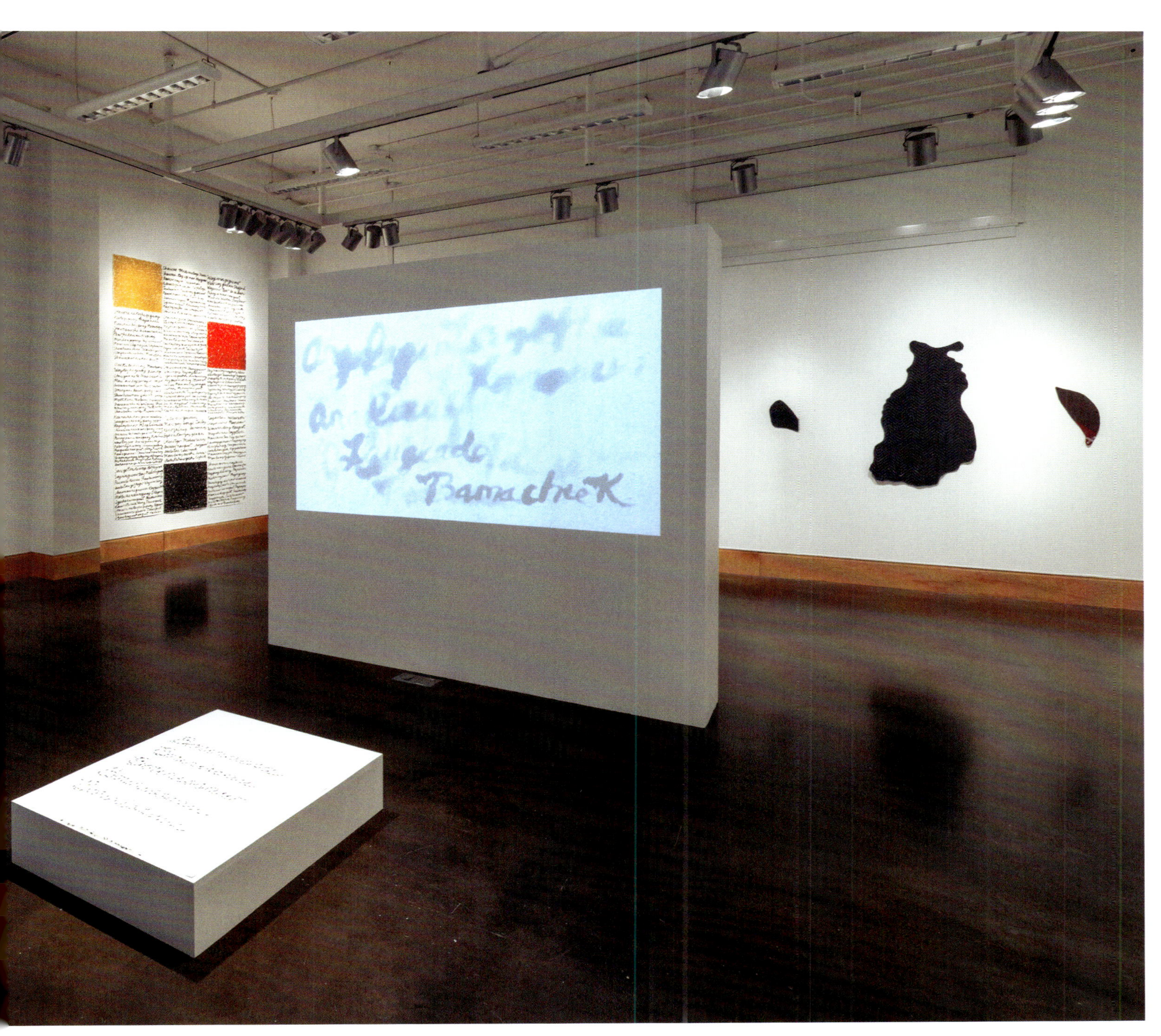

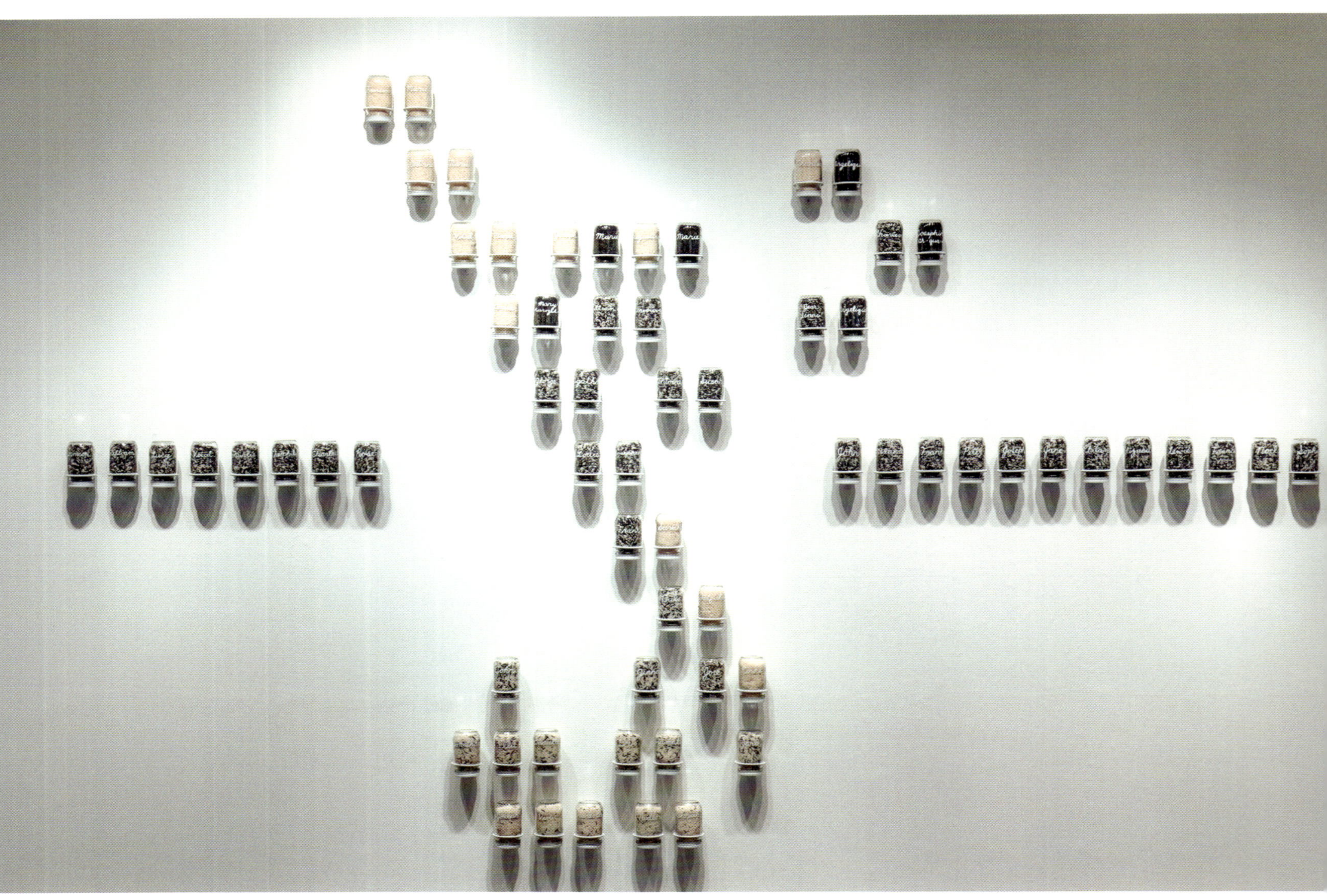

33
How Indian Are You? (Families of Lewis Bourissaw and Josephine Paquin), 2021
"Enriched" white rice, wild rice harvested by the Red Lake Band of Chippewa, Ball jars, hardware, and latex
132 × 168 × 4 in.

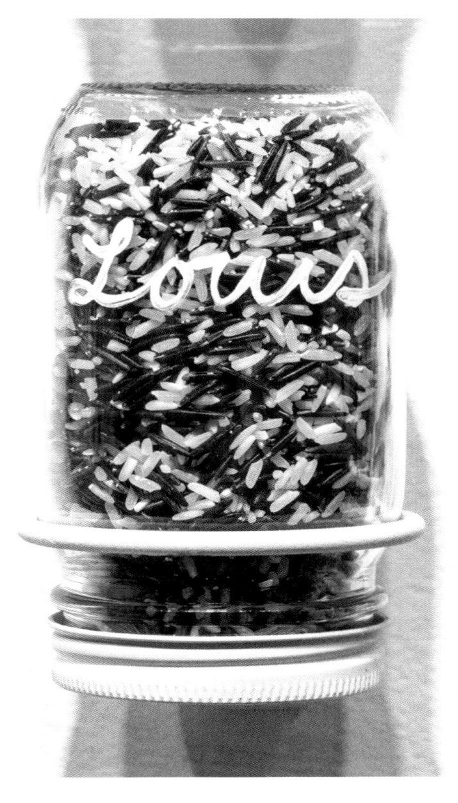
Louis

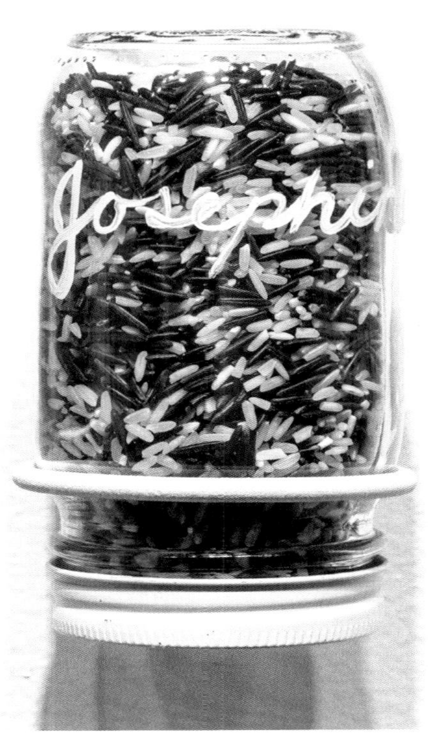

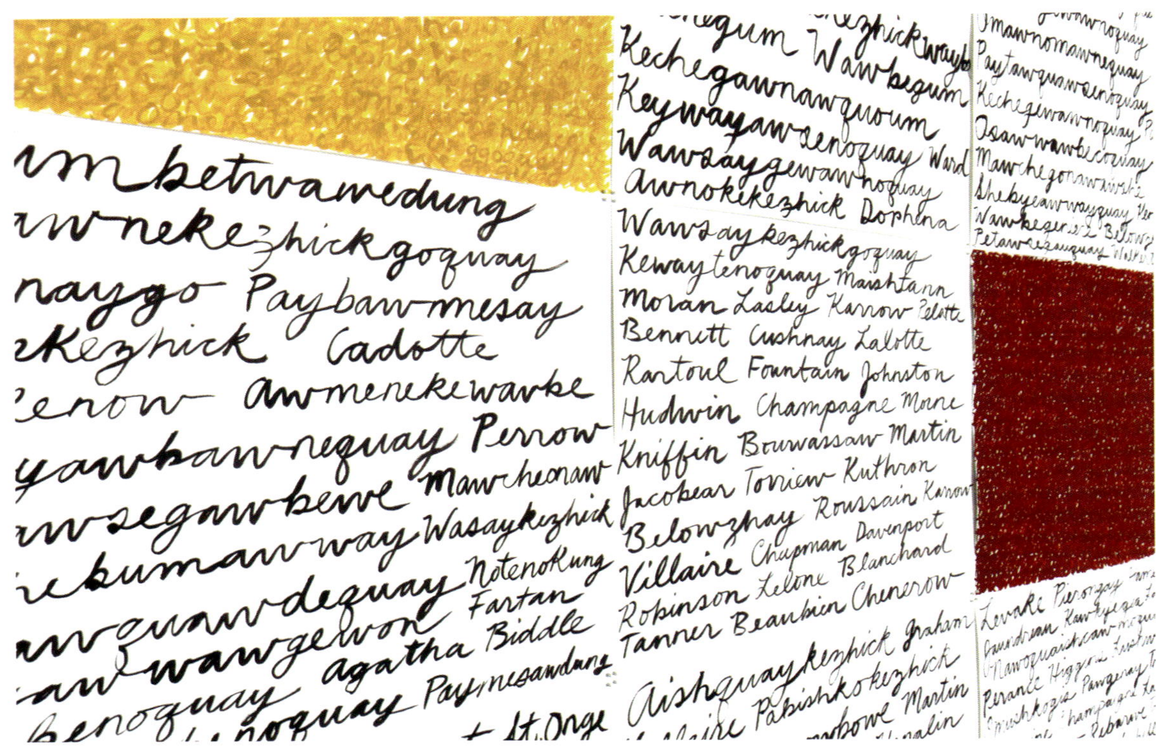

34
Memorial for Mackinac III, 2025
Sumi ink and gouache on rag paper
110 × 73 in.

Neswawsoke Pawace
Kewaykezhick LaBelle
Nawgawneguan Aslin
Nawwawchekezhickwaybe
Okechegum Wawbegum
Kechegawnawquoum
Keywayawsenoquay Ward
Wawsaygewawnoquay
Awnokikezhick Dophena

Otishquaykezhegoquay
Pawmegewawnoquay
Omawnomawnequay
Paytawquawsenoquay
Kechegewawnoquay Pond
Osawwawbecoquay
Mawchegonawawshe
Shekyeawwayquay Kenuk
Wawkegeniece Belowzhay
Petawcezauquay Walkerton

Natumbetwawedung
Negawnekezhickgoquay
Kechenaygo Paybawmesay
Wawbekezhick Cadotte
Odeskenow Awmenekewawke
Omayyawbawnequay Perrow
Neswawsegawbewe Mawheonaw
Wayzhekumawway Wasaykezhick
Wawnawguawdequay Notenokung
Mayyawwawgewon Fartan
Petawkenoquay Agatha Biddle
Nebenawshenoquay Paymesawdung

Wawsaykezhickgoquay
Kewaytenoquay Maishtann
Moran Lasley Karrow Pelotte
Bennett Cushnay Lalotte
Rantoul Fountain Johnston
Hudwin Champagne Moore
Kniffin Bouwassaw Martin
Jacobear Torriew Kuthron
Belowzhay Roussain Kanow
Villaire Chapman Davenport
Robinson Lelone Blanchard
Tanner Beaubien Chenerow

Laslin Davenport St. Onge
Belowzhay Menawsaw
LeBlanc Louisignon
McGalphin Valencourt
Lancour Maillet Rice
Martin Bezenette Harrow
LeDuke Robinson La Pien
Thompson Walsh Closs
Peltier Valier Aishcawbaywis
Nawwekezhegoquay Anse

Aishquaykezhick Graham
Villaire Pabishkokezhick
Payshegogawbowe Martin
Waywegawnaybe Hanalin
Belonzhay Omushkogos
Ogemawweminne Levake jr
Ogawbaygezhegoquay
Mayseswayweninne Pond
Bodwaince Macanuckgo
Rebaskaw Bourassa Hubert
Bennette Lorley Mesawtego

Levake Pierongay Hamlin
Jaundreau Kawkyegea Labutt
Nawoquaishcawmoquay
Perance Higgins Lushway
Omushkogis Pawgenay Trombly
Bodwaine Champaigne Lazaine
Shawnegaw Rebarwe Truckey
Segenack Rocklae LaBelle
Meswayoninne Newton Grandain
Awdayreme Shawbwayway
Nawqueishcum Andrews Kaw
Aimehemekewawke Bazinette
Waygemawwawbe Shawbawno

Wawsawnawquodequay
Maishcawtayquose
Bazenet Fountain Andrews
Awbewaynay Shawbawno
Nawoqueawmequay
Karrow Pazickwabe LaPien
Dumon Wawwawsemoquay
Ance Alick Anderson
Andres Askin Achambo
Achambo Altiman Agosa
Annemequong Besoyea Byers
Belongea Bunaway Baddeau

Belonghay Bebineau
Brooks Bellow Boyles
Beaman Bourassa Berlin
Bourissaw Bouchard Bailey
Bazinaw Bellair Boucha
Bodwin Bolton Bellant Bryce
Beheydt Bourroughs Berry
Boda Bath Bucha Cotey Cube
Campbell Carow Chevalier
Cadron Cheeseman Cox Cable
Chart Coughlin Corp Clausen
Culp Crosby Chamberlain

Compean Cadotte Doucette
Cloud Driver Daphena Drake
Duffina Davis Demonow Deshna
Deloria Dunwald Decature Desy
Donner Doneville Donavan
Dumas Dewey Derry Duklin
Dailey DeLong Dupont Durfee
Dixon Erskine Fisher Foltz Frazer
Feurt Genie Gibson Goulier Gillard
Golden Gallagher Grundain
Garrison Gamble Goudreau
Gillespie Grant Goudreau Hall
Grondin Guyer Holmes Hudson

Hildreth Hammond Harris Jake
Hipkins Henry Johnson Jarvie
Jewett Jenkins Jones Joseph
Kniffin Kush Killar Kintzel
Keaton Kanonskay Keller Kelly
Kinridge King Larson Levar
Louis Laquea Lishman Lasley
Lincoln Legget LaPine Lanayont
Landry Lafond Lazon Lalotte Lavake
LaJill Larsen LaForest LaPoint
Ludec Misho Madigan Menard
Martell Muscoe Marshall Myers
Mastaw Moreau McGulpin Moore
McCarty Morris McCauley McNaughton
Mason McDermott Michalke McGuire
McIntosh Massey Mesawtego Misatago

Mellon McDermott Miles McGulphin
McDonald Neswawsoke Obey Owen
Osawogan Oleson Perkins Parker
Peterson Plant Plaunt Pero Pool
Parper Pease Paquin Poirier Prue Pront
Pamble Payzhick Redmond Restool Reid
Rankin Russell Ross Richmond Roby
Shakway Stephenson Simmons Smith
Sheffield Stafford Sayles Santago Sageon
Sweetland Sebastian Simpson Stone
Shedowin Slocum Schelier Shomin
St. Louis Tuskenow Terrient Terrien
Taylor Timms Valliere View Vallie
Walker Wilsey Whitney Williams
Willybrand Wilmette Walters
Wahbegeniece Wawsaykezhick Young

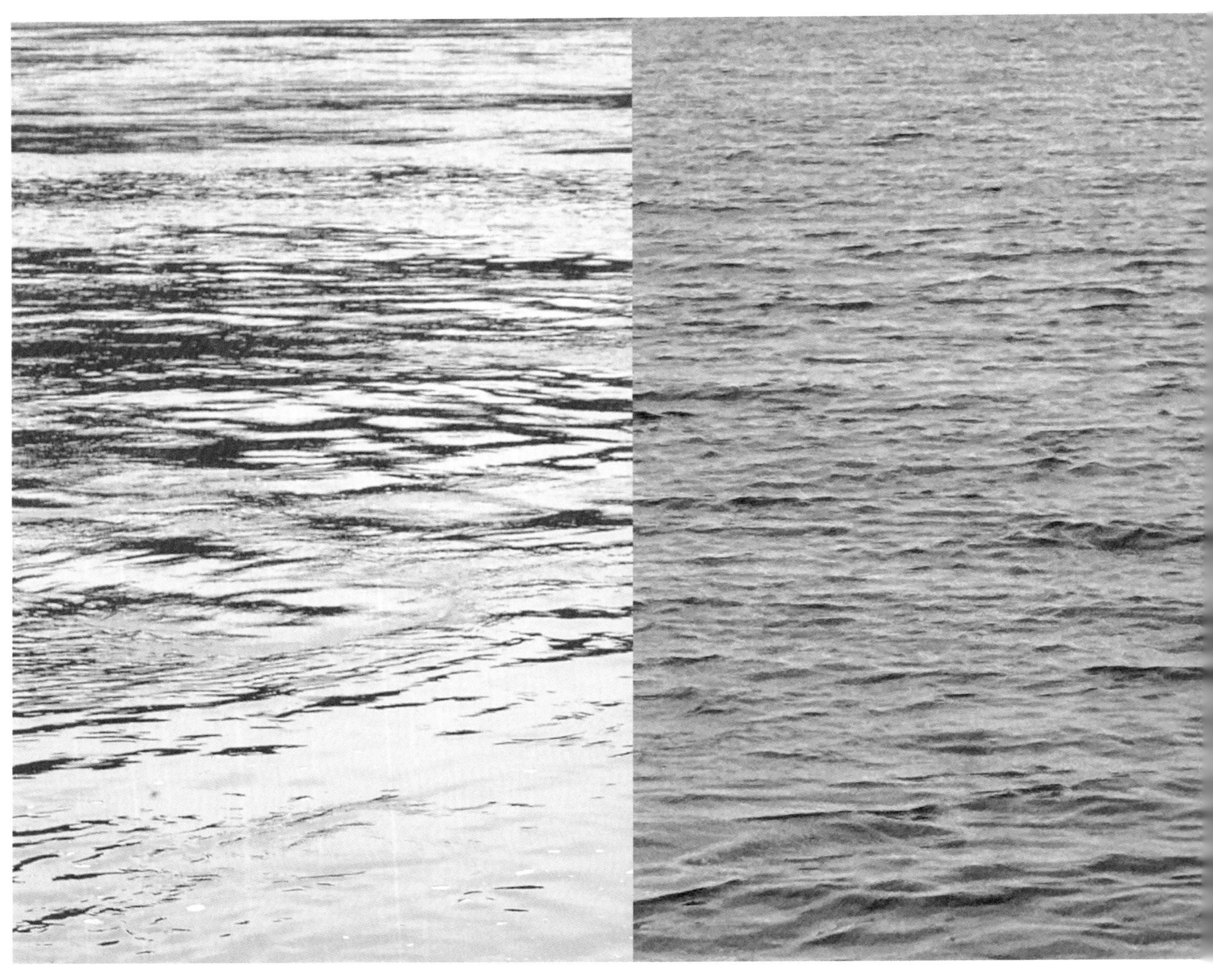

35
Song for the Water (detail), 2025
Photographs printed on silk and bathed in sacred water, cedar, copper, and glass seed beads
Dimensions variable

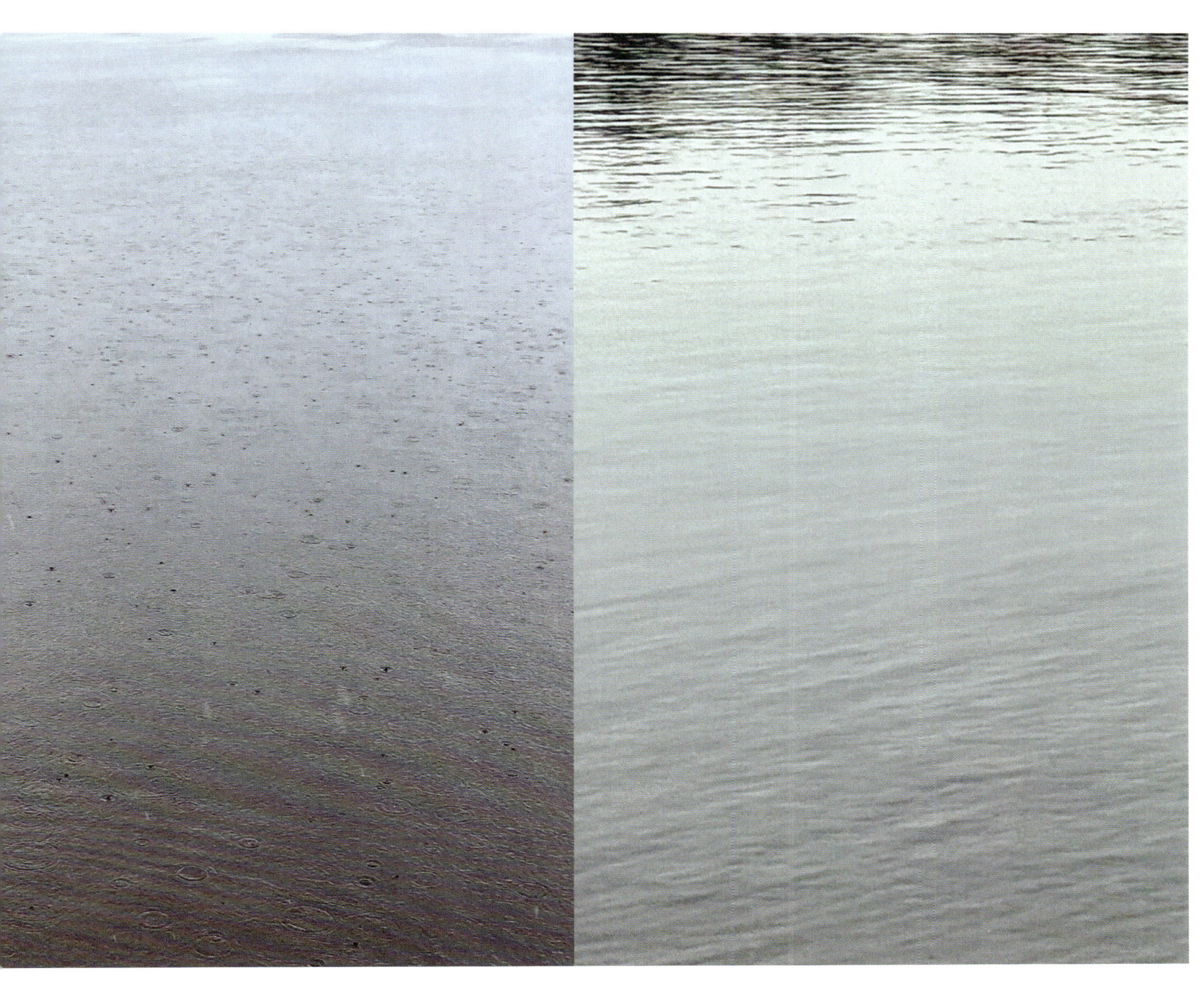

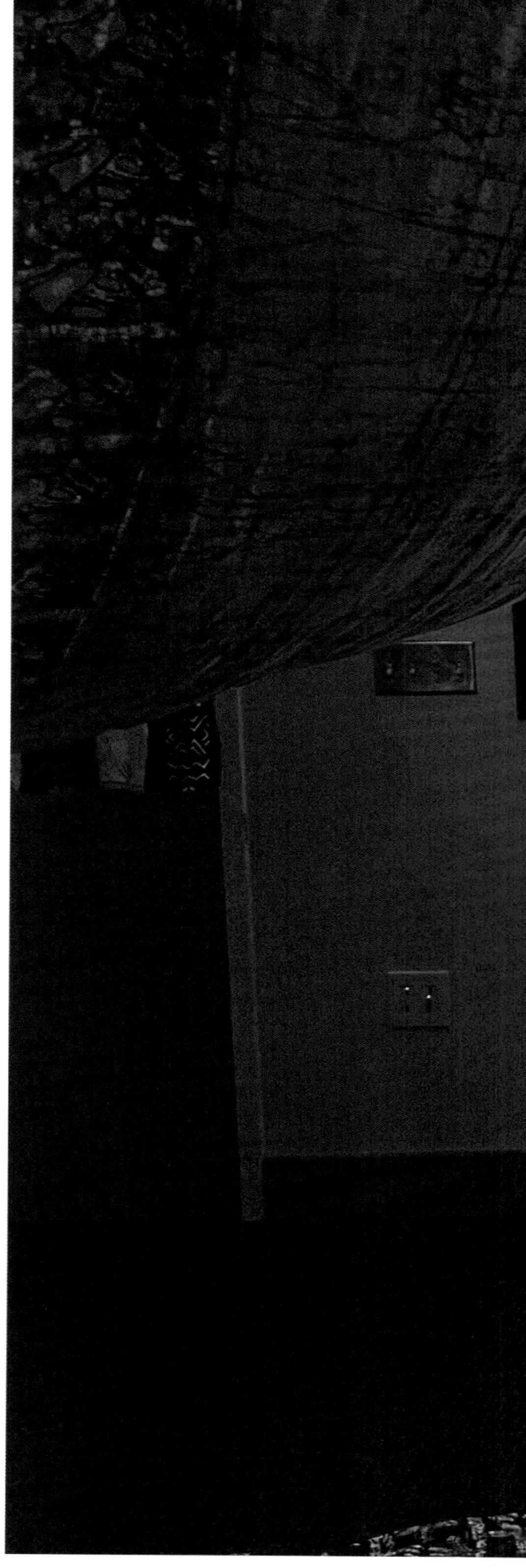

36
Culture Commodity (detail), 2023
Mixed-media installation (video, fabric, painting on cloth, and spinning wheel)
Dimensions variable
Courtesy of the artist, in memory of her late mother
Installation view, Vanderbilt University Divinity School, 2023

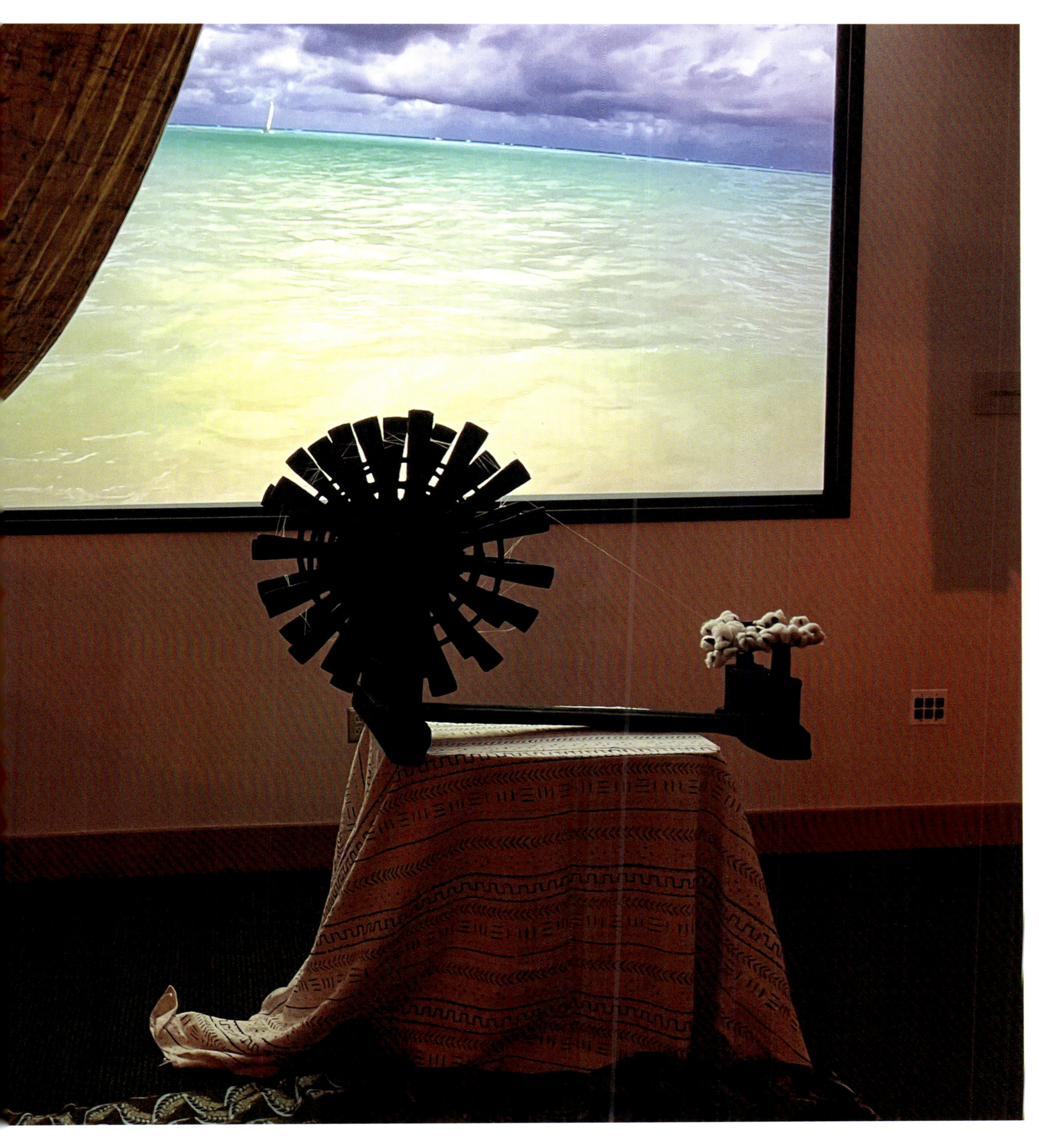

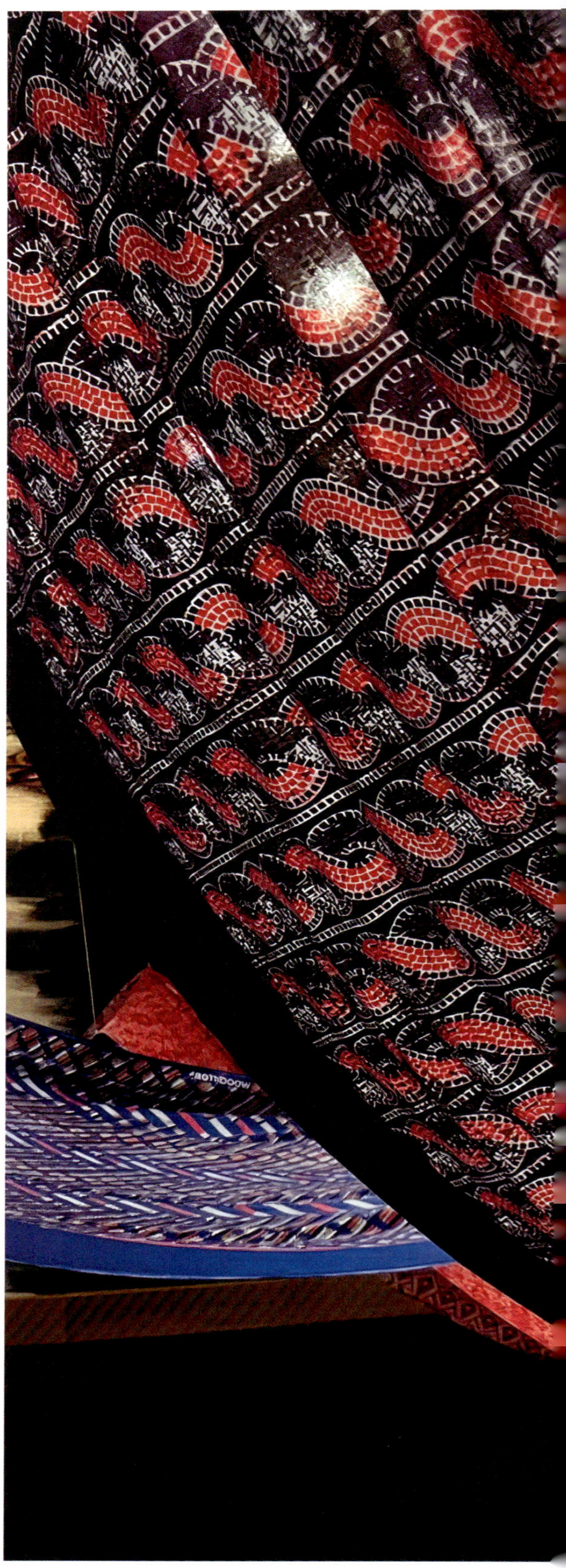

37

Culture Commodity (detail), 2023

Mixed-media installation (video, fabric, painting on cloth, and spinning wheel)

Dimensions variable

Courtesy of the artist, in memory of her late mother

Installation view, Vanderbilt University Divinity School, 2023

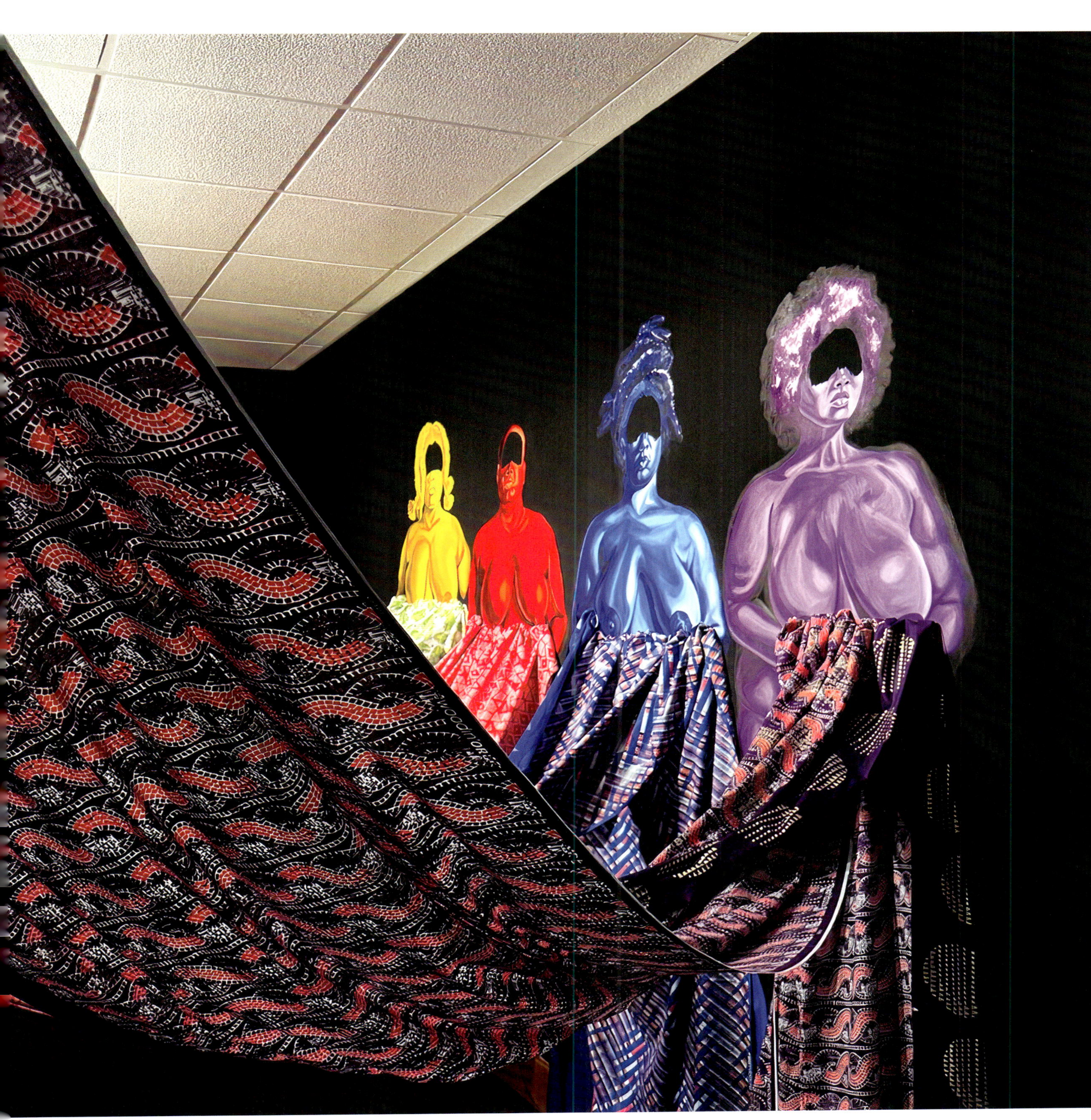

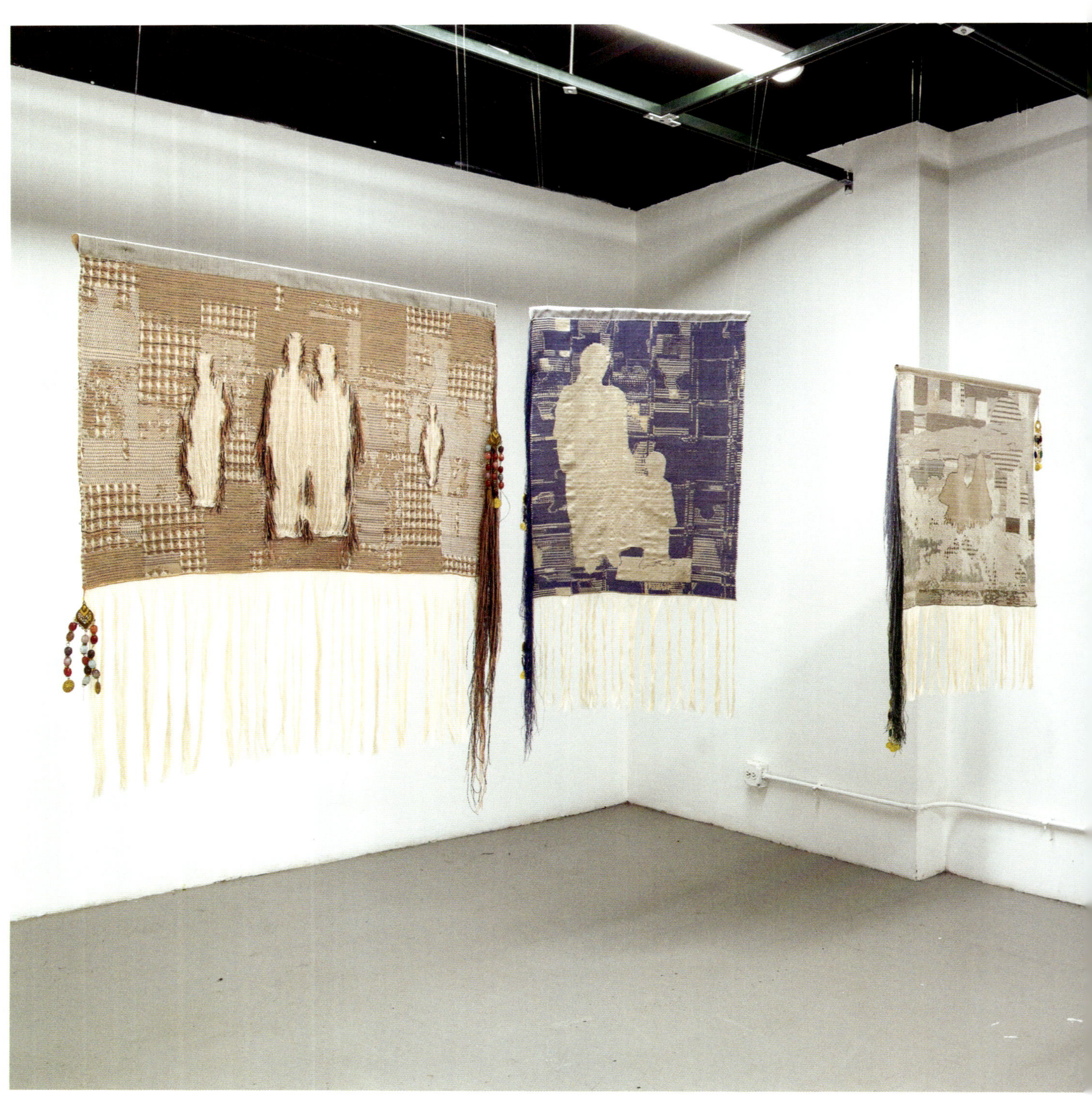

38
Installation of four handwoven tapestries
School of the Art Institute of Chicago, 2025

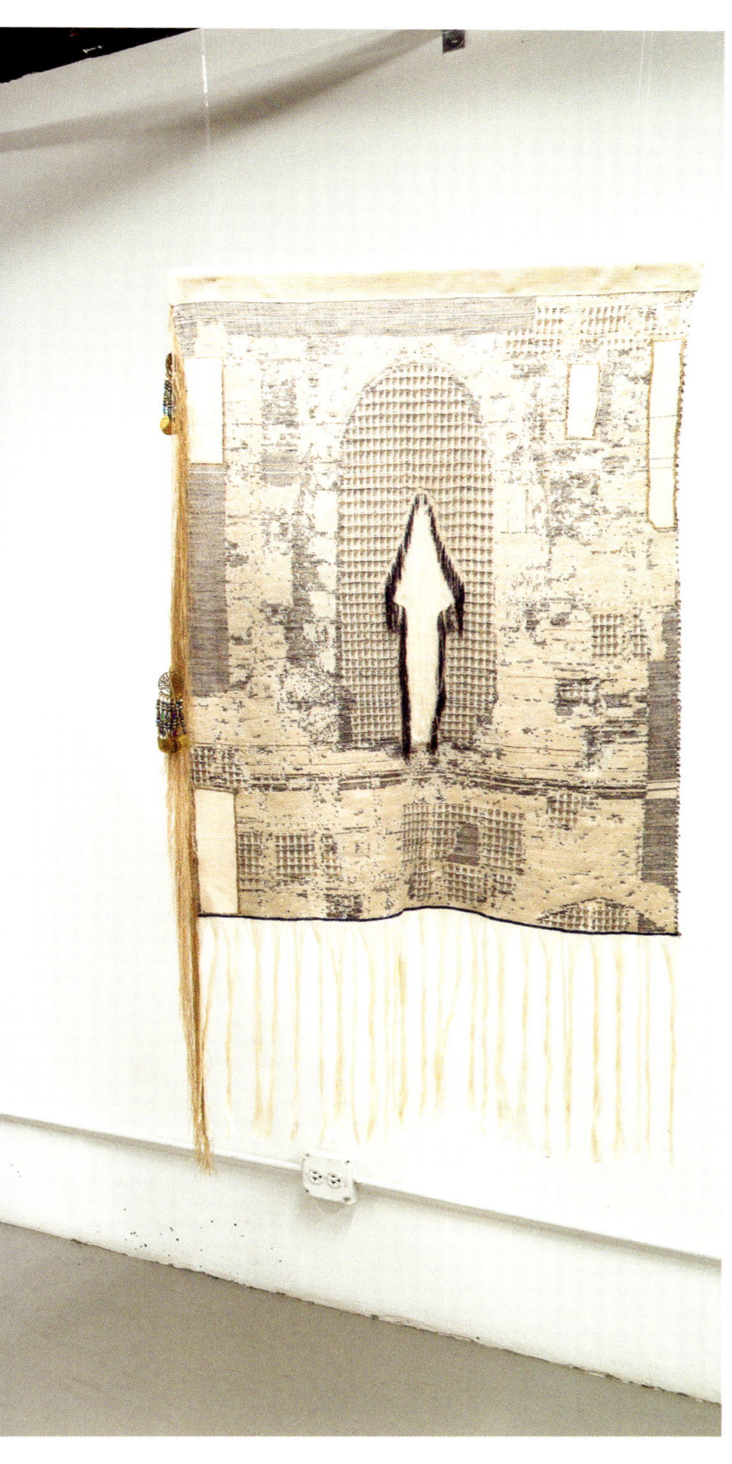

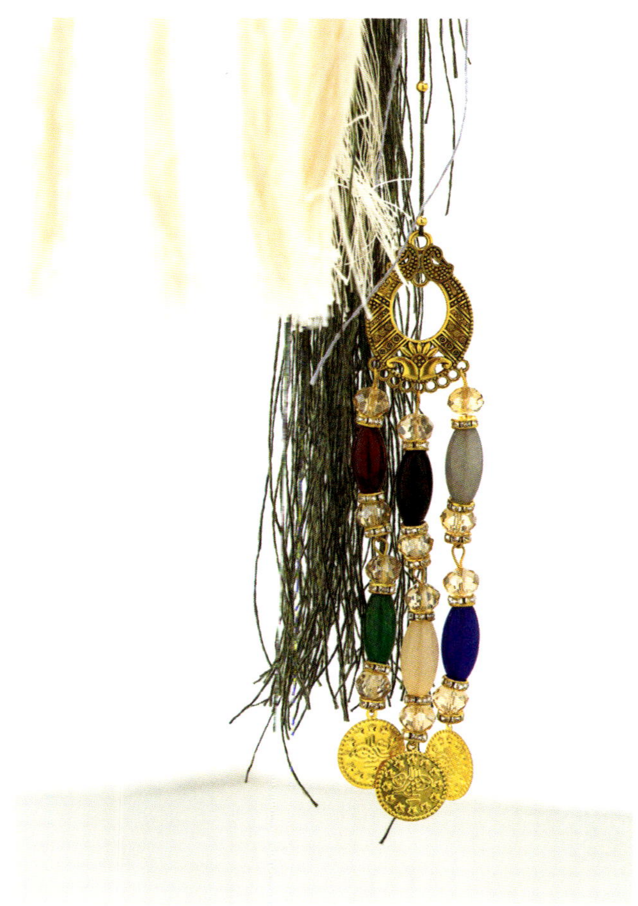

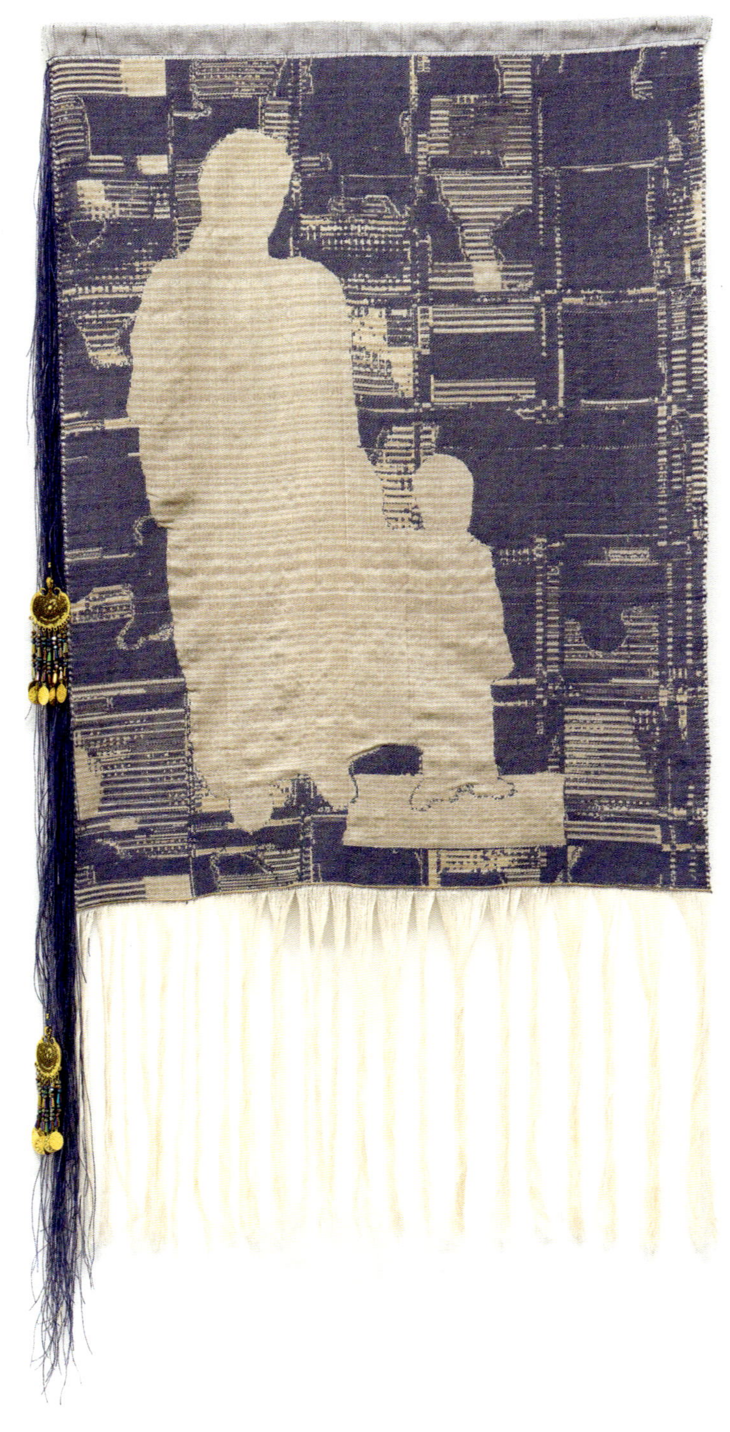

39
in the shifting ground, I found the shape of my mother's voice, 2025

Polyester, cotton, and amulets

51 × 27½ in.

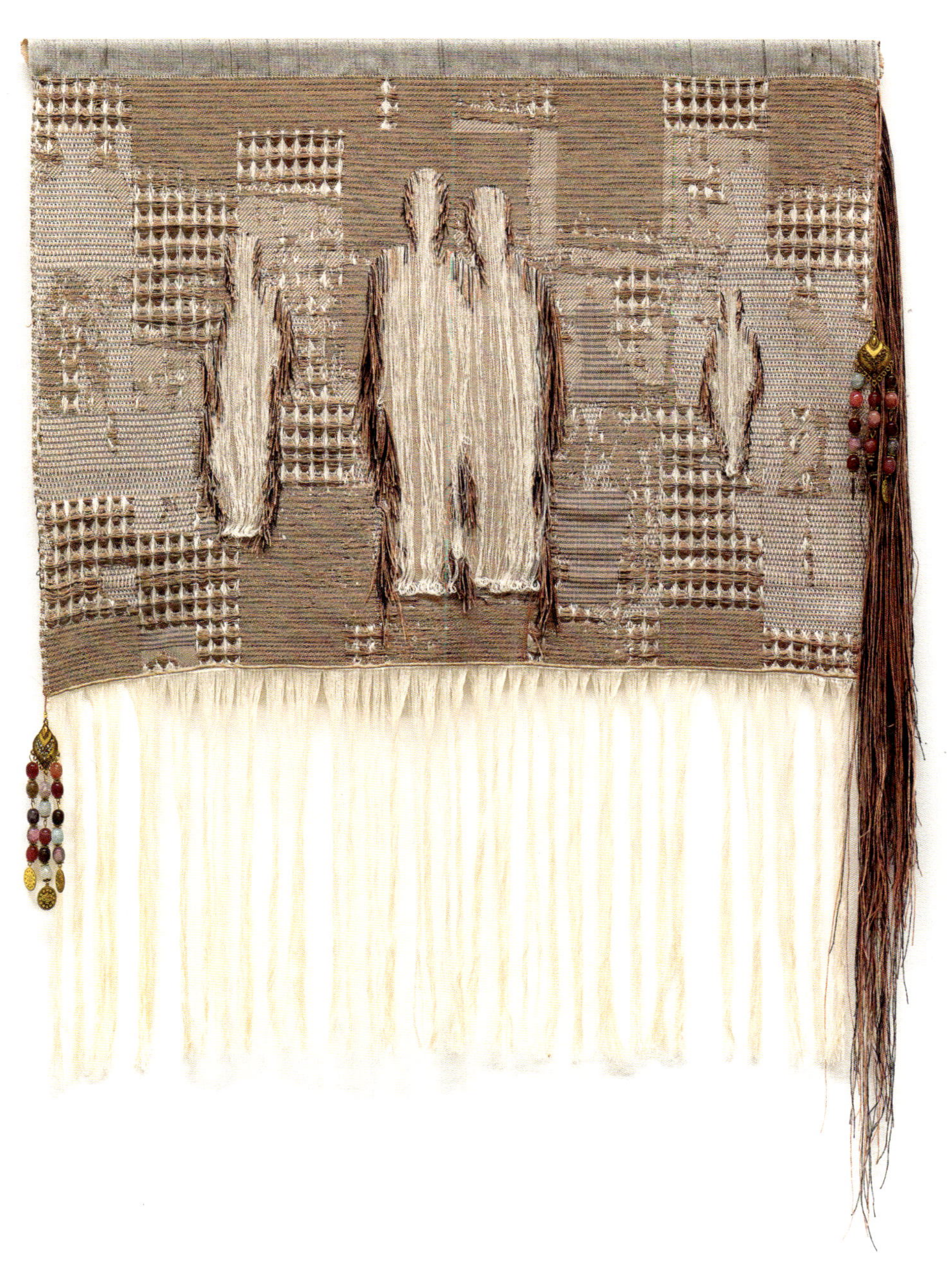

40
whispers in the warp, 2025
Polyester, cotton, and amulets
40 × 28½ in.

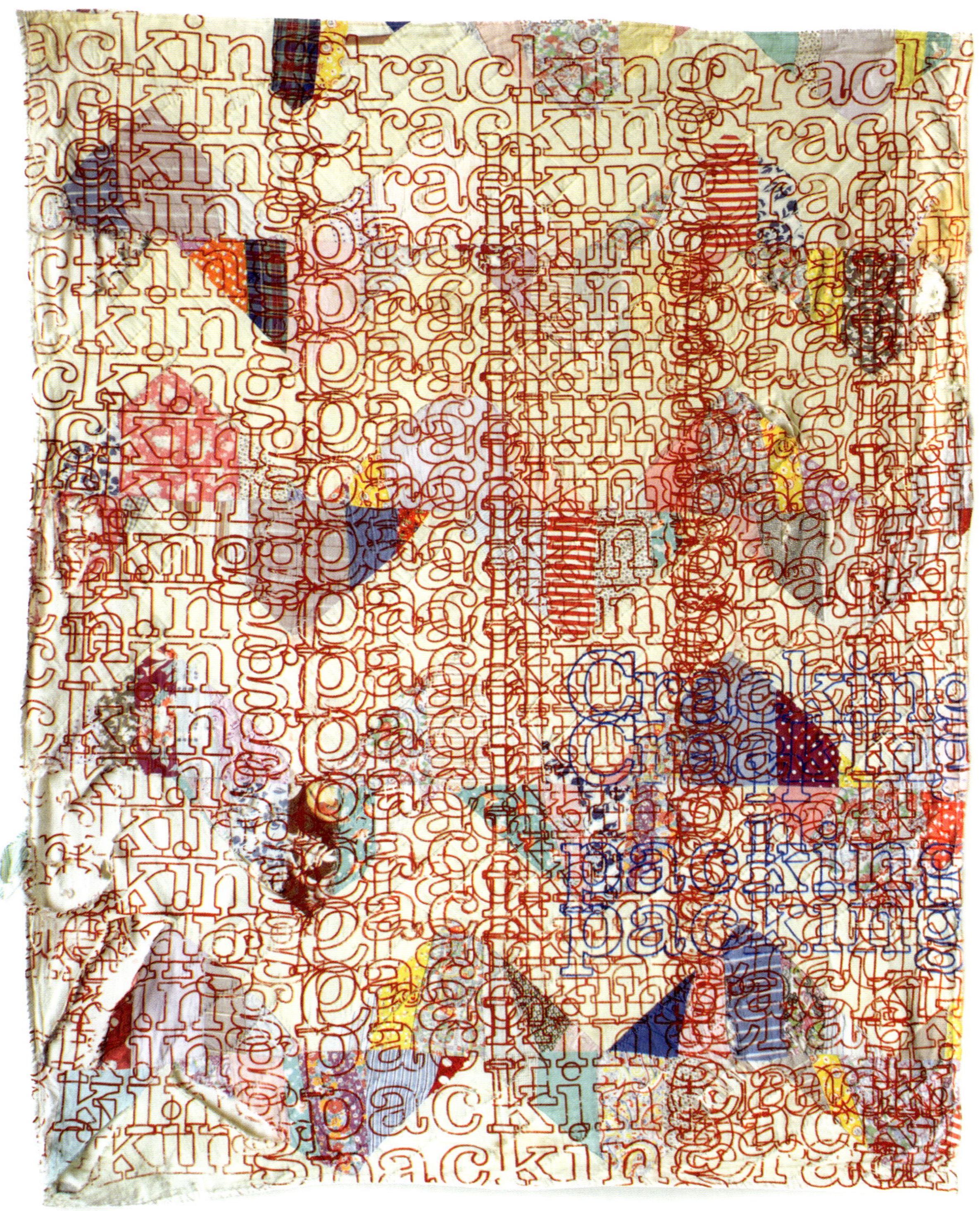

41

Packing and Cracking, 2022

Screen print on antique quilt on wood

54 × 41 in.

Courtesy of the artist and Red Arrow Gallery

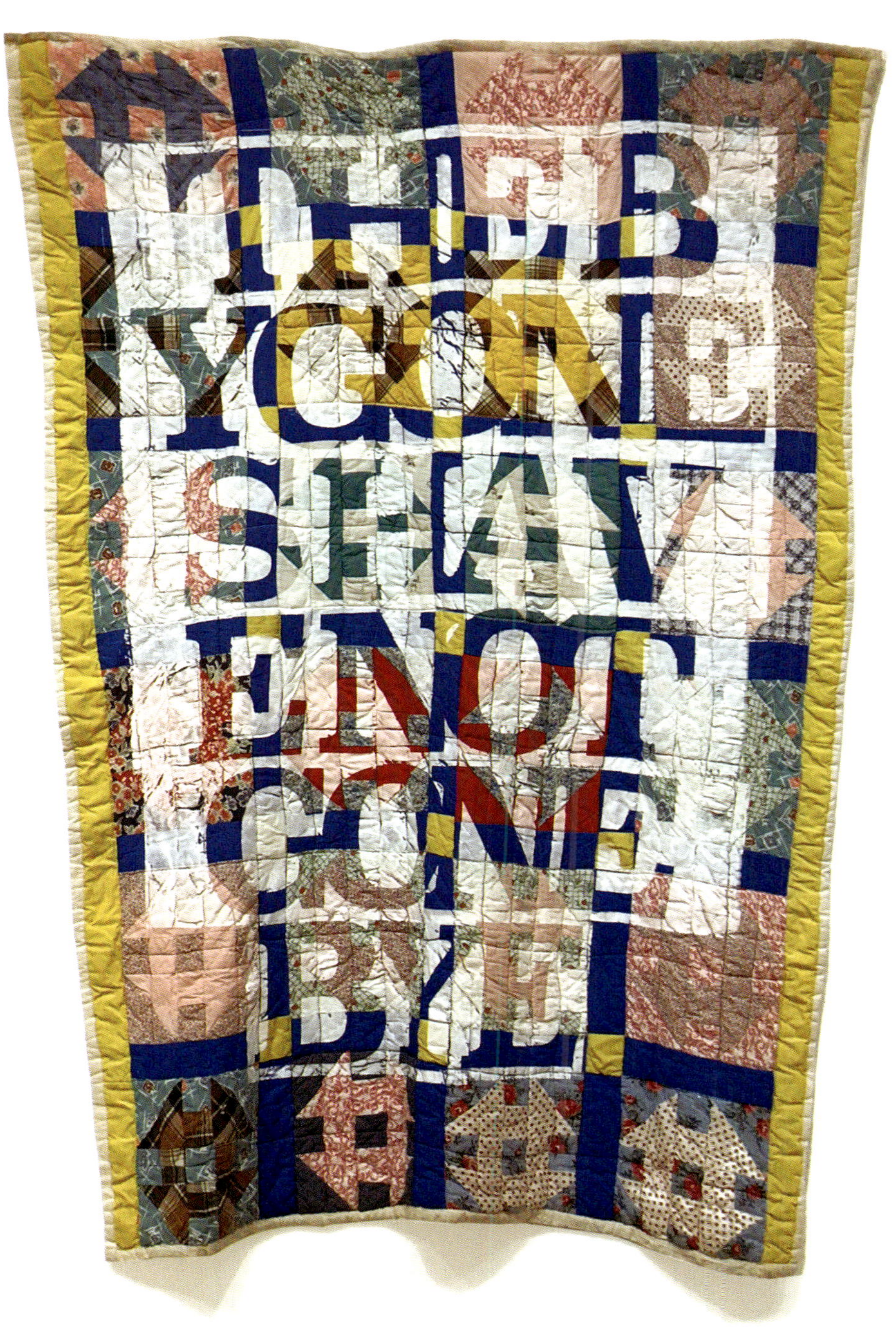

42
Can't Let Go, 2023
Screen print on antique quilt
70 × 60 in.

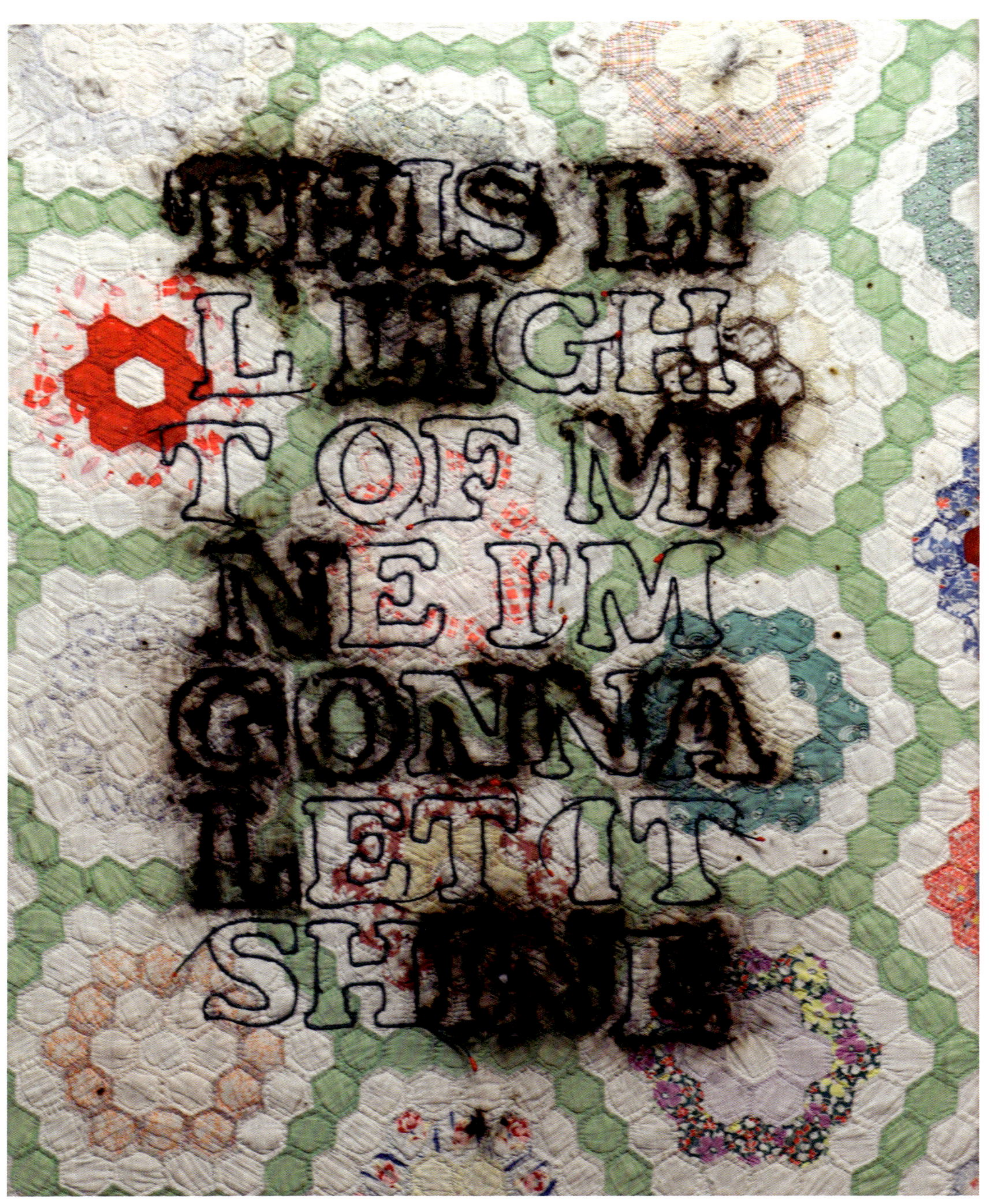

43

Never Burnout, 2024

Stitched fuses on burned antique quilt

38 × 30 in.

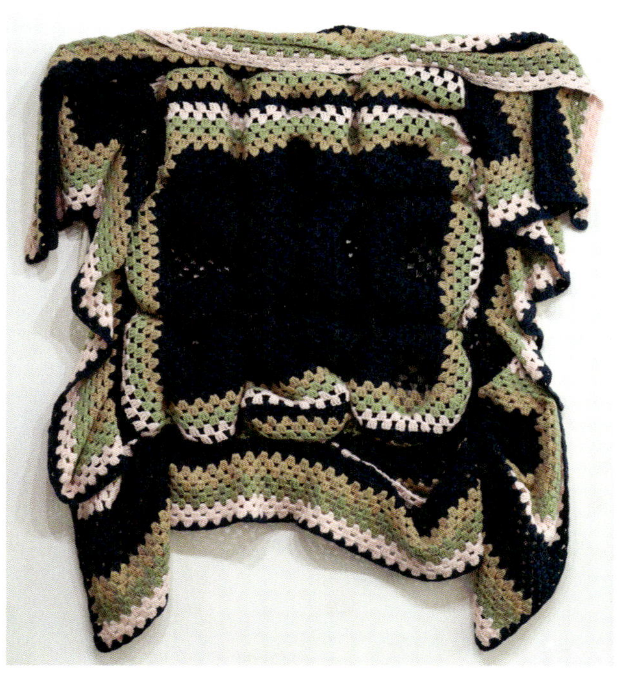

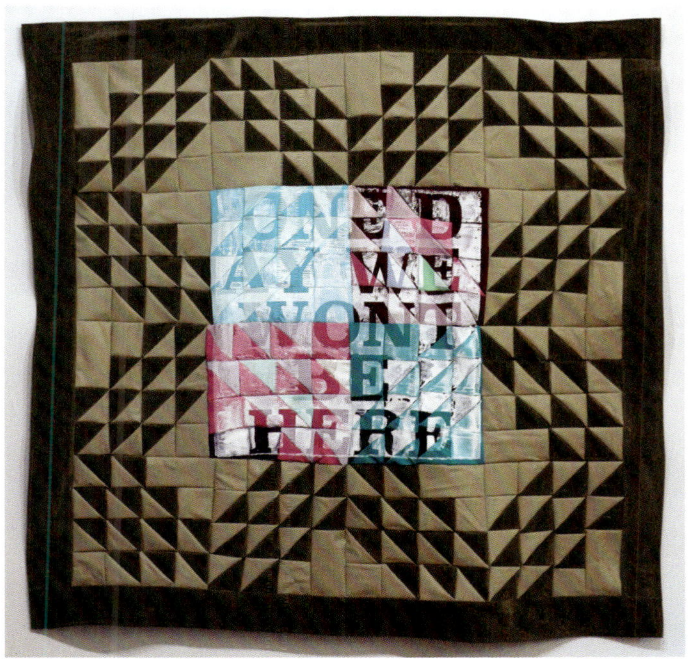

44
Well I, 2024
Crocheted blanket over shaped foam
34 × 36 × 3 in.

45
Second, Minute, Hour, Day, Month, Year, Decade, 2024
Screen print on fabric with sewn inflatable mattress
37 × 37 in.

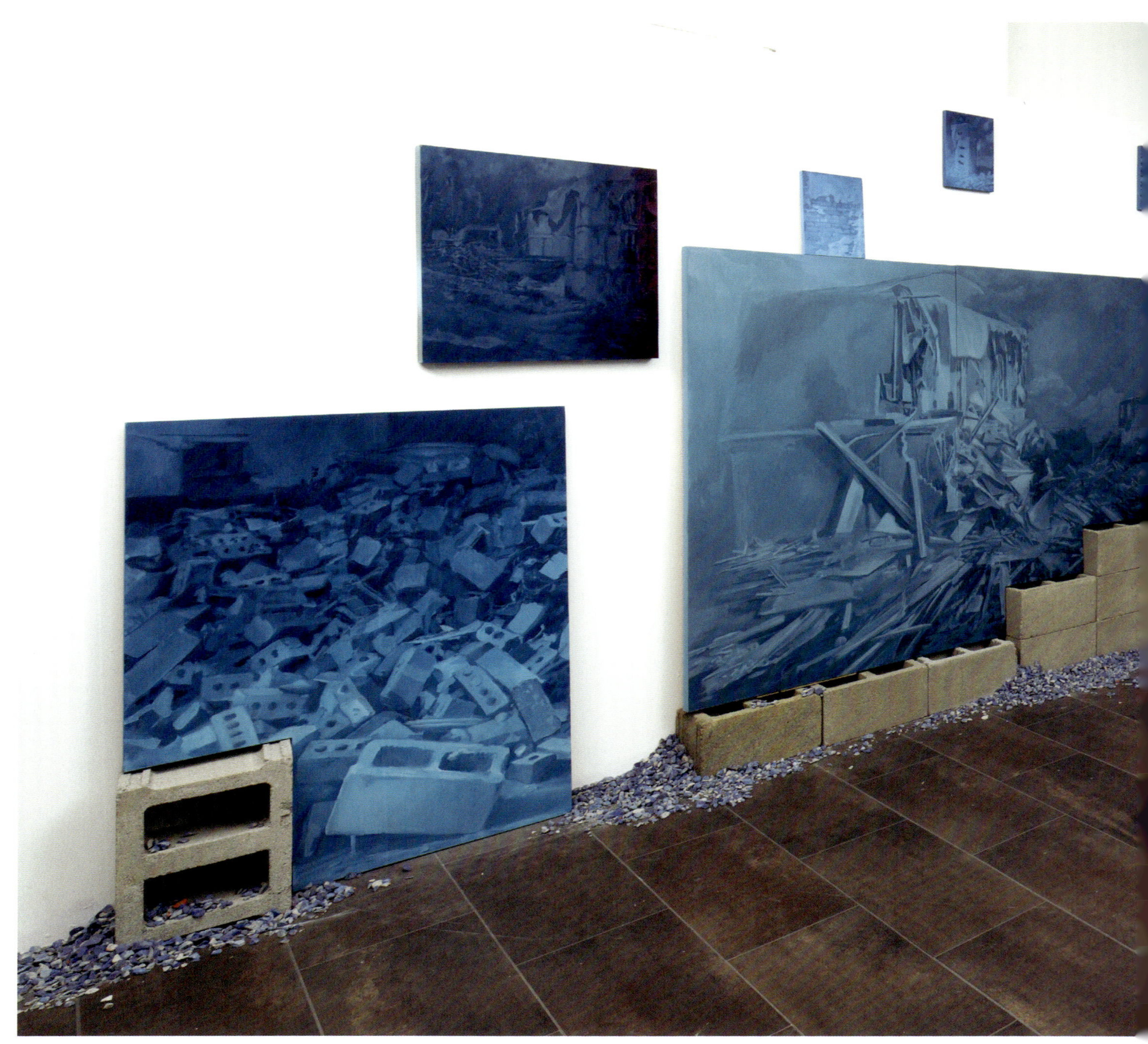

46

Material and Metaphor Series, 2023–25

Acrylic on panels, supported by cinder blocks

LEFT TO RIGHT:

Material and Metaphor I, 2023. 48 × 36 in.; *Lapse II*, 2025. 24 × 24 in.; *Face to Face*, 2025. 60 × 120 in.; *Stack and Mortar*, 2023. 12 × 9 in.; *Fit*, 2003. 12 × 9 in.; *Hold*, 2023. 12 × 9 in.; *We Lived*, 2023. 20 × 16 in.; *We Slept Easily*, 2023. 40 × 30.; *Which Way the Wind Blows*, 2025. 36 × 48 in.; *Scramble*, 2023. 12 × 9 in.; *Lapse I*, 2025. 24 × 24 in.; *Provisions*, 2023. 30 × 40 in.; *We Lived Happily*, 2023. 30 × 40 in.; *Brick Stack*, 2023. 12 × 9 in.; *Material and Metaphor II*, 2023. 48 × 36 in.; *Lapse III*, 2025. 24 × 24 in.

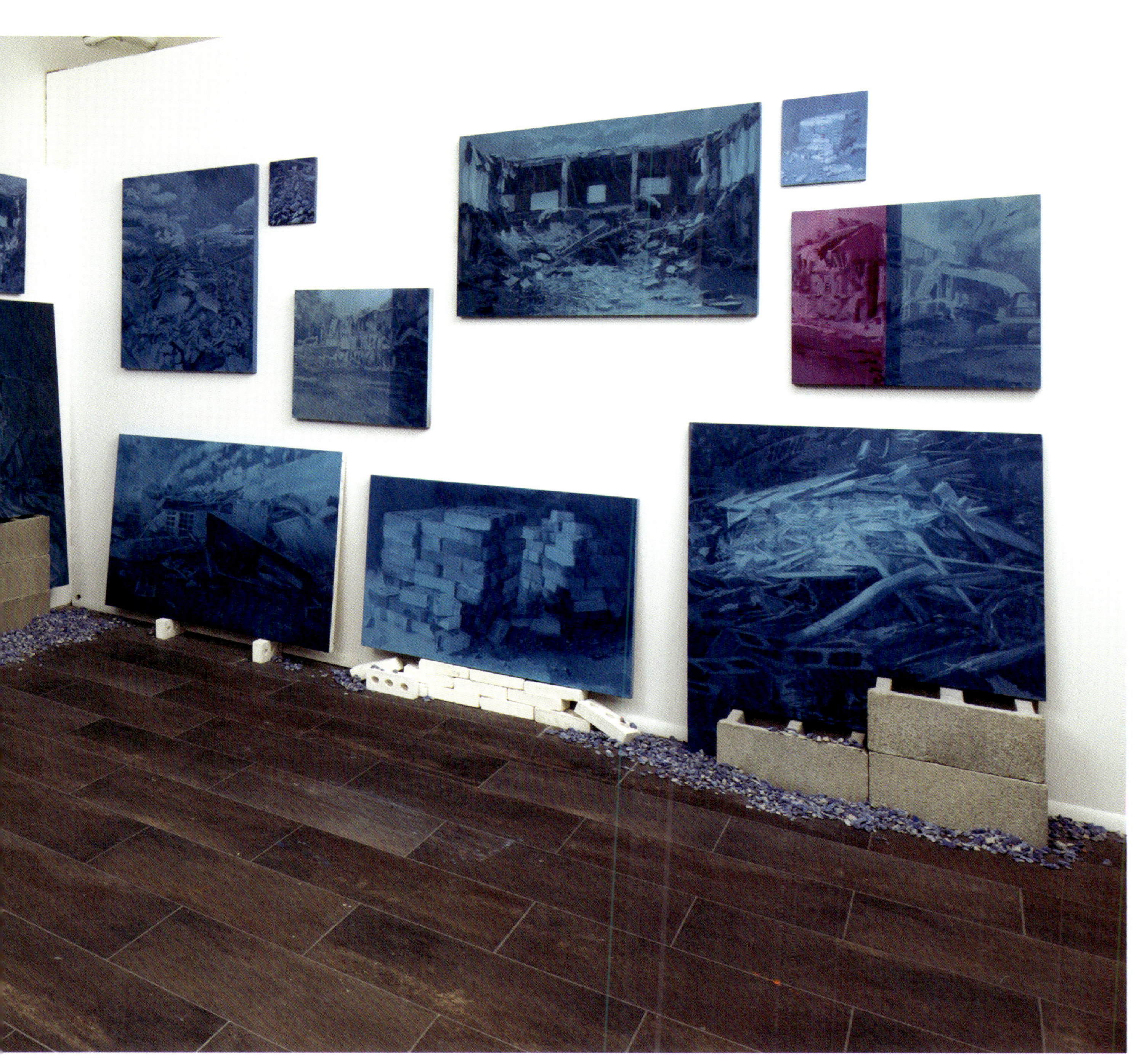

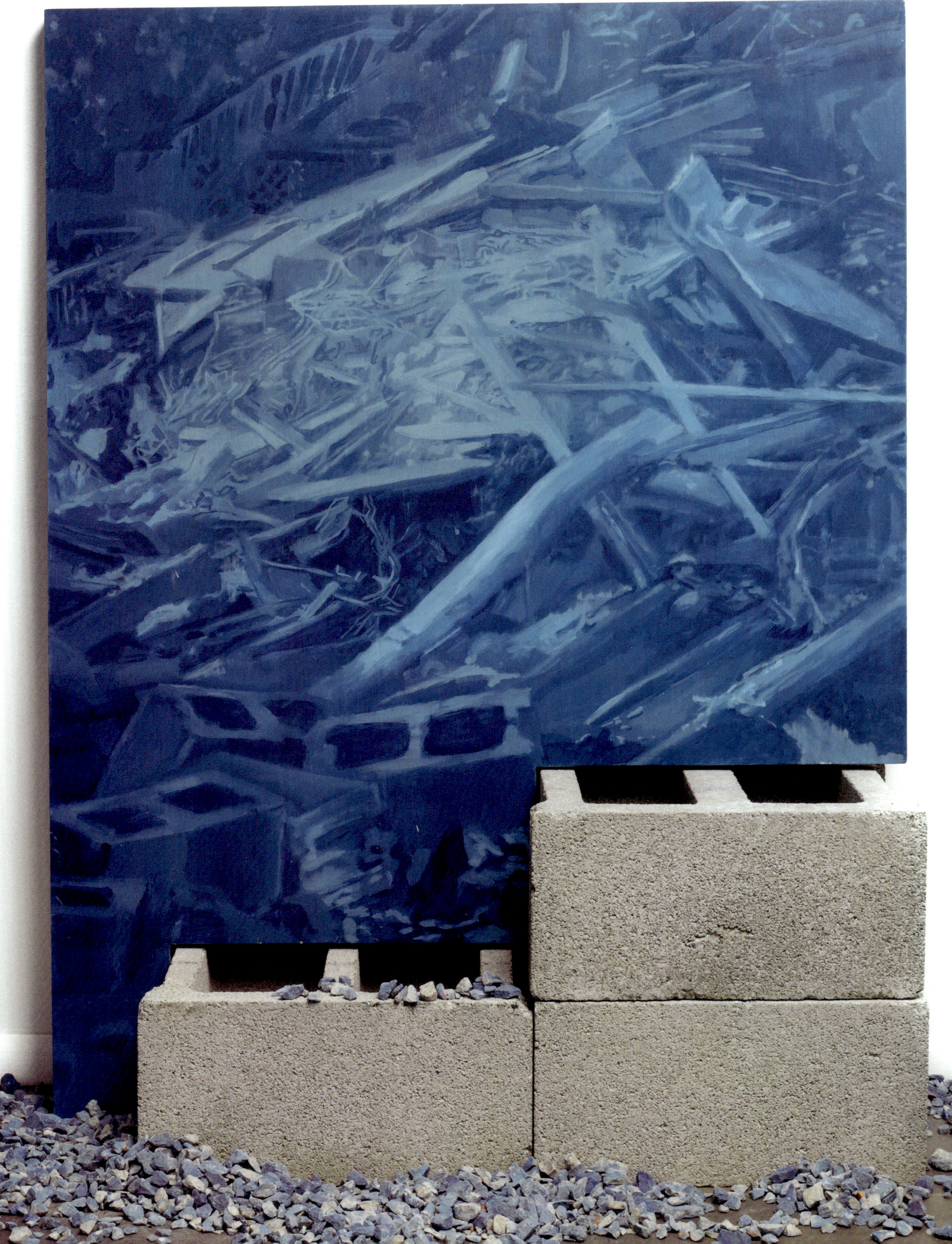

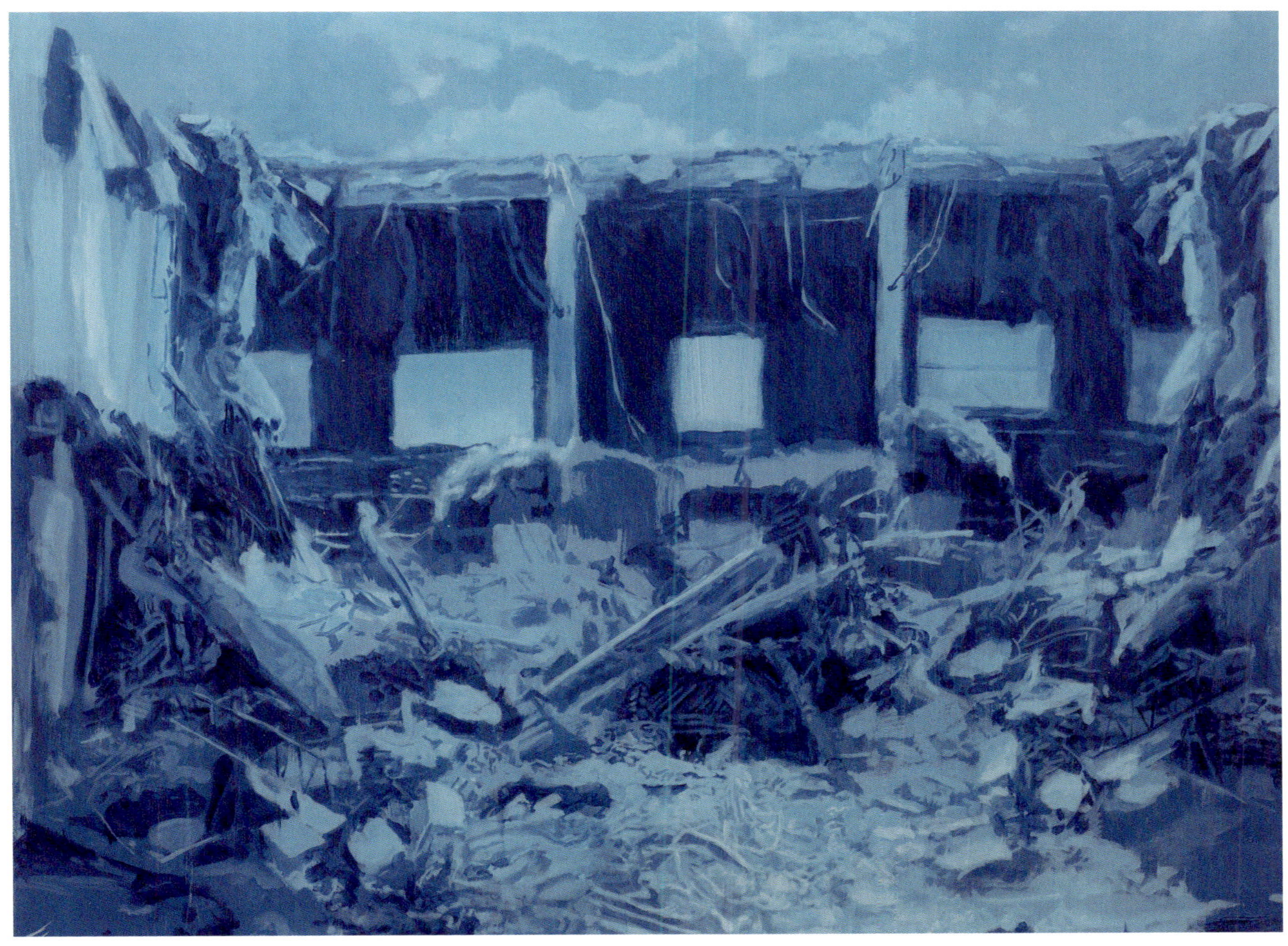

48
We Lived Happily, 2023
Acrylic on cradled panel
30 × 40 in.

47
Material and Metaphor II, 2023
Acrylic on shaped and cradled panel, supported by cinder blocks
48 × 36 in.

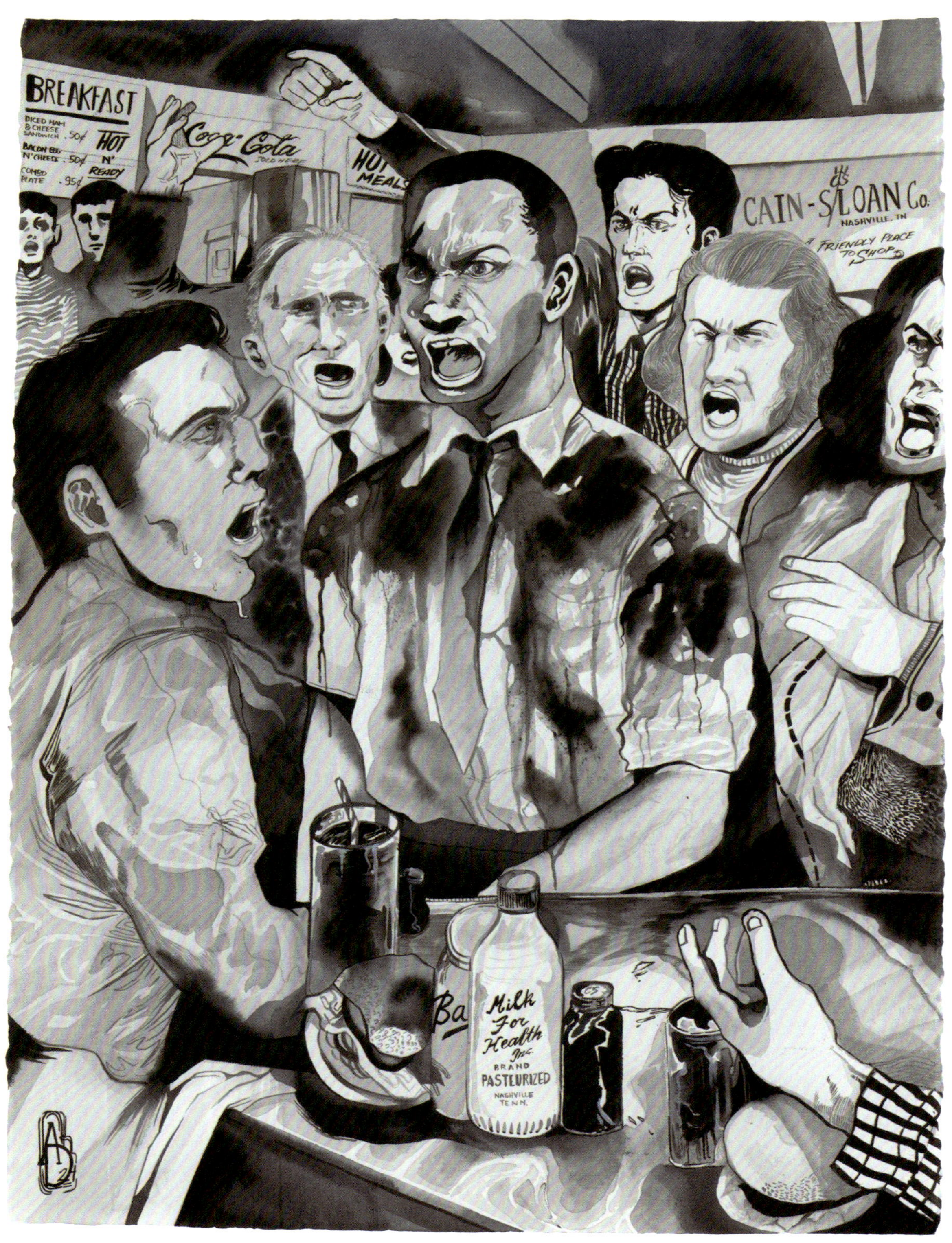

49

Battle (Cain Sloan), 2024

Sumi ink on Arches cold-pressed watercolor paper

30 × 22 in.

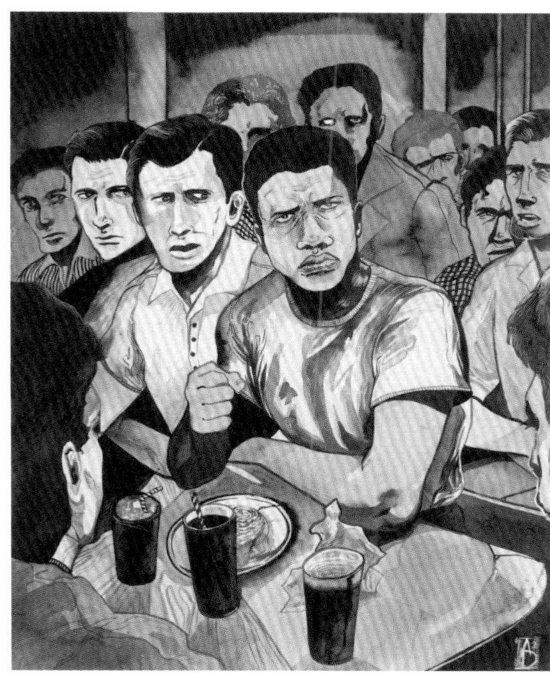

50
John, 2024
Sumi ink on cotton board
20 × 16 in.

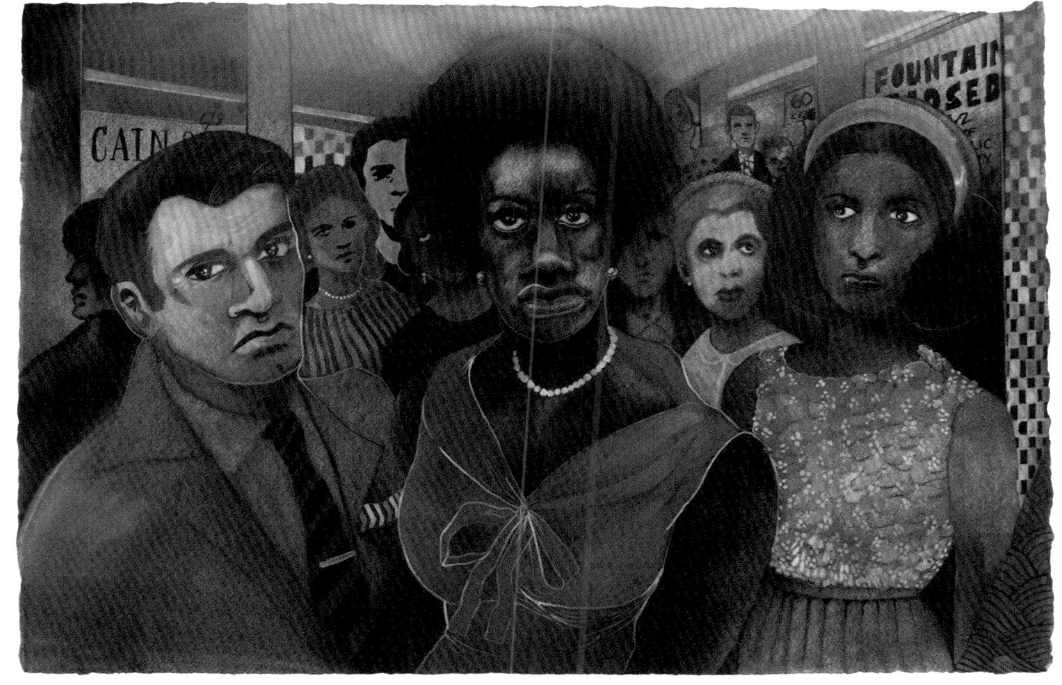

51
A Friendly Place to Shop, 2024
Sumi ink, graphite, conté, acrylic, and soot on Arches cold-pressed watercolor paper
15 × 22 in.

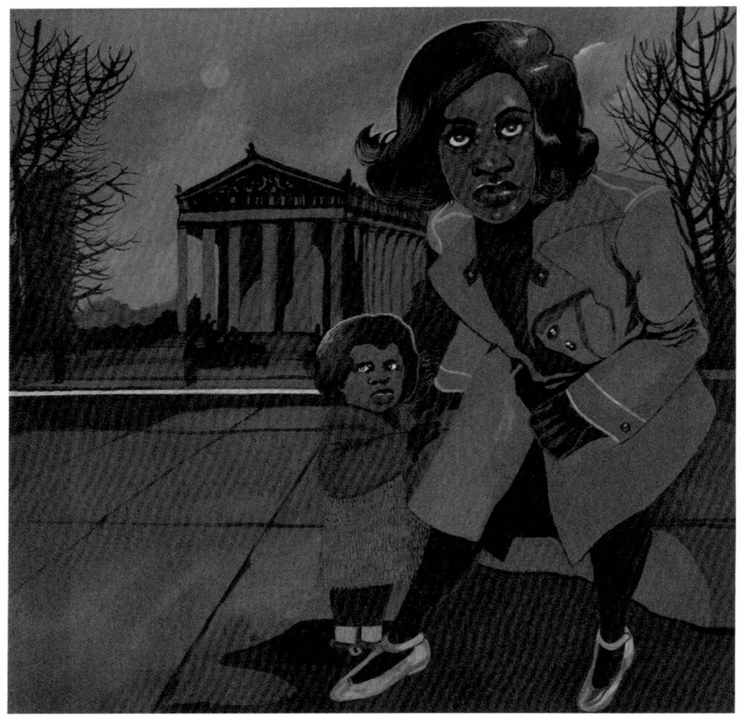

52
Shield, 2024
Oil, acrylic, graphite, soot, and polymer on linen
16 × 16 in.

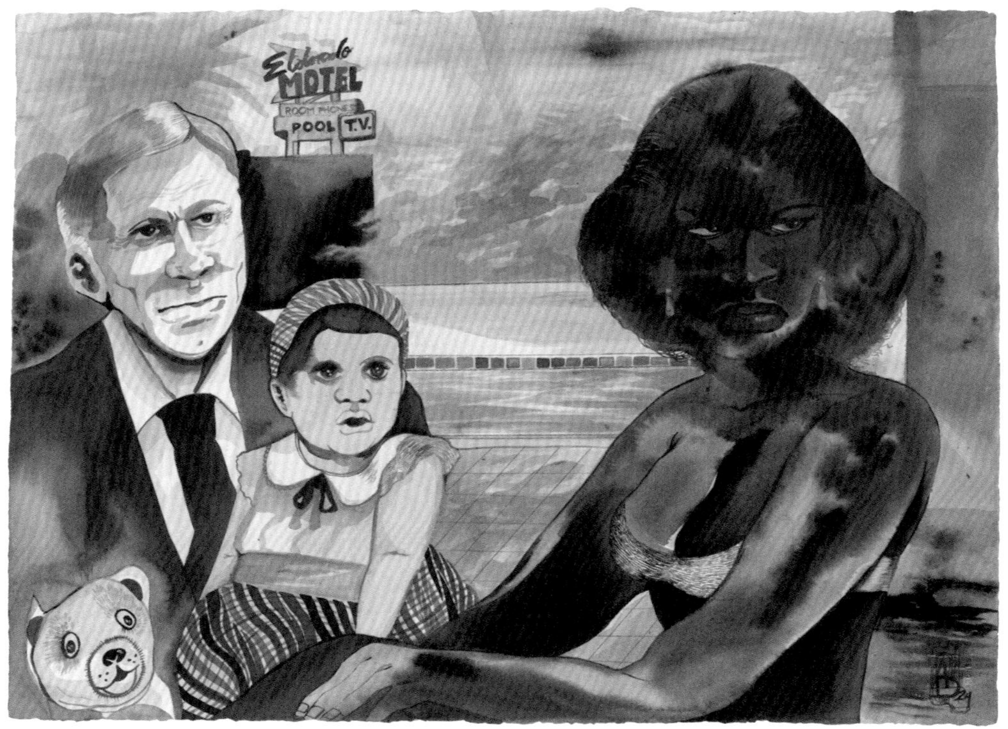

53
El Dorado, 2024
Sumi ink, wash, acrylic and graphite on Arches cold-pressed watercolor paper
22 × 30 in.

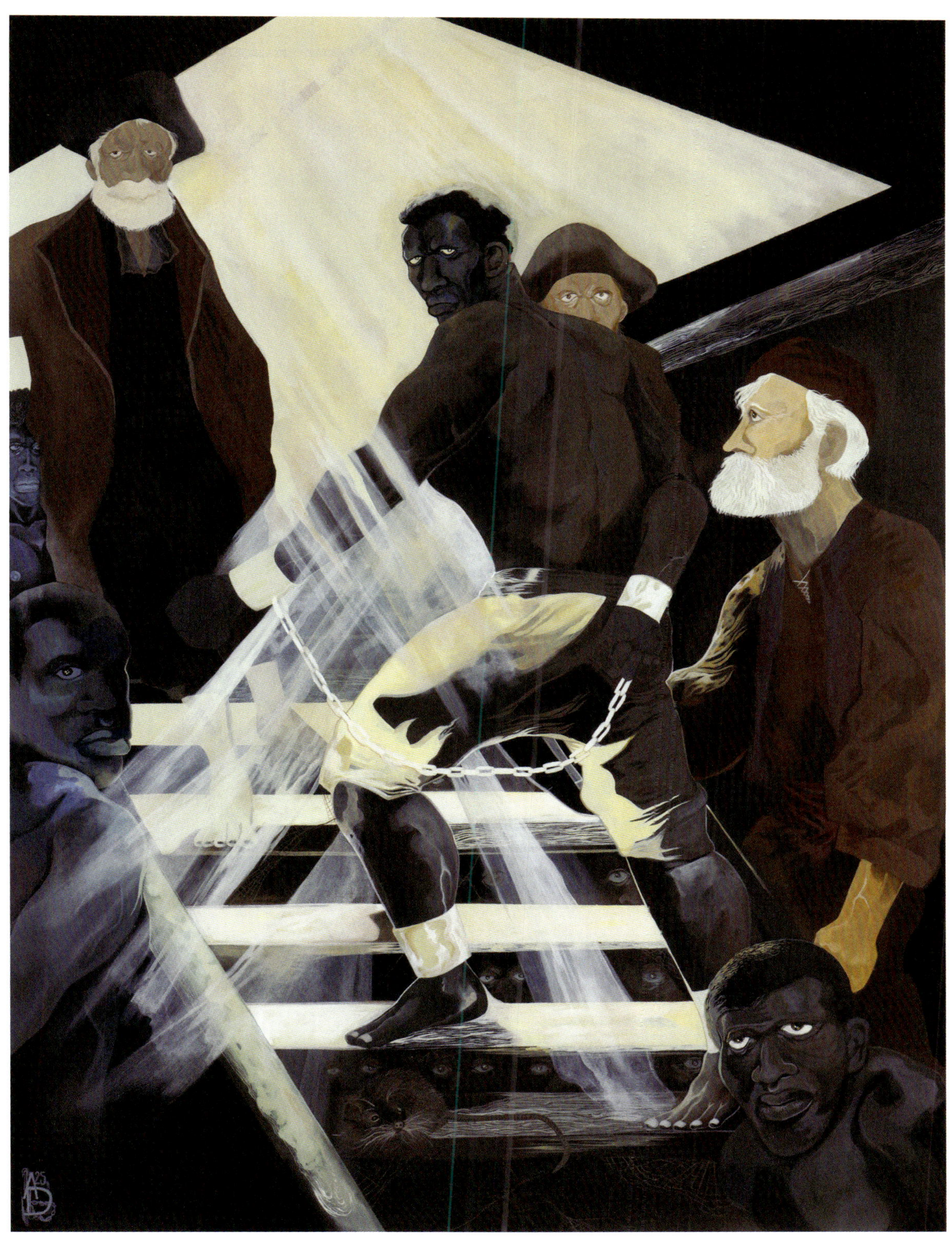

54
Hull, 2025
Oil and acrylic on linen
48 × 36 in.

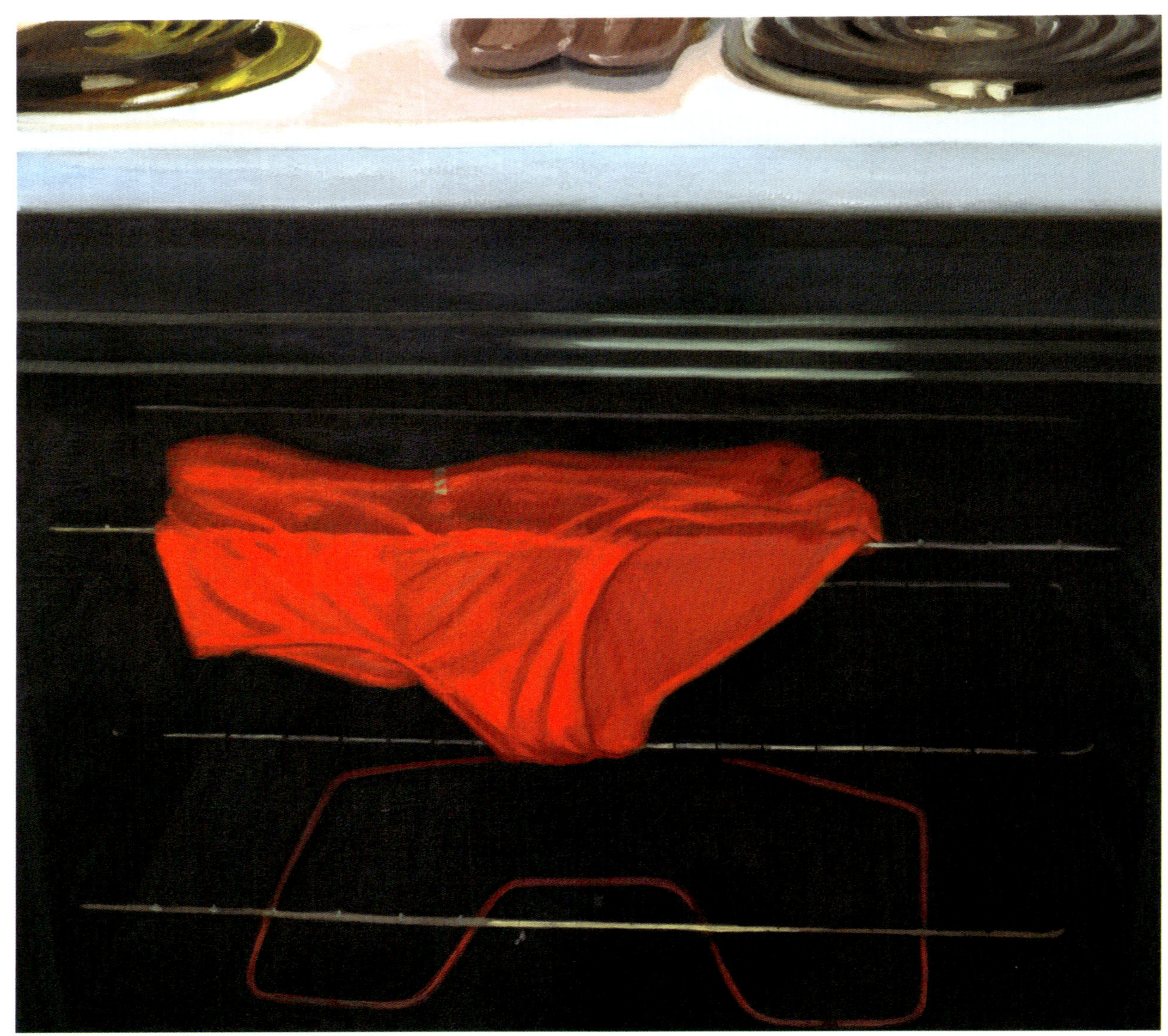

55
New Home (Oven), 2019
Oil on canvas
24 × 26 in.
Private collection, courtesy of Nina Johnson Gallery

56
Brooklyn's l'ennui, 2023
Oil on canvas
70 × 52 in.
Collection of Sandra Ballentine, courtesy of Night Gallery, Los Angeles

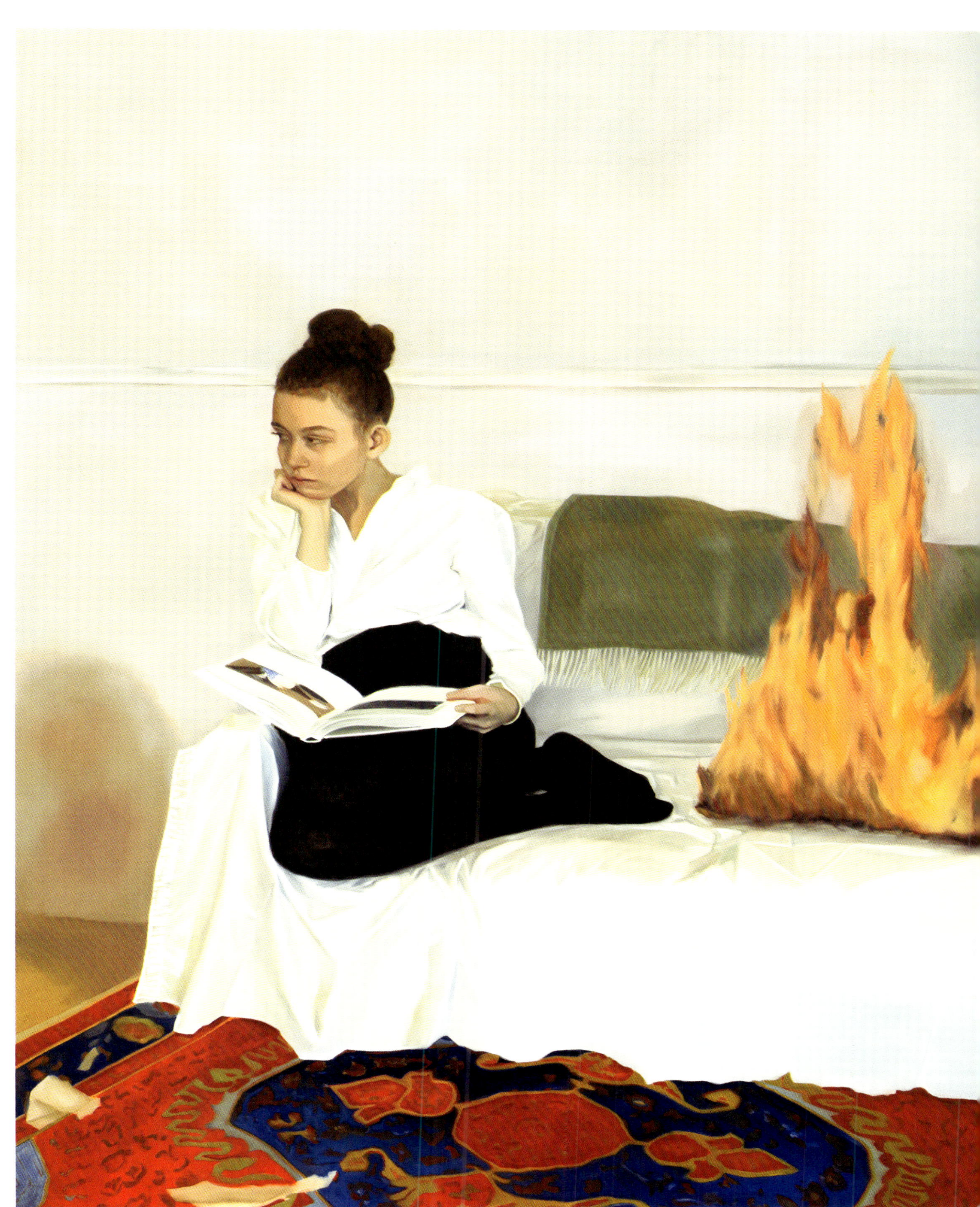

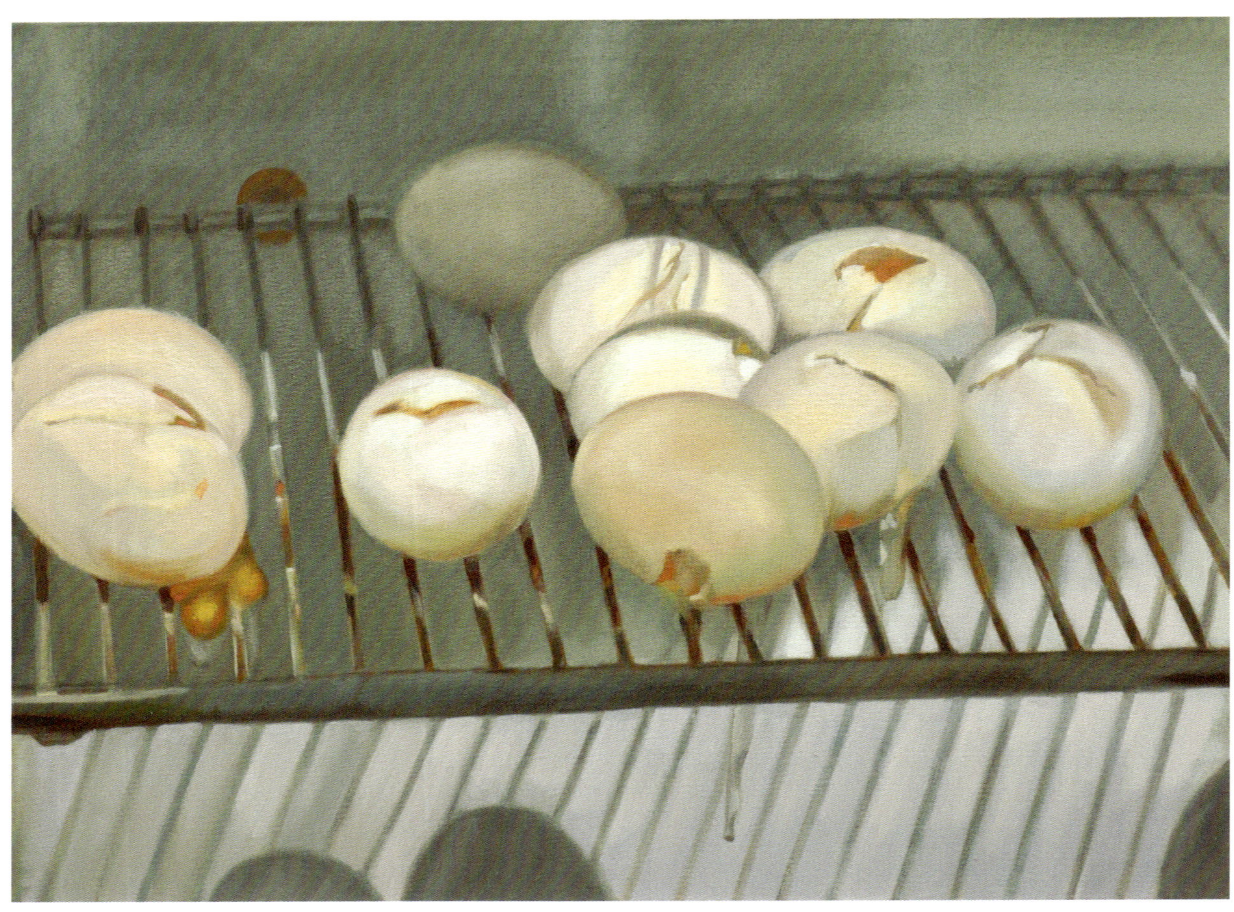

57
Our New Home (Eggs), 2019
Oil on canvas
21 × 28 in.
Collection of Alf and Clara Naman, courtesy of Nina Johnson Gallery

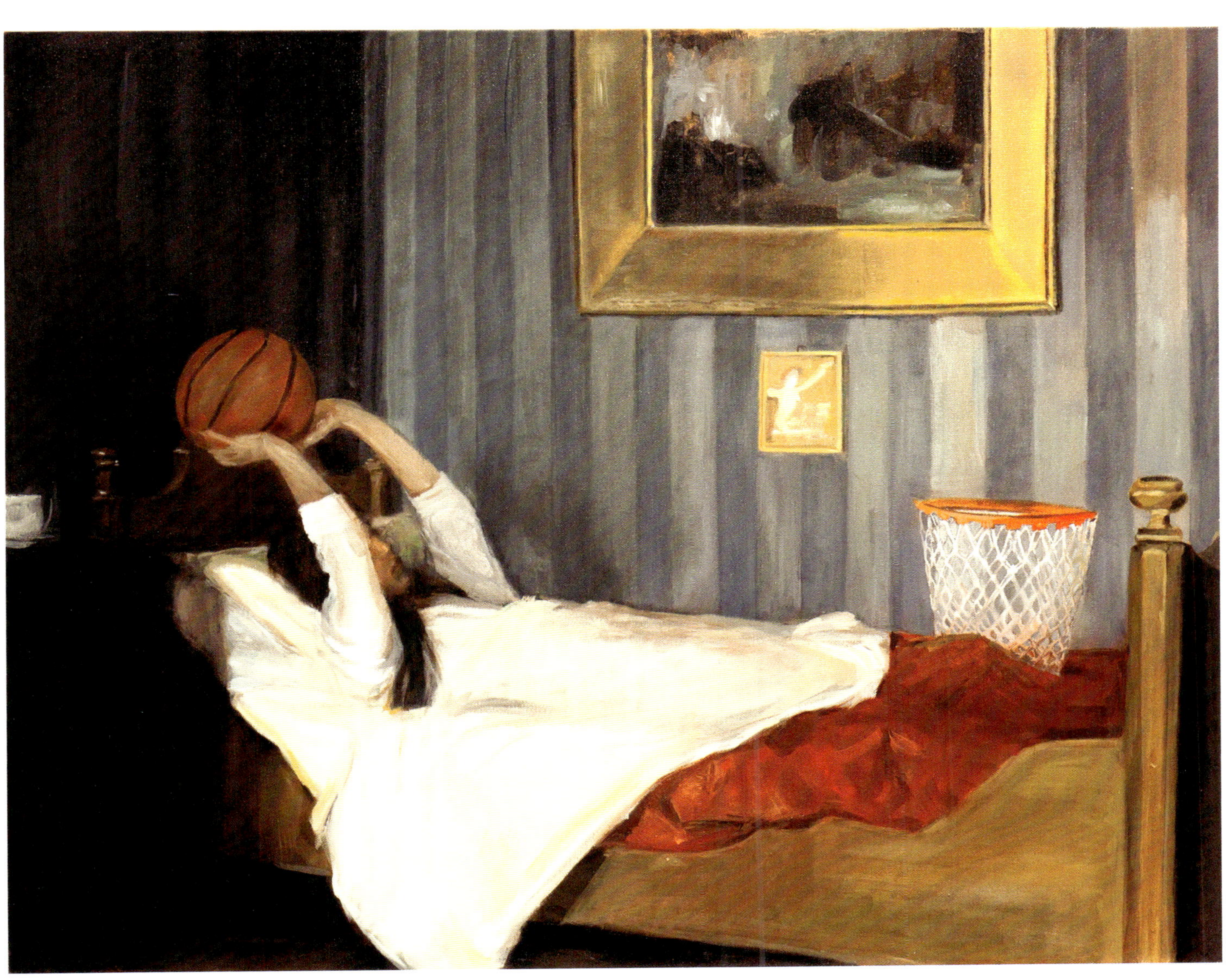

58
Bedball, 2018
Oil on canvas
24 × 30 in.
Private collection

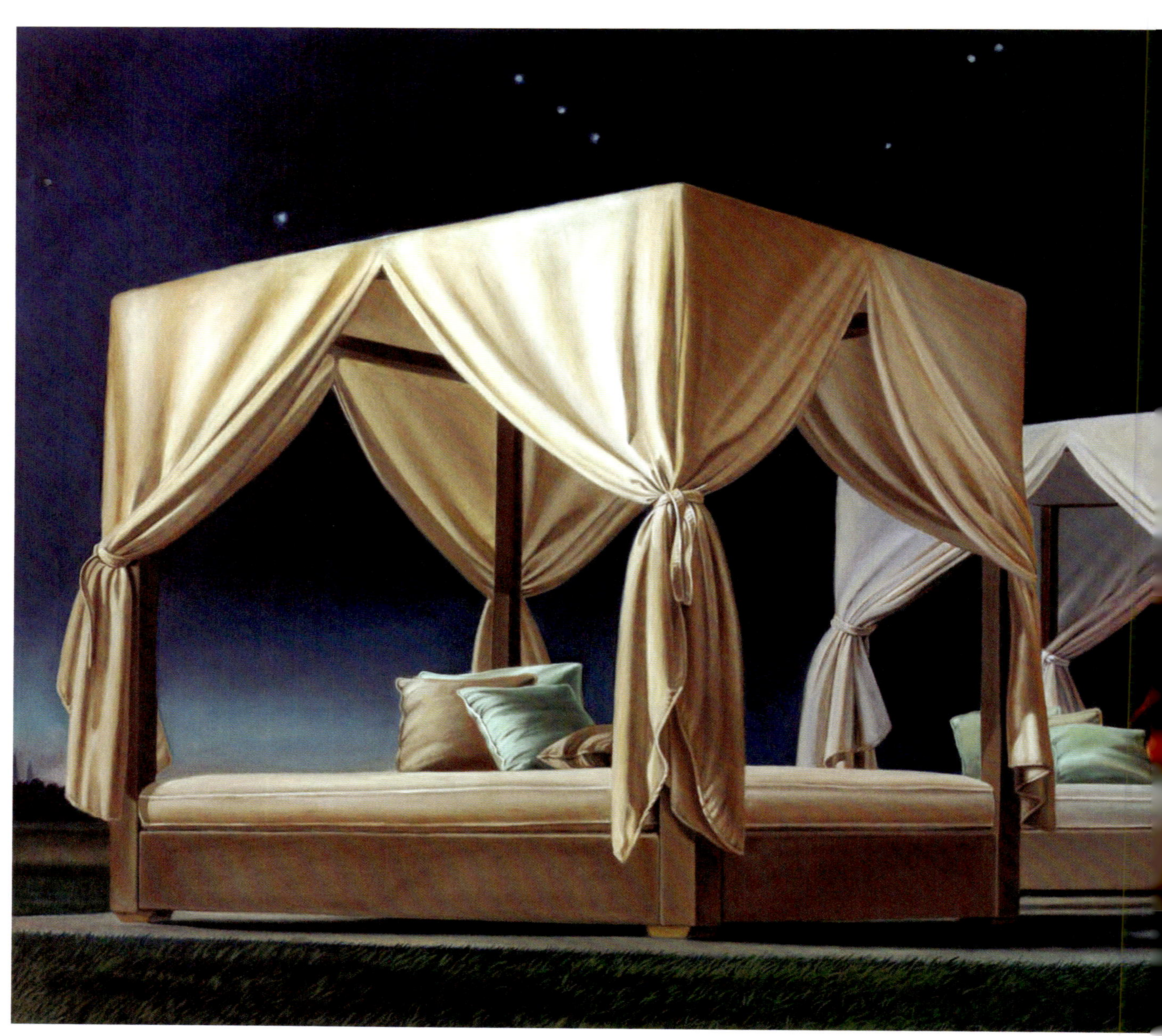

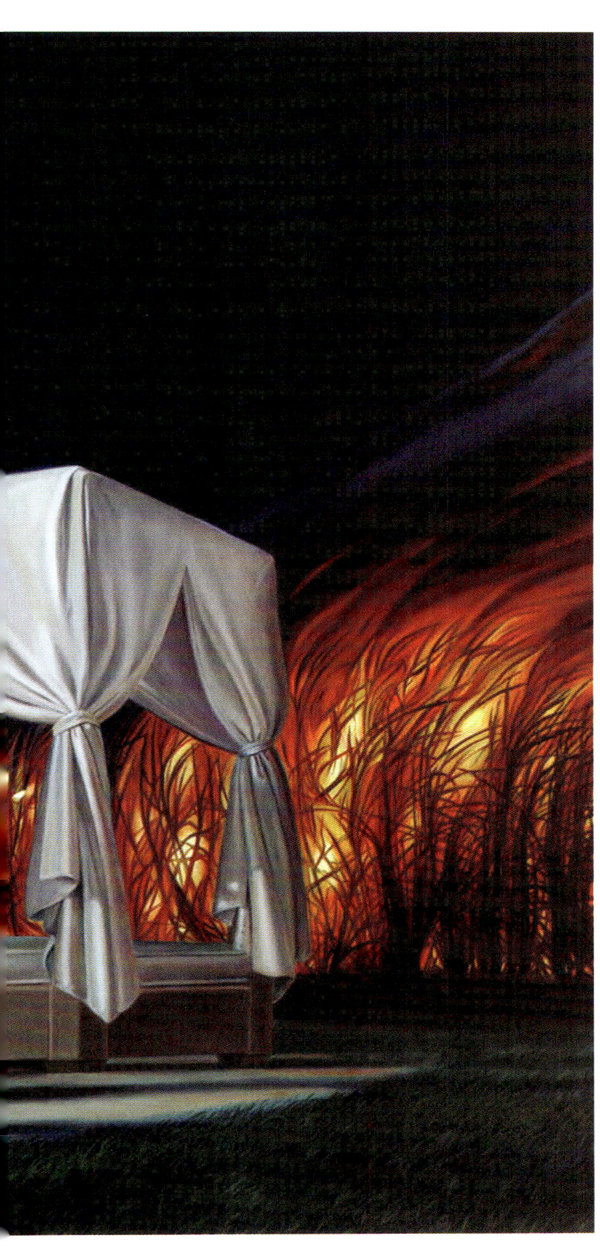

59
Air and Dreams, 2008
Oil on canvas
36 × 60 in.

60

Air and Dreams, 2020

Graphite on paper

44 × 30 in.

Collection of Eliot Michael, Nashville

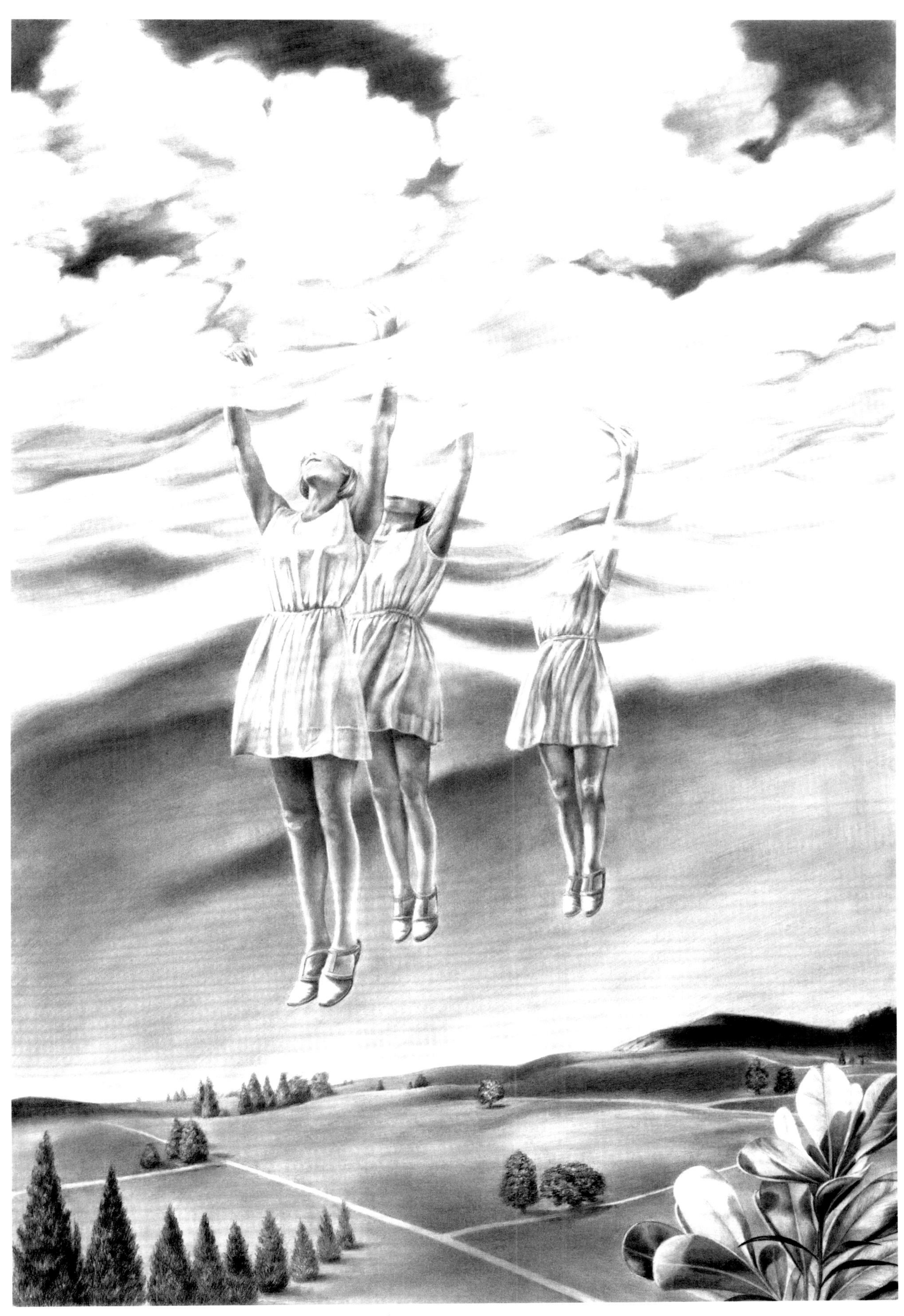

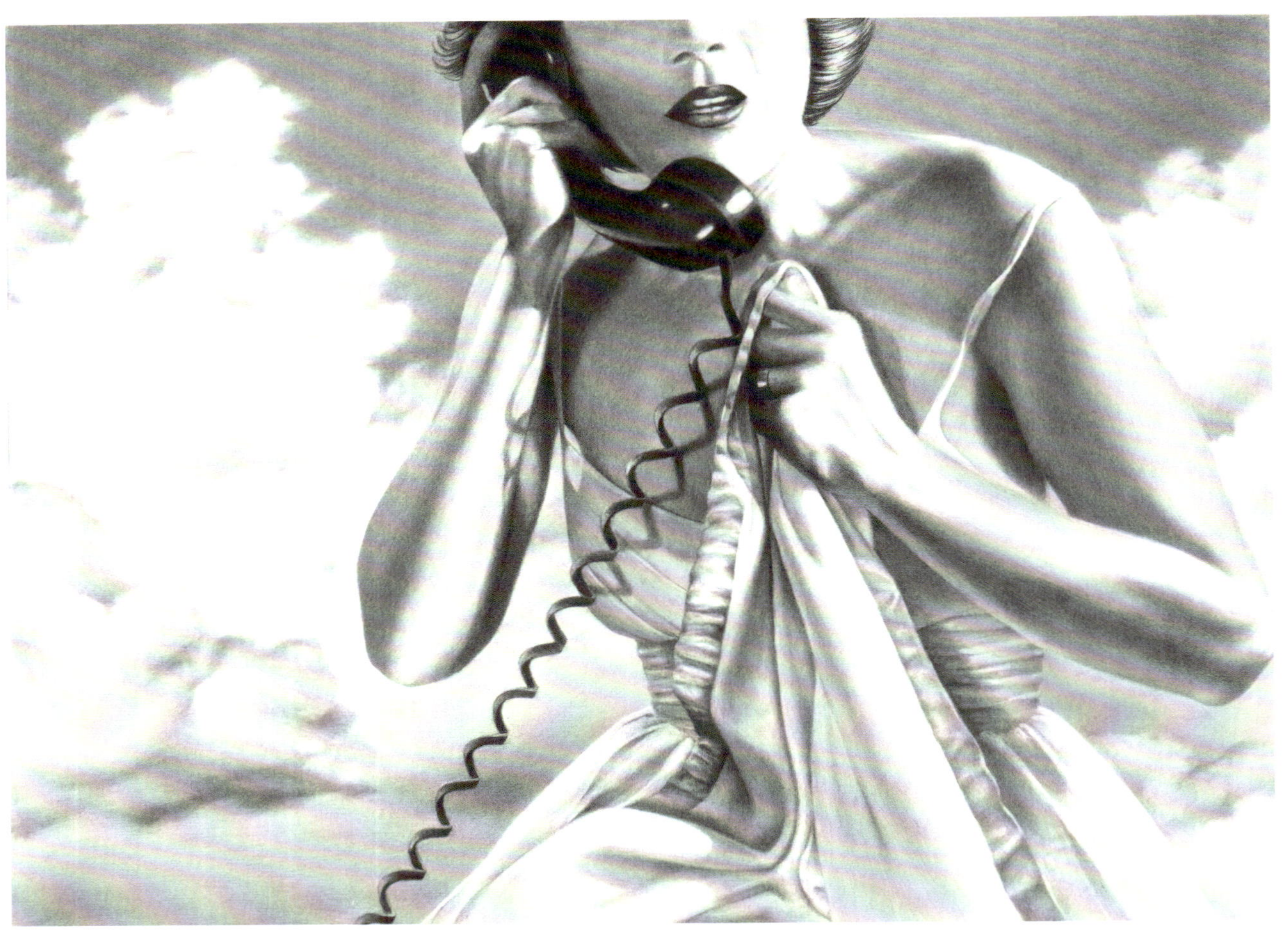

61
Call in the Night, 2018
Graphite on paper
22 × 30 in.
Collection of Mollye Brown and Paul Polycarpou, Nashville

62
Cloud Nine, 2017
Graphite on paper
22 × 30 in.
Collection of Cal Turner

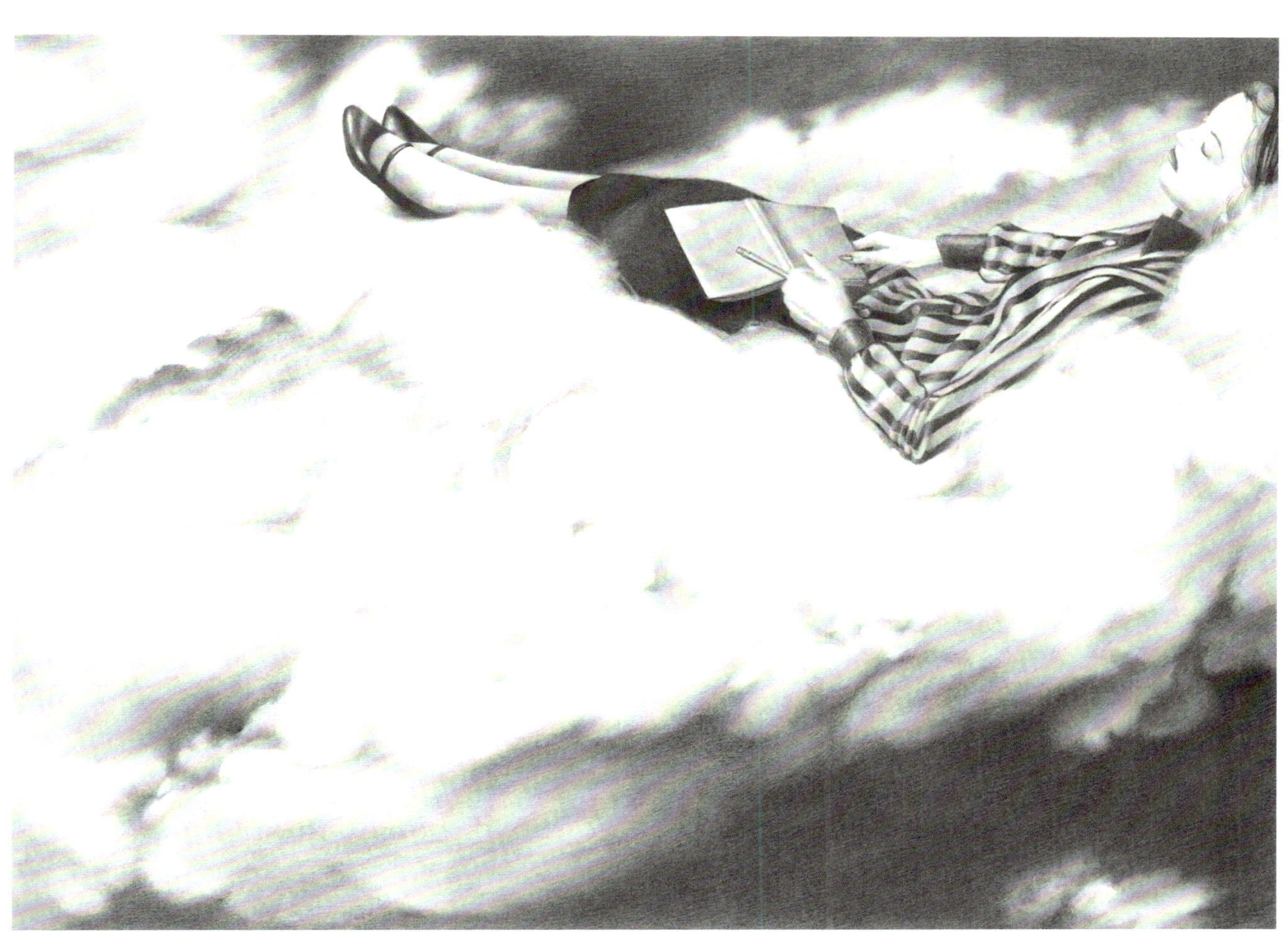

63

Complicit, 2024

Oil on canvas with maple frame and found objects

16½ × 13¾ × 5½ in.

Collection of Jesse Hale, Nashville

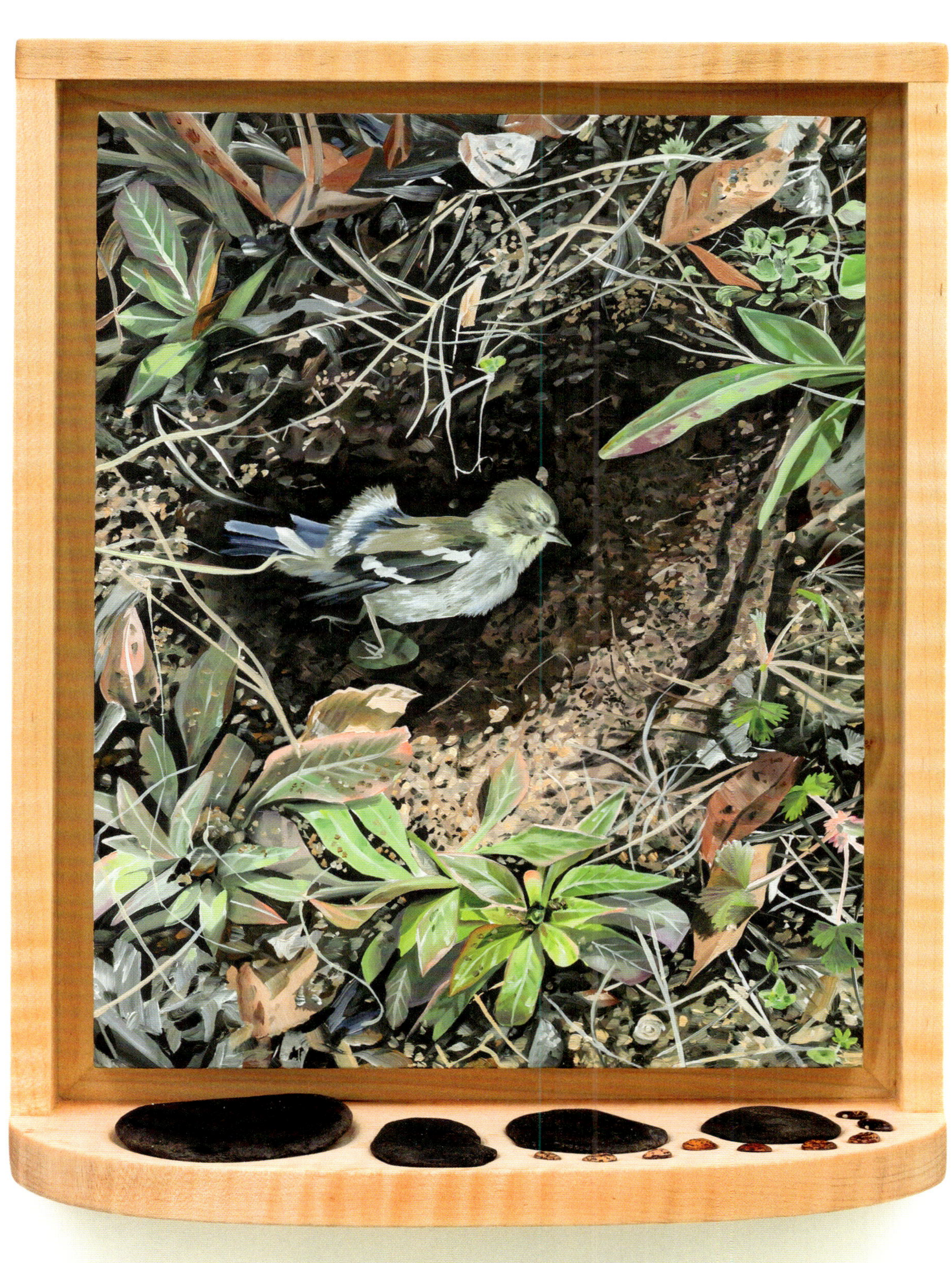

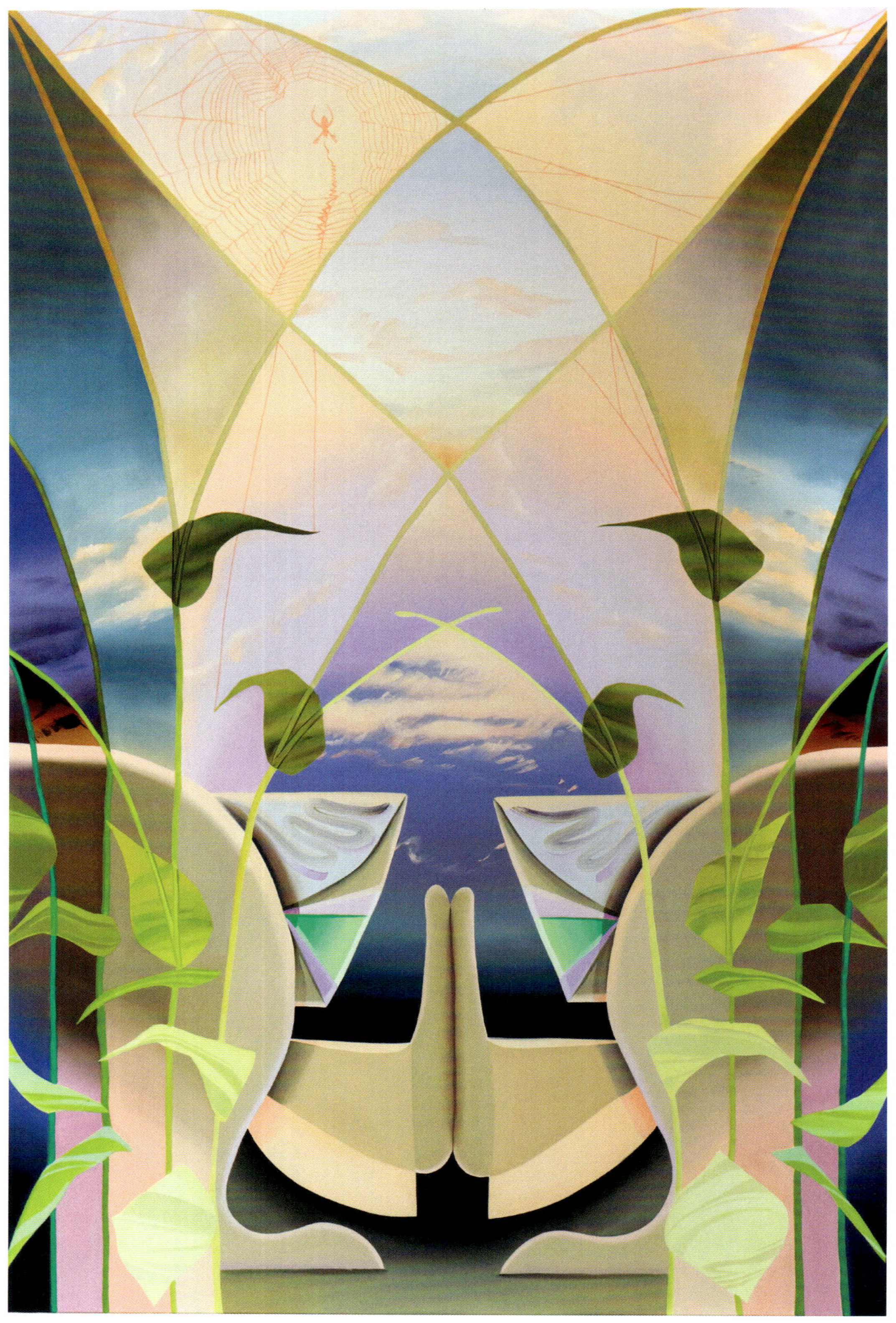

64
You Are Spring, 2023
Oil on canvas
72 × 48 in.
Collection of Sasha and Charlie Sealy

65
Seed Bomb, 2023
Oil on canvas
72 × 48 in.
Collection of Emily Leonard and Sloane Southard

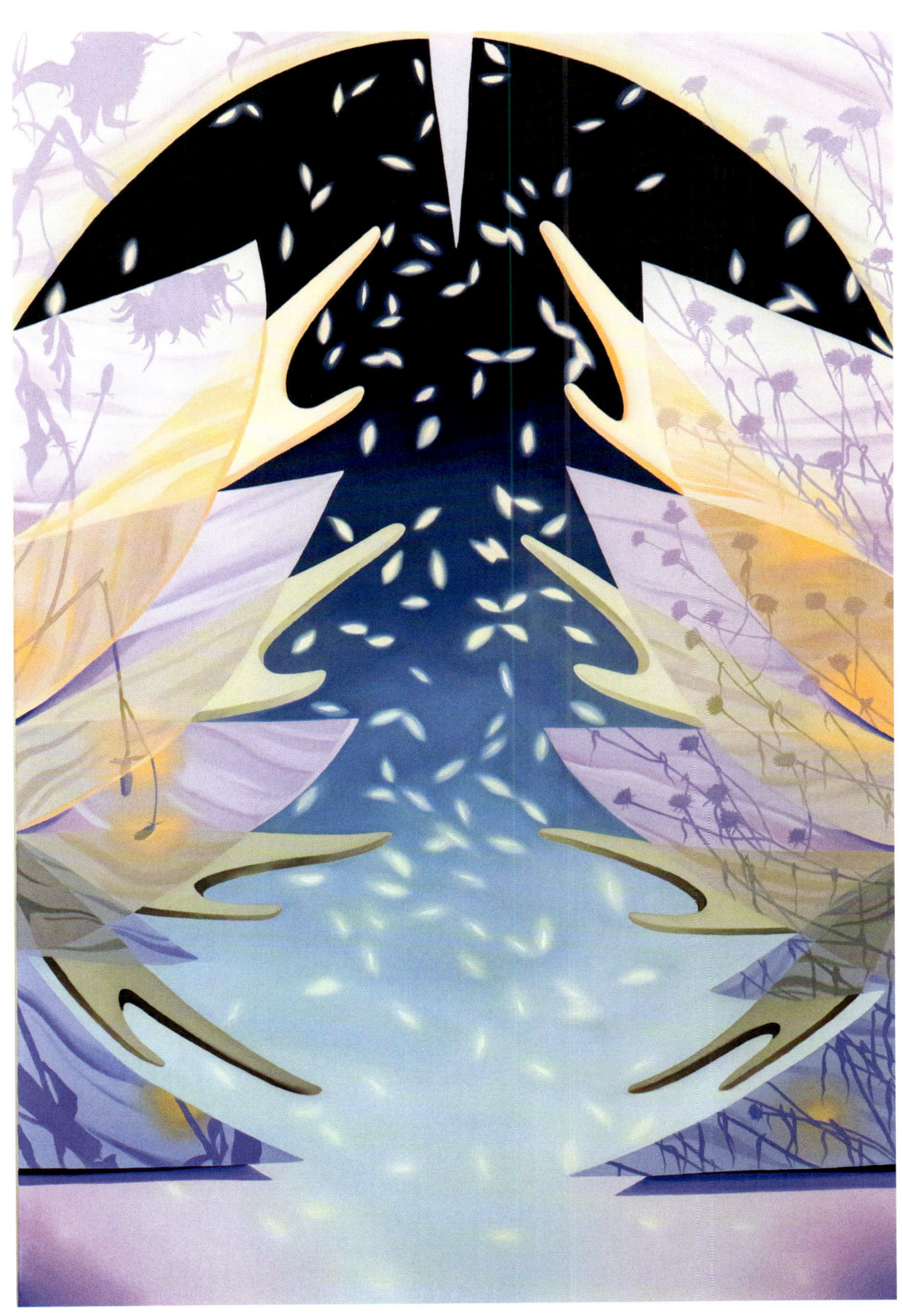

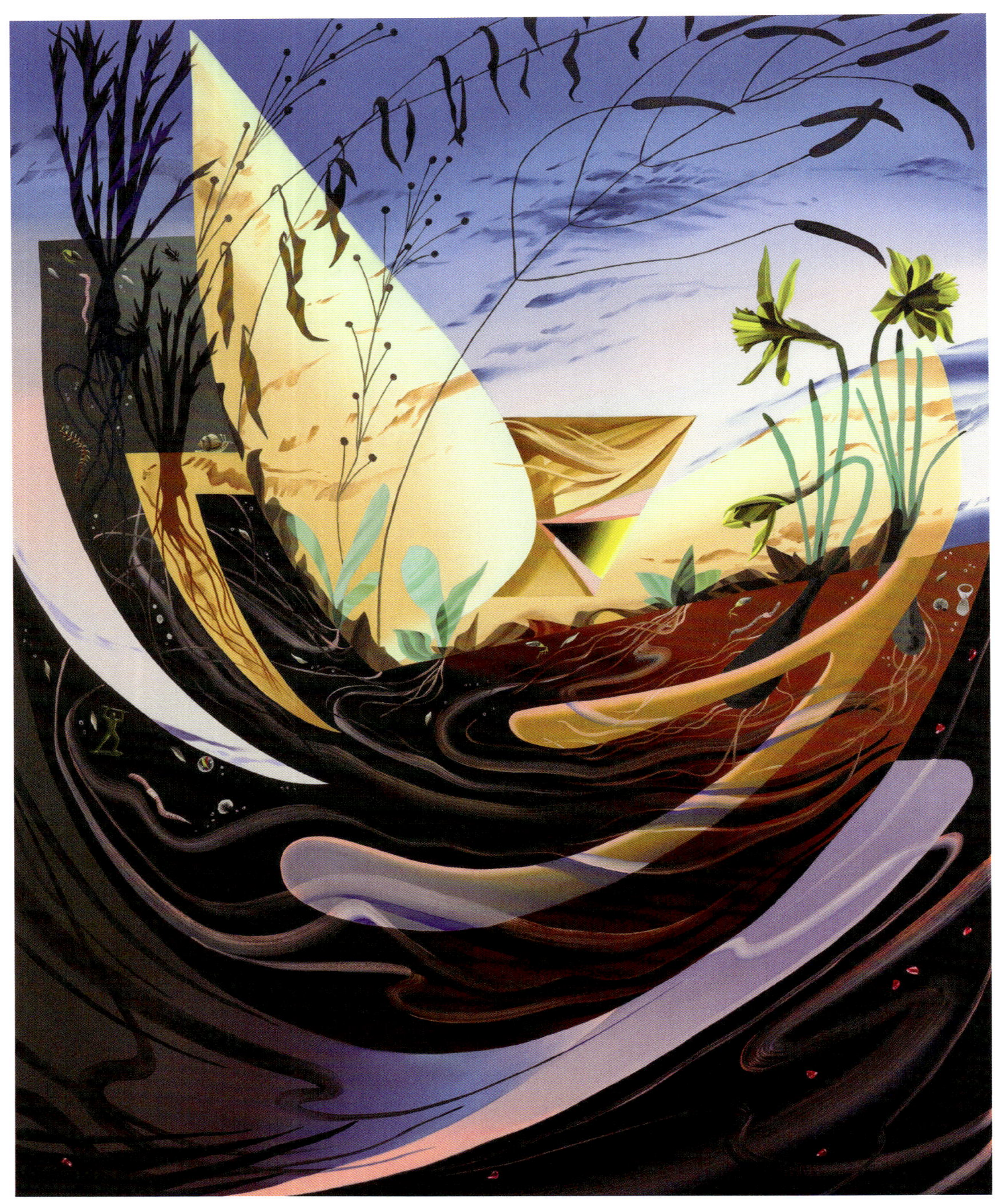

66

Persephone Emerging, 2024

Oil on canvas

60 × 48 in.

Collection of Sasha and Charlie Sealy

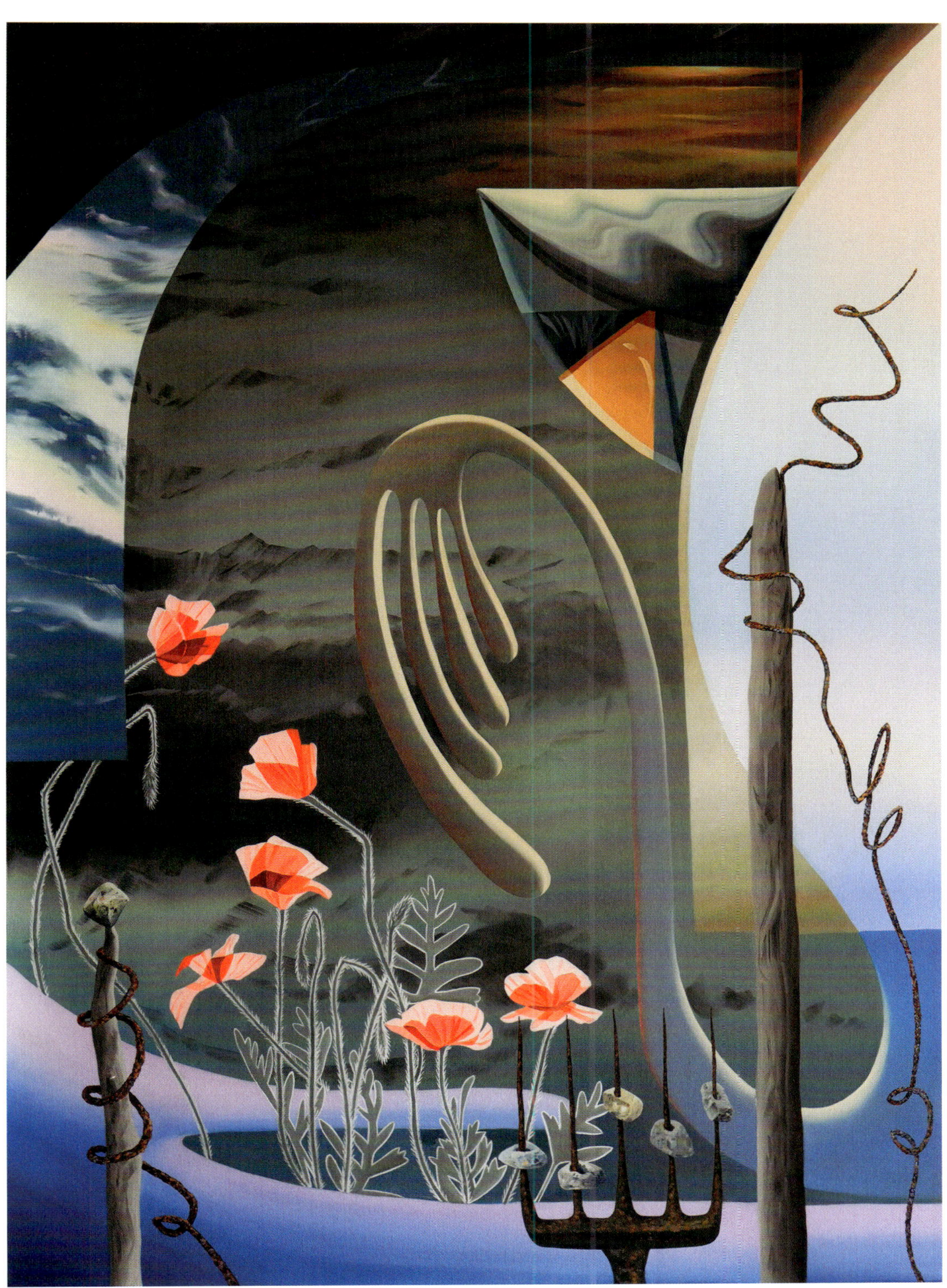

67

Saint Jarman, 2023

Oil on canvas

54 × 40 in.

Collection of Andrew Le

68
Glass Ceilings, 2024
Oil on linen in painted wood frame
50½ × 37½ × 2 in.
Collection of Sasha and Charlie Sealy

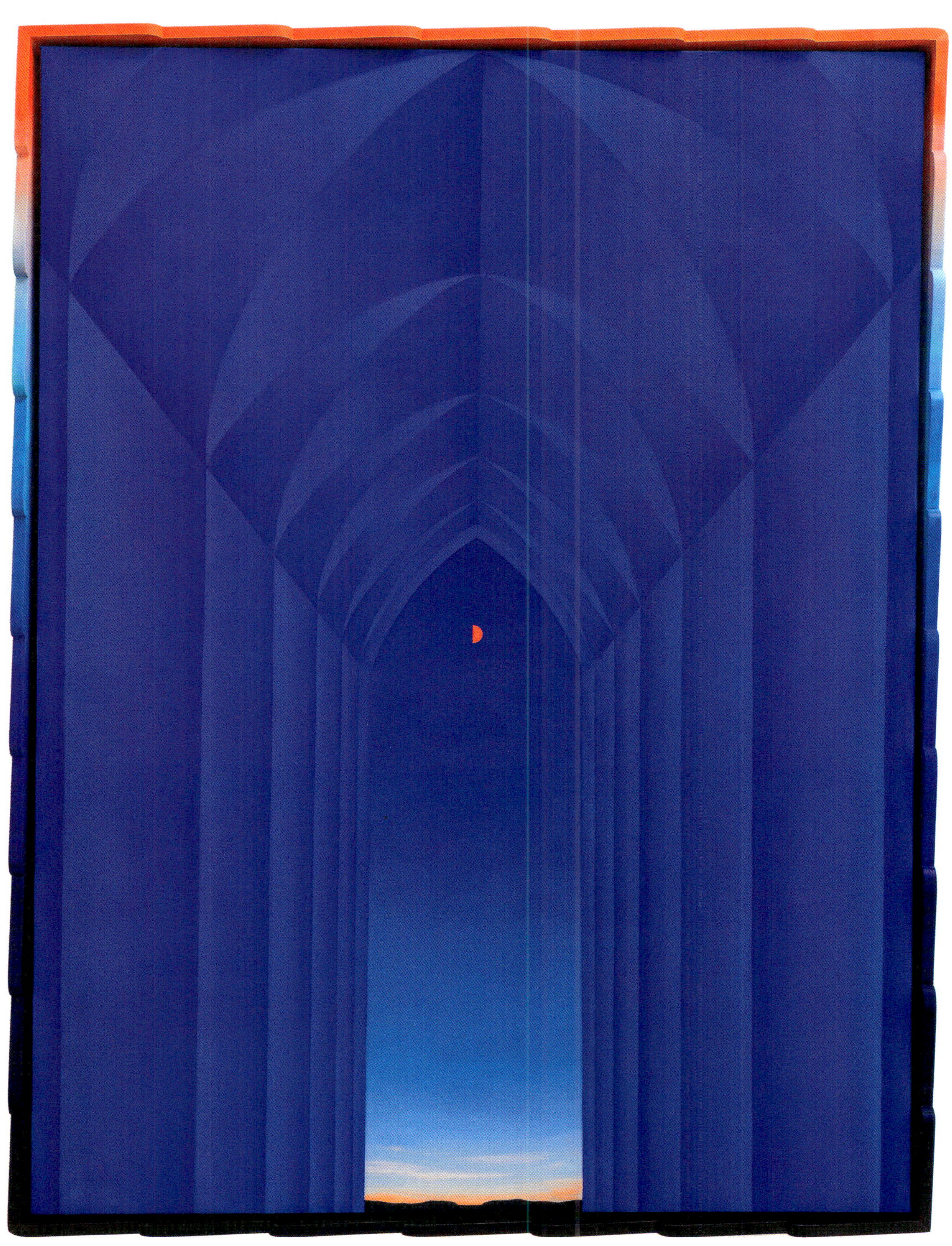

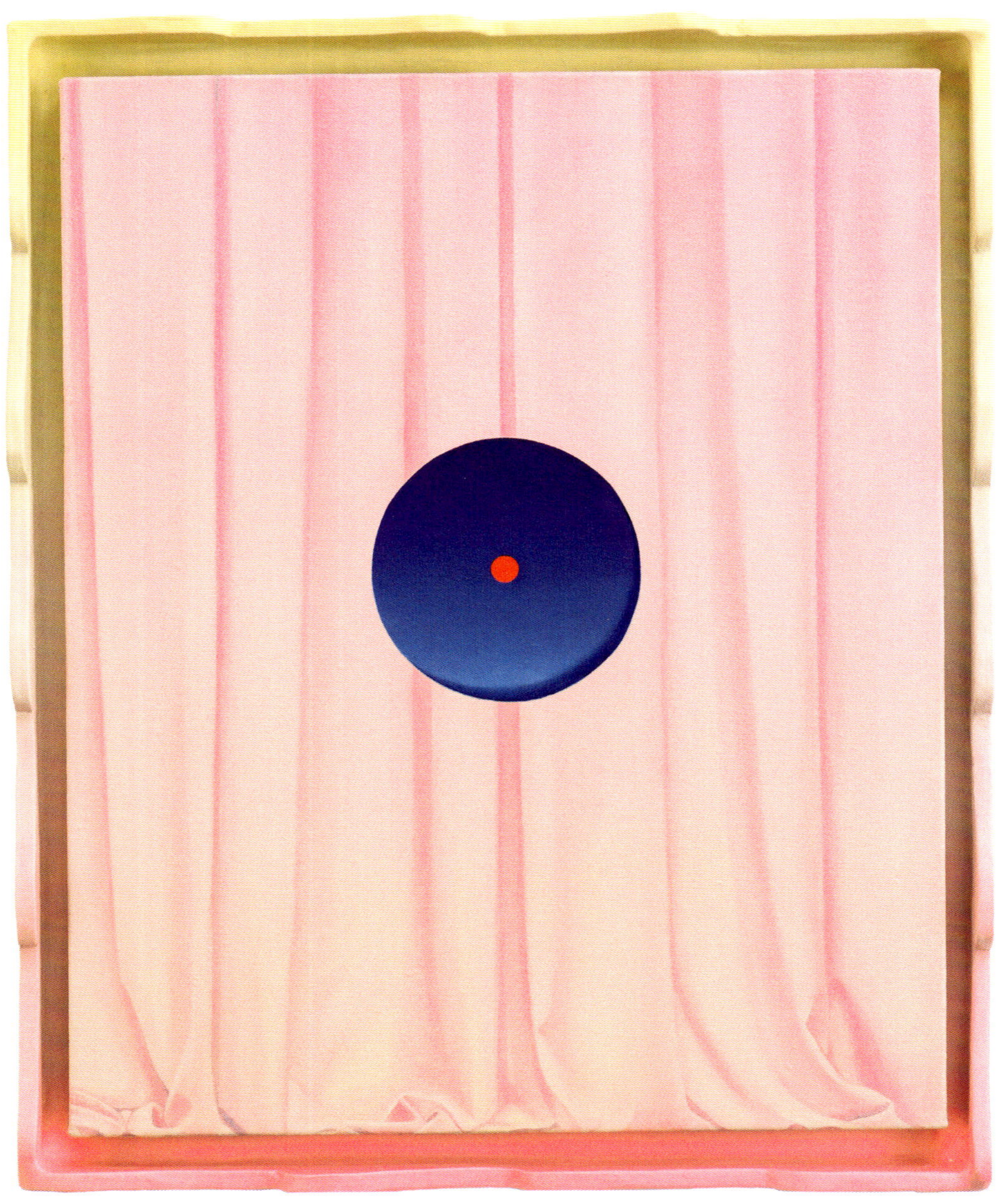

69
The Way Out Is Through, 2025
Oil on linen in ceramic frame
22 × 17½ in.
Collection of Fara White, New Jersey

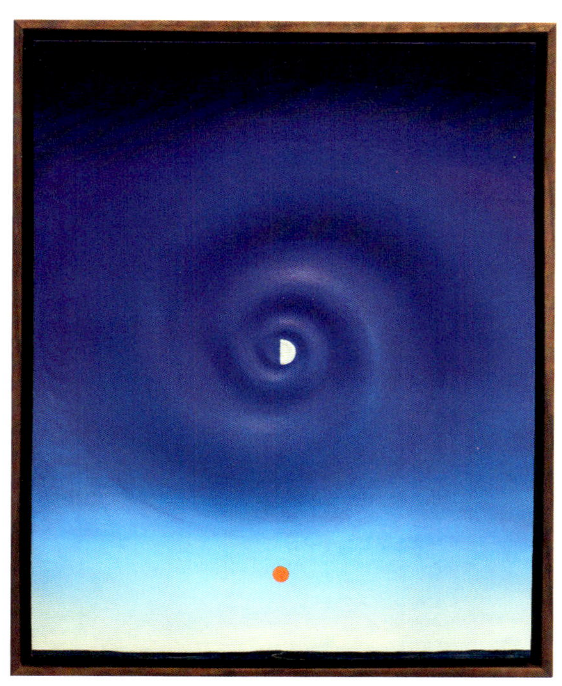

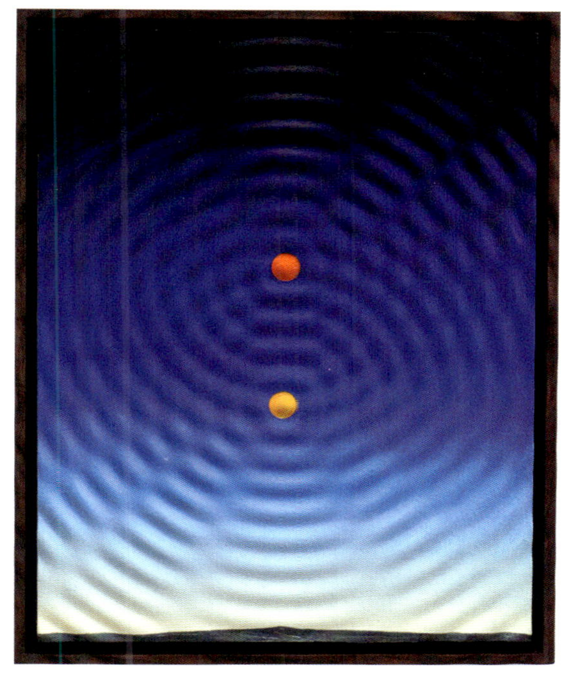

70

Centripetal, 2024

Oil on shaped medium-density fiberboard in wood frame

15 × 12 × 1½ in.

Private collection, courtesy of Red Arrow Gallery

71

Duality, 2024

Oil on shaped medium-density fiberboard in wood frame

15 × 12 × 1¾ in.

Collection of Fadi Braiteh, Nevada

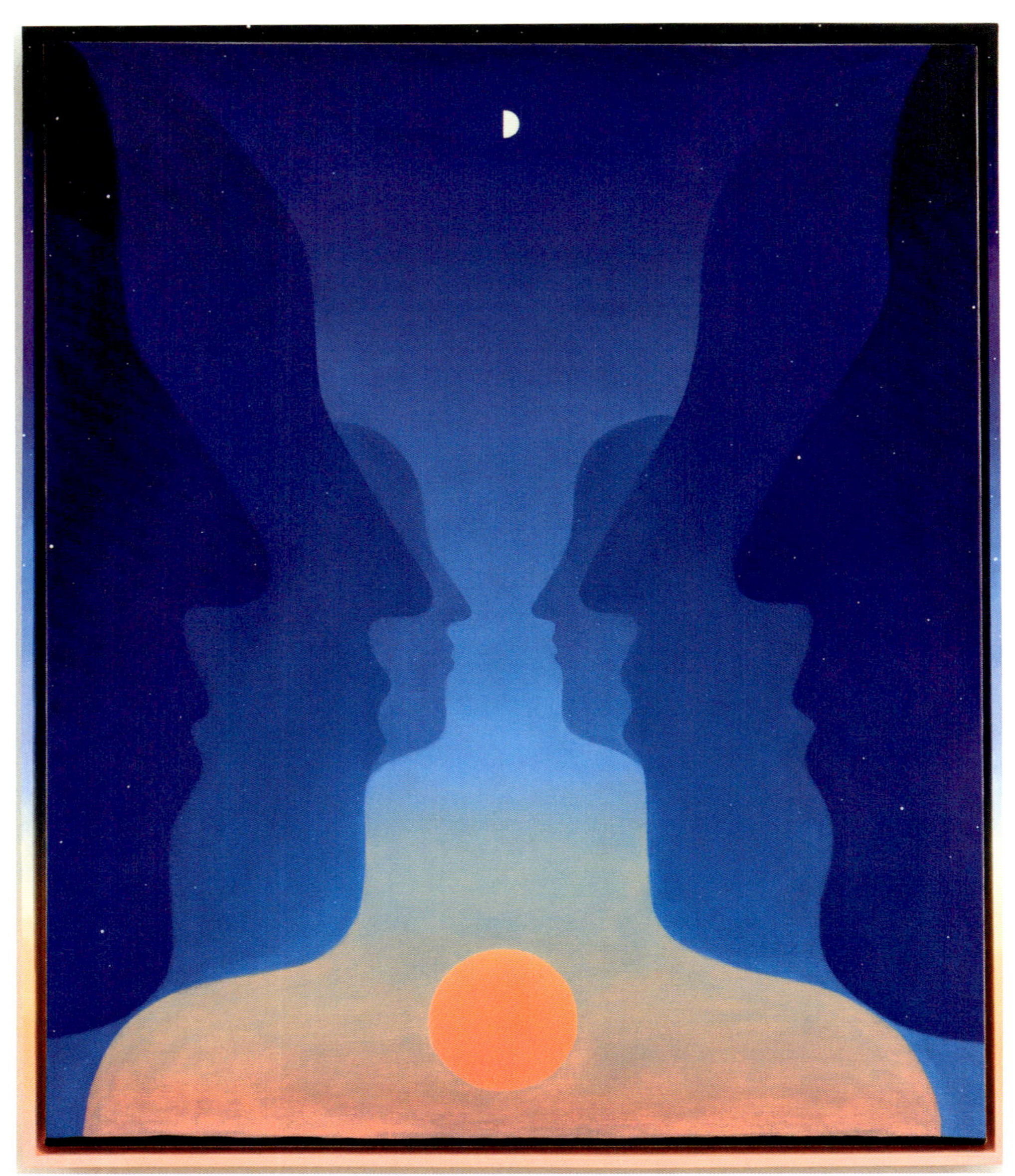

72
Mirror/Mirror, 2024
Oil on linen in painted wood frame
35 × 29 in.
Collection of Sasha and Charlie Sealy

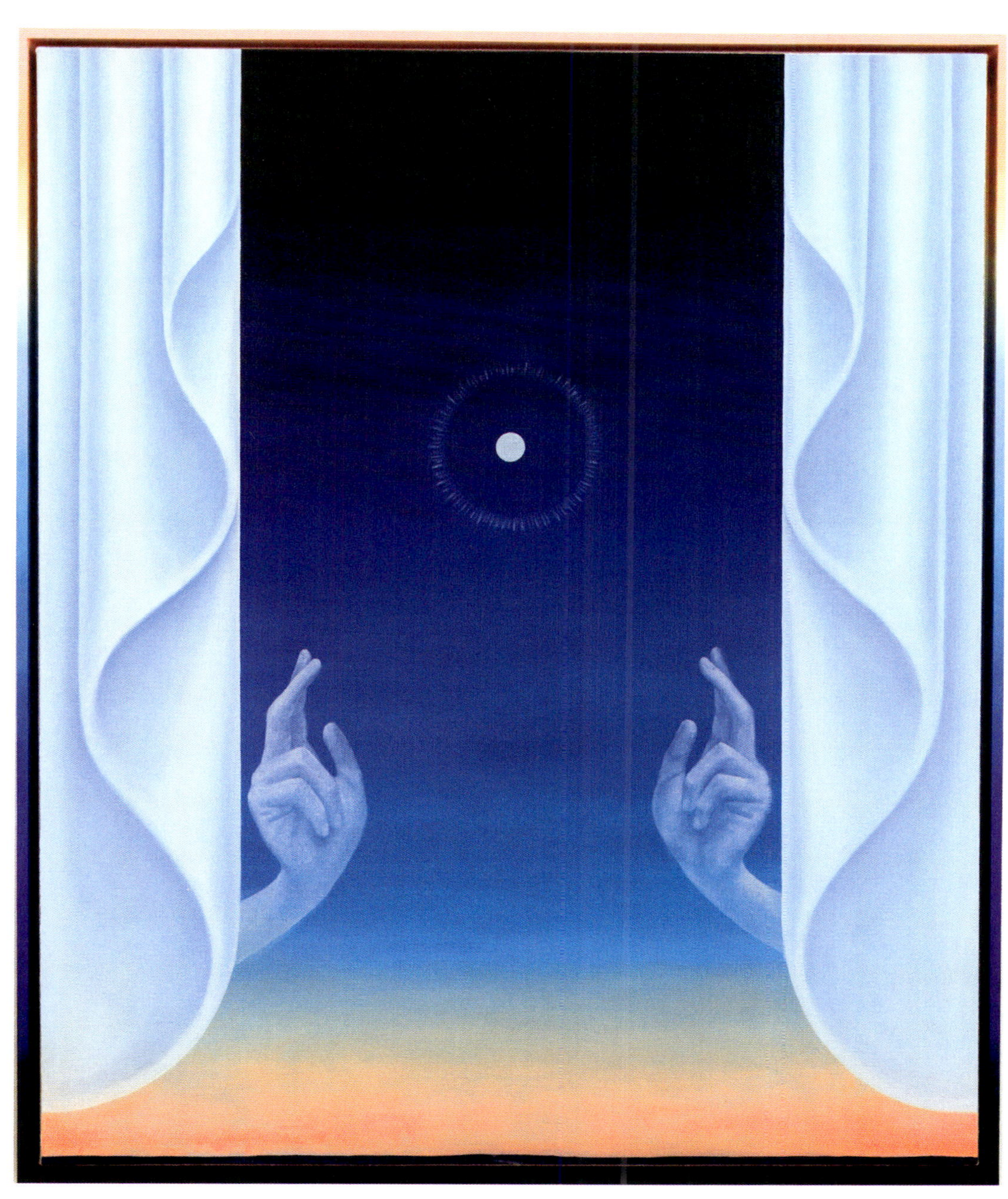

73
Mater Luna, 2024
Oil on linen in painted wood frame
35 × 29 in.
Collection of Fara White, New Jersey

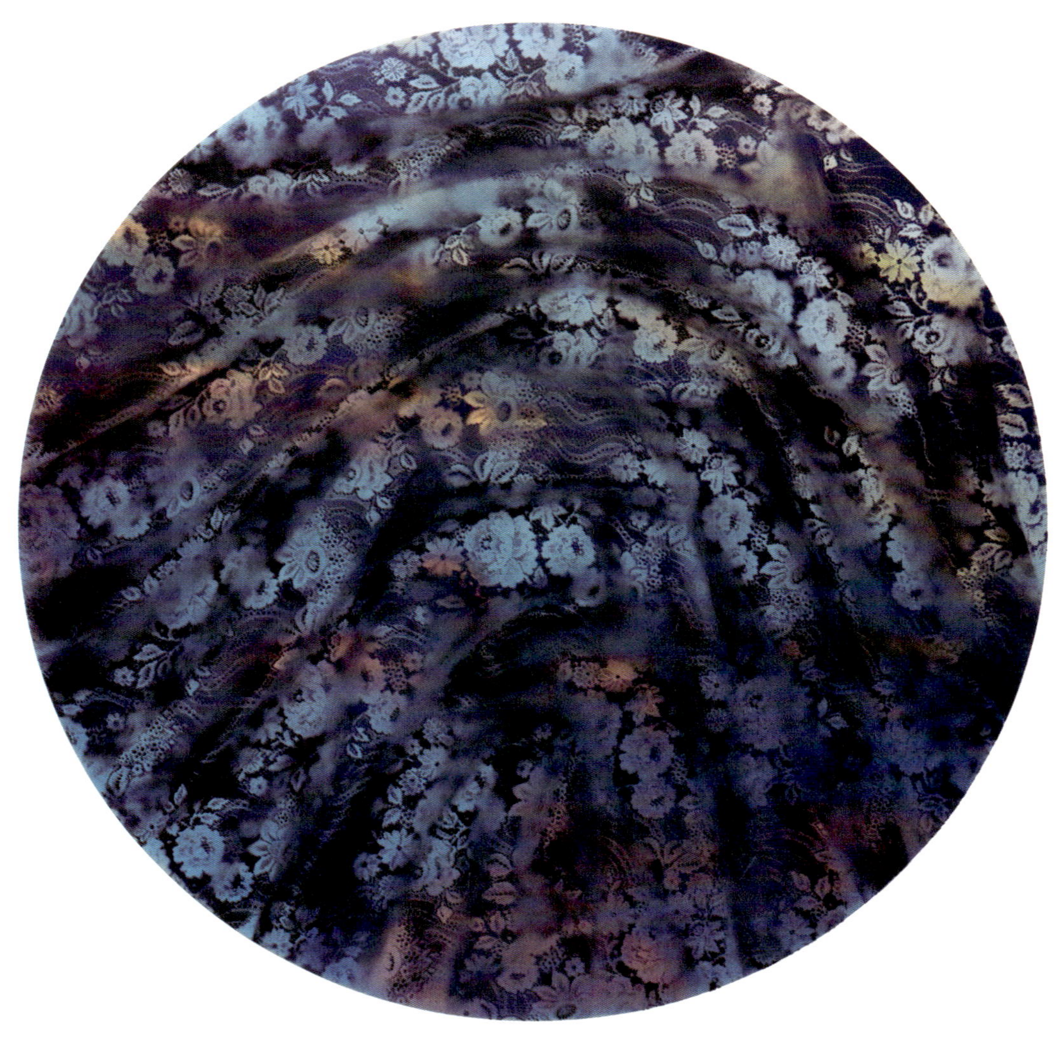

74
The Day That Just Won't End, 2023
Acrylic on wood
37 in. diameter

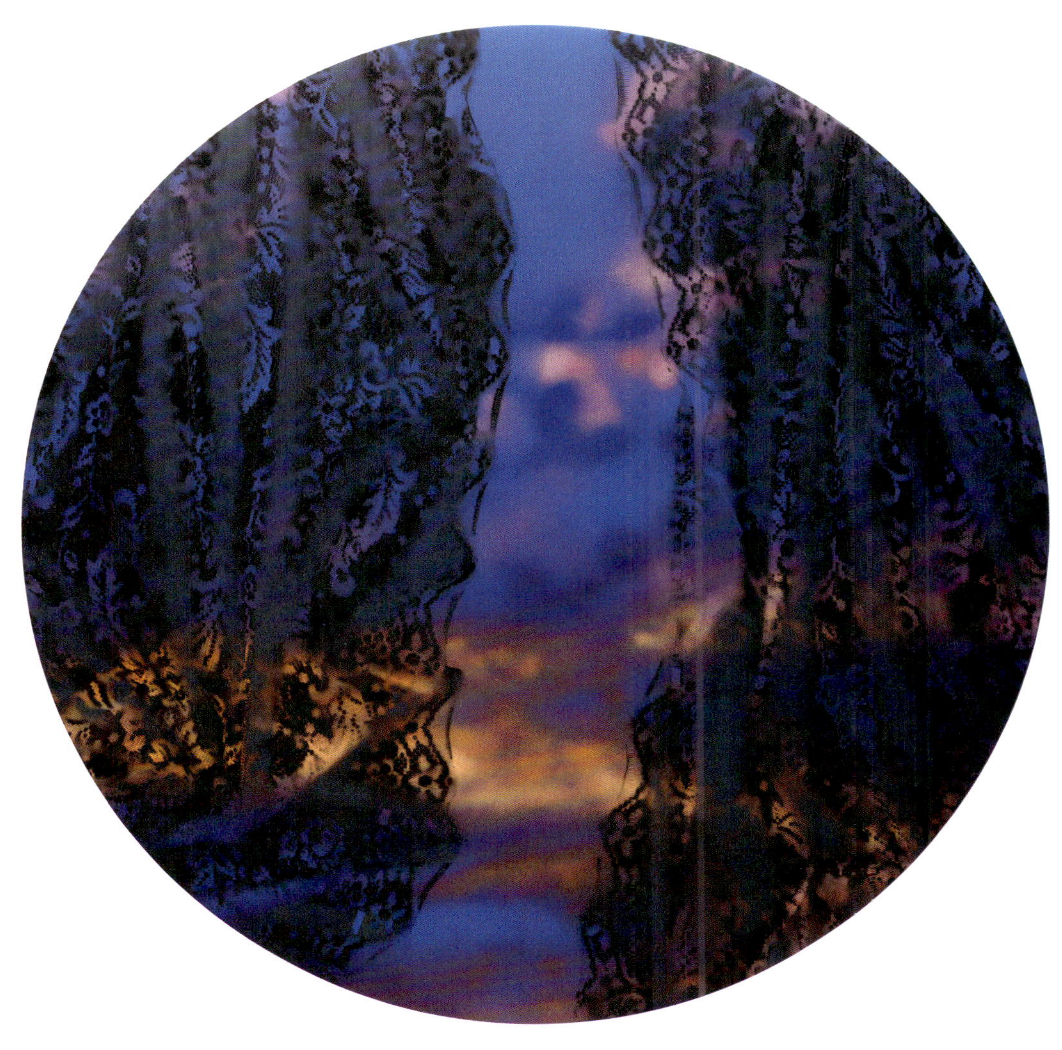

75
How Do You Spell Your Name?, 2024
Acrylic on wood
47 in. diameter

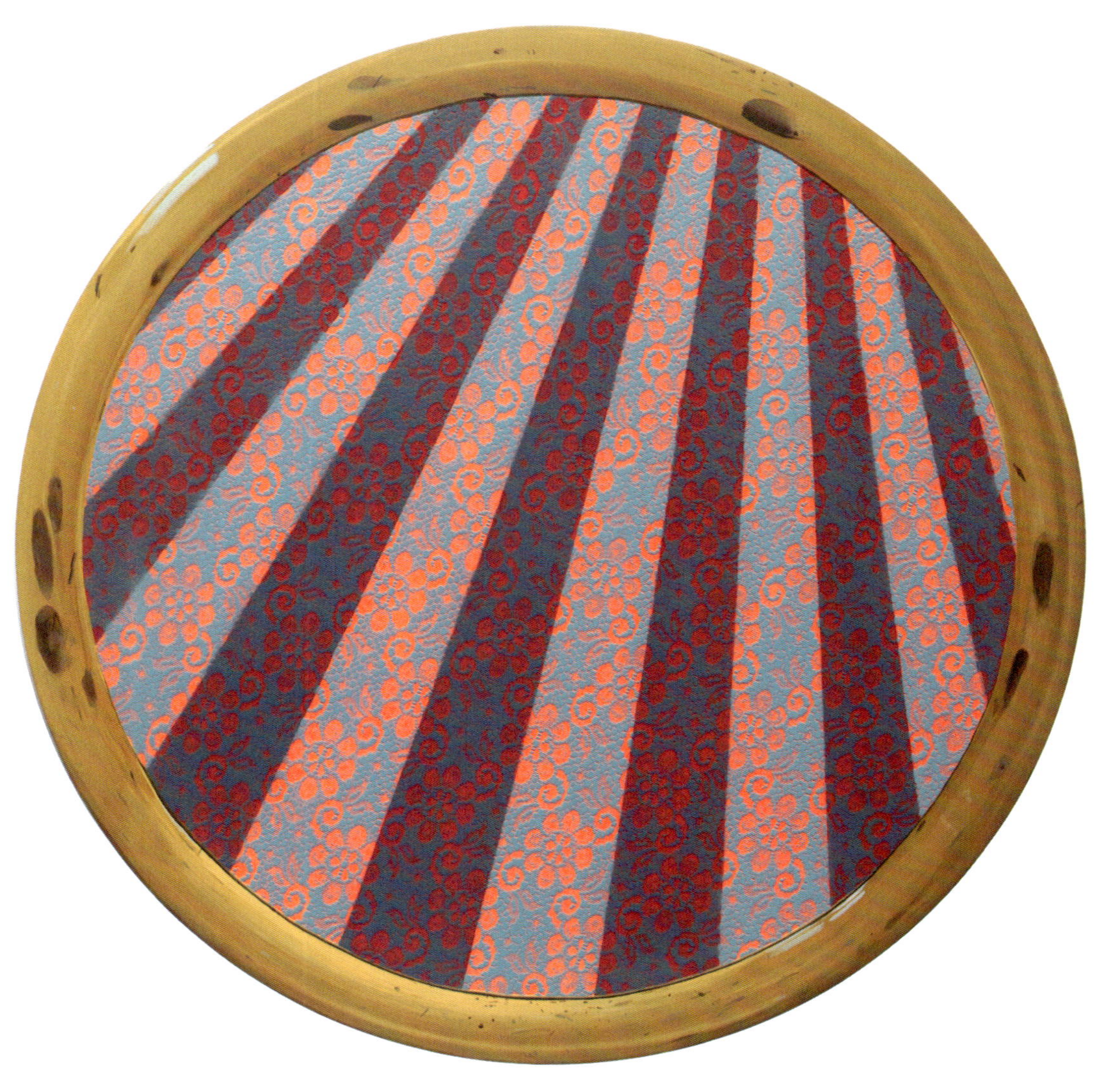

76
Knotty Pine, Pleats, 2024
Acrylic, vinyl, and oil on wood
37 in. diameter

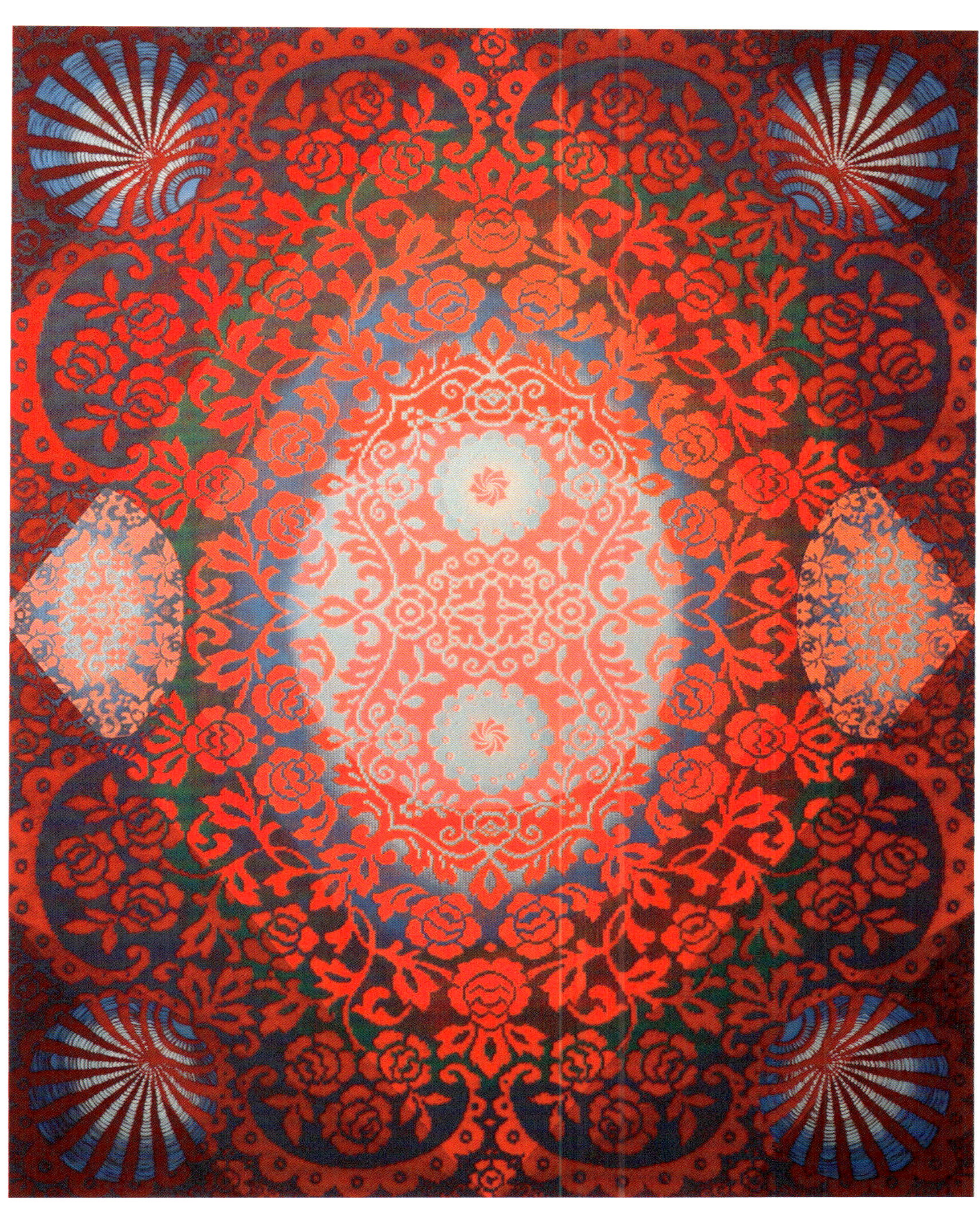

77
Double Double, 2023
Acrylic and vinyl on canvas
84 × 68 in.
Hines-T3 Wedgewood Houston Collection, Nashville

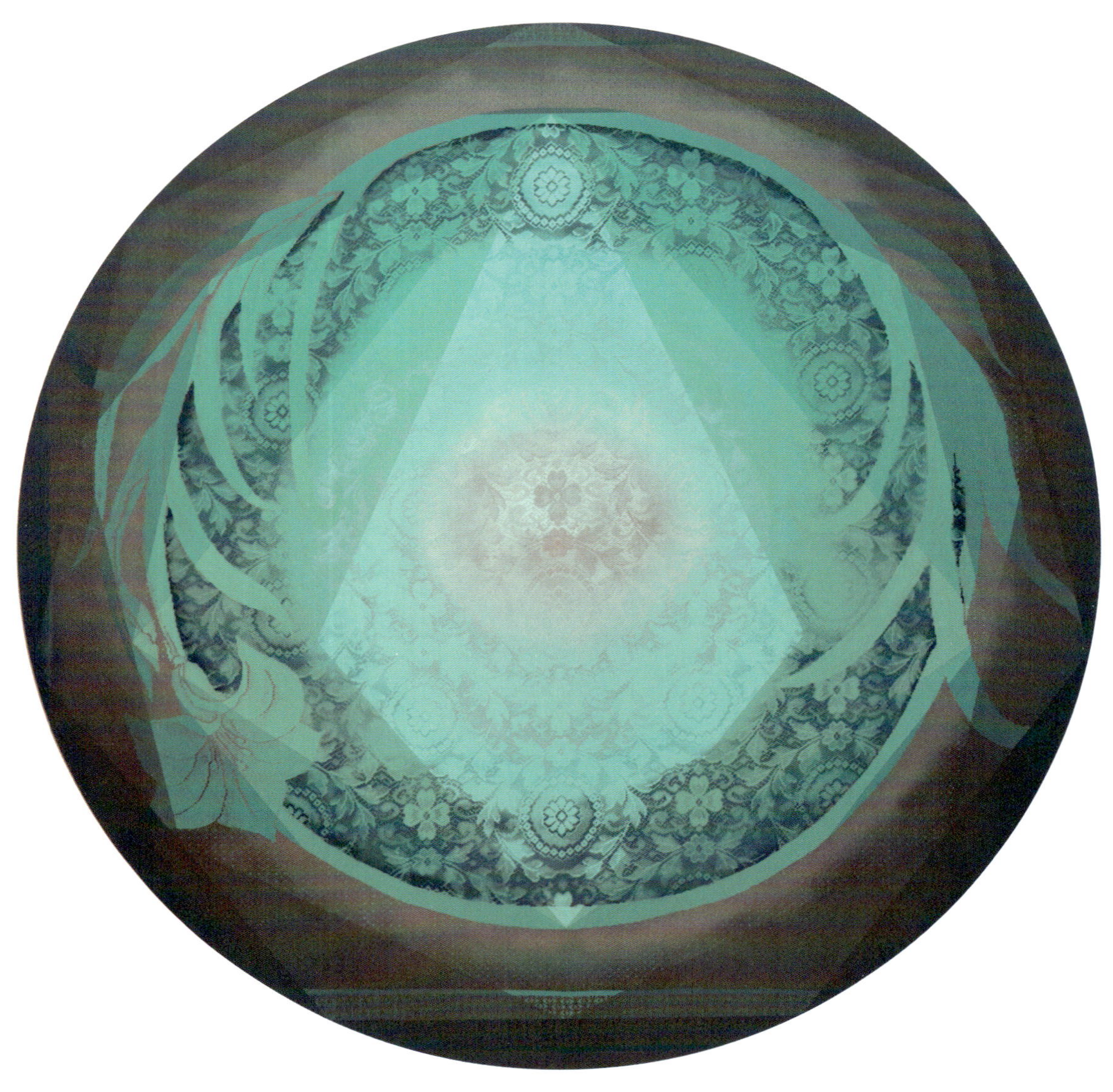

78
It Was Just the Arbutus Rustling, 2024
Acrylic on wood
59 in. diameter

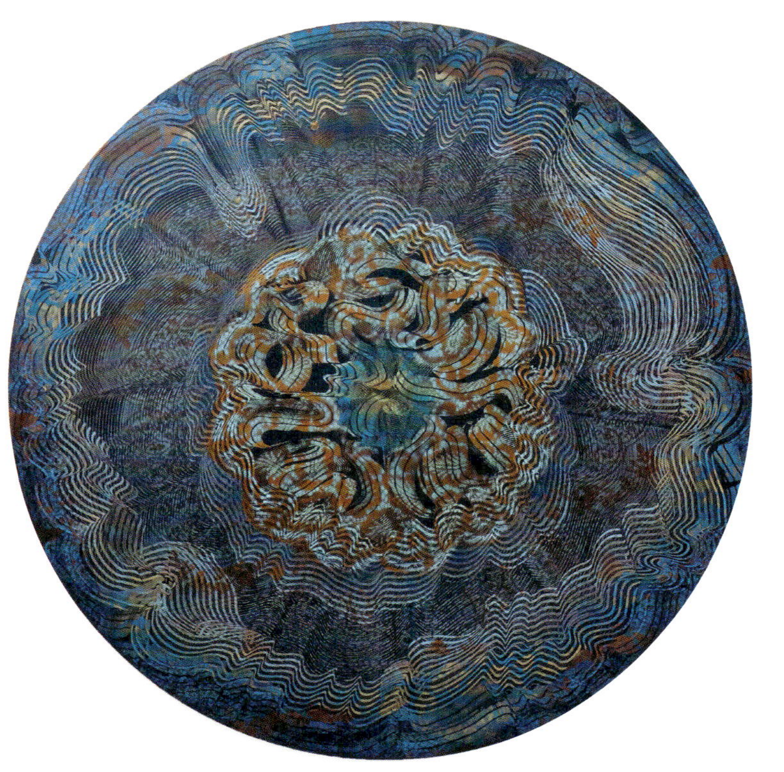

79
Last One In, 2022
Acrylic and oil on wood
47 in. diameter
Collection of Melanie and Chris Moran

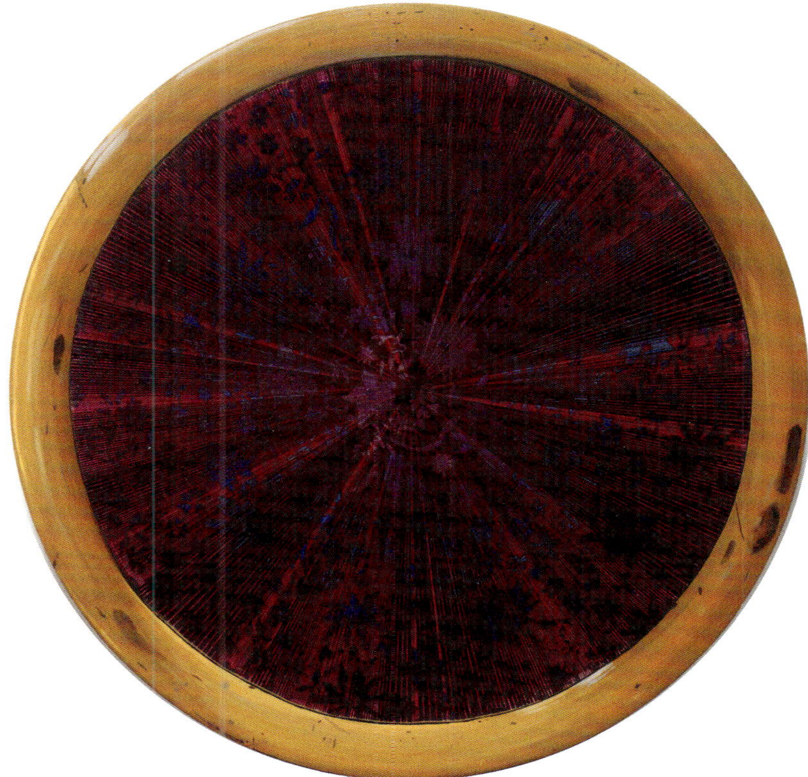

80
Selfie, 2024
Acrylic, vinyl, and oil on wood
20¼ in. diameter

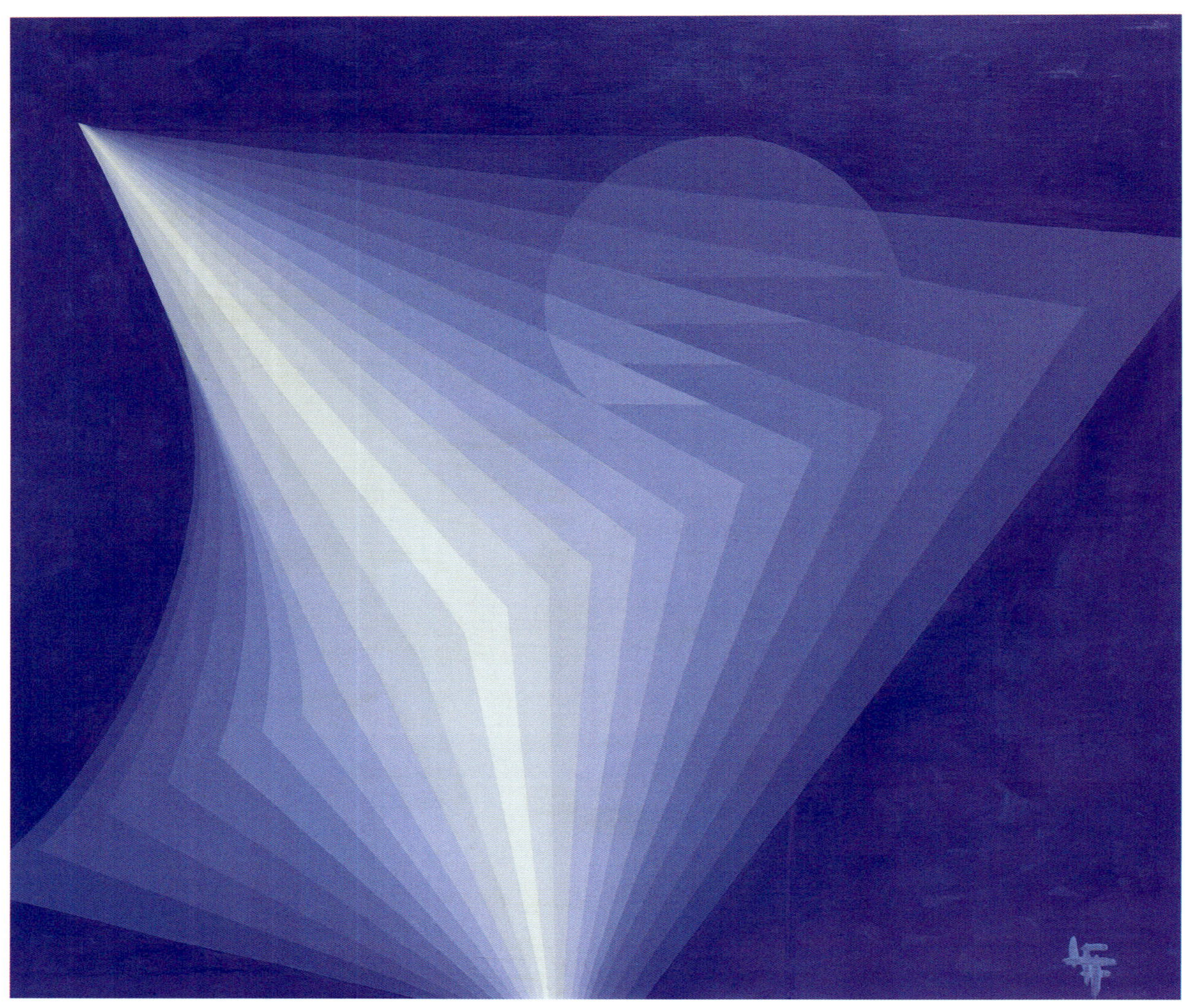

81
Indigo Sunrise, 1985
Acrylic on canvas
42½ × 48 in.

82
Radiator Building, 2014
Acrylic on canvas
20 × 16 in.

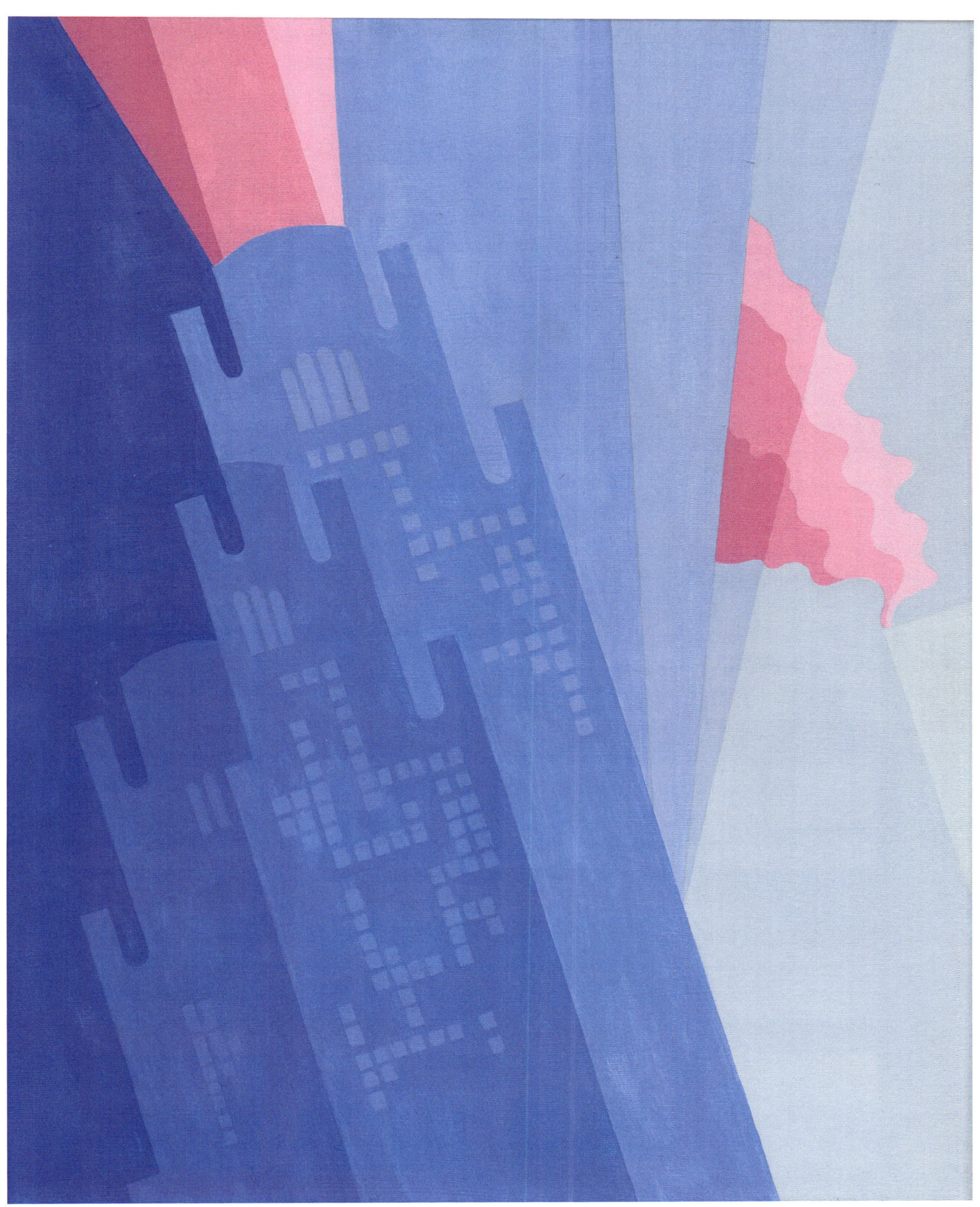

141 **LIFRAN FORT**

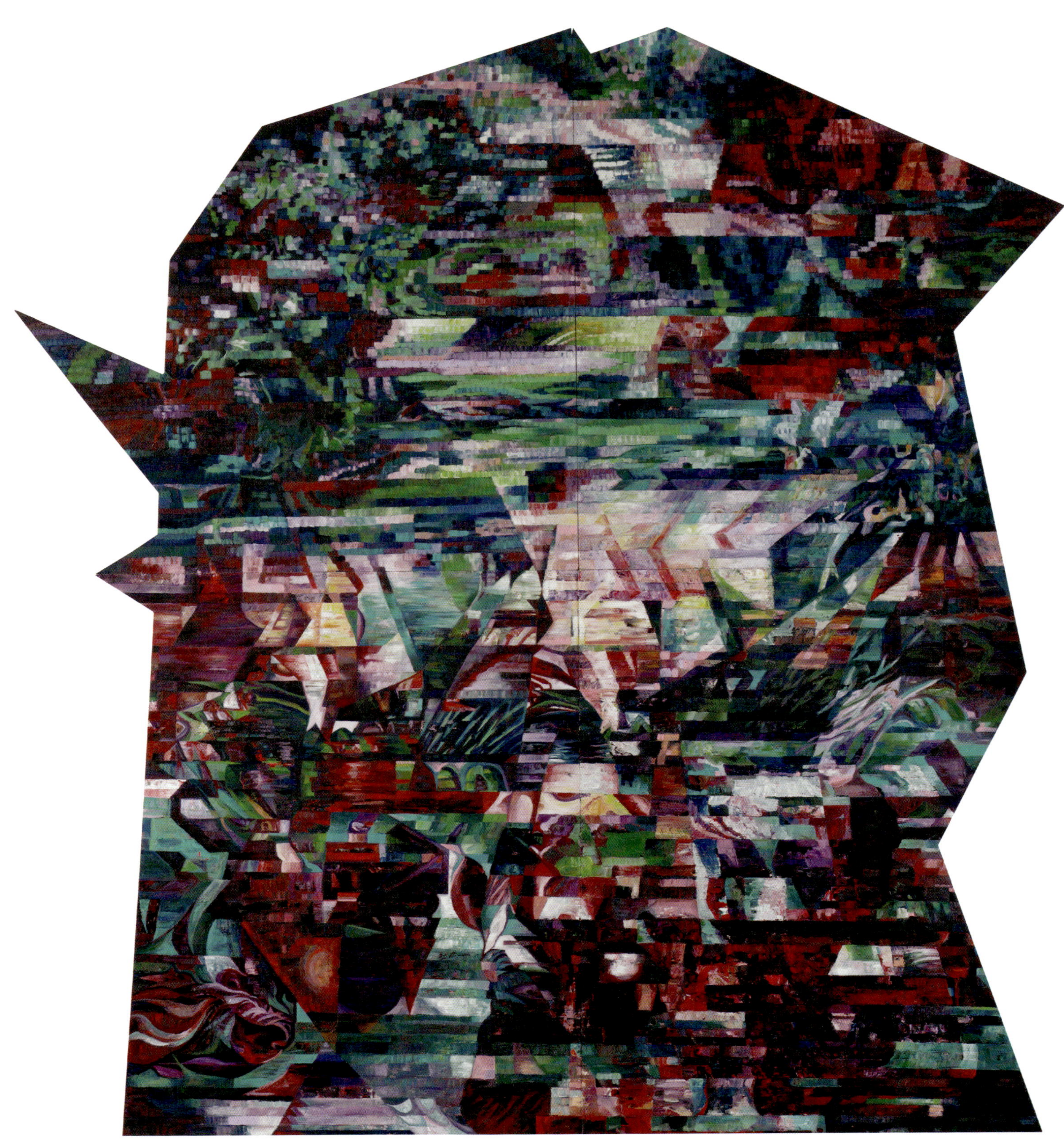

83
Birds of Prey, 2025
Oil on board
100 × 85 × 2½ in. overall

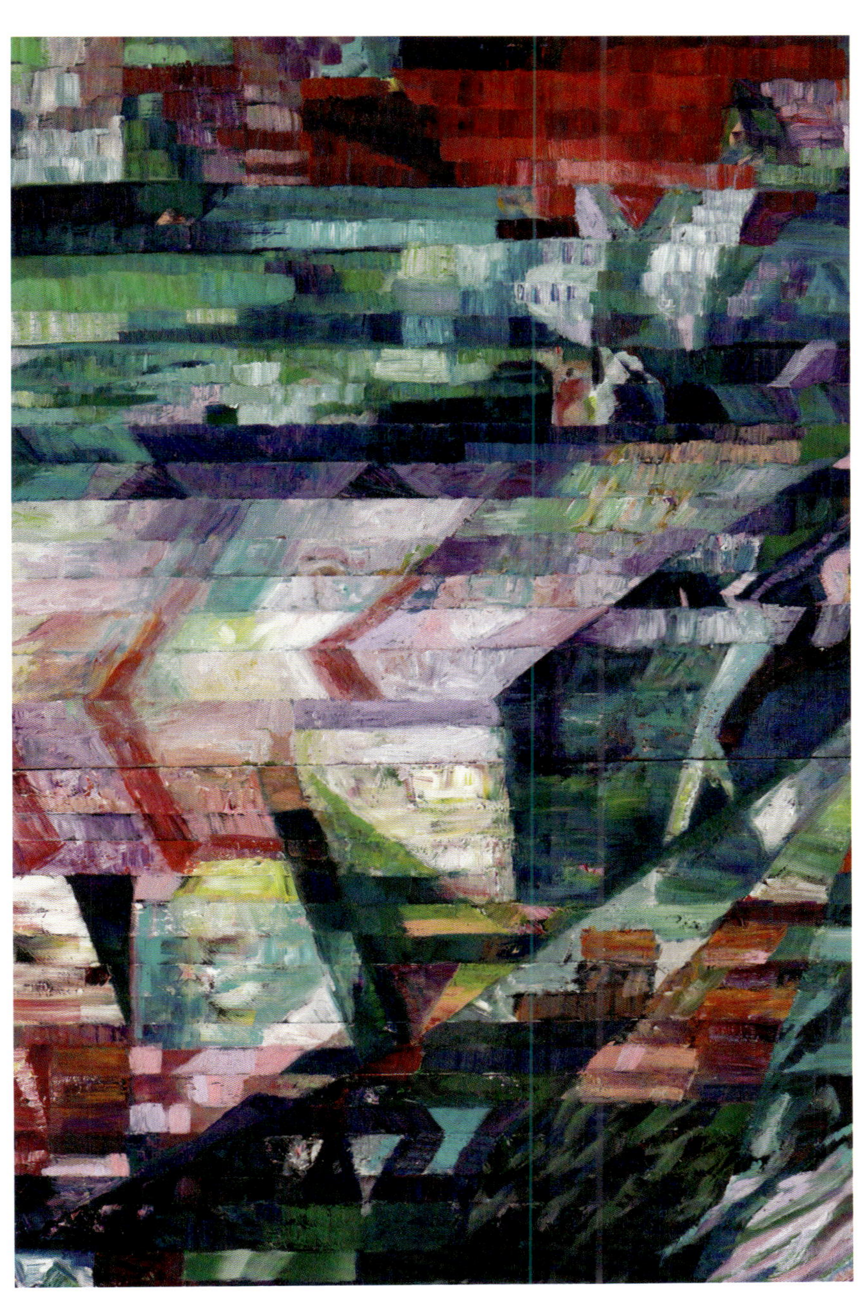

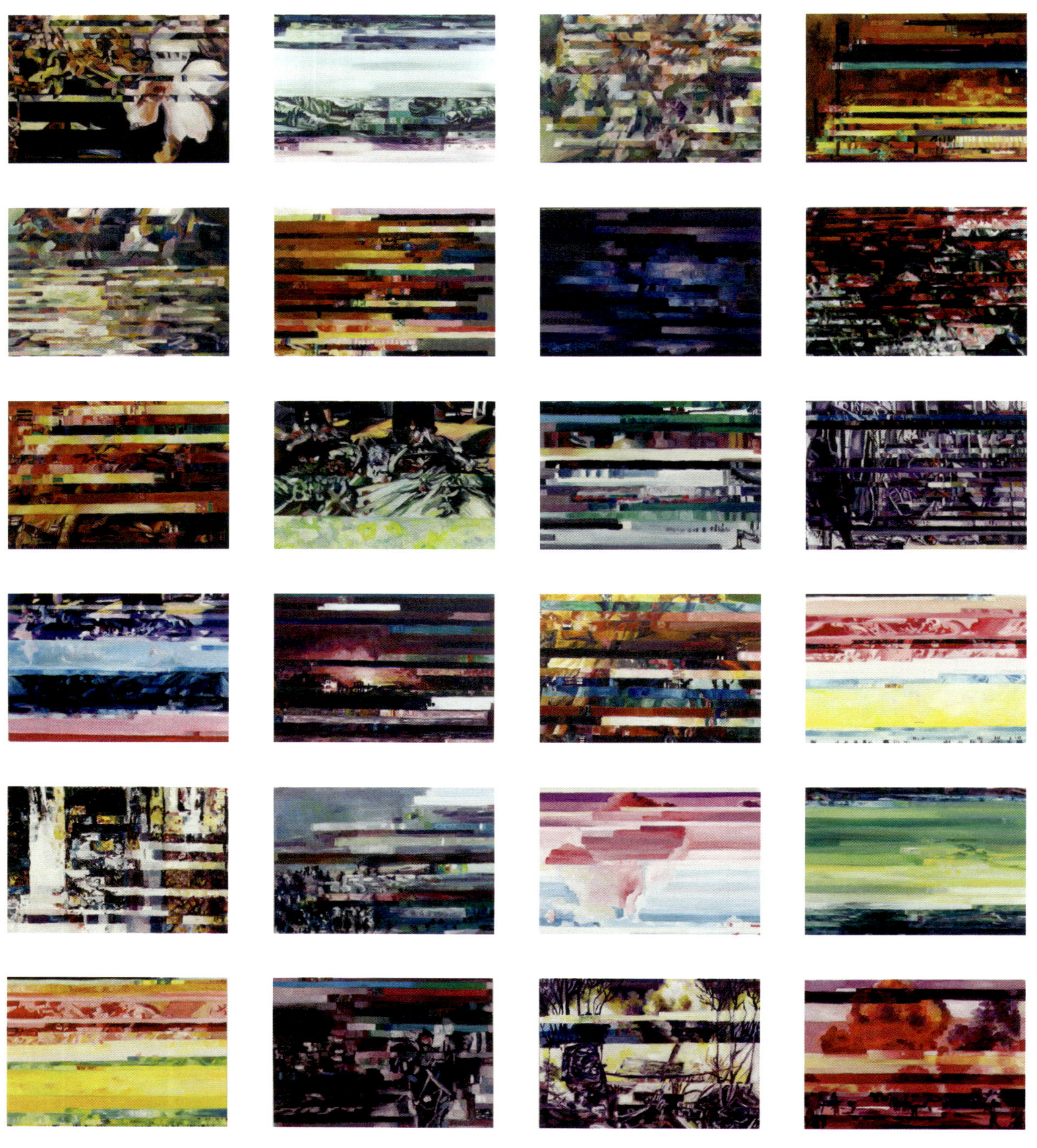

84
Whispers of Hope #21–#79, 2025
Oil on board
58 parts: 5 × 7 in. each

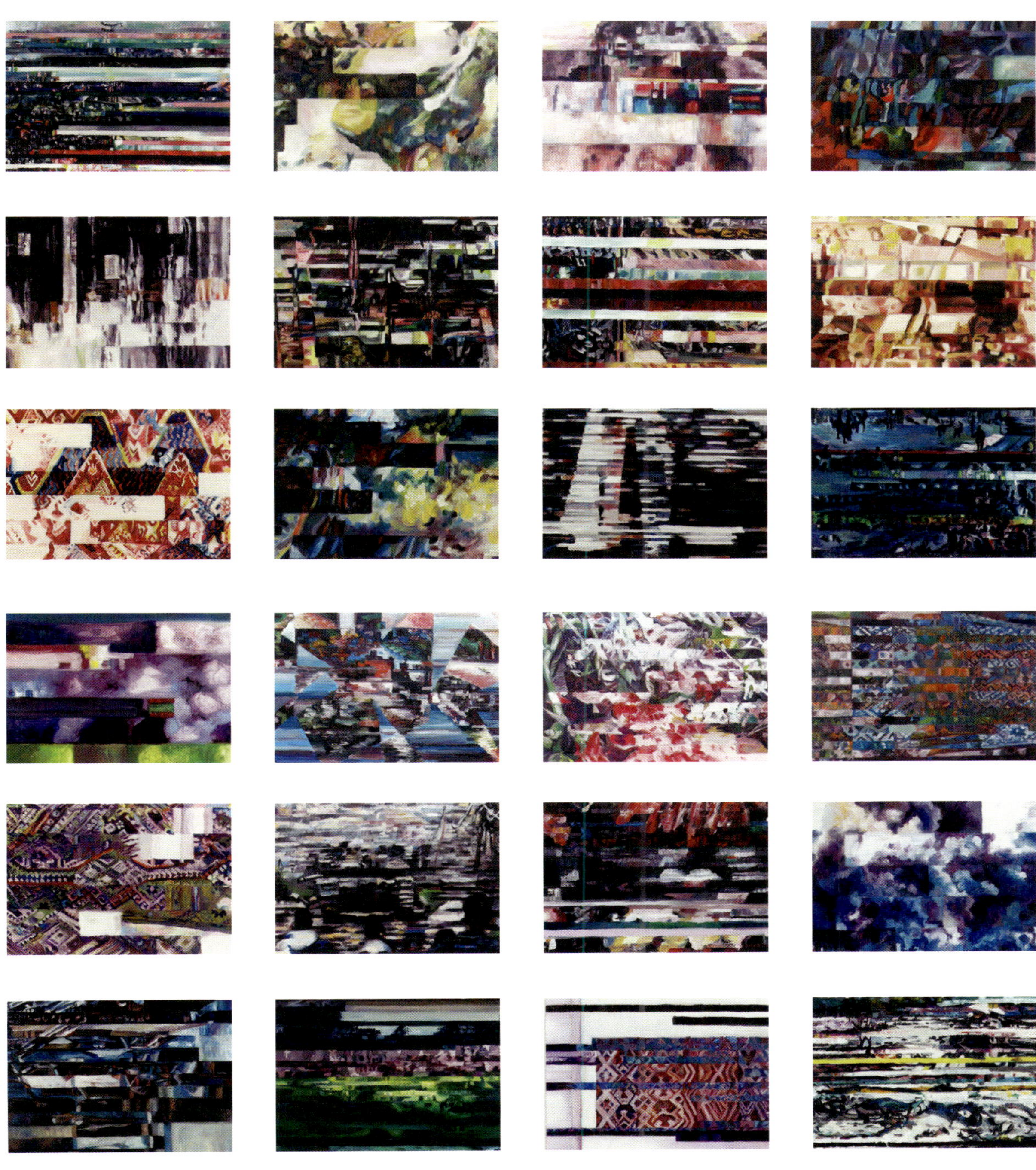

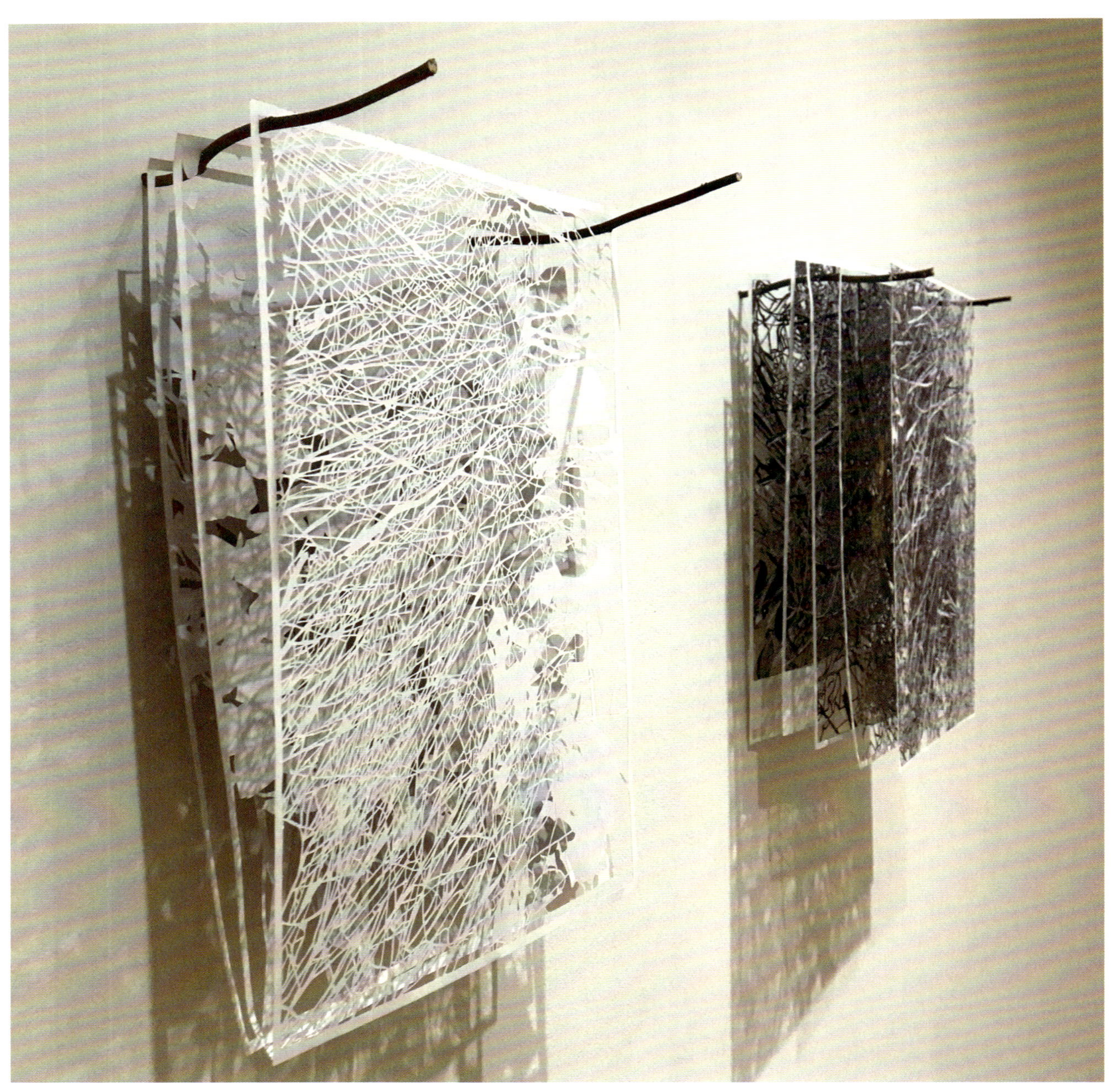

85
H.E.H., 2022–23
Cut paper and rose stems
8 parts: 17 × 11 in. each

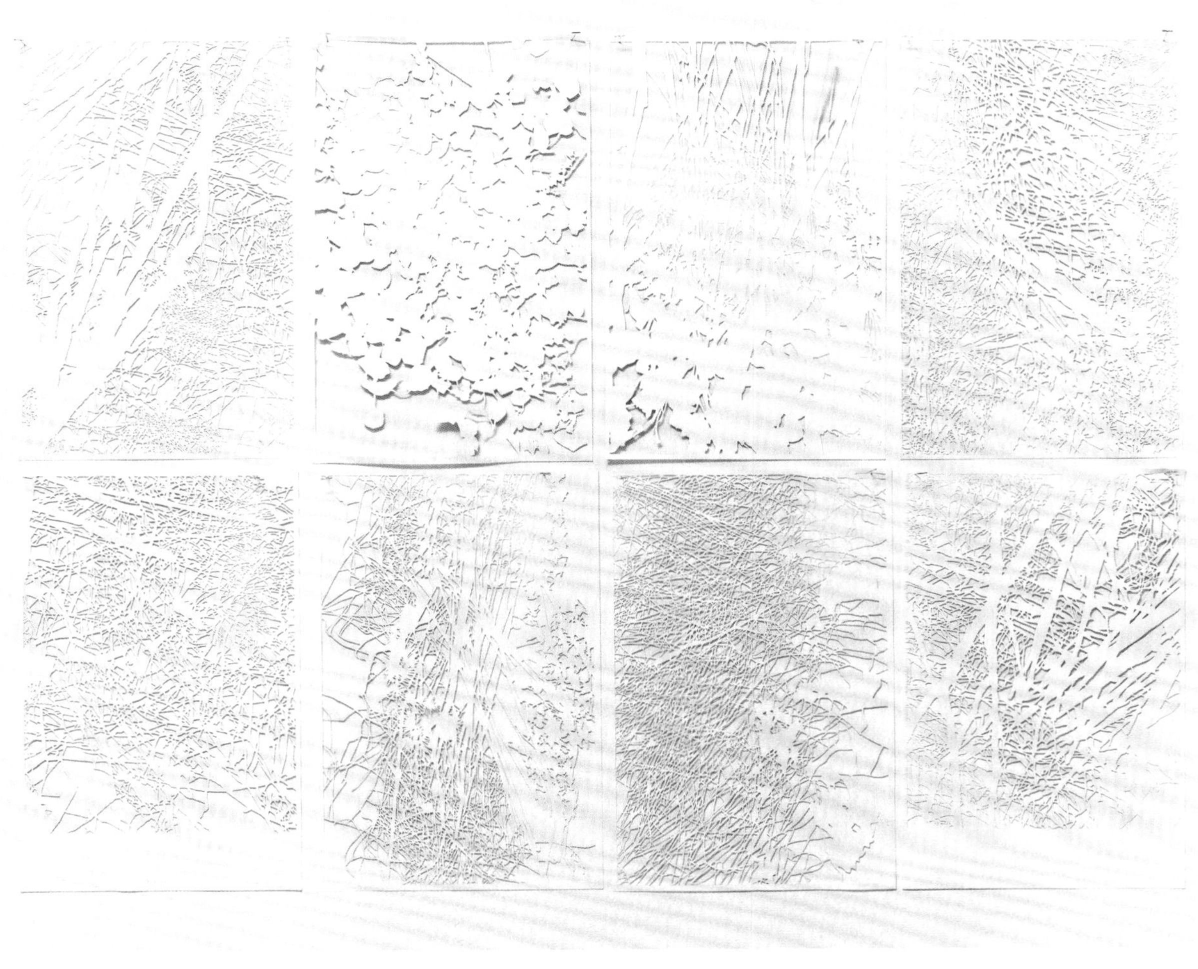

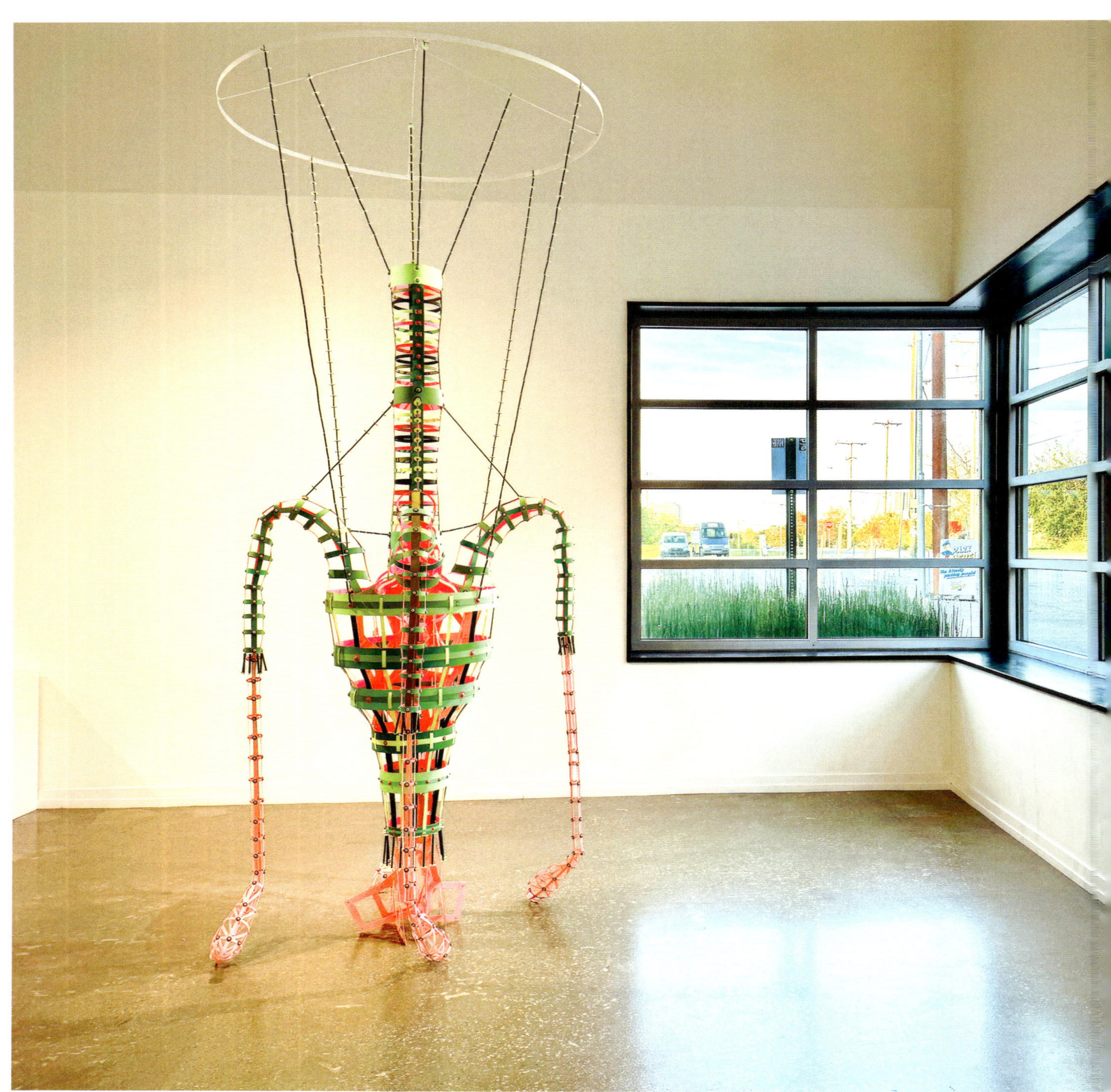

86

doily, 2024

Suspended paper, acrylic paint, metal brads, and string

102 × 48 × 48 in.

Installation view, Zeitgeist Gallery, 2025

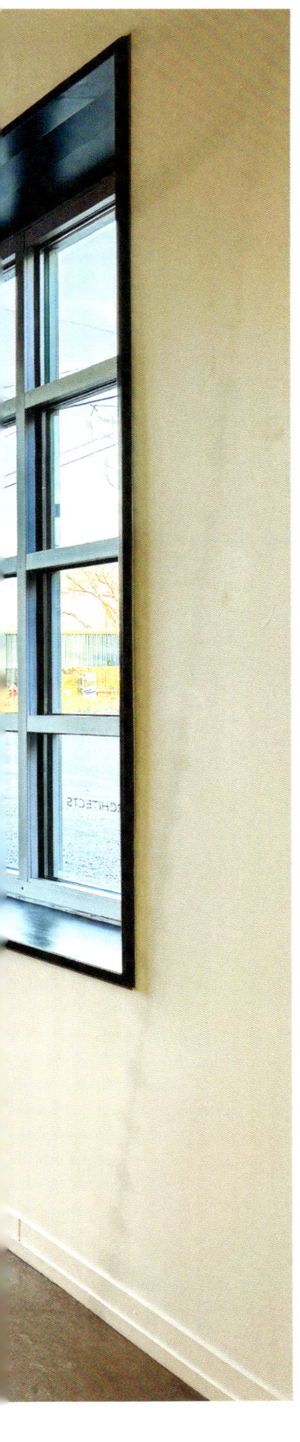

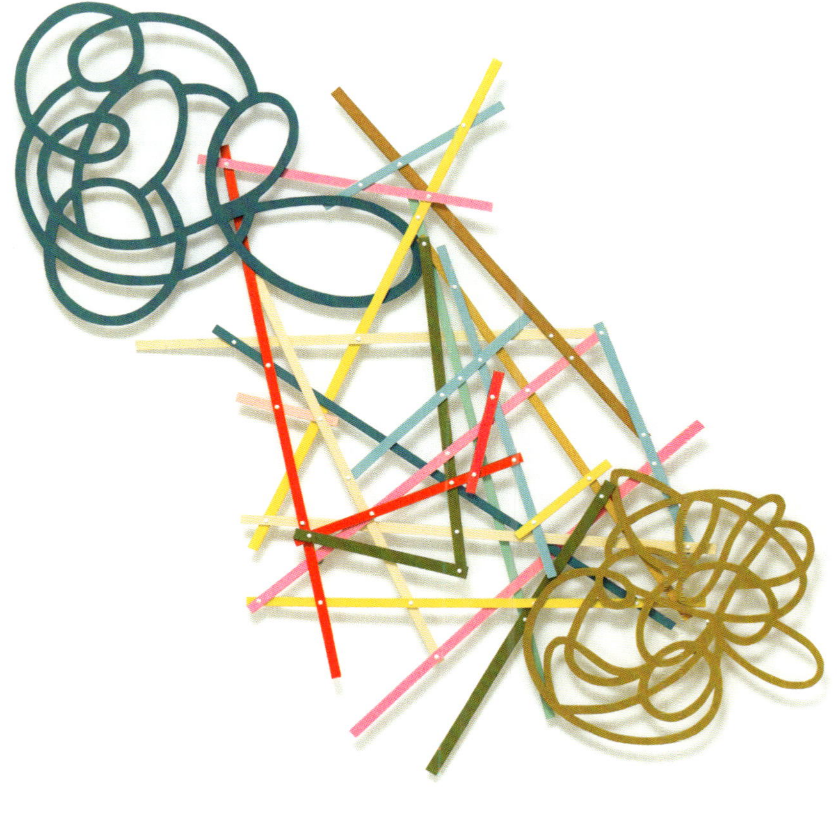

87

nest, 2022

Hand-cut paper board, acrylic paint, and metal brads

25 × 17½ in.

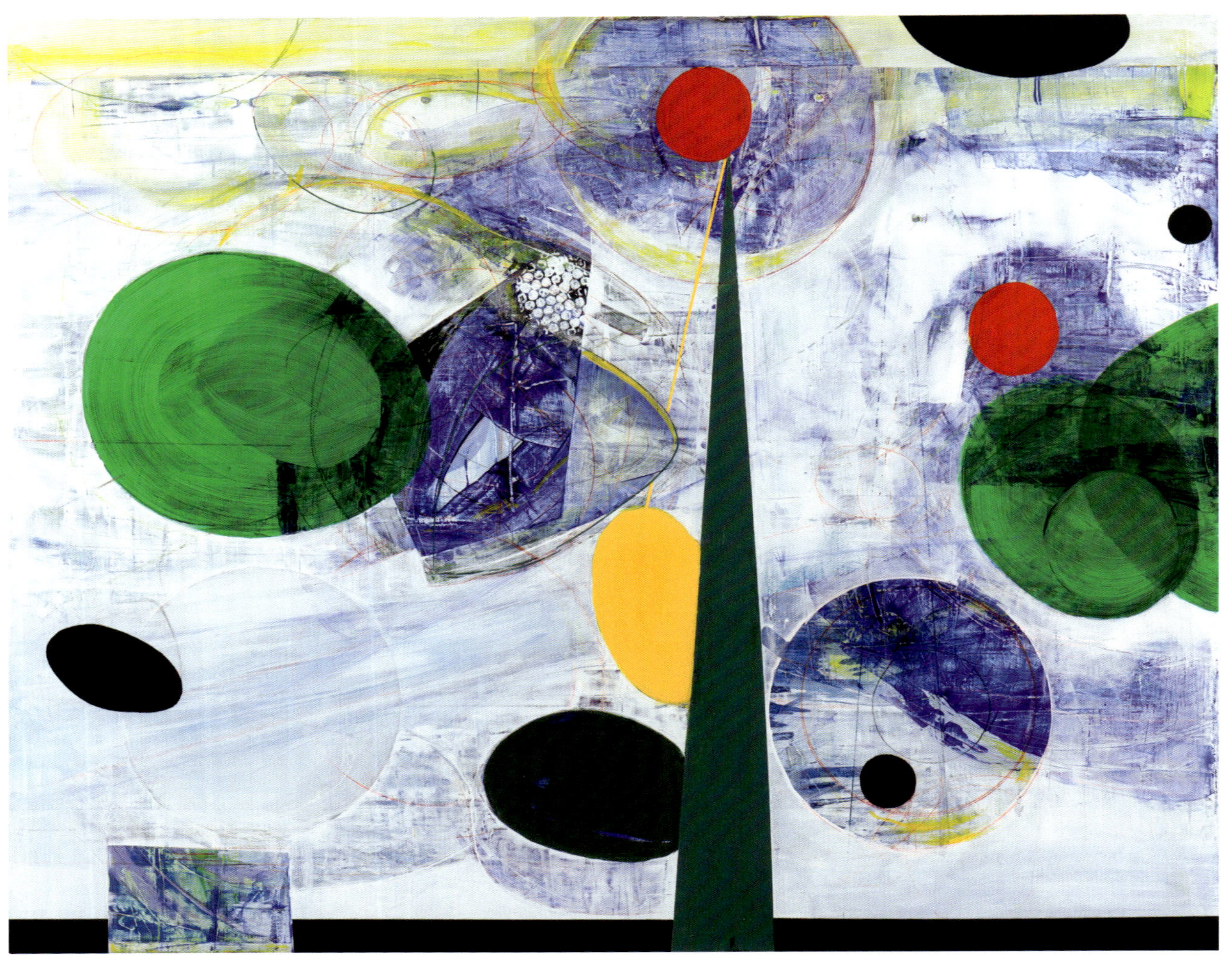

88
EMERGENCE, 2025
Acrylic on canvas
40 × 50 in.

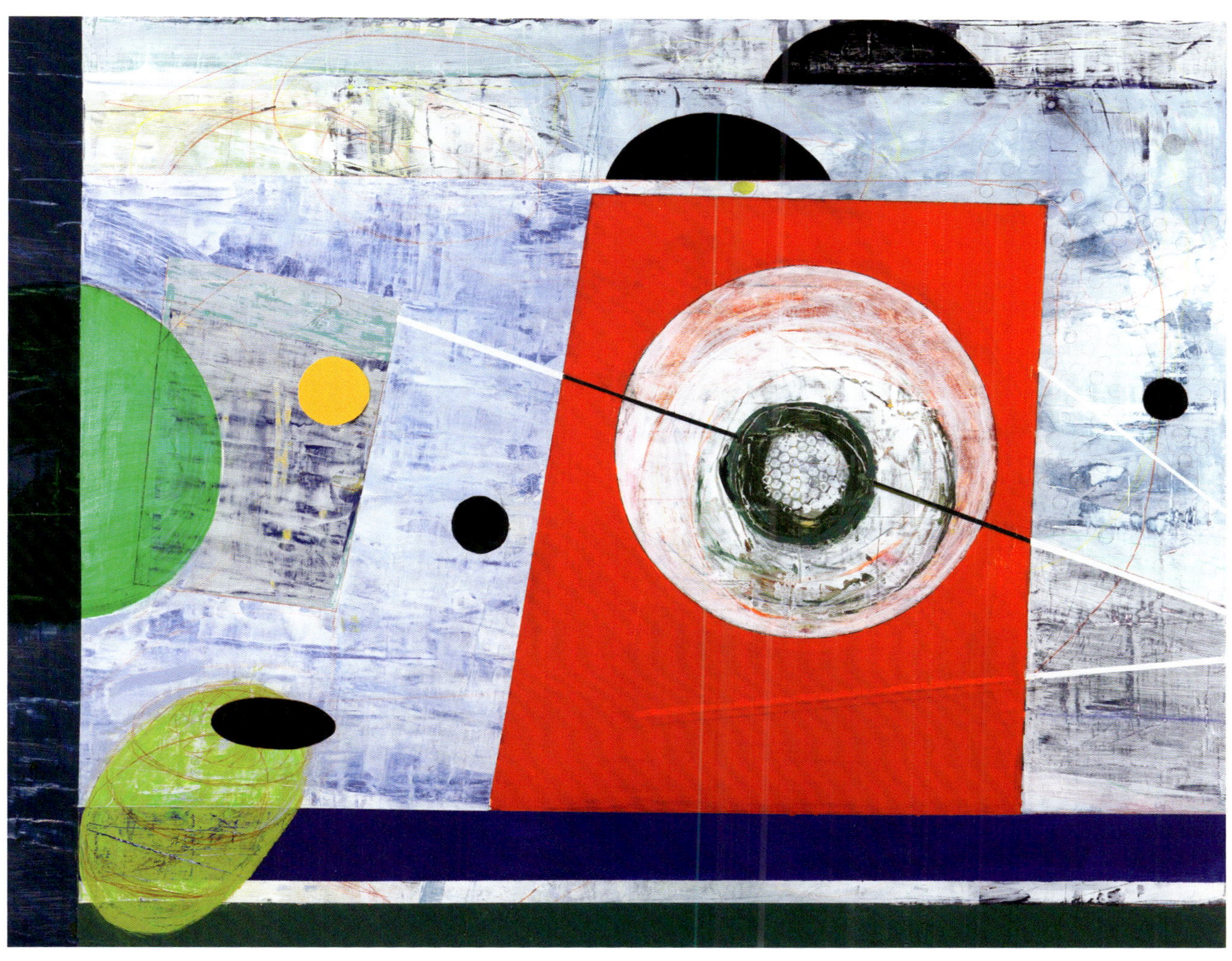

89
ENTITY, 2025
Acrylic on canvas
40 × 50 in.

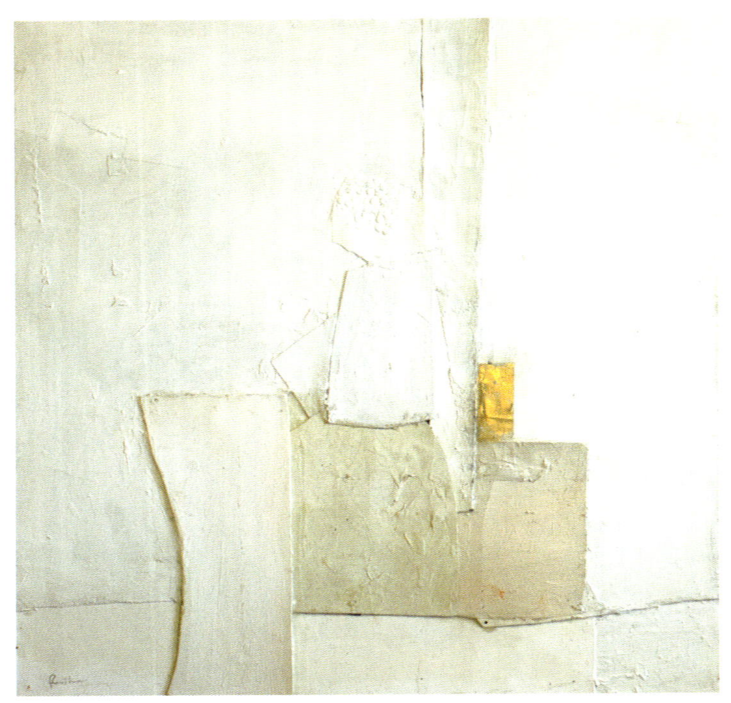

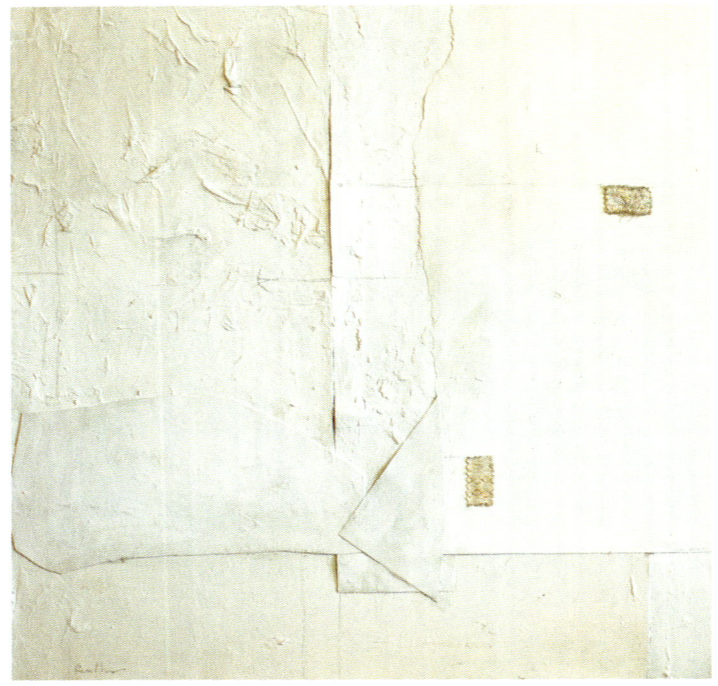

90
Untitled I, 2021
Mixed media on paper
22 × 22 in.

91
Untitled II, 2021
Mixed media on paper
22 × 22 in.

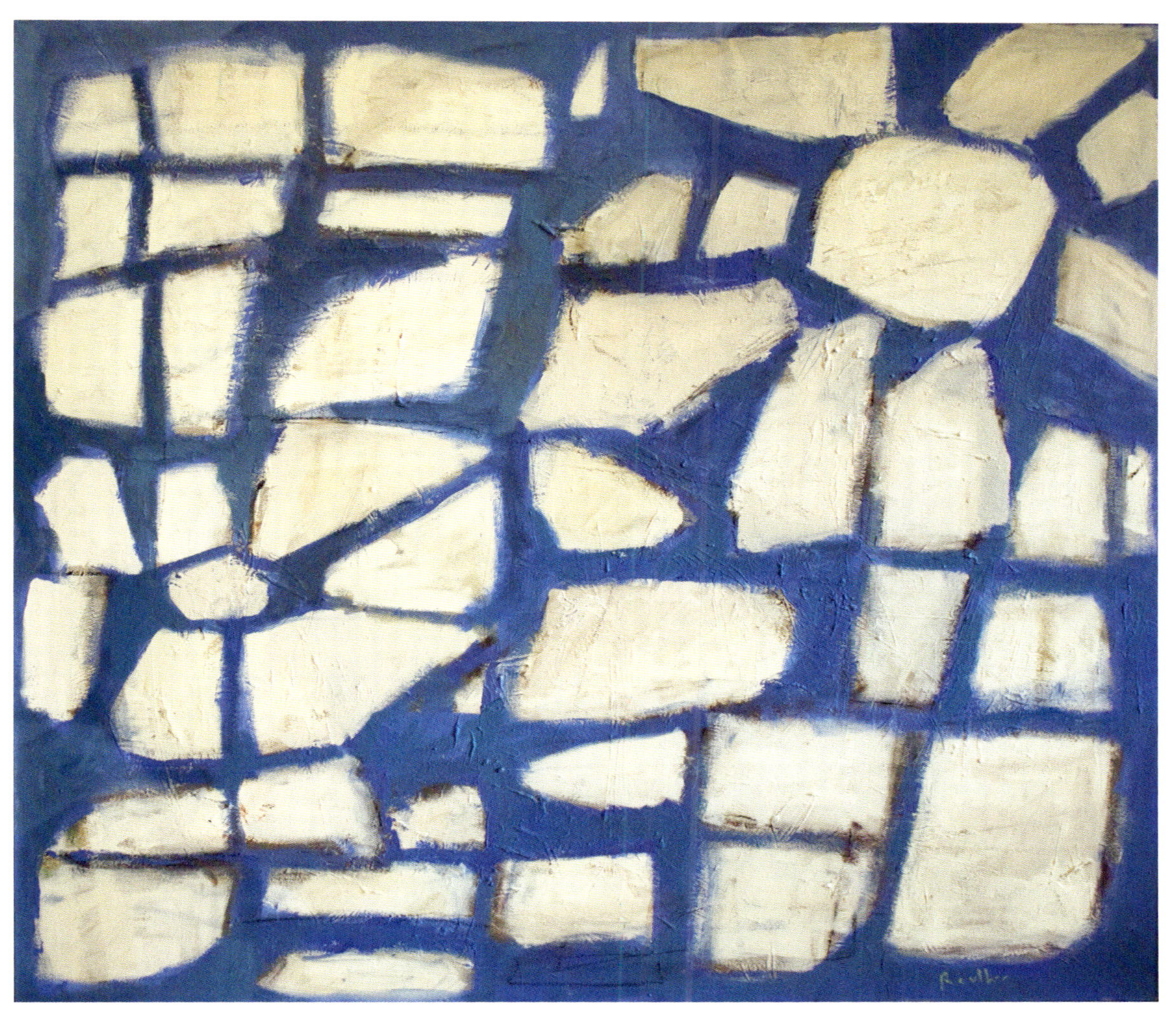

92
Sky, 2024
Oil on canvas
50 × 56 in.

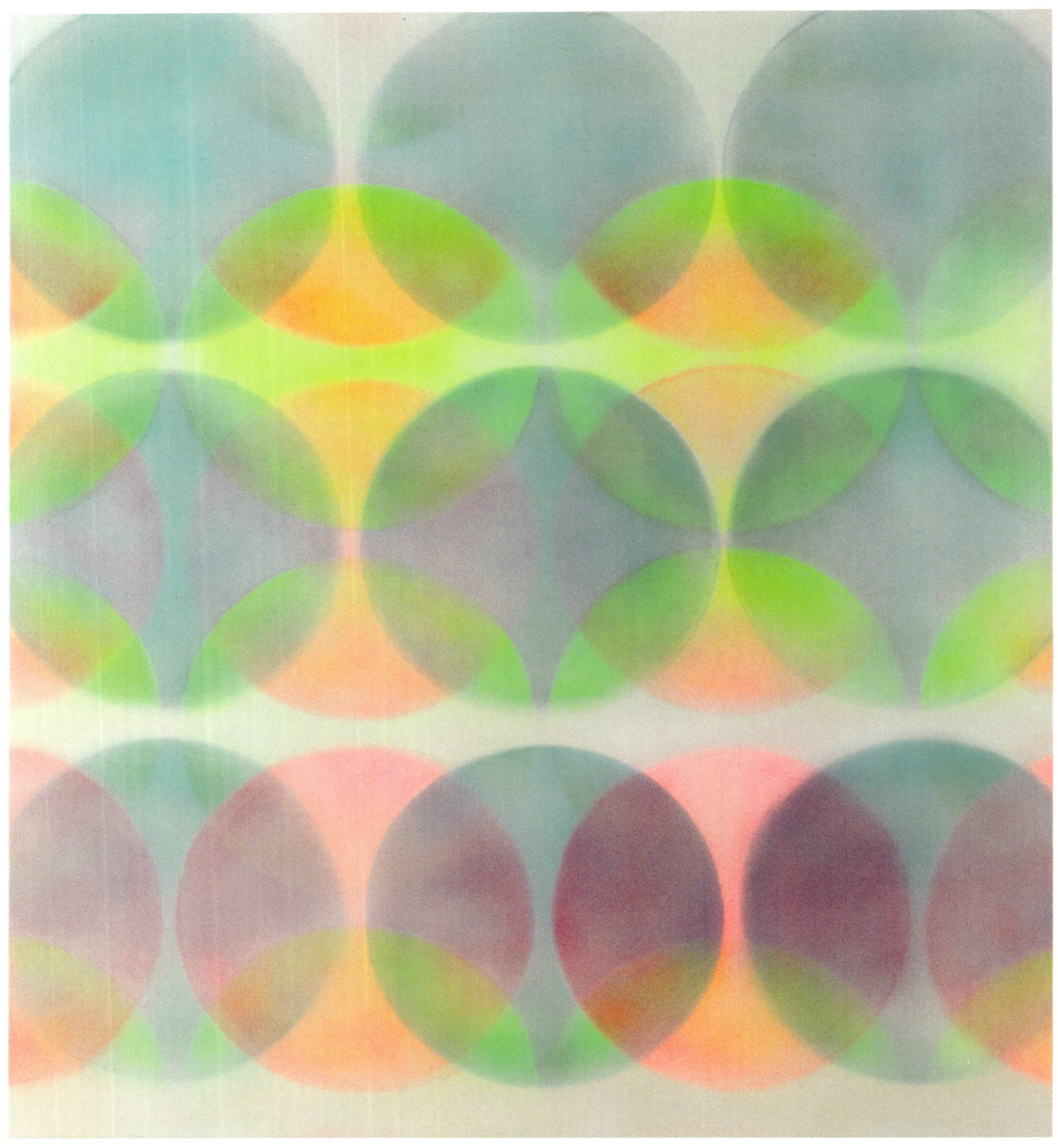

93
Sundrench, 2024
Airbrush and acrylic on linen
40 × 36 in.

94
Everlast, 2024
Airbrush and acrylic on linen
42 × 34 in.

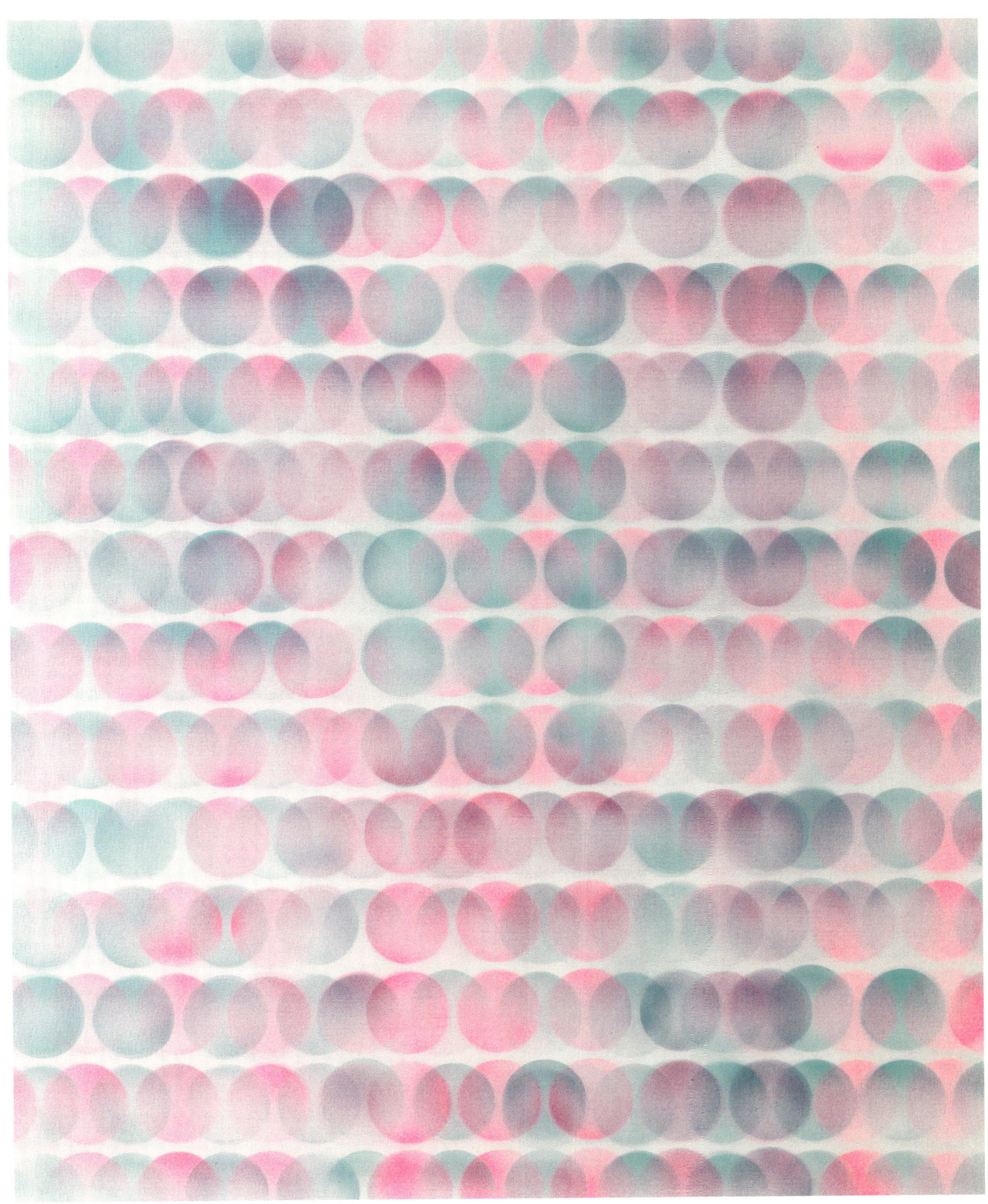

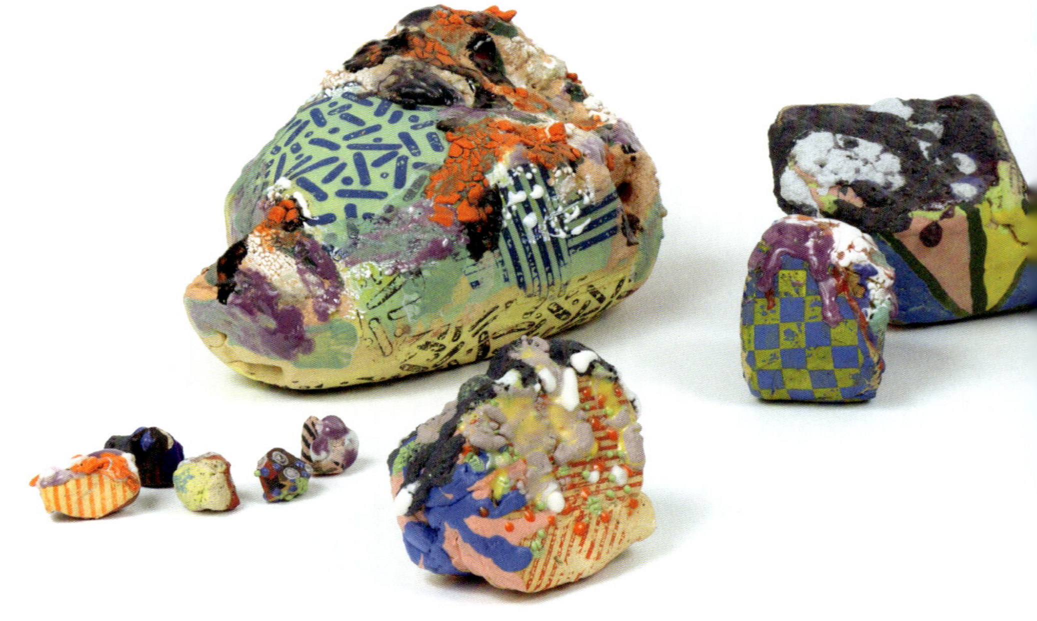

95
Assorted ceramic sculptures, 2024–25
Glazed ceramics
Dimensions variable

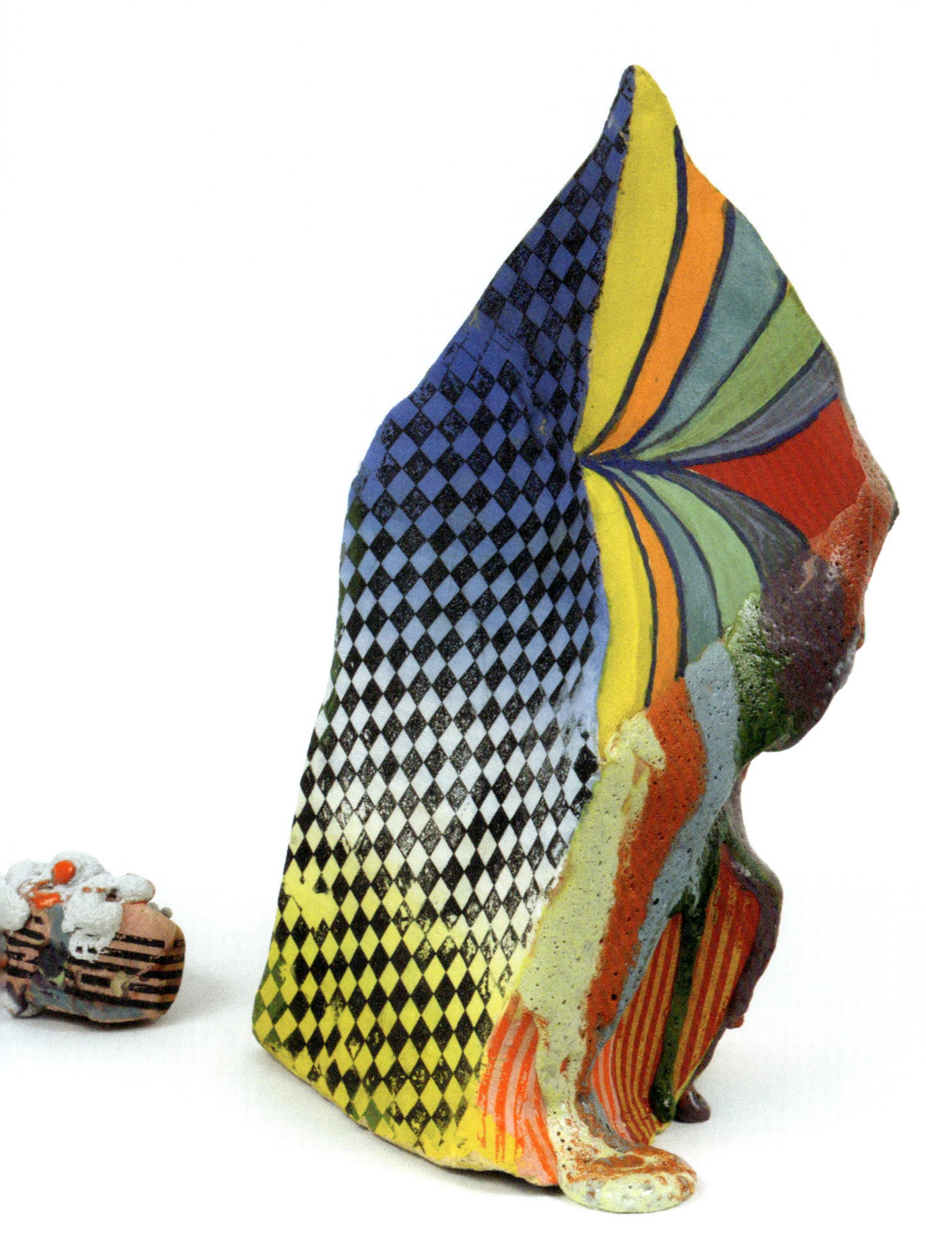

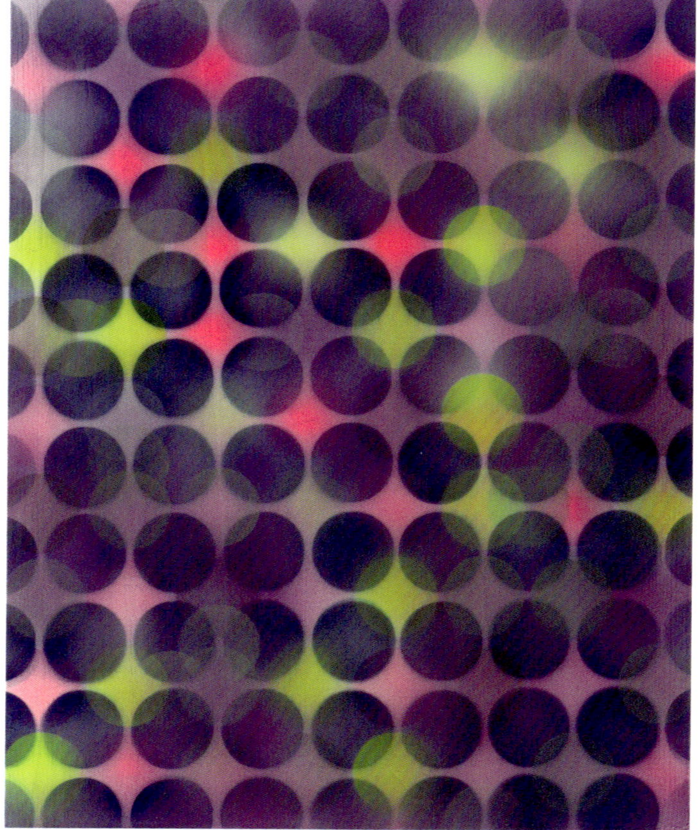

96
Midnight, 2024
Airbrush on linen
24 × 20 in.

97
Sequence, 2024
Airbrush on linen
30 × 24 in.

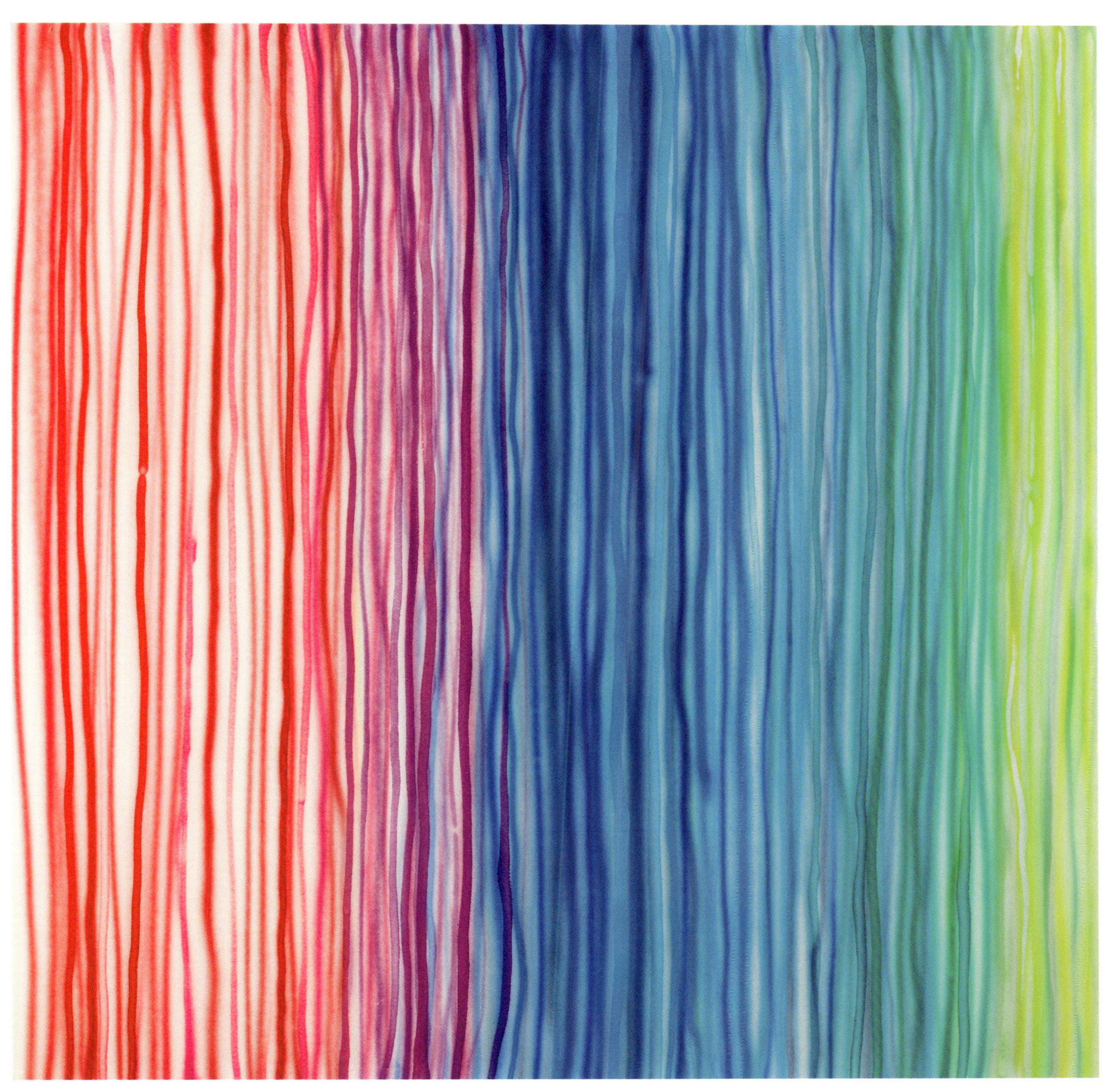

98
Waterfall, 2017
Acrylic and airbrush on canvas
48 × 48 in.

99

Crazy Brave (homage to Joy Harjo), 2025

Three parts: 60 × 60 in. each; 60 × 180 in. overall

Acrylic on canvas

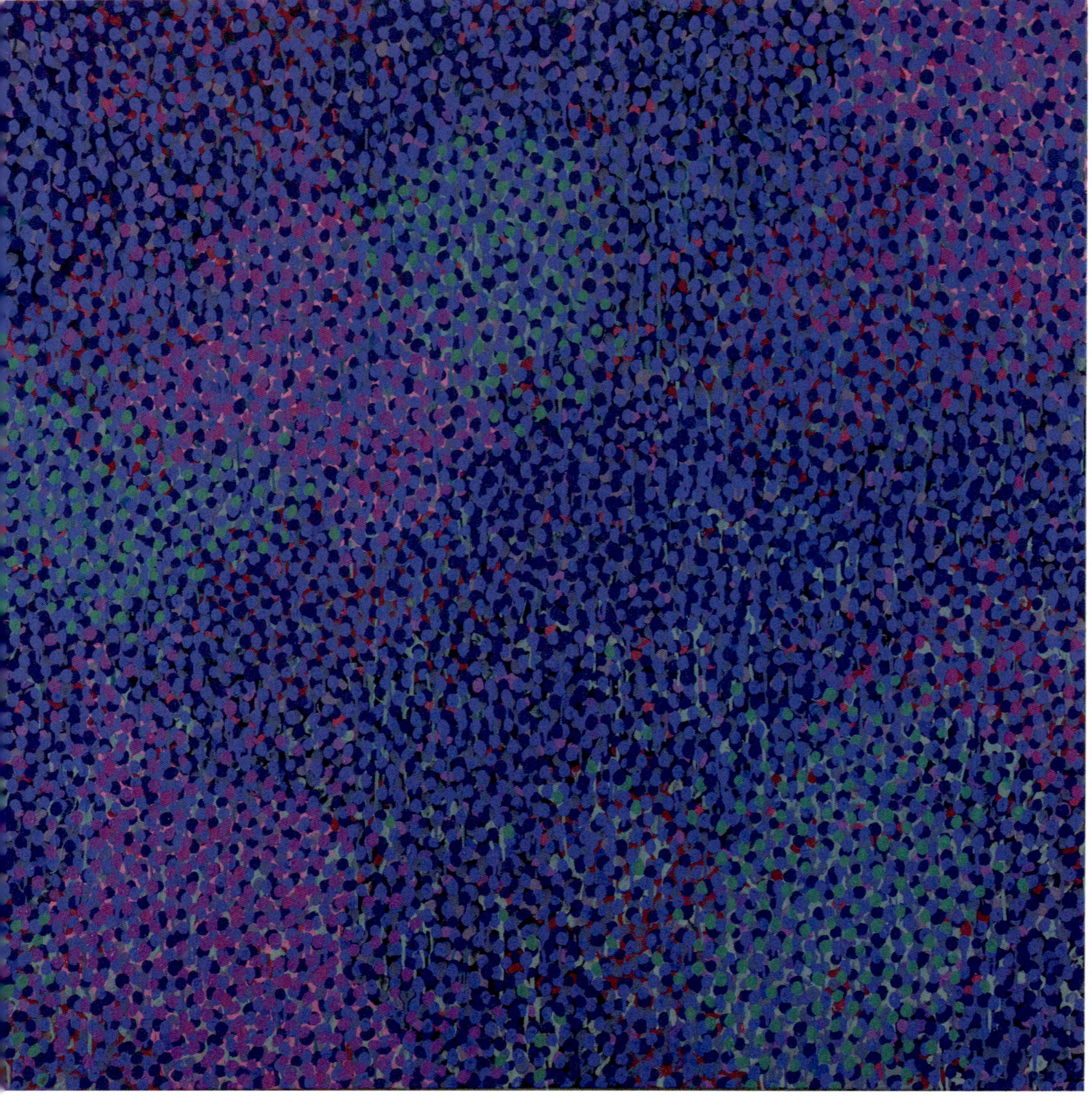

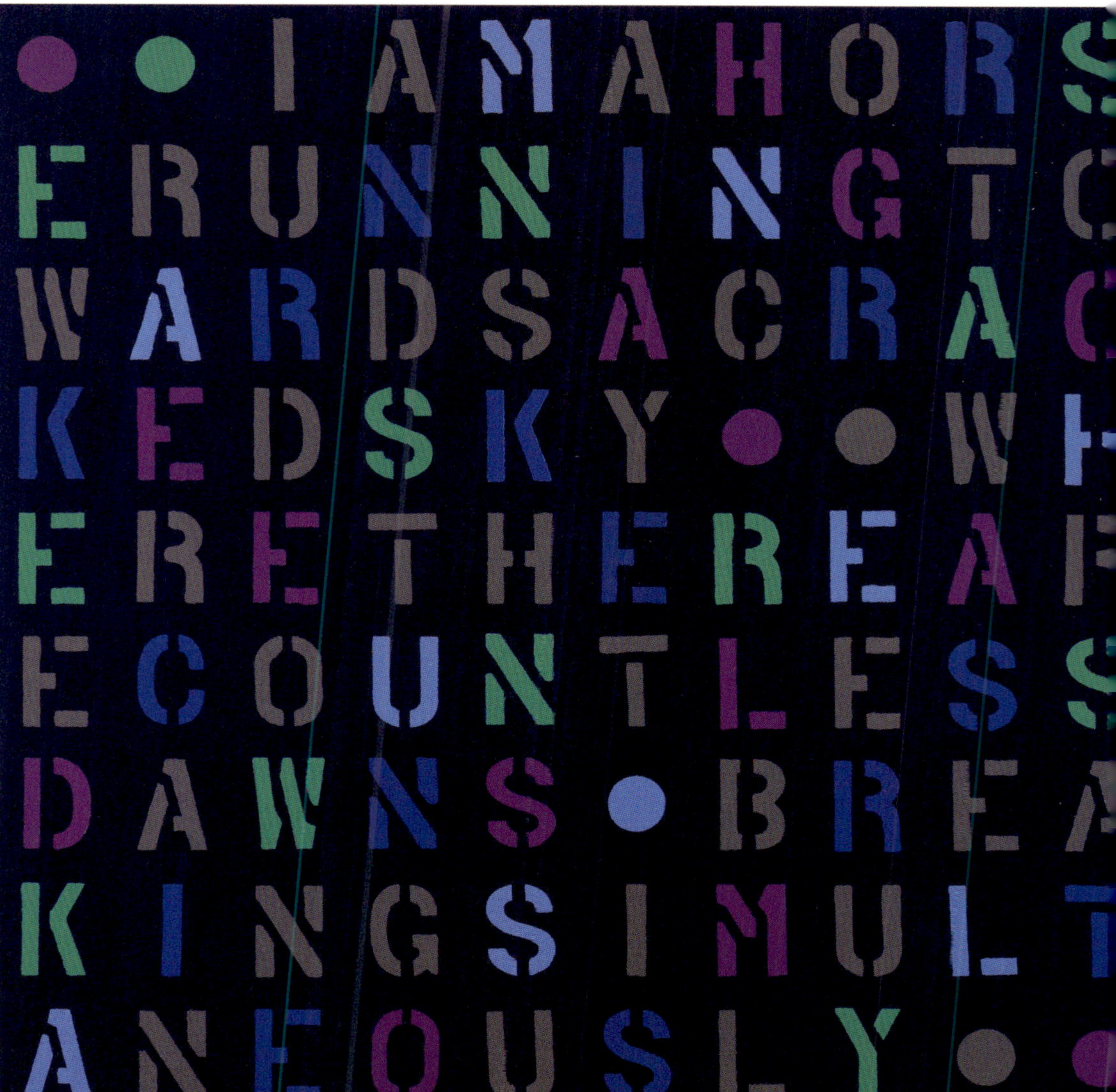

"I am a horse running towards / a cracked sky where there are countless dawns / breaking simultaneously"

—from "Two Horses" by Joy Harjo

ARTIST BIOGRAPHIES

Sai Clayton, Mac Cooper, Laura Hutson Hunter, and Mouminatou Thiaw

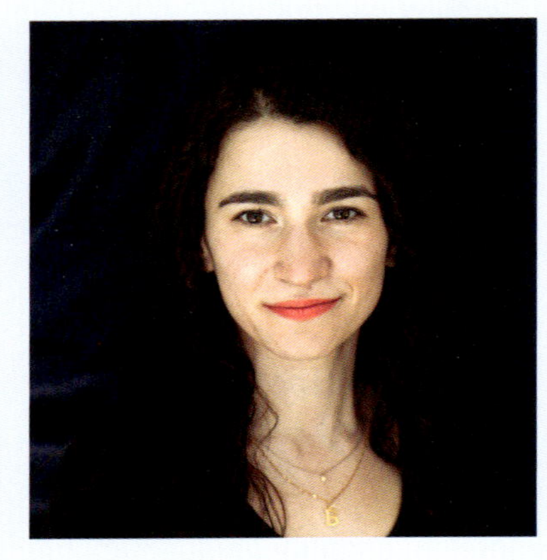

BEIZAR ARADINI

B. 1991, MARDIN, KURDISTAN

Beizar Aradini creates fiber-based works that consider her family's history and tell narratives of survival and belonging. Born in a Kurdish refugee camp after her family fled persecution in Iraq, Aradini immigrated to Nashville in 1992 as a young child. Her practice honors her family's Kurdish heritage and reflects the broader history of Kurdish resilience in the face of statelessness. Nashville is home to the single largest community of ethnic Kurds in the US—as of 2023, the estimated population was twenty thousand. Aradini's work reflects that community's influence and explores the enduring challenges of dislocation and the adaptability required to preserve identity in the face of cultural loss. Using traditional embroidery and weaving techniques, Aradini creates detailed portraits and community scenes drawn from memories and family photographs. Her innovative use of tulle and dissolvable embroidery sheets allow threads to act as loose, gestural marks.

Aradini completed a BFA in studio art at Middle Tennessee State University, Murfreesboro, in 2017. She has participated in artist residencies at Arquetopia International, Urubamba, Peru, and Arrowmont School of Arts and Crafts, Gatlinburg. She is the recipient of multiple awards, including Best in Show at the *Best of Tennessee Craft* exhibition at the Tennessee State Museum and the Tennessee Craft Scholarship for Professional Development. Her work has been featured in solo exhibitions at Electric Shed, Nashville, and in group exhibitions at the Brooklyn Collective Art Gallery, Charlotte, NC; the Frist Art Museum, Nashville; nGbK Gallery, Berlin; the Tennessee State Museum, Nashville; and the Vanderbilt Museum of Art, Nashville. Her art has been reviewed in *Burnaway* and *Gazete Duvar*, and she is currently an MFA candidate at the School of the Art Institute of Chicago. —SC

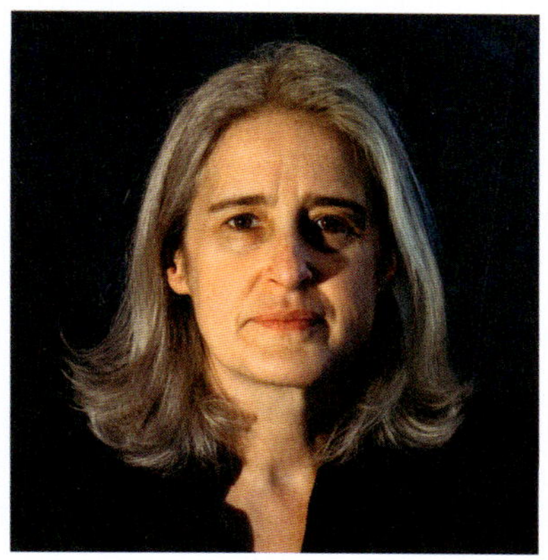

ALEX BLAU

B. 1970, AUSTIN, TEXAS

Alex Blau explores abstraction, perception, and presence through painting and ceramics. Her geometric paintings evoke rippling energies and bold, dynamic designs drawn from candy wrappers, quilts, and everyday patterns. The recurring archetypal circle serves as both a symbol of unity and a form easily disrupted, opening flowing, meandering spaces that invite pause, breath, and reflection. Her ceramic works, in contrast, are rooted in the textures of the earth: patterns in leaves, lichen on rocks, flashes of found color. These crystalline, encrusted forms celebrate surface and material, offering playful, tactile companions to her ethereal paintings.

Blau earned an MFA from the Rhode Island School of Design, Providence, and a BA from Brandeis University, Waltham, MA. She is a recipient of a Fellowship of Residency at the Vermont Studio Center, Johnson; the Joan Mitchell Fellowship; and a RISD Graduate Studies Award of Excellence. Her work has been included in several solo exhibitions, including at Anderson Ranch Art Center, Snowmass Village, CO; Firecat Projects, Chicago; Gallery Seomi, Seoul; Mark Moore Gallery, Orange, CA; the New Britain Museum of American Art, New Britain, CT; Wheeler Opera House, Aspen, CO; and Zeitgeist Gallery, Nashville. She has participated in numerous group exhibitions at such venues as Elephant Gallery, Nashville; the Frist Art Museum, Nashville; Hiram Van Gordon Gallery, Tennessee State University, Nashville; Napoleon Gallery, Philadelphia; Red Arrow, Nashville; Whitespace Gallery, Atlanta; Zeitgeist Gallery, Nashville; and others. —MC/AB

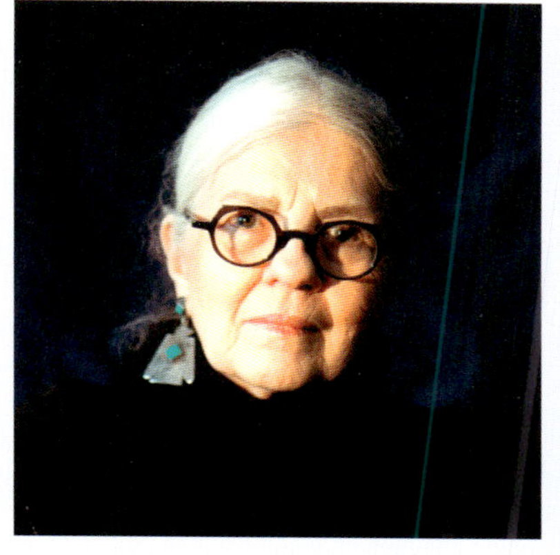

JANE BRADDOCK

B. 1946, RICHMOND, INDIANA

Jane Braddock's four-decade practice as an abstract painter explores the interplay of color, texture, and pattern. Beginning her career as a textile designer and colorist in New York City, including at the esteemed firm Brunschwig & Fils, Braddock honed a keen sensitivity to color relationships and pattern. After moving to Nashville in 1980, her focus shifted to a studio painting practice, which has developed to span three interconnected series: *Shakti*, *Text*, and *Pours*. These bodies of work often engage in dialogue with one another, linked by their shared vibrancy and complex making process. Her process incorporates diverse techniques such as stenciled text, finger-painted dots, poured drips, and glittering accents, resulting in rich, tactile surfaces that emphasize light and texture. An avid traveler, Braddock was inspired on a transformative trip to Tibet in 1996 to create her *Shakti* series, which she named after the divine feminine creative force in Hinduism. In her *Text* series, Braddock integrates meticulously stenciled fragments of quotes drawn from literature, which she loves deeply. These elements transcend linguistic meaning, merging with fields of color to evoke meditative and nonverbal states. The *Pour* paintings, by contrast, are all about chance and improvisation, with gravity and the interaction of layered colors determining the final expressive composition.

Braddock received a BFA from Syracuse University. Her work has been featured in solo exhibitions at The Arts Company, Nashville; the Country Music Hall of Fame, Nashville; and Tinney Contemporary, Nashville, as well as at Vanderbilt University Medical Center, Nashville. Selected group exhibitions include *Women of Abstraction* at Monthaven Gallery, Hendersonville, TN, and *The Art of Tennessee* at the Frist Art Museum, Nashville. Braddock's works are held in numerous public and corporate collections, including those of the Morris Museum of Art, Augusta, GA; Music City Center, Nashville; the Tennessee State Museum, Nashville; and Vanderbilt University, Nashville; as well as in private collections across the United States. —SC

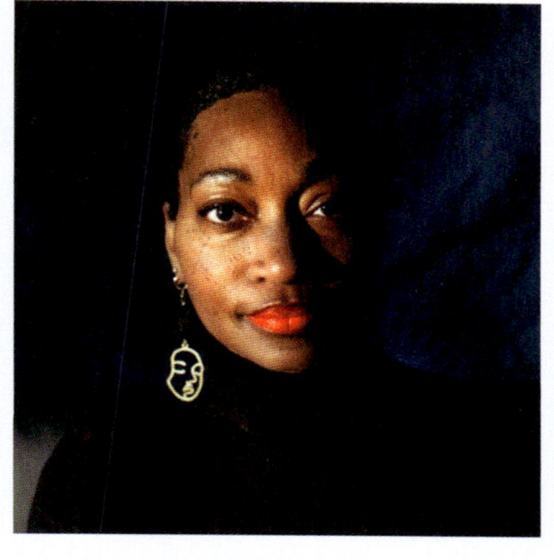

LAKESHA CALVIN

B. 1982, NASHVILLE, TENNESSEE

Artist and educator Lakesha Calvin creates paintings, drawings, collages, sculptures, and installations that center on themes of identity, memory, and belonging. Her work also references a recent personal journey of healing and transition and reflects her deep appreciation for art and desire to inspire others. Although she was born in Nashville, Calvin has a strong connection to the Caribbean—from 2010 to 2013, she lived in Saint Thomas, US Virgin Islands, where she taught art at Charlotte Amalie High School. Influenced by memories of her family and friends, she creates layered landscapes of color and form that merge dreams with materiality. She embraces the process of mixing her palette and preparing her materials, which she considers a form of meditation that is fundamental to her practice.

Calvin earned a BFA with a minor in art history from Washington University in St. Louis in 2005; an MFA with a focus in painting from the University of Tennessee, Knoxville, in 2009; and an MEd in instructional practice from Lipscomb University, Nashville, in 2016. She has taught in the Art and Design Department at Tennessee State University, Nashville, and she currently works as the gallery coordinator and leads the Art Department at Fisk University, Nashville. Her work has been exhibited at the Berry College Moon Gallery, Mount Berry, GA; Fisk University Galleries, Nashville; Nka Gallery, Nashville; Swipe Right Art, Nashville; and the Tennessee Arts Commission, Nashville, among other venues. —MT

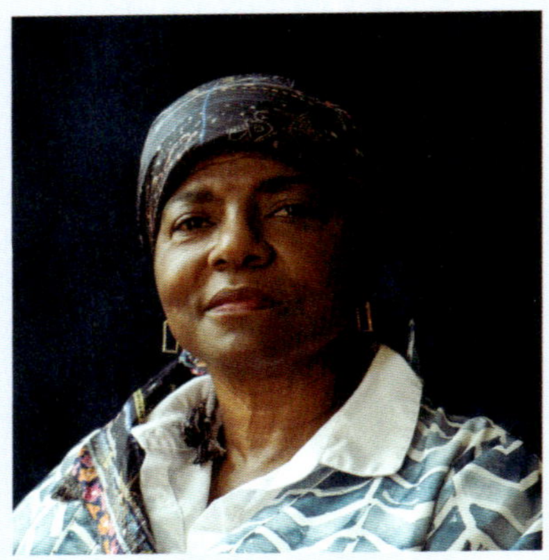

MARÍA MAGDALENA CAMPOS-PONS

B. 1959, LA VEGA, MATANZAS, CUBA

Internationally acclaimed artist María Magdalena Campos-Pons's practice centers on photography, painting, sculpture, audiovisual media, and performance. As she adapts these media to explore her Cuban identity and Nigerian and Chinese ancestry, Campos-Pons investigates how history, memory, and gender can inform identity. Her largely autobiographical work seeks to unveil the spirits of underrecognized people and places, both past and present. Influenced by the traditions, rituals, and practices of her predecessors, Campos-Pons shares untold histories of the transatlantic slave trade, including those related to the sugar industry for which her Nigerian ancestors were enslaved and brought to Cuba, and honors Santería religious practices.

Campos-Pons graduated from the National Art Schools in Havana and earned an MFA in media arts from Massachusetts College of Art and Design, Boston. From 1993 to 2017, she taught at the School of the Museum of Fine Arts at Tufts University, Boston. In 2017, she became the Cornelius Vanderbilt Chair of Fine Arts at Vanderbilt University, Nashville, where she founded the Engine for Art, Democracy, and Justice, a cross-institutional research initiative involving Fisk University, the Frist Art Museum, and Millions of Conversations. In 2023, Campos-Pons received the MacArthur Fellowship, and she was named a United States Artists Fellow in 2024.

Campos-Pons has been featured in solo exhibitions around the globe, including the major survey *Behold* that was on view at the Brooklyn Museum; the Frist Art Museum, Nashville; the J. Paul Getty Museum, Los Angeles; and the Nasher Museum of Art at Duke University, Durham, NC, as well as in the 2023 Sharjah (UAE) Biennial, documenta 14 in Kassel and Athens in 2014, and the 2013 Venice Biennale. Her work resides in the permanent collections of the Art Institute of Chicago; Harvard Art Museums, Cambridge; the Museum of Fine Arts, Boston; the Museum of Modern Art, New York; the Pérez Art Museum Miami; the Smithsonian American Art Museum, Washington, DC; the Victoria and Albert Museum, London; the Whitney Museum of American Art, New York; and many more. —MC

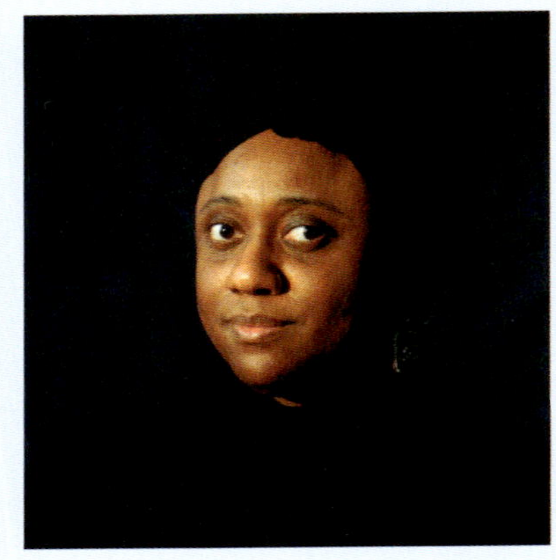

ASHLEY DOGGETT

B. 1995, NASHVILLE, TENNESSEE

Ashley Doggett's work reframes historical narratives to confront issues of race, gender, class, and cultural identity. Through painting and drawing, Doggett incorporates personal memories and familial stories while unflinchingly addressing the United States' racist history. Her use of vivid color, symbolic elements, and references to local landmarks recontextualize ideas about the American South and offer a critique of oppressive systems. She depicts unapologetic, self-aware subjects with a sense of agency, and her work honors those who fought for social equality and equity. Doggett places family members with figures of recent history within the civil rights context, emphasizing their persistence against past and present injustices. Exploring the intersection of the civil rights movement and the formative role of African Americans in American history, Doggett situates her practice within the larger discourse on race in the US.

Doggett earned a BFA from Watkins College of Art, Nashville, in 2016. She has presented solo exhibitions at Channel to Channel, Nashville; David Lusk Gallery, Nashville; Fort Houston, Nashville; Monya Rowe Gallery, New York; Steven Zevitas Gallery, Boston; and Zevitas Marcus, Los Angeles. Her work has been included in group exhibitions at Anna Zorina Gallery, New York; Channel to Channel, Nashville; Kent State University, Kent, OH; and Zeitgeist Gallery, Nashville; and in curated shows by Camilø Álvårez and Theaster Gates. —SC

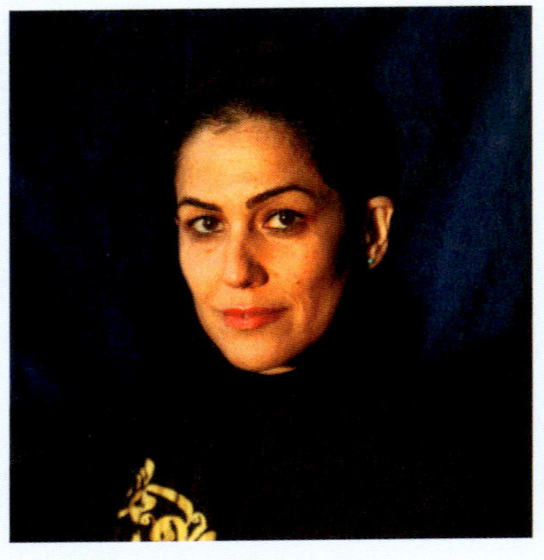

RAHELEH FILSOOFI

B. 1975, TEHRAN, IRAN

Raheleh Filsoofi is an Iranian American artist, curator, and community advocate whose interdisciplinary practice bridges clay, sound, and performance to explore themes of migration, identity, and sociopolitical dynamics. Her work challenges the boundaries of place, culture, and perception, fostering dialogue and reflection on the connections between personal experience and collective memory. Clay plays a central role in Filsoofi's art, embodying the histories, traditions, and labor of creation. She extends its material significance, reimagining ceramic vessels as containers of sound and memory. Sound, with its ephemeral and visceral qualities, serves as both a medium and a metaphor, amplifying the intersection of materiality and meaning in her practice. Filsoofi describes her artistic approach as itinerant—she makes work that reflects a continuous negotiation of cultural and geographic transitions. Her practice embodies a commitment to fostering inclusive narratives, breaking down borders, and creating spaces for dialogue across divides.

Filsoofi completed a BFA from Al-Zahraa University, Tehran, and an MFA in ceramics from Florida Atlantic University, Boca Raton. She currently teaches at Vanderbilt University, Nashville. Filsoofi is the recipient of numerous awards, including the Joan Mitchell Fellowship and the Society 1858 Prize for Contemporary Southern Art. She has held artist residencies at Franconia Sculpture Park, Shafer, MN; Loghaven Artist Residency, Knoxville; and MacDowell, Peterborough, NH. Her work has been featured in solo exhibitions and performances at Atlanta Contemporary; the Gibbes Museum of Art, Charleston, SC; the Halsey Institute of Contemporary Art, Charleston; and Telfair Museums, Savannah, GA, as well as in group exhibitions at the Crocker Art Museum, Sacramento, CA; Sharjah (UAE) Biennial; and 21c Museum Hotel, Nashville. In addition to her practice, Filsoofi has curated significant projects, including exhibitions at the International Museum of Art and Science, McAllen, TX, and the Vanderbilt Museum of Art, Nashville. —SC

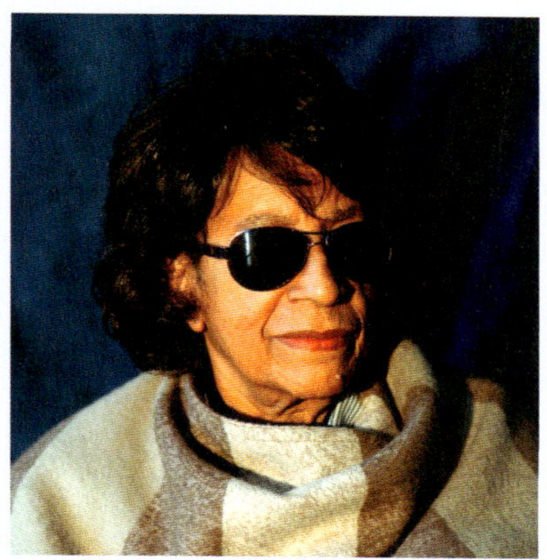

LIFRAN FORT

B. 1942, NASHVILLE, TENNESSEE

LiFran Fort's paintings and drawings speak to decades of dedication to and love for the arts. Following in the footsteps of her mentor, the esteemed Harlem Renaissance artist Aaron Douglas, Fort makes paintings that use semitransparent representational figures to not only tell personal stories but also to advocate for women's rights and evolving perspectives on Blackness. Her work often embraces a monochromatic style, using gradient color scales and straight lines drawn freehand. As the light in her paintings emanates from the darkness, Fort creates a metaphysical connection to the intrinsic good she finds in a dim world.

Fort earned an MAT with an interest in art education from the University of Chicago and a BA from Fisk University, Nashville. During her time at the University of Chicago, she received the Ford Foundation Fellowship, and at Fisk University, Aaron Douglas awarded her the Hines-Brooks Award. For more than forty years, Fort has taught art at Fisk, where she has been named Teacher of the Year four times and was entered into the university's Teachers Hall of Fame in the 1990s. Before her time at Fisk, she taught art at Washington Junior High School, Nashville, and was a staff lecturer for six years in the Museum Education Department at the Art Institute of Chicago. She has exhibited her work at Fisk University Galleries, Nashville; In the Gallery, Nashville; and the Frist Art Museum, Nashville. —MC

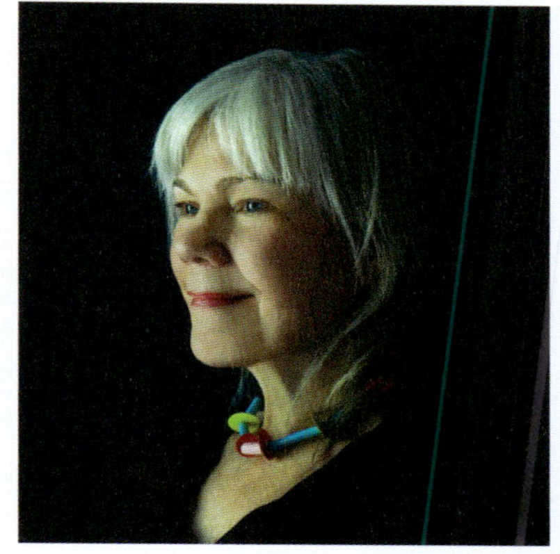

LANIE GANNON

B. 1959, DETROIT, MICHIGAN

Lanie Gannon's sculptures transform paper into intricate structures that serve as monuments to the hand-eye connection. Inspired by her experience with garment and textile construction and her background in woodworking, Gannon meticulously crafts vibrantly painted cut paper into suspended sculptural forms that reference bodices, biological matter, scaffolding, and architecture. Gannon's transition from wood to paper marked a pivotal shift in her practice, enabling her to embrace the medium's immediacy and adaptability. Using techniques such as weaving, layering, and fastening strips of paper, she creates skeletal structures from webs of joints and brads that expose worlds within.

Gannon earned a BFA in painting from Memphis College of Art and pursued graduate studies in sculpture at the Appalachian Center for Craft, Smithville, TN. She taught sculpture and 3D design at Belmont University, Nashville, from 1990 to 2007, where she established the sculpture and 3D studios. From 2014 to 2023, Gannon worked as a facilitator for the Periscope artist-entrepreneur training program for the Arts and Business Council of Greater Nashville. She has also been a visiting artist at the American Academy in Rome and has received the National Endowment for the Arts Visual Artist Fellowship and the Tennessee Individual Artist Fellowship. Her work is included in the permanent collection of the Tennessee State Museum, Nashville, and she has exhibited at CODA Museum, Apeldoorn, Netherlands; the Museum of Arts and Design, New York; and Zeitgeist Gallery, Nashville. She has held residencies at La Napoule Art Foundation, Mandelieu-La Napoule, France; Millay Arts, Austerlitz, NY; the Virginia Center for the Creative Arts, Amherst; and Headlands Center for the Arts, Sausalito, CA. Her public art installations are featured at East Tennessee Children's Hospital, Knoxville; Monroe Carell Jr. Children's Hospital at Vanderbilt, Nashville; and Valley Children's Hospital, Madera, CA. —SC

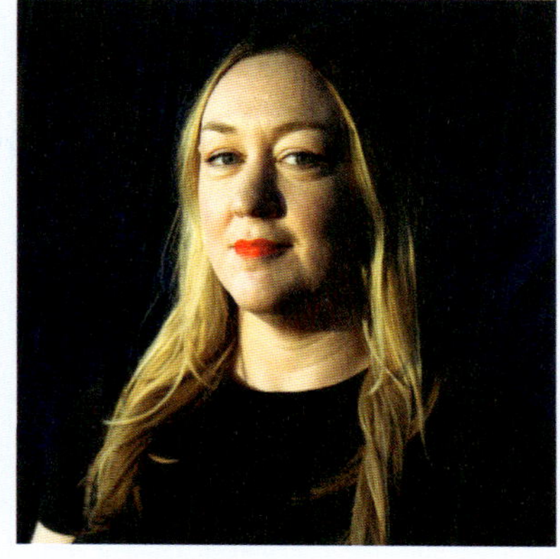

LAUREN GREGORY

B. 1983, OAK RIDGE, TENNESSEE

Lauren Gregory is a multidisciplinary artist whose practice spans painting, fiber art, and video animation. Raised in the mountains of East Tennessee, Gregory is a third-generation Southern artist who learned quilting and painting from her mother and grandmother. Their influence instilled a deep appreciation for traditional crafts, which Gregory reinterprets with humor and irony, challenging conventional boundaries between medium, composition, and content. Gregory is recognized for her innovative stop-motion oil-paint animations in which thick, impasto-style paintings are transformed into dynamic moving images. Her work also includes paintings on unconventional surfaces such as faux fur and quilts that blend kaleidoscopic compositions with symbolic imagery and pop-culture fabric sources. Guided by intuition and spontaneity, Gregory makes art that reflects an interplay between Tennessee's physical landscape and her own emotional terrain. Her playful experimentation renders a language of wit and whimsy, exploring memory, ephemerality, and the tension between capturing and releasing a moment.

Gregory holds a BFA from the University of South Carolina, Columbia, and an MFA in painting from the School of the Art Institute of Chicago. She teaches as a professor of experimental animation and painting at Parsons School of Design, New York, and as a professor of quilting and animation at Ox-Bow School of Art and Artists' Residency, Saugatuck, MI. Gregory's animations and video works have been exhibited at institutions such as MoMA PS1, Queens; the Museum of Contemporary Art, Los Angeles; and the New Museum, New York. Her collaborative projects include music videos for Bayonne, Norah Jones, and Toro y Moi. Gregory has participated in artist residencies in Hungary, Italy, and New York. —SC

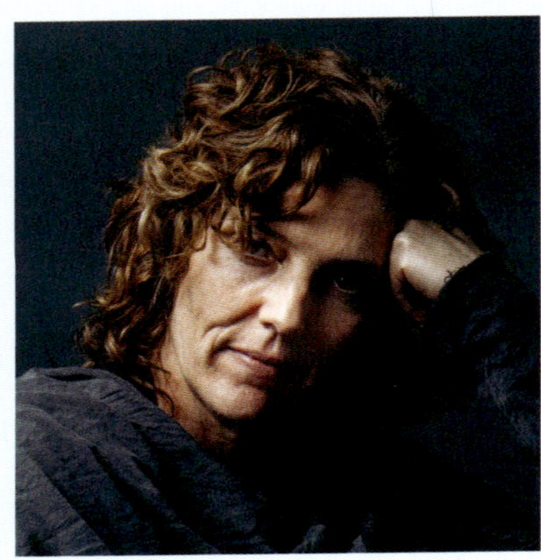

KRISTI HARGROVE

B. 1966, NASHVILLE, TENNESSEE

Well-known for her detailed pencil drawings, Kristi Hargrove considers the acts of drawing and tracing to be experimental processes not bound by representation. Relying on her intuition, Hargrove translates inspiration from the world around her into markings that refer beyond her apparent subjects. Whether in depicting the life of a deceased family member by deconstructing their lived space or revealing an iceberg's full presence underwater, Hargrove uses drawing as a method to open conversations and perspectives beyond language.

With similar exactness, recently Hargrove has also made intricate cut-paper works, sometimes in combination with photographs. The ethereal images created by the negative space evoke a sense of loss, specifically of her father, who recently passed away, or of the grand magnolia tree that stood in her yard for many years. She has found that cutting, rearranging, and layering the cut-outs generates a new sense of movement in the studio. Throughout her practice, she balances observation with traces of dissonance.

Hargrove earned an MFA from Vermont College of Fine Arts, Montpelier, and a BA from Vanderbilt University, Nashville. Since 1992, she has taught at Watkins College of Art, Nashville (now part of Belmont University), where she is currently the chair of the MFA program and an associate professor. Her work has been exhibited in several solo and group shows, including at Belmont University's Leu Gallery; Cumberland Gallery, Nashville; David Lusk Gallery, Nashville; the Frist Art Museum, Nashville; Meinblau Projektraum, Berlin; Middle Tennessee State University, Murfreesboro; Stove Works, Chattanooga, TN; and Vanderbilt University, Nashville. —MC

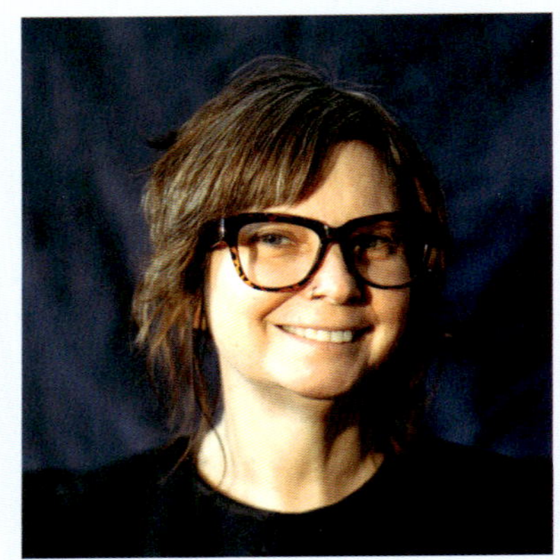

BRIENA HARMENING

B. 1980, MCMINNVILLE, TENNESSEE

Briena Harmening's work combines humor, critique, and Southern identity in the transformation of domestic and recycled textiles. Utilizing sewing, quilting, and sculptural techniques, she creates unexpected surfaces where stitched and screen-printed text interacts with nostalgic materials like quilts, kaftans, tarps, and tablecloths. Her pieces play with word spacing, repetition, and masking, creating visual puzzles that challenge how viewers process text. Harmening's work is rooted in Southern vernacular and storytelling and draws from familial sayings, regional politics, and the complexities of inherited traditions. Raised in Tennessee by a grandmother who was a seamstress and a mother who was a needleworker, she considers her work a collaboration with the women who originally crafted the textiles she deconstructs and reimagines.

Harmening graduated from Florida Gulf Coast University, Fort Myers, and earned an MFA from the University of Tennessee, Knoxville, in 2010. She currently teaches art at James Lawson High School, Nashville. Her work has been exhibited at Coral Springs Museum of Art, FL; ArtFields, Lake City, SC; Strata Gallery, Santa Fe, NM; View Arts Center, Old Forge, NY; and the Browsing Room, Nashville, among other venues. —SC

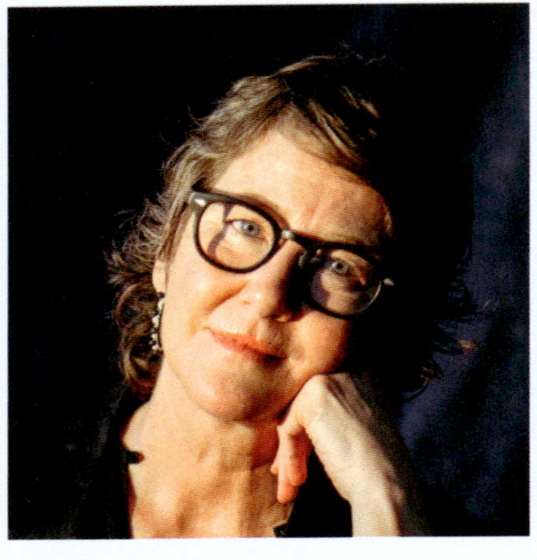

JANA HARPER

B. 1970, WASHINGTON, DC

Jana Harper is an interdisciplinary artist whose work navigates the tensions between the material and the transcendent. While working across different media—including performance, sculpture, painting, and photography—Harper transforms the burdens of human history with compassion, love, and empathy. Much of her work reflects the history of her tribe, the Mackinac Bands of Chippewa and Ottawa Indians. Whether acknowledging the spiritual traces of migration or her forebears' language and homeland, Harper seeks to honor and voice the unforgettable legacies of her ancestors.

Harper graduated with an MFA from Arizona State University, Tempe, and a BA from Evergreen State College, Olympia, WA, and she was a Core Student Fellow at Penland School of Crafts, Bakersville, NC. She is currently a professor of the practice of art at Vanderbilt University, Nashville, and previously taught art at Washington University in St. Louis. She is the recipient of several awards, including an Art Works grant from the National Endowment for the Arts; the Cité International des Arts residency, Paris, France; the Corporation of Yaddo residency, Saratoga Springs, NY; the Current Art Fund from Tri-Star Arts and the Warhol Foundation; the Good Hart Artist Residency, Good Hart, MI; a Mellon Foundation Digital Humanities Fellowship; a Smithsonian Artist Research Fellowship; the Southern Constellations Fellowship, Elsewhere Museum, Greensboro, NC; a Tennessee Arts Commission Individual Artist Fellowship; and a Thrive grant from Metro Arts Nashville. She has also exhibited and performed at numerous institutions, including the American University Museum at the Katzen Arts Center, Washington, DC; Basile Gallery, Indianapolis; Brick Aux, New York; Governor's Island, New York; the Havana Biennial, Matanzas, Cuba; the International Museum of Art and Science, McAllen, TX; Napoleon Gallery, Philadelphia; the National Gallery of Art, Washington, DC; OZ Arts Nashville; Powell Gardens, Kingsville, MO; and the Tarble Arts Center, Charleston, IL. —MC

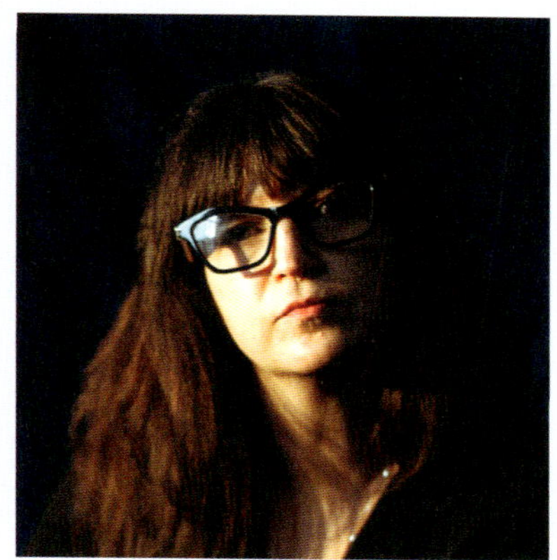

JODI HAYS

B. 1976, HOT SPRINGS, ARKANSAS

Jodi Hays is a painter and collage artist whose practice pushes the boundaries of abstraction and expands the definition of painting. After immersing paper, textiles, or cardboard into dye and bleach baths, Hays creates assemblages that embody the familiar patterns and designs found in textiles. Throughout this process, she considers the history of these found materials and their connections to resourceful labor, which resonates deeply with the historical legacy of crafts created by women. Hays views her work as building upon the visual vocabulary of the South, weaving together new material and cultural narratives that reflect the region's heritage and evolving transformations.

Hays earned an MFA from Vermont College of Fine Arts, Montpelier, and a BFA at the University of Tennessee, Knoxville, and studied at the School of Visual Arts, New York. She is a recipient of the Foundation for Contemporary Arts Grant from the New York Foundation for the Arts and the Rauschenberg Foundation and other grants. She has been awarded several residences, including at Yaddo, Saratoga Springs, NY; the Cooper Union, New York; the Hambidge Center, Rabun Gap, GA; Ox-Bow School of Art, Saugatuck, MI; Stove Works, Chattanooga, TN; and the Vermont Studio Center, Johnson, VT. Her work has been shown in monographic and group exhibitions at Johnson Lowe Gallery, Atlanta; David Lusk Gallery, Nashville and Memphis; McClain Gallery, Houston; Night Gallery, Los Angeles; Ortega y Gassett Projects, New York; Red Arrow, Nashville; Susan Inglett Gallery, New York; 21c Museum Hotel, Nashville; the University of Mississippi, Oxford; Weatherspoon Art Museum, Greensboro, NC; Western Kentucky University, Bowling Green; Vanderbilt University, Nashville, and other venues. Hays's work can be found in the permanent collections of the Arkansas Museum of Fine Arts, Little Rock; the Birmingham Museum of Art, AL; the City of Nashville; the School of Visual Arts, New York; Soho House Collection, Nashville; and the Tennessee State Museum, Nashville. —MC

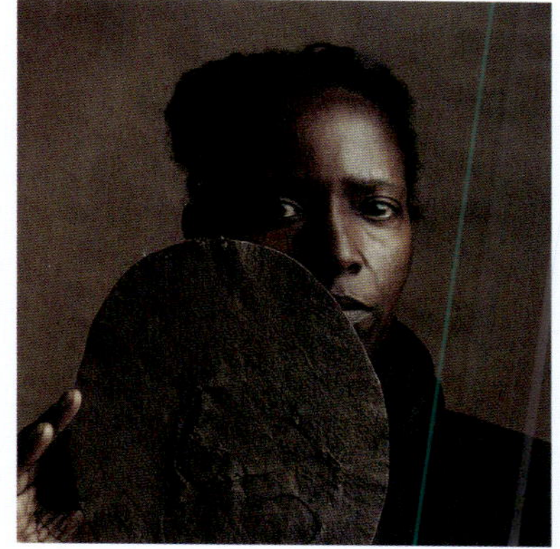

ALICIA HENRY

B. 1966, CHICAGO, ILLINOIS; D. 2024, NASHVILLE, TENNESSEE

Beloved professor and artist Alicia Henry passed away during the planning of this catalogue and accompanying exhibition. Her textile and mixed-media installations seek to understand the innate connections between the individual human form and society. Crafted from felt, linen, leather, or paper board, Henry created amorphous figures whose faces often have distinguishable features or whose bodies have missing limbs. The artist considered her figures to be a multitude of individuals, taking inspiration from the interactions humans have with one another and the communities they foster. While acknowledging their presence in the fluid landscape of race, culture, and gender, Henry activated her figures with a transcendent joy meant to overcome the isolating nature of a society that critiques standards of beauty, the body, and identity.

Henry received a BFA from the School of Art Institute of Chicago; attended the Skowhegan School of Painting and Sculpture, Madison, ME; and earned an MFA from Yale University School of Art, New Haven. After she received her MFA, she volunteered with the Peace Corps in Ghana for two years, where she was inspired by the creation and functions of African crafts and masks. From 1997 until her death in 2024, Henry was an art professor at Fisk University, one of the oldest historically Black colleges and universities in the country and the oldest of the four in Nashville. She was a recipient of numerous awards, including the Ford Foundation Fellowship, the Guggenheim Fellowship, the Joan Mitchell Fellowship, and the Society 1858 Prize for Contemporary Southern Art. Henry's work has been in numerous monographic and group exhibitions at venues including the Art Gallery of Nova Scotia, Halifax; Cheekwood Estate and Gardens, Nashville; the Frist Art Museum, Nashville; Fruitlands Museum, Harvard, MA; the Hunter Museum of American Art, Chattanooga, TN; the Huntsville Museum of Art; the Museum of Contemporary Art Australia, Sydney; the Power Plant Contemporary Art Gallery, Toronto; Provincetown Art Association and Museum; the Tennessee State Museum, Nashville; Tiwani Contemporary, London; Wiregrass Museum of Art, Dothan, AL; and Zeitgeist Gallery, Nashville. —MC

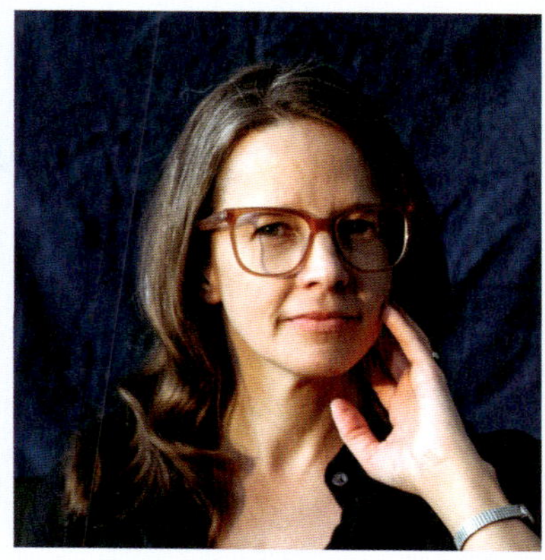

MANDY ROGERS HORTON

B. 1977, FORT BENNING, GEORGIA

Mandy Rogers Horton is a painter and mixed-media artist whose works connect painting and raw construction materials with the ongoing formation of human lives. Inspired by demolition sites—and at times including scavenged rubble, scaffolding, and tarps from the same sites—Rogers Horton's work explores the vocabulary of transformation. By focusing on architectural structures in states of flux, her paintings suggest both strength and fragility.

Rogers Horton earned a BA in psychology and art from Anderson University, IN, and an MFA in painting from American University, Washington, DC. Since 2022, she has been an assistant professor of art at Watkins College of Art at Belmont University, Nashville. She has also taught art at Lipscomb University, Nashville; University of Alabama, Tuscaloosa; and Middle Tennessee State University, Murfreesboro. She was a 2024–25 artist in residence at Arcade Arts Nashville. She is a recipient of the Pentaculum residency at Arrowmont School of Arts and Crafts, Gatlinburg; the Tennessee Arts Commission professional development support grant; and the Vermont Studio Center residency, Johnson. In 2010, she became a founding member of Coop Gallery, Nashville. Her work has been exhibited at ArtFields, Lake City, SC; Chauvet Arts, Nashville; Gallery 121, Belmont University; the Kresge Gallery, Lyon College, Batesville, AR; the Leu Art Gallery, Belmont University; the University of Alabama; Zeitgeist Gallery, Nashville; and other venues. —MC

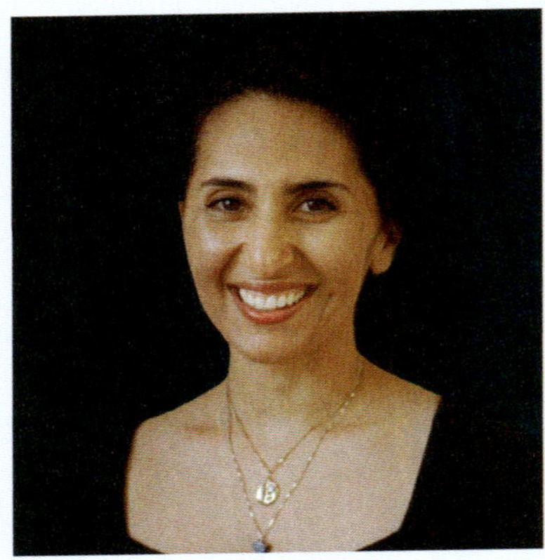

KIMIA FERDOWSI KLINE

B. 1984, NASHVILLE, TENNESSEE

Kimia Ferdowsi Kline is a Persian American artist and curator, born to Bahá'í Iranian parents whose migration to the American South shaped her understanding of belonging and identity. Kline's paintings merge two visual languages: the flat, symbolic stylization of Persian miniatures and carpets, and the textured, expressive figuration of Western painting traditions. Working primarily on salvaged wood and Egyptian papyrus, she layers paint with thread, beads, and gemstones—gestures that reference mending, ornamentation, and feminine labor. Papyrus, one of humanity's oldest storytelling surfaces, links her practice to an ancient lineage, while reclaimed wood carries histories of growth, decay, and renewal. Drawing as well from Southern folk art and modernism, she merges Eastern symmetry and ornament with Western figuration, bridging the cultural dualities that define her work. The resulting tactile, devotional surfaces evoke acts of care and repair, holding space for memory, resilience, and belonging while affirming the persistence of beauty in the aftermath of upheaval.

Kline earned an MFA from the San Francisco Art Institute and a BFA in painting from Washington University in St. Louis, where she was awarded the prestigious Danforth Scholarship. Guest lectures and teaching positions include Brooklyn College, NY; the Chautauqua Institution, NY; the Fashion Institute of Technology, New York; the Tyler School of Art and Architecture, Temple University, Philadelphia; Vanderbilt University, Nashville; Wayne State University, Detroit, MI; and Yale University, New Haven, CT. She is the recipient of the Bed Stuy Artist Residency, Brooklyn; the Macedonia Institute Residency, Chatham, NY; the New York Foundation for the Arts Basil Alkazzi Detroit Residency; and the 68projects residency, Berlin. Her work has been in group and solo exhibitions at Ceysson & Bénétière, Luxembourg City; Diane Rosenstein, Los Angeles; the Drawing Center, New York; Galerie Julien Cadet, Paris; Turn Gallery, New York; Vanderbilt University, Nashville; and several other venues. —MC/LHH/KFK

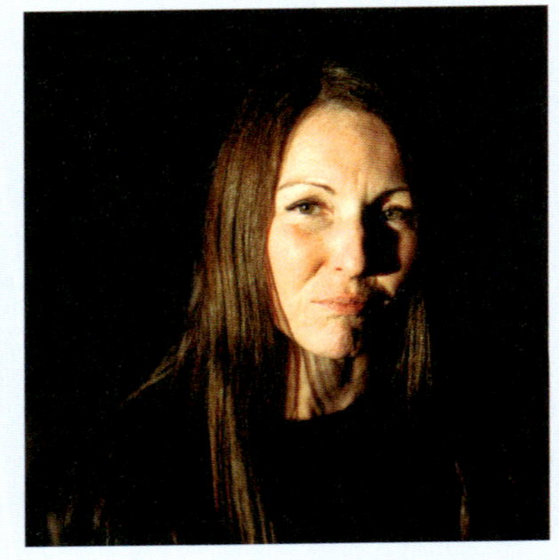

SHANNON CARTIER LUCY

B. 1977, NASHVILLE, TENNESSEE

Shannon Cartier Lucy is a painter who imposes surrealist encounters onto seemingly familiar scenes. She studied painting at New York University, where she took classes under noted figurative artist Lisa Yuskavage. After moving back to Nashville in 2011, Lucy began to study psychoanalysis, an interest that grew out of her father's battle with chronic schizophrenia. She employs the aesthetic language of modernist painters like Édouard Manet to create work that is undeniably contemporary—filled with cinematic compositions and a foreboding, often humorous, sense of the uncanny.

Lucy earned a BA from New York University and an MS in experimental psychology from the University of Tennessee. Her work has been exhibited at Edward Cella Art and Architecture, Los Angeles; Galerie Hussenot, Paris; Lubov, New York; Massimo de Carlo, Milan and Hong Kong; Night Gallery, Los Angeles; Pinakothek Der Moderne, Munich; Soft Opening, London; and other venues and has been acquired by collectors worldwide. —MC/LHH

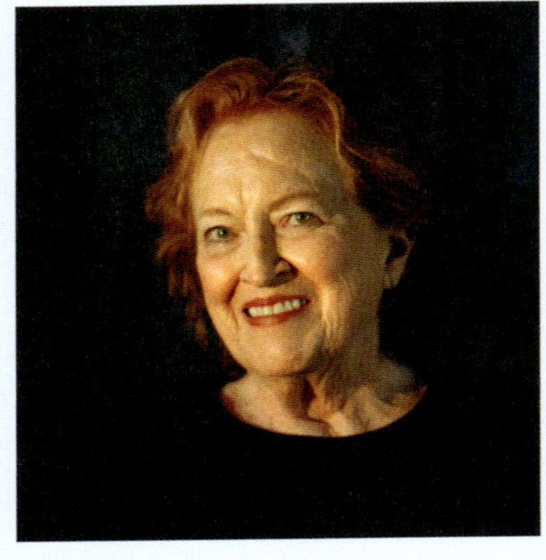

CAROL MODE

B. 1943, ST. LOUIS, MISSOURI

Carol Mode is an abstract painter whose work explores the interplay of composition, color, and visual perception in paintings that negotiate the relationships between form, space, and time. Her practice involves uncovering, reconstructing, and reorganizing surfaces; the resulting canvases are rich in color, with shapes and lines that interrupt and interact with textured paint strokes. Her abstract paintings, known for their bold exploration of sequence and process, invite viewers into a dynamic space of discovery and reinvention.

After graduating with a BFA from Washington University in St. Louis, Mode's professional career began in Venice, Italy, while accompanying her husband, the art historian Robert "Bob" Mode, on a Fulbright fellowship. Mode's early work gained recognition in Italy, where she received her first invitation to exhibit. She has since been awarded several prestigious residencies, including by the Christoph Merian Foundation, Basel, Switzerland; the Helene Wurlitzer Foundation of New Mexico, Taos; the Ucross Foundation, Ucross, WY; and the American Academy in Rome, where she also served as a visiting artist. Her paintings have been featured in numerous national and international exhibitions and were included twice in *New American Paintings*. Mode's work is held in private and public collections across the United States and abroad, and she has completed major commissions at Music City Center and the Pinnacle at Symphony Place in Nashville. —SC

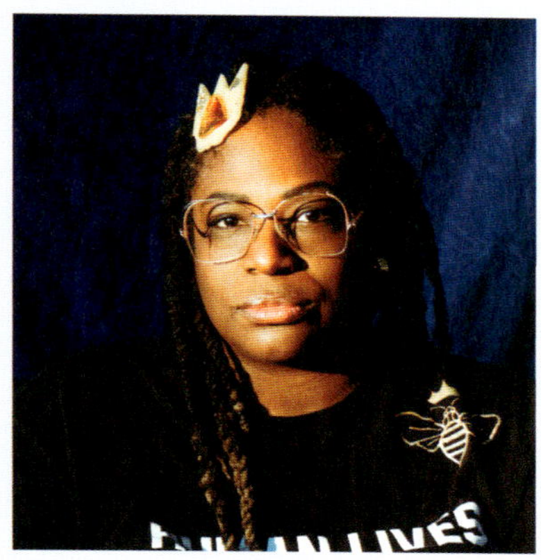

ELISHEBA ISRAEL MROZIK

B. 1984, MEMPHIS, TENNESSEE

Elisheba Israel Mrozik is a multidisciplinary artist and active member of the North Nashville arts community. Her public murals, studio paintings, sculptures, and multimedia installations venerate the experiences and value of Black women in particular. To champion a Pan-African philosophy, she often adorns her forms with Ankara fabrics and Afrocentric motifs, hairstyles, body piercings, and scarifications. She situates these empowered figures within landscapes filled with motifs and graphics suggesting Afrofuturistic worlds.

Mrozik earned a BFA in computer arts from Memphis College of Art in 2006. She moved to Nashville in 2007 and has since championed local Black artists. In 2011, she became the first licensed Black tattoo artist in Middle Tennessee, and her business, One Drop Ink Tattoo Parlour and Gallery, was a central stop on the Jefferson Street Art Crawl. She is the founder of the North Nashville Arts Coalition. Her murals can be found at many sites around Nashville, including on Jefferson Street, Buchanan Street, Chestnut Street, the Elizabeth Duff Transit Center on Herman Street, and Jefferson Street. Her art has been exhibited at the Boheme Collectif, Nashville; the Carl Van Vechten Art Gallery, Fisk University, Nashville; Columbia State Community College, TN; Corvidae Gallery, Nashville; the Frist Art Museum, Nashville; and the Vanderbilt University Divinity School, Nashville. —MT

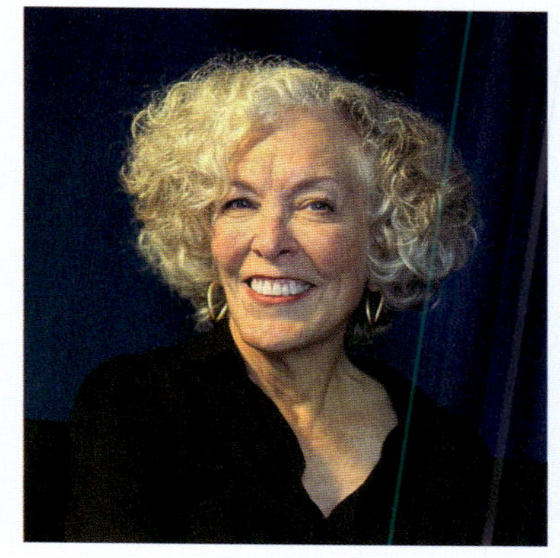

MARILYN MURPHY

B. 1950, TULSA, OKLAHOMA

Marilyn Murphy's paintings and colored-pencil and graphite drawings transform familiar worlds into dreamlike visions. Inspired by magazines from the 1940s and '50s, as well as the geography and weather of Oklahoma, Murphy places her out-of-scale human figures and the objects they chase in curious, often-improbable situations. Her use of strong lighting and tempestuous shadows creates worlds that challenge the act of seeing itself.

Murphy earned an MFA from the University of Oklahoma, Norman, and a BFA from Oklahoma State University, Stillwater. She is a professor emerita of art at Vanderbilt University, Nashville, where she taught from 1980 until 2017. She has earned numerous awards, including the Chancellor's Award for Research from Vanderbilt University; the Award for Outstanding Artwork from Tulane University, New Orleans; and the Distinguished Faculty Award from Vanderbilt University, and was included in the National Endowment for the Arts Visual Artists Fellowship Archive at the Smithsonian American Art Museum, Washington, DC. Her works can be found in the collections of Bridgestone Americas, Nashville; the Metro Nashville Arts Commission; the Huntsville Museum of Art; the Modesto Art Museum, CA; the Oklahoma City Museum of Art; the Siena Art Institute, Italy; the Tennessee State Museum, Nashville; and other institutions. —MC

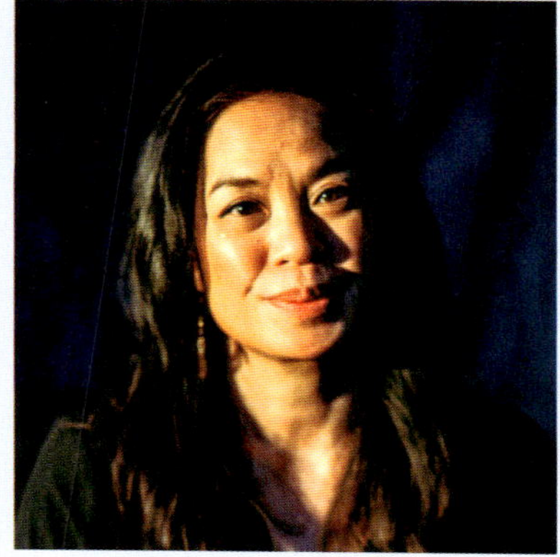

SISAVANH PHOUTHAVONG HOUGHTON

B. 1976, VIENTIANE, LAOS

Sisavanh Phouthavong Houghton is a Laotian American interdisciplinary artist whose work examines refugee identity, displacement, and the collective experiences of the Southeast Asian diaspora. Working in both painting and installation, she reflects on the "Secret War" of 1964 to 1973—when the United States dropped more than two million tons of bombs on Laos—and the impact of her family's journey from the Nong Khai refugee camp in Thailand to Winfield, Kansas. Phouthavong Houghton's paintings are dynamic compositions of saturated colors, undulating lines, and fragmented forms that reference glitches, pixels, and the fractured nature of time. Her abstract language evokes the disruption, reconstruction, and reconfiguration of memory, identity, and culture. Examining systems of information and the spread of mis- and disinformation, Phouthavong Houghton merges personal history with broader diasporic narratives, preserving untold stories and fostering dialogue about war's enduring consequences. Her work celebrates resilience, cultural preservation, and diversity while confronting the complexities of migration and memory.

Phouthavong Houghton earned a BFA in painting from the University of Kansas, Lawrence, and an MFA from Southern Illinois University, Carbondale. She has been a professor of studio arts in painting at Middle Tennessee State University, Murfreesboro, since 2003 and has taught workshops at institutions such as Arrowmont School of Arts and Crafts, Gatlinburg. Phouthavong Houghton is a recipient of multiple grants and awards, including the Tri-Star Arts Current Art Fund from the Andy Warhol Foundation for the Visual Arts grant. Her work has been featured in solo exhibitions at Tinney Contemporary, Nashville, and the University of the South, Sewanee, and in group exhibitions at the Hunter Museum of American Art, Chattanooga, TN; the Knoxville Museum of Art; and the Minnesota Museum of American Art, Saint Paul. Her paintings are held in public and corporate collections including the Hunter Museum of American Art; Pinnacle Financial, Nashville; and Prime Health Services, Franklin. —SC

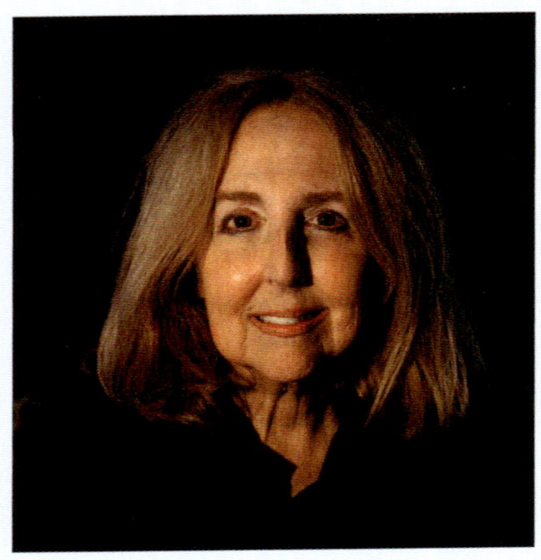

KIT REUTHER

B. 1957, NASHVILLE, TENNESSEE

Kit Reuther is a self-taught artist whose abstract paintings and sculptures recall those of the early modernists. In her paintings, she often uses a muted palette and energetic brush strokes to deconstruct representational forms like gardens, houseplants, or clouds. In her sculptures, Reuther abstracts and elongates human faces or shapes, emphasizing a multitude of rough textures and embracing a totemic essence. The artist's work navigates spatial tension and animates the familiar with new energies.

Reuther is a graduate of the O'More College of Design, Franklin, TN (now part of Belmont University). Her work has been featured in several solo shows at David Lusk Gallery, Memphis and Nashville; Hodges Taylor, Charlotte, NC; Renee George Gallery, Charlotte, NC; Sandler Hudson Gallery, Atlanta; and Sarratt Gallery at Vanderbilt University, Nashville. Her work can be found in permanent collections such as those of Music City Center, Nashville, and the Tennessee State Museum, Nashville. —MC

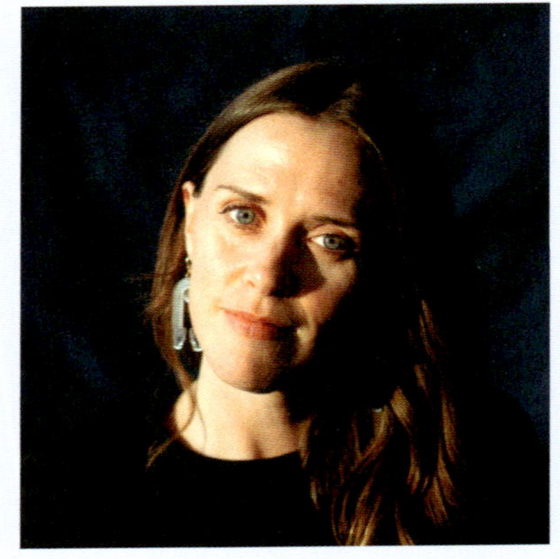

KAREN SEAPKER

B. 1982, PITTSBURGH, PENNSYLVANIA

Karen Seapker's paintings navigate physical, emotional, and intellectual connections through intensely saturated colors, historical references, shifting lines, and disrupted spaces. While employing strong geometric patterns, her dynamic, gestural style embraces movement and alludes to the power of human relationships and the natural world. Many of the paintings Seapker has produced in the last decade incorporate the garden she tends just outside her studio, which she says functions as a sanctuary and a teacher in relation to our greater world.

Seapker graduated with a BA in studio art and art history from Muhlenberg College, Allentown, PA, and an MFA in painting from Hunter College, New York. Her work has been exhibited in spaces including the Andy Warhol Museum, Pittsburgh, PA; James Cohan Gallery, New York and Shanghai; Plato Gallery, New York; Red Arrow Gallery, Nashville; Rhona Hoffman Gallery, Chicago; Sargent's Daughters, Los Angeles; the Shepherd, Detroit; and Zeitgeist, Nashville. Seapker's work was also included in Crystal Bridges Museum of American Art's survey of contemporary art *State of the Art 2020* and was acquired as a part of the museum's permanent collection. She has received numerous recognitions for her work, including the Austin Peay State University Center of Excellence for the Creative Arts Tennessee Artist Fellowship; the ChaNorth residency, Pine Planes, NY; two nominations for the Joan Mitchell Fellowship; and two *New American Paintings* Southern Competition features. Her work is included in private collections worldwide, and reviews of her work have been in publications including *ArtForum*, *Burnaway*, *Hyperallergic*, and *The Wall Street Journal*. —MC

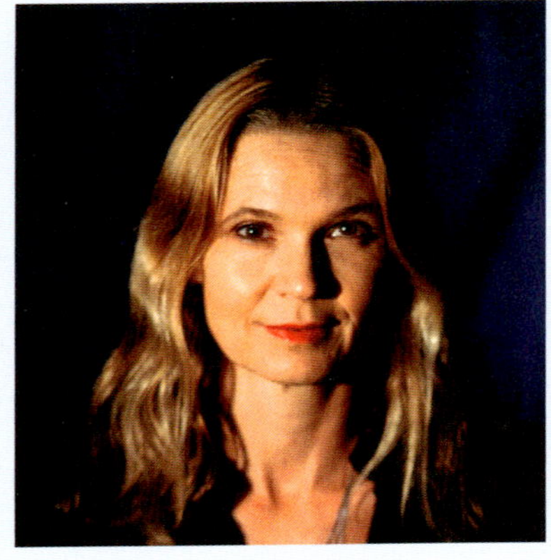

VADIS TURNER

B. 1977, NASHVILLE, TENNESSEE

Vadis Turner creates a variety of mixed-media works—typically wall-based or 3D textile-driven sculptures that challenge narratives historically associated with women and female characters. She complicates the domestic and gendered associations of materials like ribbons, curtains, and bedsheets and combines those materials with steel, concrete, and brick dust. By subverting the intended uses of such materials, she demonstrates how women can defy expectations and behavioral norms. In addition to rewriting the tales of archetypal figures such as Venus and Ophelia, Turner engages with one of the most compelling structures in modern art: the grid. The materials she uses bring a fluidity and poetic structure to the otherwise rigid form.

Turner completed her BFA and MFA at Boston University. She taught at Pratt Institute, New York, for ten years and has been a lecturer at Vanderbilt University, Nashville, since 2015. Turner has received several grants, most notably the Joan Mitchell Foundation Painters and Sculptors Grant and the Tri-Star Arts Current Art Fund from the Andy Warhol Foundation for the Visual Arts grant. Her work has been featured in solo exhibitions at the Frist Art Museum, Nashville; Huntsville Museum of Art; University of Alabama at Birmingham; and University of Colorado Boulder, and in group exhibitions at the Andy Warhol Museum, Pittsburgh, PA; Bunker Artspace, West Palm Beach, FL; Brooklyn Museum, NY; Hunter Museum of American Art, Chattanooga, TN; LongHouse Reserve, Northwest Harbor, NY; Zuckerman Museum of Art, Kennesaw, GA; Museum of Arts and Design, New York; and 21c Museum Hotel, Nashville. Turner has been an artist in residence at the Corporation of Yaddo, Saratoga Springs, NY; Materials for the Arts, New York; and the Vermont Studio Center, Johnson. Her work is held in several museum collections, including those of the Brooklyn Museum, Hunter Museum of American Art, and Museum of Arts and Design, New York. —MC

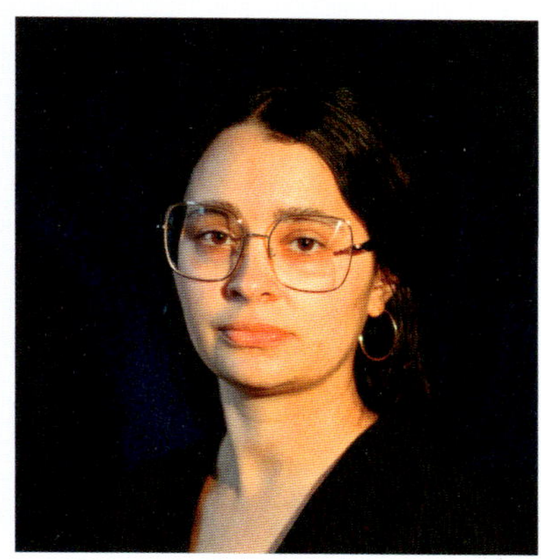

YANIRA VISSEPÓ

B. 1992, SANTURCE, PUERTO RICO

Yanira Vissepó creates vibrant compositions that bridge the landscapes and flora of her birthplace in Puerto Rico and her adopted home in the American South. She blends dreamy, color-soaked washes with crisp, cut-out depictions of plants in a dynamic interplay of minimal and immersive elements that delicately balance defined and undefined forms. Deeply informed by her experience living in the Puerto Rican diaspora, her work addresses themes of identity, transition, and environmental histories. Her techniques, such as stain painting, linocut printmaking, cyanotype, dye resists, and hand embroidery, emphasize the resilience and fragility of the natural world. The plants she portrays—native to Puerto Rico and Tennessee—serve as symbols of healing and connection, weaving ecological and cultural ties between her two homes.

In 2019, Vissepó studied printmaking at the Kyoto International Mokuhanga School, where soft gradients and refined forms became central to her practice. She has held residencies at Coop Gallery, Nashville; the Mokuhanga Innovation Laboratory, Echizen, Japan; and the Nashville Public Library. Vissepó has also worked as a teaching artist at the Frist Art Museum, Nashville, and the Nashville Public Library. Her work is included in collections such as those of the Metro Arts Lending Library, Nashville; Soho House Nashville; and the Vanderbilt Museum of Art, Nashville. Vissepó's solo exhibitions include shows at Lyndon House Arts Center, Athens, GA; Elephant Gallery, Nashville; and Sheet Cake Gallery, Memphis; and she has participated in group exhibitions at venues such as 21c Museum Hotel, Nashville, and the Vanderbilt Museum of Art. —SC

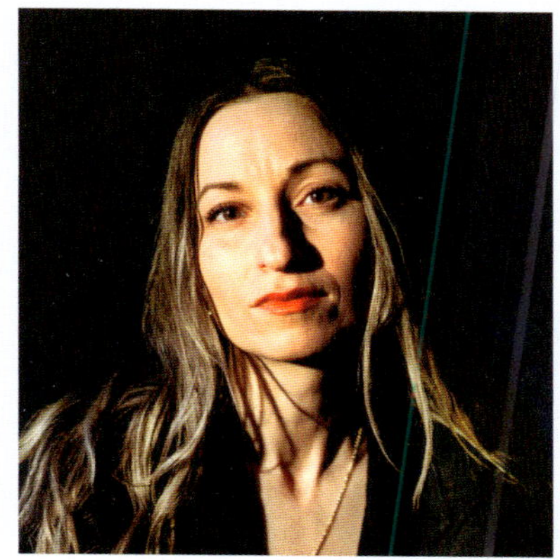

EMILY WEINER

B. 1981, BROOKLYN, NEW YORK

Emily Weiner is a painter who creates surrealist landscapes that consider how archetypal symbols passed through generations may be revolutionized to spawn new, collective meanings. Her work, often set in ceramic or hand-painted wood frames, envisions primordial imagery—such as moons, spirals, and hand gestures found in folklore, theater, dreams, and nature—through a nonhierarchical, feminist, and Jungian lens. Using her intuition and layers of oil paint, the artist questions how representational imagery may be shaped, shared, and translated.

After Weiner graduated with a BA from Barnard College, Columbia University, New York, she earned an MFA in fine art from the School of Visual Arts, New York, where she later served as a faculty member. Since 2021, she has taught at Watkins College of Art at Belmont University, Nashville, and was previously a visiting assistant professor and lecturer of fine arts at Pratt Institute, Brooklyn. She is a winner of multiple awards and grants, including the Tri-Star Arts Current Art Fund from the Andy Warhol Foundation grant, the Hopper Prize, and the Pratt Faculty Development Fund grant, and was nominated for the Joan Mitchell Fellowship in 2022 and 2023. Her work has been featured in several solo and group exhibitions at venues including Red Arrow, Nashville; König Berlin and Mexico City; Miles McEnery Gallery, New York; Huxley-Parlour, London; Entrée, Bergen, Norway; Pentimenti, Philadelphia; Andrea Festa Fine Art, Rome; and Whitespace Gallery, Atlanta. Weiner's work resides in the permanent collections of Kunsthall Grenland, Porsgrunn, Norway, and the Pennsylvania Academy of the Fine Arts, Philadelphia. —MC

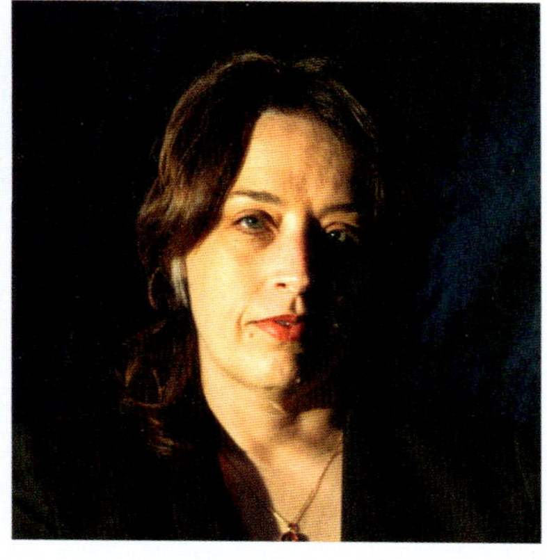

KELLY S. WILLIAMS

B. 1977, NASHVILLE, TENNESSEE

Kelly S. Williams creates oil paintings in several distinct styles: figurative realism and observational still lifes, bold abstractions often based on textiles and in the shape of tondi, and trompe l'oeil works that border on sculpture. Taking inspiration from benign objects such as bedsheets, house plants, tabletops, or tarot cards, Williams explores the subtleties of these familiar objects with a combination of artistic mastery and conceptual deftness.

Williams earned a BA in studio art from Vassar College, Poughkeepsie, NY, and an MFA from the School of the Art Institute of Chicago. As an undergraduate, Williams was honored with the Ellen Battell Stoeckel Fellowship at the Yale Norfolk School of Art, CT. After receiving an MFA, Williams participated in the Terra Summer Residency, Giverny, France, and she has also held residencies at the Chelsea Music Festival, New York; the Harpeth Hall School, Nashville; the International Center for the Arts, Monte Castello di Vibio, Italy; and the Ora Lerman Charitable Trust Soaring Gardens Artists Retreat, Laceyville, PA. Williams has taught at the School of the Art Institute of Chicago; the University of Wisconsin, Milwaukee; and Watkins College of Art, Nashville. She has exhibited in multiple monographic and two-person shows at venues including Belmont University, Nashville; the Suburban, Oak Park, IL, and Milwaukee, WI; and Turner Center for the Arts, Valdosta, GA, and in group exhibitions through the Art in the Embassies Program at the US Ambassador's Residence, Abu Dhabi; Elephant Gallery, Nashville; High Line Nine, New York; and Red Arrow, Nashville. Williams's work is included in the permanent collections of the US Department of State, Washington, DC; the US Embassy and Consulates in Pakistan, Islamabad; and the Waldorf Astoria New York, among other notable institutions. —MC/LHH

SETTING THE STAGE

A Selected Chronology of the Nashville Art World, 1949–2001

Susan W. Knowles

Nashville is and always has been a uniquely diverse and creative city—a market town in rural surroundings with an economy based in traditional mercantilism and manufacturing combined with modern banking and insurance. During the 1980s and 1990s, the rise of corporate healthcare and a burgeoning entertainment economy grown from humble country music roots changed Nashville into a city on the rise. This chronology is a tribute to those who helped make the New Nashville a welcoming place for artists. Supporters and promoters of this culture include a disproportionate number of women who led organizations, opened exhibition spaces, and gathered public support for the arts in the decades leading up to the opening of the Frist Art Museum in 2001.

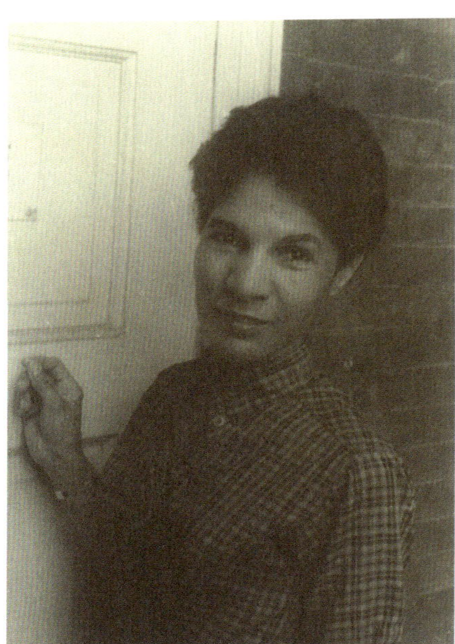

FIGURE 8.1. Portrait of Pearl Creswell. Carl Van Vechten Gallery, Fisk University, 1957.

1949 Georgia O'Keeffe donated a portion of the Alfred Stieglitz Collection to Fisk University. University President Charles S. Johnson appointed Pearl Creswell curator of the newly founded **Carl Van Vechten Gallery**, a role she filled until her retirement in 1990.

1950 The first organizational meeting of a professional art guild happened at Vanderbilt University. Of twenty-six charter members of the **Nashville Artist Guild**, twelve were women, including Louise LeQuire. Over the seventy-five years of its history, the Nashville Artist Guild has had forty-seven woman presidents.

1972 The first **Centennial Park Crafts Fair** was produced by the Tennessee Association of Craft Artists (Alice Merritt became its first paid director in 1989). Nancy Saturn bought the Craft Cranny on Bandywood Drive, later transforming it into the **American Artisan Gallery** in 1981. Lucienne Reed became a codirector of the Craft Cranny (the American Artisan Gallery), a position she would hold until 1998.

1974 The **Vanderbilt Sarratt Student Center** opened. The first director of Sarratt Gallery, located in the public lobby, was Jane Ann Dill.

1976 Barbara Chazen, director of corporate public affairs at **Commerce Union Bank**, began to provide corporate support for Nashville arts organizations. By the mid-1980s, the bank was hosting local contemporary art exhibitions in their public lobby downtown. Nancy Saturn started what became the **American Artisan Festival**, which brought national attention to both Nashville and the artisan craft movement. **Martin Wiley Gallery** was opened by Terry Martin and Wiley Eugene (Gene) Sizemore at 2122 Acklen Avenue, with fine art prints from Brooke Alexander, Marian Goodman Gallery, and Parasol Press. Lois Riggins advised on craft artists shown at the gallery.

1978 **Cumberland Art Conservation Center** was founded by art conservator Cynthia Kelsey Stow; Dee Minault became a partner in 1983. Wesley Paine was appointed as director of **the Parthenon**.

1980 **Cumberland Gallery** opened on Bandywood Drive in Green Hills. Originally owned by Susan O'Neill, Susan Hammond, and Carol Stein, the gallery first exhibited works on paper.

1981 **Nashville Parks and Recreation** board member Anne Roos raised funds for and oversaw the production and installation of *Sea Serpent* at Fannie Mae Dees Park by Pedro Silva and community volunteers. **The Studio/L'Atelier** was opened on Acklen Avenue by Danièle Folon and Noëlle Rigsby. By 1989, the gallery had moved to Bandywood Drive in Green Hills and been renamed the **Folon-Rigsby Gallery**. The **Tennessee State Museum** expanded, moving from the War Memorial Building to the lower levels of the Tennessee Performing Arts Center; Lois Riggins was named its director. Art conservator Shelley Reisman Paine had been overseeing the removal of the state's collection to the new location since 1979.

1982 Anne Brown was named the director of the **Metro Nashville Arts Commission (MNAC)**. Ann R. Williams opened **Ann Kidwell and Associates**, a framer and gallery on West End Avenue; renamed **AKA Gallery** after its move to Twelfth Avenue South, it eventually became a contemporary art venue before closing in 1995.

1984 Victoria Boone was appointed director of visual arts and craft media at the **Tennessee Arts Commission**. JoEl Logiudice transformed **Sarratt Art Gallery** into a contemporary art space—solo shows during her tenure (1984–2001) included presentations of the work of Susan Bryant, Sherri Warner Hunter, Sue Mulcahy, and Adrienne Outlaw.

1985 **Cumberland Gallery**, now co-owned by Carol Stein and Caroline Boyd Stevens, moved to a modern building designed by architect Robert Anderson on Hillsboro Circle in Green Hills; solo exhibitions in the 1980s featured work by *In Her Place* artists Jane Braddock, Lanie Gannon, Carol Mode, and Marilyn Murphy. MNAC commissioner Alice Zimmerman and Nancy Saturn opened **Zimmerman Saturn Gallery** in the downtown historic district. Zimmerman also founded the downtown **Summer Lights Festival** with Anne Brown. Celia Walker was hired to curate Hospital Corporation of America's corporate collection, and Yvonne Boyer was hired as the curator for Northern Telecom. Vanderbilt University Medical Center had also begun acquiring art in the 1980s. All boosted the Nashville art economy by purchasing from local artists.

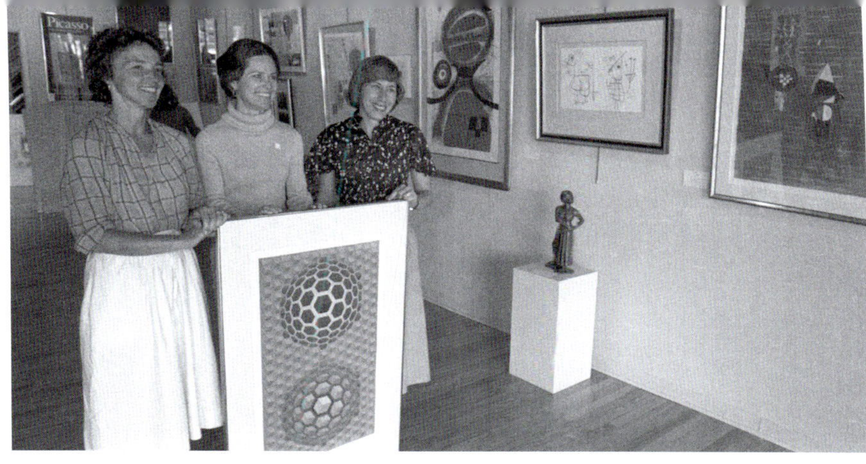

FIGURE 8.2. Cumberland Art Gallery opening (left to right: Susan O'Neill, Susan Hammond, and Carol Stein), 1980.

1987 Carlton Wilkinson opened **In the Gallery** in a historic building on Jefferson Street in North Nashville and later founded the not-for-profit **Nashville African American Artists Association (N4Art)** with Barbara Bullock, Lynn Norris, and Walter Whitmore. **Arts in the Airport**, a program that oversees site-specific installations, temporary exhibitions, and a permanent art collection at the Nashville International Airport, was founded under the direction of MNAC and overseen by its visual arts director Susan Knowles.

1988 **Vanderbilt Art Gallery** interim director Christine Kreyling curated *4 × 4: Jane Braddock, JoEl Logiudice, Carol Mode, Marilyn Murphy*. **An Artrageous Evening**, an art party benefiting Nashville agencies providing direct services to people with AIDS and their loved ones, was spearheaded by the American Artisan Gallery, Cumberland Gallery, Metro Arts Commission Gallery, and Zimmerman Saturn Gallery—all run by women. The event continued for years as a fundraiser for Nashville Cares under the auspices of the Nashville Association of Art Dealers, which comprised Finer Things Gallery, directed by Kim Brooks; In the Gallery, directed by Carlton Wilkinson; and Midtown Gallery, directed by Ron York.

1989 The Cheekwood Museum of Art (now Cheekwood Estate & Gardens) presented *Harlem Renaissance: The Art of Black America*, organized by the Studio Museum of Harlem. Kevin Grogan, director of the Cheekwood Museum of Art, coordinated a citywide collaboration with the Nashville Chapter of the Links, Incorporated. At the invitation of Alice Zimmerman, New York gallerist Bernice Steinbaum facilitated exhibitions at local galleries that presented works by Emma Amos, Camille Billops, and Faith Ringgold. **The Sinking Creek Independent Film Festival** moved from Greeneville, Tennessee, to Vanderbilt's Sarratt Student Center. Meryl Truett succeeded

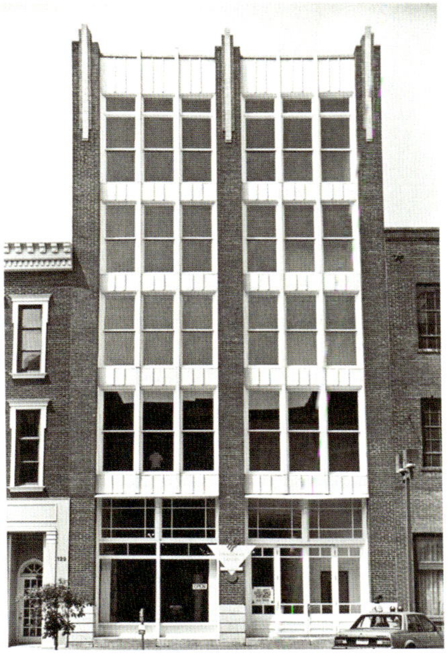

FIGURE 8.3. Zimmerman-Saturn art gallery, 131 Second Avenue North, 1985. Built in 1892, this handsome five-story brick structure was renovated by architect Earl Swensson.

founder Mary Jane Coleman as its executive director, and the festival grew expansively under her leadership. Its name was changed to the Nashville Independent Film Festival in 1998.

1990 **Belmont University's Leu Gallery** director Elena Graves hosted Kit Reuther for her first solo exhibition. Over the next few years, the Leu Gallery exhibited the work of Lanie Gannon, Donna Glassford, Linda Marks, and Meryl Truett.

1991 **Visual Arts Alliance of Nashville (VAAN)**, a not-for-profit arts group, secured and renovated the Alamo storefront at Fourth Avenue and Broadway; VAAN's founding officers were Susan Knowles, Andrée LeQuire, Linda Marks, and Sue Mulcahy. **Untitled: Uncensored Art for Unlimited Audiences** began producing large, all-inclusive, often one-night-only shows at various temporary venues.

1992 Kristi Hargrove was hired as an adjunct instructor at the **Watkins Institute** on Church Street. Hargrove is now a faculty member of the Watkins College of Art at Belmont University.

1993 *Tennessee: From the Mountains to the Mississippi* opened at the **National Museum of Women in the Arts, Washington, DC**; it was organized by project curator Susan Knowles and project director Celia Walker, with invited juror Eleanor Heartney. Nashville artists included were Armanda Balsamo, Barbara Bullock, Annie Freeman, and Margaret Krakowiak. A related show with thirty finalists was presented at the **Tennessee State Museum**; in addition to the artists shown in Washington, DC, it included

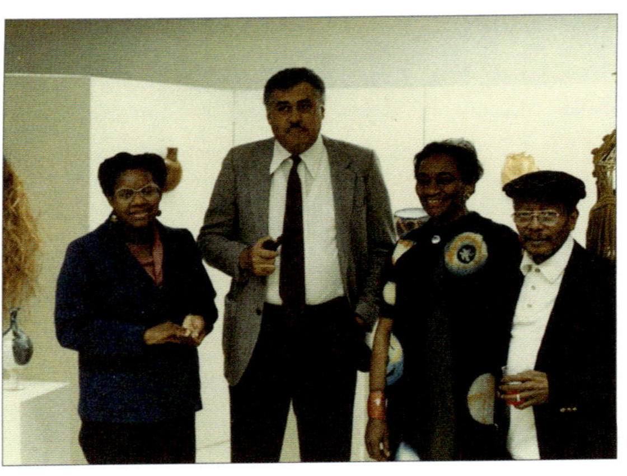

FIGURE 8.4. Left to right: Viola Marietha Wood, Tennessee State University president Fred Humphries, Dolores Ashley Harris, and Earl J. Hooks at TSU, 1985. Harris (a textiles instructor) and Wood (a ceramic sculptor who had studied under Hooks at Fisk University) were longtime art faculty members at TSU.

Nashville artists Lanie Gannon, Sherri Warner Hunter, Renée LaRose, Marilyn Murphy, and Kathryn Schoepflin.

1994 **Zeitgeist Gallery** opened in Cummins Station, a 1907 warehouse repurposed by architect Manuel Zeitlin; founder Janice Zeitlin was joined in 1996 by curator Lain York. In September, Zeitgeist Gallery presented a solo show of Lanie Gannon's work.

1996 Anne Brown opened **The Arts Company** gallery on Fifth Avenue North. Curator Terri Smith began the popular **Temporary Contemporary series** at **Cheekwood Estate & Gardens**, a series of solo shows presented in the upper-level hallway of the museum; the series later moved to a dedicated gallery space, converted from horse stables, in 1998. Exhibitions included a posthumous tribute to Barbara Bullock and installations by Alicia Henry, Carrie McGee, and Donna Tauscher.

1997 **Ruby Green**, an artist studio and gallery space created by Chris Campbell, opened on Fifth Avenue South. In 2005, Ruby Green became Nashville's first recipient of a Warhol Foundation grant.

1998 **Fugitive Art Center** was founded on Martin Street in Wedgewood-Houston by Bryan Hunter and Greg Pond; board members included Carol Mode, Lesley Patterson-Marx, Donna Tauscher, and Iwonka Waskowski. Adrienne Outlaw became the first art feature producer for **Nashville Public Radio**.

1999 **Watkins College of Art** moved to a temporary location in One Hundred Oaks Mall before relocating to Metro Center in 2002; **Zeitgeist Gallery** moved to Hillsboro Village. **Nashville Cultural Arts Project** (whose not-for-profit designation was later passed on to **Nashville Area Arts / Seed Space**) sponsored the **Outta Site** lecture series featuring architects, designers, and artists at the Neuhoff complex in Germantown. Founders included Mel Chin, Stephen McRedmond, Anita McRedmond Sheridan, and Helen Nagge.

2001 **Plowhaus Artists' Cooperative** was opened in East Nashville by Franne Lee, Lesley Patterson-Marx, and J. D. Wilkes.

April 8, 2001: **The Frist Art Museum** opened on Broadway in the city's former postal headquarters.

Through these decades, the following art writers promoted local galleries, museums, and artists.

1950s–90s *Nashville Banner*'s Louise LeQuire, Corinne Franklin, Julie Pursell, Susan Quick, Kittler Zibart, and Beth Monin

1960s–90s *The Tennessean*'s Clara Hieronymus and Alan Bostick

1990s *Nashville Scene*'s John Bridges, Susan Knowles, Christine Kreyling, David Ribar, and David Maddox

PHOTOGRAPHY CREDITS

FRONT COVER

Photo: Sam Angel. Courtesy of the artist. © 2026 Karen Seapker

BACK COVER

Photo: John Schweikert. Courtesy of the artist. © 2026 Yanira Vissepó

DETAILS

pg. ii: Jodi Hays. Detail of pl. 5 • pg. iv: Kelly S. Williams. Detail of pl. 75 • pg. viii: Alex Blau. Detail of pl. 98 • pg. x–xi: Alex Blau. Detail of pl. 98 • pg. xiv: Lauren Gregory. Detail of pl. 14 • pg. 6: María Magdalena Campos-Pons. Detail of pl. 25 • pg. 12: Jane Braddock. Detail of pl. 99 • pg. 26: Lakesha Calvin. Detail of pl. 18 • pg. 30: Emily Weiner. Detail of pl. 72 • pg. 176: LiFran Fort. Detail of pl. 81

FIGURES

0.1: Courtesy guerrillagirls.com. © Guerrilla Girls • 1.1: Photo: Mindy Solomon. Courtesy of Andrea Zieher • 1.2: Courtesy of the artist. © 2026 Beizar Aradini • 1.3: Courtesy of the artist. © 2026 Sisavanh Phouthavong Houghton • 2.1: Photo: Sam Angel. Courtesy of the artist. © 2026 Vadis Turner • 2.2: Courtesy of the artist. © 2026 Kelly S. Williams • 2.3: Digital image © The Museum of Modern Art/Licensed by SCALA / Art Resource, NY • 2.4: Photo: John Schweikert. Courtesy of the artist. © 2026 Kimia Ferdowsi Kline • 3.1: Courtesy of the artist. © 2026 Marilyn Murphy • 3.2: Courtesy of the artist. © 2026 Carol Mode • 3.3: Courtesy of the artist. © 2026 Lanie Gannon • 3.4: Courtesy of Carlton Wilkinson • 4.1: Photo: Erika Barahona Ede. Estate of Louise Bourgeois/Licensed by VAGA at Artists Rights Society (ARS), New York, NY • 4.2: Courtesy of the artist. © 2026 Lenka Clayton • 4.3: Photo: Tina Gionis. Courtesy of the artist. © 2026 Jodi Hays • 4.4: Photo: Sam Angel. Courtesy of the artist. © 2026 Karen Seapker • 4.5: Photo: Rocky Horton. Courtesy of the artist • 5.1: Photo: Carlos Limas. Courtesy of the artist • 5.2: Photo: Faith Rodriguez. Courtesy of the artist • 5.3: Courtesy of the artist • 6.1: Courtesy of Samantha Saturn • 6.2: Courtesy of Julia Martin • 6.3: Photo: © Alan Poizner – USA TODAY NETWORK via Imagn Images • 6.4: Photo: Andrés Bustamante. Courtesy of Ashley Layendecker • 7.1: Photo: Gina R. Binkley • 7.2–7: Photo: Jerry Atnip. Courtesy of Fisk University Galleries. © 2026 Artists Rights Society (ARS), New York / VG Bild-Kunst, Bonn • 8.1: Photo: Carl Van Vechten. Library of Congress, Prints & Photographs Division, Carl Van Vechten Collection • 8.2: Photo: Bob Ray for the *Nashville Banner*. *Nashville Banner Archives*, Special Collections Division, Nashville Public Library • 8.3: Photo: Bob Schatz. Zimmerman Saturn Gallery Archives. Used with permission by Robyn Zimmerman Rubinoff • 8.4: David C. Driskell Papers, MS01.11.01.P0476. David C. Driskell Center for the Study of Visual Arts & Culture of African Americans & the African Diaspora, University of Maryland

PLATES

1: Courtesy of Trépanier Baer Gallery. © 2026 Artists Rights Society (ARS), New York / VG Bild-Kunst, Bonn • 2: Courtesy of Zeitgeist Gallery. © 2026 Artists Rights Society (ARS), New York / VG Bild-Kunst, Bonn • 3: Photo: Jerry Atnip. Courtesy of Fisk University Galleries. © 2026 Artists Rights Society (ARS), New York / VG Bild-Kunst, Bonn • 4–5: Photo: Nik Massey. Courtesy of the artist. © 2026 Jodi Hays • 6: Photo: Aaron Harper. Courtesy of the artist. © 2026 Jodi Hays • 7–8: Photo: Sam Angel. Courtesy of the artist. © 2026 Vadis Turner • 9: Photo: John Schweikert. Courtesy of the artist. © 2026 Vadis Turner • 10: Photo: Sam Angel. Courtesy of the artist. © 2026 Vadis Turner • 11: Photo: John Schweikert. Courtesy of the artist. © 2026 Vadis Turner • 12: Photo: Sam Angel. Courtesy of the artist. © 2026 Vadis Turner • 13: Photo: John Schweikert. Courtesy of the artist. © 2026 Vadis Turner • 14–15: Photo: John Schweikert. Courtesy of the artist. © 2026 Lauren Gregory • 16: Courtesy of the artist. © 2026 Lauren Gregory • 17–21: Photo: John Schweikert. Courtesy of the artist. © 2026 Lakesha Calvin • 22–23: Courtesy of Northern Clay Center. © 2026 Raheleh Filsoofi • 24: Photo: Silvia Ros. Courtesy of the artist. © 2026 Raheleh Filsoofi • 25: Courtesy of the artist and Gallery Wendi Norris, San Francisco. © 2026 María Magdalena Campos-Pons • 26: Photo: John Schweikert. Courtesy of the artist. © 2026 Yanira Vissepó • 27: Photo: Sam Angel. Courtesy of the artist. © 2026 Yanira Vissepó • 28: Photo: John Schweikert. Courtesy of the artist. © 2026 Yanira Vissepó • 29: Courtesy of the artist. © 2026 Kimia Ferdowsi Kline • 30–31: Photo: John Schweikert. Courtesy of the artist. © 2026 Kimia Ferdowsi Kline • 32–33: Courtesy of the artist. © 2026 Jana Harper • 34: Photo: John Schweikert. Courtesy of the artist. © 2026 Jana Harper • 35: Courtesy of the artist. © 2026 Jana Harper • 36–37: Photo: Katie Delmez. © 2026 Elisheba Israel Mrozik • 38–40: Photo: Eugene Tang. Courtesy of the artist. © 2026 Beizar Aradini • 41: Courtesy of the artist and Red Arrow Gallery. © 2026 Briena Harmening • 42–45: Courtesy of the artist. © 2026 Briena Harmening • 46–48: Photo: John Schweikert. Courtesy of the artist. © 2026 Mandy Rogers Horton • 49–54: Photo: John Schweikert. Courtesy of the artist. © 2026 Ashley Doggett • 55: Courtesy of the artist. © 2026 Shannon Cartier Lucy • 56: Photo: Nik Massey. Courtesy of the artist. © 2026 Shannon Cartier Lucy • 57–58: Courtesy of the artist. © 2026 Shannon Cartier Lucy • 59–62: Courtesy of the artist. © 2026 Marilyn Murphy • 63: Photo: John Schweikert. Courtesy of the artist. © 2026 Karen Seapker • 64–65: Photo: Sam Angel. Courtesy of the artist. © 2026 Karen Seapker • 66: Photo: John Schweikert. Courtesy of the artist. © 2026 Karen Seapker • 67: Photo: Sam Angel. Courtesy of the artist. © 2026 Karen Seapker • 68–69: Photo: John Schweikert. Courtesy of the artist. © 2026 Emily Weiner • 70: Photo: John Schweikert. Private collection, courtesy of Red Arrow Gallery. © 2026 Emily Weiner • 71–73: Photo: John Schweikert. Courtesy of the artist. © 2026 Emily Weiner • 74–76: Photo: John Schweikert. Courtesy of the artist. © 2026 Kelly S. Williams • 77: Courtesy of the artist and Red Arrow Gallery. © 2026 Kelly S. Williams • 78–79: Photo: John Schweikert. Courtesy of the artist. © 2026 Kelly S. Williams • 80: Courtesy of the artist and Hannah Deits. © 2026 Kelly S. Williams • 81–82: Photo: John Schweikert. Courtesy of the artist. © 2026 LiFran Fort • 83–84: Photo: John Schweikert. Courtesy of the artist. © 2026 Sisavanh Phouthavong Houghton • 85: Photo: John Schweikert. Courtesy of the artist. © 2026 Kristi Hargrove • 86: Courtesy of the artist and Zeitgeist Gallery. © 2026 Lanie Gannon • 87: Photo: John Schweikert. Courtesy of the artist. © 2026 Lanie Gannon • 88–89: Photo: John Schweikert. Courtesy of the artist. © 2026 Carol Mode • 90–92: Photo: Kit Reuther. Courtesy of the artist. © 2026 Kit Reuther • 93–98: Photo: John Schweikert. Courtesy of the artist. © 2026 Alex Blau • 99: Photo: John Schweikert. Courtesy of the artists. © 2026 Jane Braddock

ARTIST HEADSHOTS

All photos by Ashley Holstein except the following:
Aradini: Eugene Tang • Gannon: Gina R. Binkley • Hargrove: Sam Angel • Henry: Gina R. Binkley • Kline: Mac Cooper
Murphy: Wayne Roland Brown

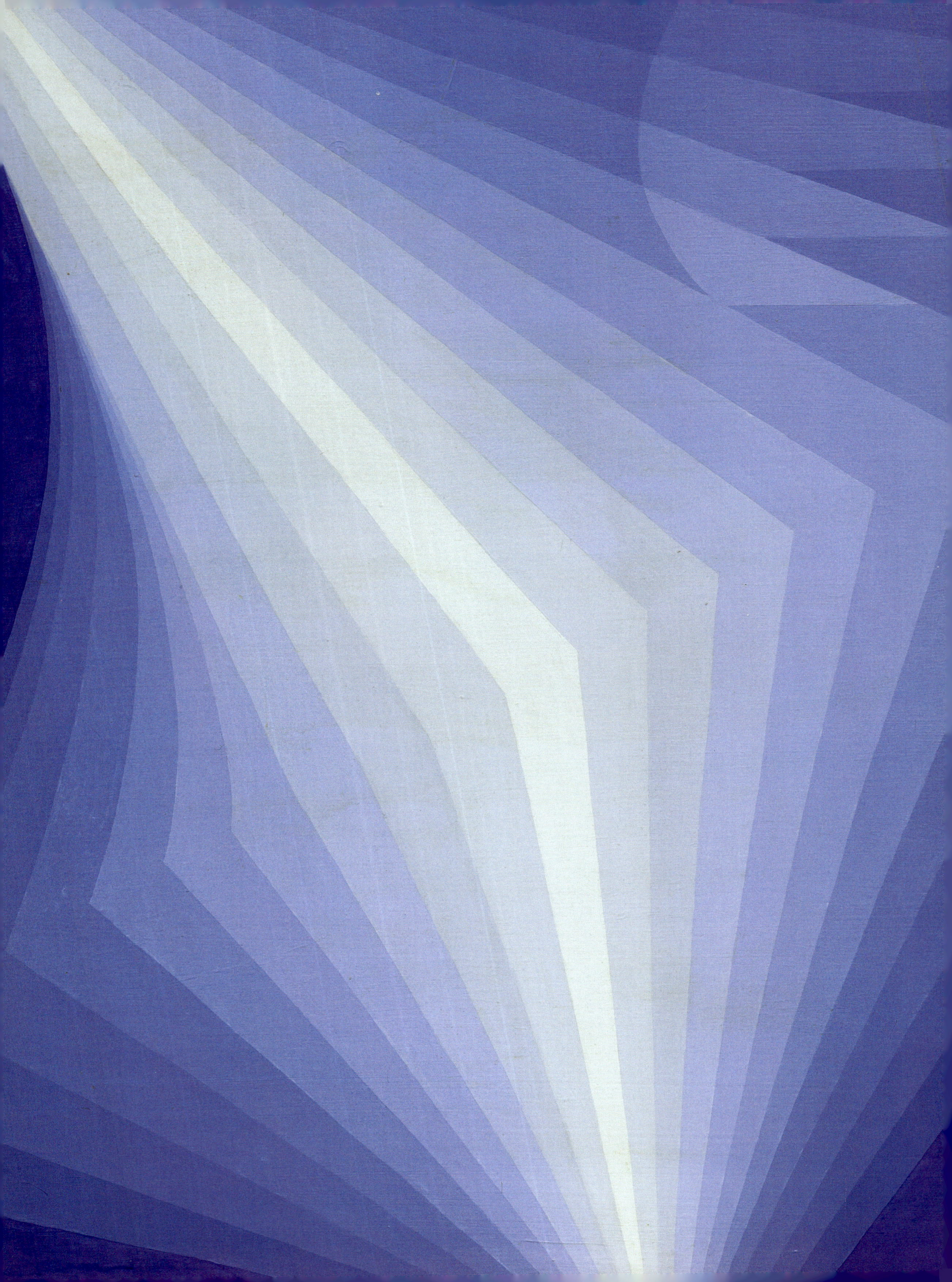

CONTRIBUTORS

Sai Clayton
artist and independent curator

Mac Cooper
curatorial assistant, Frist Art Museum

Kathryn E. Delmez
senior curator, Frist Art Museum

Michael J. Ewing
associate curator, Frist Art Museum

Michelle Millar Fisher
Ronald C. and Anita L. Wornick Curator of Contemporary Decorative Arts, Museum of Fine Arts, Boston

Vivien Green Fryd
professor emeritus, art history, Vanderbilt University

Shaun Giles
director of community engagement, Frist Art Museum

Katy Hessel
author and podcaster

Laura Hutson Hunter
writer, editor, and curator

Susan W. Knowles
digital humanities research fellow, Center for Historic Preservation, Middle Tennessee State University

Joe Nolan
artist and writer

Mouminatou Thiaw
2024–25 Susan H. Edwards Curatorial Fellow, Frist Art Museum

LENDERS TO THE EXHIBITION

Sheila Aminmadani

Sandra Ballentine

Mollye Brown and Paul Polycarpou

Fadi Braiteh

Jesse Hale

The Estate of Alicia Henry

Hines – T3 Wedgewood Houston Collection, Nashville

Jodi and Hal Hess

Anne Joyce and Peter Lawrence

Andrew Le

Emily Leonard and Sloane Southhard

Kylie Manning

Ces McCully and Jordy Kerwick

Eliot Michael

Melanie and Chris Moran

Alf and Clara Naman

Jennifer and Lee Pepper

Sasha and Charlie Sealy

Roya Shanks and Aaron Bender

Matthew Steer

Jason Stopa

Cal Turner

Fara White

And several private collections that wish to remain anonymous

Published in conjunction with *In Her Place: Nashville Artists in the Twenty-First Century*, organized by the Frist Art Museum, Nashville, and cocurated by Sai Clayton, Kathryn E. Delmez, and Shaun Giles; on view at the Frist Art Museum January 29–April 26, 2026.

PLATINUM SPONSOR

HCA Healthcare | TriStar Health
Part of the HCA Healthcare Family of Hospitals

EDUCATION AND COMMUNITY ENGAGEMENT SUPPORTER

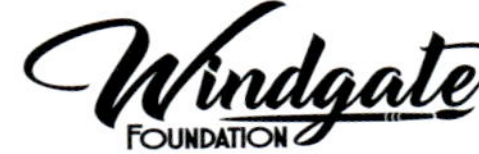

This project is supported in part by
The William Stamps Farish Fund
and the Tennessee Commission for the United States Semiquincentennial.

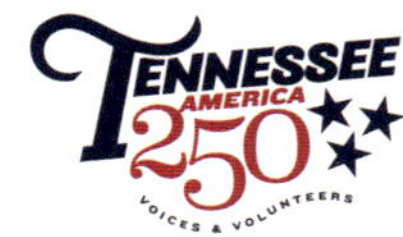

Frist Art Museum

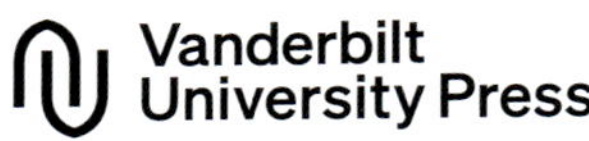

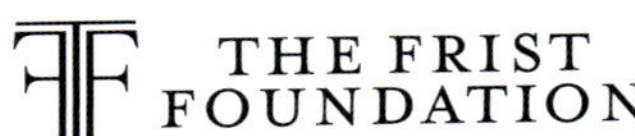

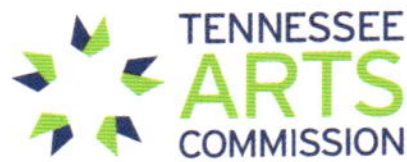

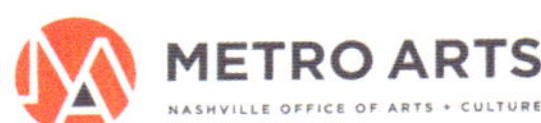

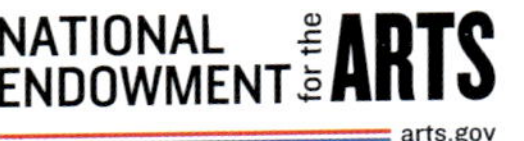

Printed in Canada

Frist Art Museum
919 Broadway
Nashville, Tennessee 37203-1948
FristArtMuseum.org

Editor: Ben Thomas
Image acquisitions: Katherine Campbell and Mac Cooper

Vanderbilt University Press
2301 Vanderbilt Place
Nashville, Tennessee 37204-1813
VanderbiltUniversityPress.com

ISBN: 978-0-8265-0834-8

Library of Congress Cataloging-in-Publication Data

Names: Delmez, Kathryn E. editor | Frist Art Museum (Nashville, Tenn.) host institution
Title: In her place : Nashville artists in the twenty-first century / edited by Kathryn E. Delmez and Laura Hutson Hunter.
Description: Nashville, Tennessee : Frist Art Museum, [2026] | Includes bibliographical references.
Identifiers: LCCN 2025045102 | ISBN 9780826508348 hardcover
Subjects: LCSH: Art, American--Tennessee--Nashville--21st century--Exhibitions | Women artists--Tennessee--Nashville--Exhibitions
Classification: LCC N6535.N37 I6 2026
LC record available at https://lccn.loc.gov/2025045102

The Frist Art Museum sits on land that Cherokee and Shawnee Native peoples, elders, and their ancestors call their homeland. We acknowledge and pay respect to them. We also acknowledge and offer deep gratitude to the land and water that support us.